Refiguring the Father

Ad Feminam: Women and Literature
Edited by Sandra M. Gilbert

Christina Rossetti
The Poetry of Endurance
By Dolores Rosenblum

Lunacy of Light
Emily Dickinson and the Experience of Metaphor
By Wendy Barker

The Literary Existence of Germaine de Staël
By Charlotte Hogsett

Margaret Atwood
Vision and Forms
Edited by Kathryn VanSpanckeren and Jan Garden Castro

The Woman and the Lyre
Women Writers in Classical Greece and Rome
By Jane McIntosh Snyder

He Knew She Was Right
The Independent Woman in the Novels of Anthony Trollope
By Jane Nardin

Refiguring the Father
New Feminist Readings
of Patriarchy

Edited by Patricia Yaeger and
Beth Kowaleski-Wallace

With an Afterword by Nancy K. Miller

Southern Illinois University Press
Carbondale and Edwardsville

Printed in the United States of America

Edited by William Jerman
Designed by Joyce Kachergis
Production supervised by Linda Jorgensen-Buhman

92 91 90 89   4 3 2 1

Illustration on title page, William Blake, *Lot and His Daughters*. Courtesy of The Henry E. Huntington Library and Art Gallery.

Excerpt from Dan Ebolo, "Star Story," reprinted by permission; © 1987 Dan Ebolo. Originally in The New Yorker.

Library of Congress Cataloging-in-Publication Data

Refiguring the father: new feminist readings of patriarchy / edited
   by Patricia Yaeger and Beth Kowaleski-Wallace.
      p. cm.
   1. American literature—History and criticism. 2. English
literature—History and criticism. 3. Patriarchy in literature.
4. Feminism and literature. 5. Sex role in literature. 6. Fathers
in literature. I. Yaeger, Patricia.
PS169.P36R44 1989
810.9'3520431—dc20   89-6118
ISBN 0-8093-1529-7   CIP

The paper used in this publication meets the minimum requirements of American National Standard for Information Sciences—Permanence of Paper for Printed Library Materials, ANSI Z39.48-1984. ∞

Contents

Ad Feminam:
Women and Literature

Ad Hominem: to the man; appealing to personal interests, prejudices, or emotions rather than to reason; *an argument ad hominem.*
—*American Heritage Dictionary*

Until quite recently, much literary criticism, like most humanistic studies, has been in some sense constituted out of arguments *ad hominem.* Not only have examinations of literary history tended to address themselves "to the man"—that is, to the identity of what was presumed to be the *man* of letters who created our culture's monuments of unaging intellect—but many aesthetic analyses and evaluations have consciously or unconsciously appealed to the "personal interests, prejudices, or emotions" of male critics and readers. As the title of this series is meant to indicate, the intellectual project called "feminist criticism" has sought to counter the limitations of *ad hominem* thinking about literature by asking a series of questions addressed *ad feminam:* to the woman as both writer and reader of texts.

First, and most crucially, feminist critics ask, what is the relationship between gender and genre, between sexuality and textuality? But in meditating on these issues they raise a number of more specific questions. Does a woman of letters have a literature—a language, a history, a tradition—of her own? Have conventional methods of canon-formation tended to exclude or marginalize female achievements? More generally, do men and women have different modes of literary representation, different definitions of literary production? Do such differences mean that distinctive male- (or female-) authored images of women (or men), as well as distinctly

vii

male and female genres, are part of our intellectual heritage? Perhaps most important, are literary differences between men and women essential or accidental, biologically determined or culturally constructed?

Feminist critics have addressed themselves to these problems with increasing sophistication during the last two decades, as they sought to revise, or at times replace, *ad hominem* arguments with *ad feminam* speculations. Whether explicating individual texts, studying the oeuvre of a single author, examining the permutations of a major theme, or charting the contours of a tradition, these theorists and scholars have consistently sought to define literary manifestations of difference and to understand the dynamics that have shaped the accomplishments of literary women.

As a consequence of such work, feminist critics, often employing new modes of analysis, have begun to uncover a neglected female tradition along with a heretofore hidden history of the literary dialogue between men and women. This series is dedicated to publishing books that will use innovative as well as traditional interpretive methods in order to help readers of both sexes achieve a clearer consciousness of that neglected but powerful tradition and a better understanding of that hidden history. Reason tells us, after all, that if, transcending prejudice and special pleading, we speak to, and focus on, the woman as well as the man—if we think *ad feminam* as well as *ad hominem*—we will have a better chance of understanding what constitutes the human.

Sandra M. Gilbert

Introduction

In Wallace Stevens's "The Auroras of Autumn" we encounter the father as Western culture has come to know him: as a grand inquisitor and whimsical bumbler who nevertheless controls law and vision, as a master "motionless and yet/ Of motion the ever-brightening origin":

> The father sits
> In space, wherever he sits, of bleak regard,
>
> As one that is strong in the bushes of his eyes.
> He says no to no and yes to yes. He says yes
> To no; and in saying yes he says farewell.[1]

An archetypal lawgiver and naysayer, Stevens's father "measures the velocities of change" but is himself changeless. How does the father come to have—and to represent—this implacable power?

In one representative scenario, Robert Con Davis describes the origins of paternal authority in Greek myth. Savvier than his voracious father Kronos, Zeus makes a law that forbids the eating of children, and in this moment "the paternal identity that Zeus fashions as protector of fathers and children institutes the law by which parents and children can coexist in a family."[2] For Davis, the father's word becomes the origin of civilization as we know it. "What makes Zeus a father is quite simple: alone of all gods and humans, he bows to no greater power—he alone holds the Greek world together" (12–13).

Wary of the perseverance of these mythic moments, feminist theorists have resisted this worshipful reading of patriarchy. Whereas for Davis we remain sojourners in Zeus's universe, grateful heirs of the father's law, feminist critics have rediscovered the originary beauty of the mother's body and language. While Davis argues that "one comes to literary texts to find and take hold of the father,"[3] feminist critics have discovered the mother's face as the "purpose of the poem."[4] While *The Fictional Father* tells us we are told that the father's "symbolic function" can only be "accepted as a gift . . . for which one assumes a castration debt in relationship" (189), feminist critics have taught us to resist this paternal "gift," to refuse not only "a castration debt" owed to the father but also the legality of the father's power.

In resisting the hunger of paternal history, feminist theory has opened a discursive field in which the father's centrality and omnipotence have been refigured. The father now enters our conversation in new ways, and it is the purpose of this collection to extend this conversation even further—to explore the father figure as a shifting, multiple field of tropes and practices that must be reconstrued and deconstructed.

In *Alice Doesn't* Teresa de Lauretis comments that "a woman (or a man) is not an individual identity, a stable unit of 'consciousness,' but the terms of a shifting series of ideological positions."[5] As feminists, we have become increasingly attentive to the ways in which woman is an ideological construction whose identify is "multiple, shifting, and often self-contradictory."[6] We are aware of woman's divided subject position, her impossible relation to language, and to the ways in which identity itself is "made up of heterogeneous and heteronomous representations of gender, race, and class, and often indeed across languages and cultures; an identity that one decides to reclaim from a history of multiple assimilations" (9). But we have yet to use these insights to inform feminist theories of the father as person or principle.

While many feminist projects thrive on an antagonism between father and daughter, it is our conviction that this antagonism is not enough. We need to think about the ways in which literary and cultural texts have not only shaped the difficult terms of the daughter-father relationship but also prescribed a role for fathers that is paradoxical and contradictory. In restricting feminist discourse about the father to refutations of the father's power as originary principle, or to diatribes against his strong authority, or even to feminist autobiography, we continue to limit the scope of our analysis. As Hortense Spillers comments in "Interstices": "Symbolic power, like the genetic parent, begets power, takes pleasure in proliferating itself. Feminist discourse, to extend the figure, keeps talking, or reproducing itself, tending to do so in its own image, on the bases of initiating symbolic gestures, against which it might struggle."[7] This collection of essays is motivated by our desire to enter into a new dialogue not only with the tenets of patriarchy but also with the "initiating symbolic gestures" of feminist discourse that have helped to maintain the father's voracious and hierarchical position in Western culture.

What does it mean for feminist discourse that father figures have been excluded from the stories of multiple identity and ideological self-construction that characterize a feminist exploration of subjectivity? When feminist writers construe the father as a metaphor for patriarchy, we lose sight of the complexities of paternity and the paternal function. The power of an individual father becomes conflated with the power of patriarchy; we miss the ways in which fathers inhabit a "shifting series of ideological positions" in which men are also misshapen by homosocial values.

Hortense Spillers is eloquent about our need to reencounter the father as "impermissible origin" in any feminist struggle with our own "regime" of images: "My point is that feminist analytical discourse that women engage in different ways and for different reasons must not only ascertain vigil over its procedures, but must also know its hidden and impermissible origins. I am remembering a folk-say from my childhood . . . 'Mama's baby, papa's maybe.' In other words, to know the seductions of the father and *who*, in fact, the father is might also help to set us free, or to know wherein we occasionally speak when we have least suspected it" (90). The problem, as we see it, is not simply to change our focus from father-as-center to mother-as-center but to reinvent the discourse of the father altogether, to move outside an oedipal dialectic that insists upon revealing the father as law, as the gaze, as bodiliness, or as the symbolic, and to develop a new dialectic that refuses to describe the father function as if it were univocal and ahistorical.

Feminist practitioners and theorists have already suggested several directions for this new practice. For example, in "The Other

Body: Cultural Debate in Contemporary British Photography," the feminist photographer Jo Spence describes the ways in which a child's entry into a "society of rigid patriarchy" is enforced by the images surrounding that child. How do these images conspire to reproduce the effects of patriarchy? Spence notices that the "paternal body" is the body that is most frequently missing from the photograph albums and histories of families. She asks, "How much is the lack of image-making about the family, the struggle for power in the domestic sphere part of a cementing process, the blocking off of those early traumas and desires which as children we are encouraged not to acknowledge? How does this relate to the 'regime of images' offered us from birth?" The goal of her photography is to allow her audience to revisit the "taboos and hidden voyeurisms" of a childhood in which men's bodies represent—in their absence—a forbidden territory.[8]

In *The Daughter's Seduction,* Jane Gallop takes this analysis one step further: "By giving up their bodies, men gain power—the power to theorize, to represent themselves, to exchange women, to reproduce themselves and mark their offspring with their name. All these activities ignore bodily pleasure in pursuit of representation, reproduction, production."[9] If Spence and Gallop point to a dissonance between the father's law and the father's desire, in *Shakespeare's Ghost Writers* Marjorie Garber points to another dissonance in the political underpinnings of patriarchy. She reminds us that "the father is always a suppositional father, a father by imputation, rather than by unimpeachable biological proof. . . . This doubt, on which paternity, legitimacy, inheritance, primogeniture, and succession all depend, is the anxiety at the root of the *cultural* failure of the paternal metaphor—that is, its failure because of its status as metaphor, its nontranslatability into the realm of proof. . . . The more the father is idealized, the more problematic is the presence of doubt, the gap in certainty that instates paternal undecidability."[10]

This notion that the idealization of the paternal function is, in part, a reaction formation designed to ward off knowledge of "paternal undecidability" informs a number of essays in this collection. The father's power is never whole or unified—its manifestations are splintered, divisive, in crisis, shot through with disorder and desire.

If, as feminist writers, we have ignored the ways in which fatherhood is fraught with somatic contradictions and shattered by undecidability, it is because we still lack the complex idioms we need to
describe the political and tropological roles that fathers play in
Western culture. For example, in *Fathers: Reflections by Daughters,*
Ursula Owen suggests that feminists possess only two locutions for
writing about the father-daughter bond. "The first is Freud's and
that of the psychoanalysts who came after him" and focuses on
the sexual bonds between father and daughter, emphasizing the
daughter's sexual feelings and her elaborate mechanisms for denying
those feelings.[11] The second discourse available to feminists writing
about the father-daughter bond emphasizes patriarchy as "the institutionalized power of the fathers," a "familial, social and political
system in which men . . . determine what part women shall or shall
not play and in which the female is everywhere subsumed under the
male." Given this dearth of expressive means, Owen gathered the
essays for *Fathers: Reflections by Daughters* to provide an "opportunity for women to try and find their own idiom for this most
complicated of relationships, to explore their own experience of
paternal authority" (x).

Our collection is also in search of new idioms, but with these
differences. First, the focus of this book is neither feminist biography nor autobiography. For Owen, each woman's relation to her
father becomes the originating point where women begin to feel
the weight of patriarchy. But as Beth Kowaleski-Wallace argues in
the final essay in this collection, by limiting ourselves to biography
or autobiography, we may limit our anger and our analysis—direct-
ing it toward a single father who, as "metaphor" for patriarchy,
seems to bear the burden of responsibility for his daughter's predicament. We do so at the risk of underestimating the complex mechanisms of male dominance: to castigate (or even praise) the father of
feminist biography or autobiography may mean to ignore the larger
mechanisms of patriarchy and promote simplistic models wherein
patriarchal trauma seems univocal and magical; it is thought to
vanish with the abolition of the individual father.

Second, we have extended the scope of this collection beyond
a traditional feminist exploration of daughter-father bonds. The

daughter-father relationship is an important source for feminist analysis, but as we develop new idioms for describing the mechanisms of patriarchy, we must recognize the father-daughter relationship as a single point of entry. We need to mobilize other theorems and other subject positions relating to fathering in order to evoke a series of different father constellations: father-son eroticism, the white father's relation to race and miscegenation, the relation of fathering to creativity and gynesis, the relation of class-rights to father-rights, as well as the father's imperfect creation of diverse family texts: from the emptiness of his patronyms to the failure of dynasties. In order to challenge old myths and paradigms, it is essential not only to explore the father's diverging jural, political, familial, racial, and psychological positions but also to examine these divergences within individual father figures.

Finally, our collection is in search of new idioms in its deviations from current Lacanian-feminist discourse about the father. With its overt privileging of the symbolic, Lacanian theory has demonstrated little interest in actual fathers. Lacan himself insists that the symbolic father is the dead father. In response to a query from Ernest Jones, he wrote: "The credit that seems to me to be accorded quite legitimately to the human capacities to observe the real [paternal function] is precisely that which has not the slightest importance in the matter."[12] Jacqueline Rose reiterates the insignificance of the actual father for Lacan: "When Lacan calls for a return to the place of the father he is crucially distinguishing himself from any sociological conception of the role. The father is a function and refers to a law, the place outside the imaginary dyad and against which it breaks."[13] The Lacanian father is a disembodied entity, a law or function who is essentially bodiless. Yet is it precisely this bodilessness that so compels and obsesses his daughters.

If the Lacanian view denies the father a body, it also denies him a plural history, for the Symbolic father operates beyond the bounds of time or space. It is our conviction that feminist analyses must recognize the father both as a historical product and an ideological construct. As Althusser writes in a footnote to his essay on Freud and Lacan, "It is not enough to know that the Western family is patriarchal and exogamic (kinship structures)—we must also work out the ideological formations that govern paternity, maternity, conjugality and childhood: what are 'husband- and wife-being,' 'father-being,' 'mother-being' and 'child-being' in the modern world?"[14] Theorists like Althusser challenge us to strike a subtle balance—to reconstruct the father as historical being without over-investing in the terms of psychoanalysis.

It may be possible to reconcile a Lacanian view of a disembodied, "dead" father with a historical view by creating a model of the family that is reflective of psychic experiences and configurations and yet, at the same time, descriptive of historical changes in the structure of the family—that is, rooted in history. Such a model has been proposed by Marie Christine Hamon in her description of parental splitting. Writing about the figure of the mother in Freud, Hamon distinguishes among the mother's many figures and describes the splitting of the actual mother from her parental imago; while the actual mother lives in history, the mother as parental imago is a function of the unconscious.[15] By describing the mother as a multiple figure, Hamon allows us to consider the maternal function on several levels, and what she suggests about the mother may be true for the father as well: he may be a composite of several different father figures, Lacan's Symbolic among them.

What does it mean for feminist theory to invoke the father's self-division and plurality? Two of the essays in Ursula Owen's collection provide empirical answers to this question. In sketching out their relationships with their fathers, Sara Maitland and Alice Walker encounter a plural, divided father who cannot be wholly accounted for in either Freudian or antipatriarchal feminist idioms. Sara Maitland discovers herself split between a father who is material and biological, who "after 'a long illness bravely borne' . . . died of cancer," and another father who is "alive and well and rampaging inside me. He never goes away, although sometimes he is silent; he is never ill, never weakened, never leaves me alone. He lurks about under other names—God, Husband, Companion." Even when she abandons her biological father, the superegotistical father stays. "It is this Father that I want to kill, and dare not."[16]

For Maitland it becomes crucial to separate these two fathers: "I did not want to kill my father. . . . I had come to respect this person who happened to be my father. . . . I liked him." At his death she does not want to blame him "for everything that was difficult in my life." In talking about this double father with her brothers and sisters, Maitland discovers, "We, who all shared the same historical father, all had different fathers inside our heads. Between the six of us we had seven fathers."

In splintering the father, finding an idiom to dissect his moods and differences within the intricate psychic mix of the family, Maitland is breaking a family taboo, sending the family into disarray. "I'm challenging not just my father but the whole code by which we live, as a family." To break this taboo is liberating, but also frightening. "The love that my father had for me and expressed so fully and so generously has soured in me. It was so exactly, uncannily, precisely that paternal love which a deeply anti-woman society uses to control its uppity women. I suppose it's not his fault. But should he have known?" (27).

In "The Democratic Order: Such Things in Twenty Years I Understand," Alice Walker also finds a tragic division within her father—but this division speaks of another familial experience and a different paternal history. "Actually, my father was two fathers. To the first four of his children he was one kind of father, to the second set of four he was another."[17] After years of backbreaking work to feed and clothe his family, Walker's father is in poor health; he is overweight, he has diabetes. But the difference between these two fathers is also spiritual and political. As Walker reimagines his past, her father separates into several psychic and social beings. Active in his youth in protest movements—he fought to win Afro-Americans a vote and a place for Afro-Americans in the biracial community—Walker's father knows only bitterness and defeat in Walker's lifetime. But in the midst of his bone-weary despair and cynicism, "for no apparent reason, he'd come out with one of those startlingly intelligent comments about world affairs . . . and I would be reminded of the father I didn't know" (227).

The importance of these divisions within individual fathers as well as the splintering effects of varying class, race, and sexual positions within patriarchy means that feminist discourse about the father must describe a range of paternal configurations. With this in mind, our collection is divided into three sections, each investigating another aspect of the father's cultural and symbolic status. In Part I, The Father's Desire, contributors reveal the nature of the father's desire and discuss the social consequences of disembodying or disguising the father's yearning. In "The Father's Breasts" Patricia Yaeger argues that while "*somatophobia,* or fear of the body's fleshliness and mutability,"[18] qualifies our vision of women's bodies, "*asomia,* or bodilessness, characterizes our way of describing and thinking about the father." In separating a preoedipal narrative privileging the mother's body and an oedipal narrative privileging the father's law, we maintain this *somatophobia* and *asomia* as cultural symptoms. To renegotiate these symptoms, both oedipal and preoedipal plots must be mapped onto the father's body. This means reconstruing not only the father's lacks but his somatic surplus, discovering a father with breasts.

For Jerry Aline Flieger, in "Colette and the Captain: Daughter as Ghostwriter," the father's desire re-creates the father as paradox and enigma. Colette's father, "the Captain," an amputee, is "a silent poet," an "Orpheus dismembered," a figure of castration who asks his daughter as ghostwriter to give shape to his desire. The daughter's "mourning-work" for her dead father means his "re-membering," but in this remembering the dead father is also refigured through the echolalias of the daughter's desire.

While Flieger suggests that writing must be predicated upon the daughter's recognition of her father's wounding, Susan M. Griffin reminds us in "Screening the Father: The Strategy of Obedience in Early James," that the very notion of the father's desire is frightening insofar as it reminds us of the father's essential "lack." In Henry James's early fiction the father's desire is a sign of his incompleteness and the child's complicity in the father's law is the sign of a coverup: mother and child act as accessories to the father's authority because "if the father lacks, they do too." What emerges from Griffin's reading of early James is a portrait of just how destabilizing the discovery of the father's desire can be, as well as the ways in which disempowered family members not only share in but profit from the myth of the father's authority.

In "Renegotiating the Oedipus: Theseus and Hippolytos," Nancy

Sorkin Rabinowitz isolates and identifies the father's erotic desire for his own son in Euripides' *Hippolytos*. In describing the destabilizing effects of paternal desire, she argues that the play is organized around the father's desire "for one like himself," and she describes the hostility and intolerance for the son that covers up the father's unspoken desire. Although *Hippolytos* has been seen as an archetypal play about female desire, Rabinowitz suggests that the play enacts "the destruction of (not the desire for) the mother, and the desire for (not the destruction of) the father."

In "The Name of the Daughter: Identity and Incest in *Evelina*," Irene Fizer also writes from a historical perspective about the "unstable paternal position" in Fanny Burney's eighteenth-century novel *Evelina*. Illuminating the double power of a sexualized and legalized father, Fizer asserts that this "double standard" means that "the father can exercise his bodily pleasures without giving away his entitlement to the law." The father is an unstable term who evades the daughter's recognition and tantalizes her desire with his own. Even as *Evelina* affirms the power of paternal law to bring family stability, the central question of the novel deconstructs this stability: How will Evelina know the proper father?

A father's double identity is also at stake in Vanessa D. Dickerson's essay, "The Naked Father in Toni Morrison's *The Bluest Eye*." For the narrator of Morrison's novel and her sister, the father possesses two sides, one obscure, unknowable, the other naked and familiar. Yet the novel sets out to explain how the "most provocative" father, Cholly Breedlove, becomes "desperately extreme" in his nakedness. His familiarity destroys his own daughter, and Morrison's novel offers a parable of how a "nontraditional father operating in a traditional Dick-and-Jane society ruins himself and his own."

The essays in Part 2, Oedipal Hermeneutics, suggest a number of ways in which feminist critics can renegotiate Freud's oedipal design. In *Anti-Oedipus* Deleuze and Guattari argue that "the father and the mother exist only as fragments, and are never organized into a figure or a structure able both to represent the unconscious . . . they always shatter into fragments that come into contact with these agents, meet them face to face, square off with them, or settle the differences with them as in hand-to-hand combat."[19] The contributors to this section would agree, but also see the father as an organizing principle that helps us examine the ways in which "the terms of the Oedipus do not form a triangle, but exist shattered into all corners of the social field" (Deleuze and Guattari, 62). For Heather Hathaway the father is a profoundly political figure operating in a field of familial and racial tensions. In "'Maybe Freedom Lies in Hating': Miscegenation and the Oedipal Conflict," Hathaway suggests that in miscegenous relationships the violation of racial identity "exacerbates oedipal motivations." In her analysis of short stories by Charles Chestnutt and Langston Hughes, Hathaway dramatizes the way in which two mulatto protagonists redefine their white fathers, challenging a racist principle of paternal abstraction.

In contrast, Linda Kauffman insists on the paternal abstraction in *Lolita*. In "Framing *Lolita:* Is There A Woman in the Text?," Kauffman describes the importance of reading Humbert Humbert not only as Lolita's lover but as her father. While most critics find "aesthetic bliss" in the text's satiric playfulness, Kauffman also insists on the importance of reading Nabokov's text referentially. Her analysis moves between that moment when the "material body of the child Lolita" can be reinscribed in Nabokov's text and the moment when the representational fallacy can be tested by situating Nabokov's text "dialogically in relation to other texts." This allows Kauffman to analyze both "the horror of incest" and the pressure of the father's body that most critics of *Lolita* ignore.

For Susan Fraiman, the father's significance is political as well as sexual. It lies in his central position within the "system of homosocial relations underlying the institution of heterosexuality." In "The Humiliation of Elizabeth Bennet" Fraiman describes two fathers in *Pride and Prejudice,* one who is initially enabling and the other who seems disabling because of his "excessive social authority." Fraiman charts the collapse of the enabling father into the disabling one and the results of this collapse upon Elizabeth Bennet as she follows a "trajectory of humiliation."

If Fraiman suggests that the heroine of *Pride and Prejudice* is humiliated by a system of homoerotic relations, Helena Michie analyzes the ways in which novelistic heroines are often subject to greater violence; they are literally killed off in a genre of nineteenth-century fiction that foregrounds the daughter's dying body and places her in the middle of a struggle between competing ideologies. In "Dying Between Two Laws: Girl Heroines, Their Gods, and Their Fathers in *Uncle Tom's Cabin* and the *Elsie Dinsmore* Series," Michie finds the dying heroines positioned between "two competing fathers who embody two competing laws." In these stories, familial relations are more than oedipal. Instead, both works "participate in a fantasy of female potency that unites body and word in the struggle against the earthly father and the power he represents." In this, as in other essays in this section, oedipal relations are recast in terms encompassing not only psychic but political and social life as well.

In Part 3, Beyond the Figure of the Father, contributors go beyond an implacable image of paternal authority to demonstrate that the Name-of-the-Father is not an absolute. Rather, the father's authority can be subverted, disembodied, or dissipated in a variety of fictional and political tropes. We have included two essays on Faulkner in order to demonstrate not only the father's division and plurality but also the diversity of methodologies that can be summoned to a feminist project of refiguring the father. In "Creation by the Father's Fiat: Paternal Narrative, Sexual Anxiety, and the Deauthorizing Designs of *Absalom, Absalom!*," Joseph A. Boone questions the standard association of "the materials of male procreativity" with "metaphors of narrativity." According to Boone, the father's authority should be seen as an ambiguous construction "founded on a profound anxiety about the meaning of masculinity itself." Boone's project is both deconstructive and reconstructive. In challenging Sutpen's "self-proclaimed authority," he also affirms the presence, in texts read beyond the shadow of the Oedipus, of a vulnerable father whose presence "problematizes the patriarchal ethos."

Minrose C. Gwin also suggests the patriarchal plot's "impossibility," but instead of challenging the oedipal hypothesis she challenges our literary investment in character. In "(Re)Reading Faulkner as Father and Daughter of His Own Text," Faulkner's fictional daughters not only undermine his fictional fathers but also undermine

Faulkner's own narrative position of father-author. Using psychoanalytic and deconstructive insights developed by Helene Cixous, Alice Jardine, and Barbara Johnson, Gwin analyzes the ways in which Faulkner's female characters decenter and deride his/her fictional projects—making Faulkner-as-father/daughter both usurper and usurped.

In the last three essays of the collection, patriarchy surfaces as a political and social function perpetuated by language itself, a function that must be rewritten by feminist critics. In "Where the Absent Father Went: Alcott's *Work*," James D. Wallace demonstrates the ways in which an individual father figure in Louisa May Alcott's *Work* is dissolved into a patriarchal principle. Wallace argues that in Alcott's fictions, men and their discourse become tropes for the patriarchal system, which Alcott sets out to subvert, splintering the father's individual image in the process. Wallace analyzes the puzzling disappearance of the father into a linguistic abstraction. Similarly, in her essay on the epic tradition, Adrienne Munich shows how the father is created by means of the mother's buried voice. In "Engendering the Literary Father, or, The Law-of-the-Mother," Munich examines the position of the mother in the construction of the epic hero, uncovering images of paternal fragility and scenes of mutual desire between mother and son. While the son must bury the nurse who threatens his sense of self, the mother arms the son so that "the voice and the written language of the Mother exert a great, even decisive force in the canonical creation of the hero as Father." Finally, in "Reading the Father Metaphorically," Beth Kowaleski-Wallace proposes that we need to read patriarchy as both metaphor and synecdoche. Examining the ways in which our perception of patriarchy has been shaped by a series of linguistic conventions, she discusses the perils of reading the individual father as a substitute for patriarchy. We must, she argues, revise our way of thinking and acting toward a man who seems a "gargantuan oppressor."

In "My Father's Penis," the afterword to this collection, Nancy K. Miller takes this refiguring of the father's language and body to new extremities. Recounting a mystery from her childhood, Miller describes her fascination with the opening in her father's string pajamas; she defines her father's genitals in terms of a lacuna, a gap. Her response to this opening offers us the counter-imperative of the female gaze. In "My Father's Penis," the "autobiographical penis and the theoretical phallus" come unstrung. What is the phallus-penis, Miller asks, and how do we relate to the crack in its double name?

The essays in this collection remind us that the father is not a singular character who autonomously creates himself but a figure supported and uplifted by many imaginations. If we privilege one figure of the father over all others, we will fail to see the complex ways in which we construct "the" father even as we are structured by him. Since the father's power is plural, shattered, amorphous, and contradictory, we must relinquish our investments in an over-wrought picture of the father as culpable patriarch, even as we recognize our victimization at his hands. This achieved, we might be free, as feminists, to acknowledge the fleeting but extraordinary presence in our lives of a paternal gift that is not linked to castration.

Alice Walker discovers such a gift in "The Democratic Order: Such Things in Twenty Years I Understand." Fearing the destructive potential of her father's words, Walker nevertheless accepts his celebration of her physical being. "A woman's hair is her glory," Walker's father said in her youth, and Walker discovers in middle age a power in uncut hair she had little expected—the power of the racially untamed, the sexually undomesticated, the wild. She re-creates this fragile gift when she recasts her father's words in her own style: "a wildness about the head, as the Rastas have discovered, places us somehow in the loose and spacious freedom of Jah's universe" (228).

Beth Kowaleski-Wallace
Patricia Yaeger

Notes

1. Wallace Stevens, "The Auroras of Autumn" in *The Collected Poems of Wallace Stevens* (London: Faber and Faber: 1966), 414.
2. Robert Con Davis, "Critical Introduction: The Discourse of the Fa-

ther" in *The Fictional Father: Lacanian Readings of the Text*, ed. Robert Con Davis (Amherst: University of Massachusetts Press, 1981), 12.

3. Robert Con Davis, "Epilogue: The Discourse of Jacques Lacan," in *The Fictional Father*, 189. Subsequent references will be cited parenthetically in the text.

4. Wallace Stevens, "Auroras of Autumn," 413.

5. Teresa de Lauretis, *Alice Doesn't: Feminism, Semiotics, Cinema* (Bloomington: Indiana University Press, 1984), 14.

6. Teresa de Lauretis, "Feminist Studies/Critical Studies: Issues, Terms, and Contexts," in *Feminist Studies/Critical Studies*, ed. de Lauretis (Bloomington: Indiana University Press, 1986), 9. Subsequent references will be cited parenthetically in the text.

7. Hortense Spillers, "Interstices: A Small Drama of Words," in *Pleasure and Danger: Exploring Female Sexuality*, ed. Carole S. Vance (Boston: Routledge and Kegan Paul, 1984), 90.

8. Jo Spence, quoted by Tim Norris in *The Other Body: Cultural Debate in Contemporary British Photography* (Boston: Boston Resource Center at Boston University, 1987), 9.

9. Jane Gallop, *The Daughter's Seduction: Feminism and Psychoanalysis* (Ithaca: Cornell University Press, 1982), 67.

10. Marjorie Garber, *Shakespeare's Ghost Writers* (New York: Methuen, 1987), 133.

11. Ursula Owen, *Fathers: Reflections by Daughters* (New York: Pantheon, 1983), x.

12. Jacques Lacan, *Ecrits: A Selection*, trans. Alan Sheridan (New York: Norton, 1982) 199.

13. Jacqueline Rose, "Introduction II" in *Feminine Sexuality: Jacques Lacan and the école freudienne*, eds. Jacqueline Rose and Juliet Mitchell (New York: Norton, 1982), 39.

14. Louis Althusser, "Freud and Lacan" in *Lenin and Philosophy and Other Essays*, trans. Ben Brewster (London: NLB, 1971), 194.

15. Marie Christine Hamon, "The Figure of the Mother: A Study," in *M/F* 8 (1983), 34.

16. Sara Maitland, "Two for the Price of One" in *Fathers: Reflections by Daughters*, ed. Owen, 19.

17. Alice Walker, "The Democratic Order: Such Things in Twenty Years I Understood" in *Fathers: Reflections by Daughters*, ed. Owen, 226. Subsequent references will be cited parenthetically in the text.

18. See Elizabeth Spelman, "The Erasure of Black Women," *Quest*, vol. 4, no. 4 (1982), 36–62.

19. Gilles Deleuze and Felix Guattari, *Anti-Oedipus: Capitalism and Schizophrenia* (Minneapolis: University of Minnesota Press, 1983), 97. Subsequent references will be cited parenthetically in the text.

Part 1   *The Father's Desire*

I *The Father's Breasts*
Patricia Yaeger

We can read Elizabeth Bishop's "Crusoe in England" playfully, from the fantastic perspective of a female Crusoe who has returned—with some regret—to England. This Crusoe has inhabited a wild zone, a world elsewhere, an island that is "still / un-rediscovered, un-renamable." But while the island's flora and fauna offer limited resources, Crusoe finds other ecstasies. She makes "home-brew" and plays her "home-made" flute. "Dizzy" she whoops and dances "among the goats," until:

> Just when I thought I couldn't stand it
> Another minute longer, Friday came.
> (Accounts of that have everything all wrong.)
> Friday was nice.
> Friday was nice, and we were friends.
> If only he had been a woman!
> I wanted to propagate my kind,
> and so did he, I think, poor boy.
> He'd pet the baby goats sometimes,
> and race with them, or carry one around,
> —Pretty to watch; he had a pretty body.[1]

In depicting neither a female Crusoe attracted to men, nor a typically male Crusoe with homoerotic inclinations, but a lesbian Crusoe who views Friday as a dear, but alien companion, "Crusoe in England" offers a poignant erotica. It becomes a poem about a woman desiring another woman and offers us a man's world made over in a woman's image. "A whole new poetry invented here," as Adrienne Rich has said, and a whole new criticism has begun to respond to it. As we move out upon this heady circumference, why write another book about the father? To what end? Have not all books in the last decades, centuries, eons, been to, for, or about the father? Is it possible to offer readings of the father that "whoop and dance," that move into nonpatriarchal space?

In "Envy: or With Your Brains and My Looks," Rosi Braidotti argues that this move is unlikely in the presence of men. "It feels quite uncomfortable to coexist with men under this (book) cover," she says. "It is a form of cohabitation . . . laden with potential for destruction." In composing an essay for Alice Jardine's and Paul Smith's *Men in Feminism*, Braidotti remembers her adolescent obsessions for men with distaste—especially those days when the presence "of 'men' seemed to contain an answer to the question" of female "identity as not just *a*, but rather as *the* woman." For Braidotti, writing an essay about men still invites new and masochistic forms of regression: "My entire conditioning, enforced by a whole sociopolitical system, pushes me to rejoicing at having yet another opportunity to think talk dream about 'men.' " Braidotti is ambivalently ecstatic about the forbidden desire awakened by the subject of her essay—the desire to be invited, from within feminist space, to dream about masculinity. "And so I hesitate. There is something both appealing and suspect in the ease with which the topic pops up, offering itself to my attention. I am against compulsory heterosexuality, even of the sublimated kind."[2]

The feminist who writes for, or reads, or edits a book about the father risks this compulsion. The danger is real. Nevertheless, I want to push against this closure—first by exploring the oedipal boundaries defined in two meditations on the father by Marguerite Duras and Terry Eagleton, and second, by discovering an anxiously sublimated erotica in Coleridge's poetry—the erotica of the father's breasts. The oedipal fragments by Duras and Eagleton will seem at first to confirm Braidotti's warnings about a feminist compulsion to write about men and suggest that the feminist critic should stay away from the father's body. But these meditations will also help me set a puzzle for the reader, to ask whether we can discover a feminist paradigm for analyzing the father problem in Western culture without being seduced once again by a Western machismo.

For Marguerite Duras, the father's name is unmentionable. It is something monstrous that must be exorcised, that hides in the mouth. As Xaviere Gauthier explains: "Marguerite Duras, in order to write, had to choose her own name (what we call a pseudonym). When I asked her if a woman could write if she kept her father's name, she told me: 'That's something which never seemed possible, not for one second. Like many women I find this name so horrible that I barely manage to say it.' "[3] For Gauthier and Duras, the father's name is a subterfuge, a dementia. Commenting on Duras's choice, Gauthier writes, "Women . . . do not have a proper name. . . . Knowing, more or less consciously, that in order to make a name for themselves in literature, women have to be men, they often used masculine pseudonyms" (p. 163). For Gauthier, the father's name intrudes as nonchoice, as legal imperative. But for Eagleton, the father's name is a salvo, a song:

> Der der, deary didi! Der? I? Da! Deary? da!
> Der I, didida; da dada, dididearyda.
> Dadareder, didireader. Dare I die
> deary da? Da dare die didi. Die derider!
> Didiwriter. Dadadidididada.
> Aaaaaaaaaaa! Der i da.[4]

For all his hostility toward Derrida as "deary da," Terry Eagleton plays with the father's name as if this playing were pleasurable. He gets inside this name's demanding syllables and throttles them; he rearranges vowels to find a cozy space. A change of letter promises a change of state. "Dare I die" becomes "Der i da": the son dares to become the father he hates by taking over his name. These oedipal positions—the daughter's mimetic outrage at the father's power and the son's dissolute play with his name—are the repetition compulsions of Western culture, but are these compulsions inevitable? How can we move beyond these oppositional categories and find other ways to describe a "new" feminist reading of the father?

I begin with a caveat. In writing feminist criticism we may be too comfortable playing a binary game; we fetishize one story of the father over another and then proceed oppositionally, as if every argument had only two or three sides, and each of these sides existed in the same dimension of meaning. We might begin to envision, not only for ourselves, but for our reading of men and patriarchy, a stranger model of analysis: a model drawn from Foucault's description of the *heteroclite*.

For Foucault the *heteroclite* is the dimension of the 'incongruous'; it describes a multiplicity of zones that cannot be read simultaneously. The *heteroclite* describes "the linking together of things that are inappropriate; I mean the disorder in which fragments of a large number of possible orders glitter separately in the dimension, without law or geometry. . . . The *heteroclite* . . . should be taken in its most literal, etymological sense: in such a state, things are 'laid,' 'placed,' 'arranged' in sites so very different from one another that it is impossible to find a place of residence for them, to define a *common locus* beneath them all."[5] This looking for a "common locus" pervades feminist readings of the father. In focusing on the patronym, or the phallus, or the father's law, we seek theoretical consensus or codification of the phallogo- and femino-centric when each of these "centrics" may be happening in several different and incommensurable dimensions at once. This is not a plea for patriarchy's beneficence, but rather a call for the recognition of differing zones of gendered reading and being that are not simultaneously mappable; a call for a starring of women's texts that notices their "heteroclissory," a starring of men's texts that could move beyond the "name" or "no" of the father and speak—without coercion or bedazzlement—of the father's breasts.

Is it dangerous to feminist principles, to our renegotiation of women's priority and power, to give the father a body, to speak about a father with breasts? In their introduction to *The (M)other Tongue*, Shirley Nelson Garner, Claire Kahane, and Madelon Sprengnether suggest that we can name only two kinds of familial plots. "Oedipally organized narrative is based on the determining role of the father and of patriarchal discourse" and "tells a different story from preoedipal narrative, which locates the source of movement and conflict in the figure of the mother."[6] The editors add that these narratives can co-exist in the same fictive space, but their relation is oppositional, "the emphasis shifting as one co-opts or is set in opposition to the other." I, for one, am uncomfortable with this opposition and want to suggest that these narrative structures need to be mapped onto one another, to be read simultaneously. For example, in playing with Derrida's name, Eagleton is involved in an oedipal battle for power with the father, but this battle is waged with preoedipal weapons; he attempts to exorcise the father's power by returning to a state of prelinguistic pleasure in which nonsense syllables can become paradoxical terms of self-dispersion and self-empowerment. And while Eagleton celebrates the power of preverbal pleasure to reinscribe oedipal trauma, Gauthier emphasizes "the determining role of the father and of patriarchal discourse" in Duras's repudiation of her father's name. The father figure offers Duras impetus for another kind of orality, for a glissade toward the preoedipal, but only insofar as the daughter fixates upon the father's oedipal game. Thus neither Eagleton nor Duras fit into neat oppositional categories. Their stories suggest preoedipal and postoedipal questions. Do these fragments lead us toward a nonoedipal father— or mother? Might a preoedipal father be as dangerous—or more dangerous—than an oedipal father? What happens to the *nom* or "no" of the father when his discourse fades into preverbal bliss?

We can explore these questions only if both oedipal and preoedipal plots are mapped onto the father's body—a mapping suggested in Sharon Olds's "My Father's Breasts":

> Their soft surface, the polished silk of the hair
> running down them delicately like
> water. I placed my cheek—once,
> perhaps—upon their firm shape,
> my ear pressed against the black
> charge of the heart within. At most
> once—yet when I think of my father
> I think of his breasts, my head resting
> on his fragrant chest, as if I had spent
> hours, years, in that smell of black pepper and
> turned earth.[7]

Beth Kowaleski-Wallace and I belong to a feminist literary theory group that recently enjoyed a lively discussion of "My Father's Breasts." Those present made a number of apt comments—someone noted that all the senses but taste are emphasized in Olds's poem and therefore the ambivalent splitting of the father's body into good breast and bad breast so familiar in our readings of the maternal body is not present here. Someone else commented that we do not possess a code for talking about male bodies as we do for female bodies—hence the rather conventional images with which the poem begins. A third person noted that synecdoche functions differently in poems about men and women. When a part of woman's body is named in, say, a blazon poem, the part never represents the whole— that is, the whole, integral woman—but instead encodes for us the shattering of woman as she is ripped and fragmented by the male gaze, or by patriarchal discourse itself. But in Olds's poem the synecdoche—using the breast part of the father to signify his entire being—does function to convey his whole person rather than the shattering of his person into vulnerable, socially exchangeable parts.

These comments are revealing, but I want to focus on an even more obvious point: Olds talks about the father as a body—and only as a body. This kind of literary speech about the father is extraordinary; it seems to me almost unprecedented. We need to foreground Olds's choice of the father's body as poetic subject because most critical and philosophical discourse about the father evades the body altogether; it is obsessed with a father who is bodiless—who stands for Law, for the Idea, for the Symbolic.

For instance, when Paul Ricouer explains why the father figure in religious discourse "was bound to have a richer and more articulate destiny than the mother figure," he suggests that the father figure's "privileged status is no doubt due to its extremely rich symbolic power, in particular its potential for 'transcendence.'. . . The father is an unreality set apart, who, from the start, is a being of language. Because he is the name-giver, he is the name problem."[8]

In *The Fictional Father* Robert Con Davis also valorizes the father's absence. In explaining what he calls "the essential concepts for a the-ory of the father in narrative," he says that "the father is a 'no' that initiates narrative development by enfranchising one line of continu-ity over other narrative possibilities" and backs up his theory by insist-ing on the importance of the father's absence in the *Odyssey* and the New Testament: "in Trinitarian theory the Son . . . is knowledge of the Father, knowledge beginning with the awareness of difference and exclusion. That is, to know the Father, Trinitarian theory shows that the Son must be excluded from the Father's immediate presence—from sharing the Father's being—in order to be the Mind . . . that has an object of awareness outside of itself."[9]

Finally, in Barthes's *Pleasure of the Text* the writer-son and the mother who provides his text with a "mother-tongue" both possess bodies—but the father figure is bodiless. "The text is . . . that uninhibited person who shows his behind to the Political Father." For Barthes the Political Father has neither breasts nor "behind": "If there is no longer a Father, why tell stories? Doesn't every narrative lead back to Oedipus? Isn't storytelling always a way of searching for one's origin, speaking one's conflicts with the Law?" Barthes asks.[10] The father is an enormous abstraction; he represents the invisible force of conscience, of the discursive, of the oppressive legality regulating society itself.

In summing up these texts and their grandiose tenets, I want to make two suggestions. First, if *somatophobia,* or fear of the body's fleshliness and mutability, characterizes our conflicts with women's bodies,[11] then *asomia,* or bodilessness, characterizes our way of describing and thinking about the father. Second, to divide our ways of talking about narrative into oedipalized narratives about patriarchal discourse and unfulfilled desire and preoedipal narratives about intimacy and nondifferentiation is to leave both this *somatophobia* and this *asomia* in place. Hence, one of the main projects in a reconstructive feminist criticism is to give the father a body, to reconstruct the father as a somatic being, as a being with breasts.

What are the implications of embodying the father? The power stakes are high. As Elaine Scarry explains in *The Body in Pain:*

In discussions of power, it is conventionally the case that those with power are said to be "represented" whereas those without power are "without representation." It may therefore seem contradictory to discover that the scriptures systematically ensure that the Omnipotent will be materially unrepresented and that the comparatively powerless humanity will be materially represented by their own deep embodiment. But to have no body is to have no limits on one's extension out into the world; conversely, to have a body, a body made emphatic by being continually altered through various forms of creation, instruction (e.g., bodily cleansing), and wounding, is to have one's sphere of extension contracted down to the small circle of one's immediate physical presence. Consequently, to be intensely embodied is the equivalent of being unrepresented and . . . is almost always the condition of those without power.[12]

In the Old Testament, it is God's bodiless voice that becomes the source of eternal life. Ejected from paradise, "man and woman move outside the garden to the realm of the troublesome body, permanently blocked from the verbal category" (210). But woman is particularly marked by this exile. According to Scarry: "Throughout the Hebraic scriptures, the question of having or not having a body arises not only in man's relation to God but also in man's relation to man. Even among human beings, the one with authority and power has no body for his inferiors" (210).

The appeal of transforming the figure father from a punishing imago to someone who is vulnerably embodied is clearly a power play—a toppling of the father into the zone women have always inhabited. But Scarry adds that the desire to shine forth and be revealed in one's "fragility and vulnerability" is also part of the dynamic of embodiment: "Having a body means having sentience and the capacity to sense the sentience of others, reciprocity, compassion. Having a body means being not everywhere but somewhere, no longer hidden" (233).

If we ask the father's body to come out of its closet, "to sense the sentience of others," what will we see? Dan Ebalo's recent poem from *The New Yorker,* "The Star Story," insists that the experience of pressing the absent father into embodiment can be poignant and strange. Ebalo's poem begins in darkness; the speaker (as we discover later, a son searching for his father) looks for light and convergence:

> I wait
> for the stars
> to emerge from their dark
> canyons.
>
> I know them well;
> they rise
> above me every evening
> like balloons,[13]

As these stars come "rising" and "burning, / into the sky," the poem wavers toward a metaphysic—toward the father's transcendence—while the narrator-son is left behind: "I stay / to watch the stars / go higher, deeper / into the night." This embodied son who traces the father's height may remind us of Roland Barthes's insistence in *The Pleasure of the Text* that the absent father is the single source for telling tales. Ebalo's narrator is questing for this absent father. "The dead, / I was told and believed, become stars." As they dance behind a "smoky gauze / in clusters" like "Christmas lights / moving across the sky," we see that the father's locus is mysterious; it is faintly familiar, yet spectral. But even as we stride into star space, the poem veers down to earth:

> Some nights they
> are like young
> Cassiopeia,
>
> distant and solitary.
> Tonight she sits in the sky
> holding hands with war
> dead, widow-makers,
>
> and a man whose heart
> medicine is still
> in the kitchen cabinet—
> my father.

Ebalo's poem offers one example of a text in which the father's *asomia,* his bodilessness and distance, is broken open and revealed as tragedy. Cassiopeia, gallant queen, seems a bridge to revision, a woman whose body holds the sky and the sky-gods open to our sight. This openness is frightening. Ebalo's poem makes achingly clear the depth of the tension between embodiment and disembodiment that characterizes the father's relation to others and to himself.

"The Star Story" is a tragic poem with a utopian dimension; it offers an arena for feminist praxis. That is, it suggests that we can look for and talk about texts that attempt to break the cultural pattern of the father's bodilessness. But feminist analysis of the father must take another direction as well, since there are myriad texts that struggle to displace or defame the father's relation to embodiment. For example, in Coleridge's prose fragment, "The Wanderings of Cain," the father is horrified by his own guilt and embodiment and the narrative struggles to both confront and avoid this agonized knowledge:

The path was dark till within three strides' length of its termination, when it turned suddenly; the thick black trees formed a low arch, and the moonlight appeared for a moment like a dazzling portal. Enos ran before and stood in the open air; and when Cain, his father, emerged from the darkness, the child was affrighted. For the mighty limbs of Cain were wasted as by fire; his hair was as the matted curls on the bison's forehead, and so glared his fierce and sullen eye beneath: and the black abundant locks on either side, a rank and tangled mass, were stained and scorched, as though the grasp of a burning iron hand had striven to rend them; and his countenance told in a strong and terrible language of agonies that had been, and were, and were still to continue to be.[14]

"The burning iron hand" and the "terrible language" inscribed in Cain's body tell us that this is already a body striving beyond its own physicalness, a body Coleridge is describing in its animal ferocity and striving to deny. Even in the moment of depicting Cain's wretched embodiment, this prose fragment is anxious to project this struggle and bodiliness toward a metaphysical domain.

In discovering this customary subterfuge, we may wish to dismiss Coleridge's prose fragment as another version of an old, deadly tale, but in such dismissal we make two mistakes. First, we fail to estimate the power of exposing what a patriarchal metaphysic represses. To read the father as "Law" or as "the Symbolic" misses both the fracturable dimension of the father's role and the fact that the father problem is always a multiple tale: it is the product of divergent forces; not of a single, hegemonic structure or voice. Second, if we dismiss the vexed position of the father in "The Wanderings of Cain" as the same old paternal hijinks—rather than analyzing the various social and sexual formations struggling in Coleridge's narrative for a voice—we will also ignore Coleridge's own concrete life as a father. It may be worth asking what Coleridge's (or Hardy's or Hawthorne's or Hemingway's) *particular* struggle with "the paternal metaphor" meant. How did being—or not being—a "good-enough" father affect Coleridge's writing, his verse? And why have both feminist and nonfeminist critics ignored the relations between

concrete acts of fathering (or failing to father) and patriarchal productions of canonical texts? The answers may be the same—we have
not permitted ourselves to think of men, of fathers, especially, as
creatures who are embodied, whose lives and works are wrapped
up in, affected by, even coerced—by the bodies of their children.

Thus, even if a Lacanian problematic can remind us of the peculiar
self-splitting and self-divisiveness inherent in sexual divisions of
labor, insofar as we continue to focus on the paternal function as
function alone, we fail to make room in our analysis for the father's
concreteness. Lacan sets forth a grand project in which the particular
father disappears: "So as to make the link between the Name of the
Father, in so far as he can at times be missing, and the father whose
effective presence is not always necessary for him not to be missing,
I will introduce the expression *paternal metaphor*."[15] But if the father
problem is always, and only, an abstracted way of connoting the
relation of socially constructed desire to the unconscious and to the
Symbolic, this can only throw us back into the arena in which the
father's specific body and bodily functions are taken away—in which
fathers are always spoken of as father-imagoes—as paternal practices
that are the wicked enemies of feminist praxis. This is not to claim
that "real" fathers are not "imagoes"—subjects and subjective experiences mediated for themselves, their cohorts, and their children
by a network of social imperatives, but rather that this mediation is
inevitably fractured and incomplete—and that a simplistic preoccupation with the "no" or "name" of the father keeps the most tyranni-
cal aspect of this name in its place. To make this point more explicit,
I will describe one of the ways in which a feminist diacritic could
profit from an analysis of particular acts of fathering—in this instance, of Coleridge's fathering, and the effect of this fathering on
his poetry.

Coleridge's first two children were named for the philosophers
Hartley and Berkeley, but in 1799, while Coleridge was traveling
with the Wordsworths through Germany, Berkeley, his second son,
died. This child was less than a year old, and Coleridge was overcome with guilt and grief: "I thought of my own verses on the
Nightingale only because I thought of Hartley, my *only* child:—
Dear Lamb! I hope, *he* won't be dead, before I get home.—There

are moments in which I have such a power of Life within me, such a conceit of it, I mean—that I lay the Blame of my Child's Death to my absence—*not intellectually;* but I have a strange sort of sensation, as if while I was present, none could die whom I intensely loved."[16]

When Coleridge's third child was born, he broke this habit of bestowing grand, philosophic names. This son was not named after a philosopher (although "Godwin" was considered), but after a local place-name, the river Derwent. This naming represents an intriguing piece of sympathetic magic. "Sept. 27 1800—The child being very ill was baptized by the name of Derwent/ The Child hour after hour made a noise exactly like the Creeking of a door which is being shut very slowly to prevent its creeking."[17] For a child who is approaching the lull of inanimate objects this naming is apotropaic; it is an attempt to ward off the wide quiet of death. It is also a naming Coleridge associates with nourishment ("I make for the water—it runs down that Green Mountain which is so directly behind that which I first ascended. . . . I drank, & was refreshed"), and with Coleridge's wished-for powers of vision ("I . . . turned my face, and beheld [O Joy for me!] . . . Derwentwater . . . with a rim of brightness along all its tongued and indented Shores").[18] The beneficent motives behind this naming may have had their effect; within a fortnight of his baptism, Derwent's health improved remarkably, and in October Coleridge was able to turn to several unfinished projects—he attempted to finish "Christabel."

"Christabel" is a poem about parents and children that Coleridge never completed. The first part was written in 1797, long before his trip to Germany, and the second part in 1800, after his return. Did the death of one child and birth of another affect the shape of Coleridge's poem? This is not a question critics have asked. Although "Christabel" is severely fractured as a poem—broken in two by the diverging themes of each section, and by crises in Coleridge's own acts of fathering—most critics analyze the poem as if it were psychically unified.

It is my thesis that Coleridge's relation to his children had an emphatic influence on the shape of this poem. If this influence has gone unnoticed, it is because we have admitted father imagoes, but not real, physical fathers, into our readings of literary texts. This is not to plead for an essentialist reading of "fatherhood," but for a different kind of feminist analytic: one that imagines men to be affected (emotional and vulnerable) as well as affected (theatrical and narcissistic) in their relations to children, and that these affections and affectations have had considerable effects on men's prose and their verse. In this spirit, I will suggest that Margery Durham's apt reading of "Christabel" in *The (M)other Tongue* is not, for all its acumen and feminist promise, complete. (Even though I will quarrel with Durham's conclusions, I should add that her analysis is marvelous in its definitions of Coleridge's troubled relation to gender; her essay has helped to provide the terms for my own reading of Coleridge's poem.)

Durham reads "Christabel" through the Kleinian parable of the mother's good and bad breasts: "The first impulse [Coleridge] considers in *Christabel* is that of dependence on the breast, that is, on the mother. This initial dependency proves to be the psychological origin of poetry and myth. As Coleridge develops his symbol of the lost paradise, the breast becomes a metaphor of the entire nourishing environment, some loss of which occurs at each stage of individual growth."[19]

Durham's account of "Christabel" 's genesis is moving, but this story of the maternal origins of grief can prevent an assessment of the other uses of the mother figure in "Christabel," for Coleridge's poem is not only a meditation upon the ways in which "the breast and the woman who provides it . . . feed our mental as well as physical life." It is also a poem that uses images of bad mothering to describe bad fathering. The mother's breasts become a figure not only for maternal loss and primordial despair, but for the inadequacy of the father's breasts.

Durham explains that the mother and her body "may become hateful because we desire them yet cannot always and wholly possess them; we can fear the mother because we need her too much" (183). But I would suggest that in "Christabel" this maternal plot is also used to explore paternal lack. In naming Derwent after plentiful Lake District water Coleridge is both nourishing his third child and anxiously acknowledging his failure to nourish his second child.

Similarly, in the second part of "Christabel," written after Berkeley's death, Coleridge is exploring and compensating for the failure of the father's body and language. In reworking these failures in symbolic form, "Christabel" becomes a generalized meditation on the displacement and repression of the father's body as well as a private meditation on the ways in which neither the poet's language nor his physical presence have offered adequate nourishment for his children.

How does the father figure fail in "Christabel"? Sir Leoline, Christabel's father, is named, but does not appear in the 1797 version of Coleridge's poem, which focuses primarily on the lamia Geraldine's uncanny seduction and vampirizing of Christabel. However, in the partition to the poem that Coleridge added in 1800 after his return from Germany, Sir Leoline dominates; his bitter words open the section written after Berkeley's death: "Each matin bell, the Baron saith, / Knells us back to a world of death." The second half of "Christabel" is preoccupied with death and paternal maiming. Although Geraldine has functioned as a supernaturally malevolent and seductive mother figure in the first half of the poem, in the second half her role is defined within paternal history; she claims to be the daughter of an old and estranged friend of Sir Leoline's, "Lord Roland de Vaux of Tryermaine." After spending the first half of the poem traumatizing Leoline's daughter, Geraldine now offers Sir Leoline the added bliss of a reconstituted bond between men: a figurative version of the bliss involved in Coleridge's intricate bonding with Wordsworth. Sadly, the child Christabel begins to wither away when exposed to this bond. Like Berkeley, she is thrust outside the new family circle. And, true to the spirit of Margery Durham's analysis, what Christabel sees at this moment of betrayal—and what maims her—is Geraldine's bosom: "Again she saw that bosom old, / Again she felt that bosom cold, / And drew in her breath with a hissing sound."

For a feminist reader preoccupied with identifying the meaning of the mother's body in "Christabel," the poem's "central, tragic idea" is its yearning for "the origin of speech and of all achievement in the mother's touch," in its enactment of "the rage at not possessing her completely, and the guilt incurred by either remaining with her . . . or leaving her" (175). While I agree that these anxieties are marked in the poem, I would argue that Coleridge is also mapping these images onto—or out of—the father's body as well. Just as naming a child after the river Derwent is Coleridge's way of imagining his third child to be nourished by a source lacking in his own "paternal functioning," so the revisited "Christabel" offers Coleridge the chance to explore a father's guilty allegiance to the wrong child and wrong project—the project of establishing homoerotic bonds between already grown men—instead of the project and contract of bonding between father and child. Although this anxiety about inadequate fathering is present in the first half of the poem (and throughout Coleridge's work, for Coleridge duplicated his own father's absence on more than one occasion), his real grief at Berkeley's death, and the displacement of this grief onto oppositional moments of figuring and fathering, not only becomes the tragic focus of the second half of "Christabel," but these foci reshape the poem from a fantasy about mothers, daughters, and the oral vagaries of an interior muse, to a poem also focused on paternal guilt and anger.

These emotions are spelled out in particular detail when Bracy, Sir Leoline's "bard," enters the poem as a new mediator, as the carrier of love and connection between daughter and father. (Another way to establish a connection between the naming of Coleridge's children and the writing of "Christabel" is to note that "Bracy" was another name Coleridge considered for his son Derwent.) In the poem it is the father, Leoline, who challenges the bard's allegiance to Christabel and makes Bracy into the go-between who will travel between himself and Lord Roland. "Bard Bracy! bard Bracy! your horses are fleet, / Ye must ride up the hall, your music so sweet . . . And loud and loud to Lord Roland call, / Thy daughter is safe in Langdale hall!"[20] But whose child has been preserved? When Bracy has a vision of Christabel's death, Sir Leoline refuses to listen to this omen and has eyes for Geraldine alone. Geraldine in turn fixes an evil eye upon Christabel who responds with grim metamorphosis: "the lady's eyes they shrunk in her head, / Each shrunk up to a serpent's eye." Geraldine, following Leoline's lead, becomes the source of bad nourishment—here, a nourishment that involves dispensing bad images: Christabel "had . . . drunken in / That look, those shrunken serpent eyes, / That all her features were resigned / To this sole image in her mind" (ll.601–4). Vampirized by this symbolism, Christabel faints at Leoline's feet, but he merely turns away "from his own sweet maid" and leads "forth the lady Geraldine!"

The plot of "Christabel" stops here—with the story still laboring; the poem finds its conclusion in a small coda about parental desire:

> A little child, a limber elf,
> Singing, dancing to itself,
> A fairy thing with red round cheeks,
> That always finds, and never seeks,
> Makes such a vision to the sight
> As fills a father's eyes with light;
> And pleasures flow in so thick and fast
> Upon his heart, that he at last
> Must needs express his love's excess
> With words of unmeant bitterness.   (ll.656–65)

The poem's shift from an anxiety about maternal to paternal nourishment is striking. Coleridge explains that while the child amply nourishes the father, the father fails to nourish the child; he feeds it with words of bad intent. If Coleridge ends the poem by thematizing the father's guilt, his absent care and failure to nourish, it is because the father's breasts are the poem's buried, nearly irretrievable figure—a figure that comes very close to the poem's surface in the end. In this moment it is not only the figure father, but the father's figure that Coleridge is trying to recover and repress.

In conclusion, I would like to describe these rereadings of the father function in terms of several feminist projects. First, it would be useful to return to the abstract father figure or "paternal metaphor," the ache and mystery of an embodiment that, at least in the modern age, has been acknowledged only as it has been projected onto women. Second, this recovery must be complex and variable. Men of color and homosexual men in particular have been stripped of their humanity, unclothed, and overembodied by a patriarchal discourse that disvalues embodiment. Feminist analyses of the father's body must be both reconstructive and deconstructive; we must reinvent what it means to be embodied, and we must challenge the classical focus on white, heterosexual fathers as recipients and bestowers of the father's name.

A third feminist project would be to examine texts like Dan Ebalo's "Star Story" that break open this dimension of the father's physicality in a new way. A fourth project would ask for closer attention to the complexity of father figures' lives as they interact with canonical texts—especially to the ways in which the father's vulnerability, his desire and his libidinal body, are ever-present in literary and cultural texts, but as themes that are disguised, as contents under pressure.

A father figure who is busy repressing or obsessing about women's bodies is also a father busy repressing his own body—with its potential for reproductivity and decay. What we should seek in our analysis is not simply the discourse of the oppressive father whose words are like death, but also the silent voice of the repressed or hidden father who will not show his face, his class affiliations, his economic interests, his homoerotic goals. We should try to locate not only the abstracting force of patriarchal law, but the all-too-particular force of an anxious father figure who has a specific material weight, a specific material being, and specific physical worries—a father whose class anxieties and desires for homoerotic bonding are invisibly projected onto his family, his co-workers, and his own "figures" of fatherhood.

It is these invisible anxieties and desires that we must begin to make visible. While feminist critics have renegotiated our reading of patriarchy by focusing on the father's invisibility, on a father whose laws, systems, and discourses function to regulate, like the invisible hand of the market, our social desires, in the course of uncovering this invisible father, we have also begun to refigure him, to make him visible, vulnerable, carnal. We must continue to reconstruct this father as a contactable, masterable, libidinal body, as a being who can be anatomized, fragmented, shattered—or cherished—as someone who no longer operates from an abstract and transcendental realm. Even as we evoke the "black charge of the heart within" that terrorizes the father's oedipal children, we must also work our way past that invisible charge toward some awkward evidence of corporeality and discover, in the texts that we read, some visceral, damnable, dear paternal fragrance, the fragrance of the father's breasts.

Notes

1. Elizabeth Bishop, "Crusoe in England," in *The Complete Poems 1927–1979* (New York: Farrar, Straus, Giroux, 1980), 162–66.
2. Rosi Braidotti, "Envy: or With Your Brains and My Looks" in *Men in Feminism*, eds. Alice Jardine and Paul Smith (New York: Methuen, 1987), 239.
3. Xaviere Gauthier, "Existe-t-il une écriture de femme?" in *New French Feminisms*, eds. Elaine Marks and Isabelle de Courtivron (Amherst: University of Massachusetts Press, 1980), 162–63.
4. Terry Eagleton, *Walter Benjamin, Or Towards a Revolutionary Criticism* (London: Verso, 1981), epigraph, 131.
5. Michel Foucault, *The Order of Things: An Archaeology of the Human Sciences* (New York: Vintage, 1973), xvii–xviii.
6. Shirley Nelson Garner, Claire Kahane, Madelon Sprengnether, Introduction, *The (M)other Tongue* (Ithaca: Cornell University Press, 1985), 10.
7. Sharon Olds, *The Dead and the Living* (New York: Knopf, 1986), 43. I wish to thank Sonya Michel for calling my attention to this poem. For another description of the embodied father, and of the importance, for feminist praxis, of distancing the paternal body from its "counterphobic mechanism," the law, see Jane Gallop's *The Daughter's Seduction: Feminism and Psychoanalysis* (Ithaca: Cornell University Press, 1982), 70ff.
8. Paul Ricouer, *Freud and Philosophy: An Essay on Interpretation*, trans. Denis Savage (New Haven: Yale University Press, 1970), 542.
9. Robert Con Davis, "Critical Introduction: The Discourse of the Father" in *The Fictional Father: Lacanian Readings of the Text*, ed. Robert Con Davis (Amherst: University of Massachusetts Press, 1981), 17.
10. Roland Barthes, *The Pleasure of the Text*, trans. Richard Miller (New York: Hill and Wang, 1975), 47.
11. Elizabeth Spelman, "The Erasure of Black Women," *Quest*, vol. 4, no. 4 (1982), 36–62.
12. Elaine Scarry. *The Body in Pain: The Making and Unmaking of the World* (London: Oxford, 1985), 207.
13. Dan Ebalo, "Star Story," *The New Yorker*, July 20, 1987, 34.

14. Samuel Taylor Coleridge, "The Wanderings of Cain," in *The Complete Poetical Works*, ed. Ernest Hartley Coleridge, 2 vols. (Oxford: Clarendon, 1912).

15. Jacques Lacan, "Les formations de l'inconscient" in *Bulletin de Psychologie* 2 (1957–58), 8, as quoted in Jacqueline Rose's *Sexuality in the Field of Vision* (London: Verso, 1986), 62.

16. Coleridge, *Collected Letters of Samuel Taylor Coleridge*, ed. Earl Leslie Griggs (Oxford: Clarendon, 1956–71) 277.

17. Coleridge, *The Notebooks of Samuel Taylor Coleridge*, ed. Kathleen Coburn (New York: Pantheon, 1957), I:813

18. Coleridge, *The Notebooks*, I:1798.

19. Marjorie Durham, "The Mother Tongue: *Christabel* and the Language of Love," in *The (M)other Tongue: Essays in Feminist Psychoanalytic Interpretation*, eds. Shirley Nelson Garner, Claire Kahane, and Madelon Sprengnether (Ithaca: Cornell University Press, 1985), 180.

20. Coleridge, "Christabel," in *The Complete Poetical Works*, ed. Ernest Hartley Coleridge, 2 vols. (Oxford: Clarendon, 1912).

2 *Colette and the Captain*
Daughter as Ghostwriter
Jerry Aline Flieger

The Paternal Intertext

Reading Between the Lines

Colette's autobiographical accounts of childhood (*Sido*, published in 1929, and *La Maison de Claudine*, translated as *My Mother's House* and published in 1922) provide a memorable encounter with a luminous central presence, the resplendent maternal figure who assumes mythic proportions in her daughter's memory. "My childish pride and imagination," Colette recalls in *Sido*, "saw our house as the central point of a mariner's chart of gardens, no section of which lay quite beyond my mother's influence."[1] In these autobiographical vignettes, all roads lead to Sido.

A glance at the chapter titles of *My mother's House* reveals the extent of this influence ("My Mother and Animals." "My Mother and Morals," "My Mother and the Books," "My Mother and the Curé," and so forth).[2] And of course the figure of Sido—as beloved spirit—looms large in later autobiographical works as well (especially *Break of Day*, 1928, and *Evening Star*, 1945): in these works the mother's spirit returns to guide her daughter in her life and in her work, and later to accompany her on what Collete calls "The Road Back Home" to eternal slumber. Little wonder, then, that critics and commentators have so often emphasized the importance of the mother-daughter relation in Colette's autobiographical writings.

But there is, of course, a corollary absence. Or rather, a displacement. For Colette's father, hardly a father figure, is a mere *figurant*
in the tales of childhood; he is relegated to the sidelines, glimpsed
only in fleeting asides to the mother-daughter love story. Indeed,
the mother is the titular figure of an entire work *(Sido)*, and the
dominant interest of another *(My Mother's House)*, in which she is
claimed with the possessive, as *"my* mother," in no fewer than six
chapter headings. Yet the father merits only a section of *Sido*, in
which he is dubbed "the Captain," rather than being referred to by
given name; and he figures only once in the chapter headings of *My
Mother's House*, as the principal character of "Father and Madame
Bruneau" (a title that, significantly, lacks the possessive "my" and
links the father to an outsider with whom he carries on a flirtation).
A second chapter, entitled "My Father's Daughter," seems to promise an account of the Captain's filial relation with the child Gabrielle
(Colette's given name); but significantly this title turns out to be a
quote from Sido, and thus deals with the maternal grandfather
rather than with Colette's own father. "Sido" is thus literally and
figuratively her daughter's text; "the Captain" is simply intertext.

Or perhaps not so simply: psychoanalysis has demonstrated the
importance of the marginal, the in-between, the forgotten, the
trivialized. Certainly, after Freud, things have ceased to be "simply"
what they seem, especially as concerns family history. When considered in oedipal terms, to be sure, the familial nest is not a haven, an
"Earthly Paradise" (to cite the title of Robert Phelps's collection of
Colette's autobiographical writings[3]): it is rather a ménage à trois,
an arena of competition, staging a struggle for independence and
for access to subjectivity. In Lacanian theory, matters are even
further complicated by linguistics, in the largest sense of the term:
the struggle for subjectivity is played out with and through a familial
other, the Symbolic Father, and is intimately bound up with the
acquisition of language.

Reading the paternal intertext in Colette's writing, then, requires
a close attention to the complications of "earthly paradise," in order
to enrich our experience of the (maternal) text and enhance our
understanding of the (filial) subtext, the drama of "Colette" herself

as writing subject. Yet reading the intertext, encountering the fantom father, is not an easy task: the effort requires the art of displaced ("free-floating") attention, of collage, of patching and pasting, of reading between the lines.

Colette's own narrative persona almost seems to elicit this effort on the part of her reader, by the wistfulness and poignancy of her own evocations of "the captain": "it seems strange now, that I knew him so little" (*Sido*, 175); "were we not worthy, he and I, of a mutual effort to know each other better?" (184). Colette's memories of her father are couched in the optative mode, the "if and only" of nostalgia and regret: "Too late! Too late! That is always the cry of children, of the negligent and the ungrateful" (181). One anecdote (in *Sido*) is particularly poignant and particularly revealing, indicating the crucial—if elided—importance of the Captain in the familial drama and in the later emergence of his daughter's literary vocation. For Sido, as it turns out, is not the only beloved ghost to haunt the writer.

The Fantom Father

Significantly, the Captain's most memorable appearance in the autobiographical writings is as an *apparition,* a ghost who visits his daughter long after his death. In "The Captain" (the chapter in *Sido* devoted to the father), there is an account of a séance "chez Mme B" (the tantalizing initial itself conjuring up the spector of Mme Bruneau, the "other woman" with whom the father is linked in *My Mother's House*. At this séance, attended casually, almost incidentally, "at the suggestion of a friend" (193), Colette characteristically asks for the news of her mother, and is "vaguely jealous" to learn that Sido's ghost is occupied with her younger brother, the rival sibling. Mme B reports, however, that the paternal ghost is clearly present and very much concerned:

Behind you the spirit of an old man is sitting. . . . He has a spreading, untrimmed beard, nearly white, and rather long, grey, hair, brushed back. His eyebrows . . . my word! what eyebrows . . . are extraordinarily bushy . . . and as for the eyes under them! They're small, but so brilliant, one can hardly endure their gaze. . . . Do you have any idea who it might be?

Indeed I do. (194)

Mme B goes on to assert that this spirit is "very much taken up with" his daughter, and when Colette expresses her skepticism, the medium explains: "He is very much taken up with you *at present.* . . . Because you represent what he would have so much liked to be when he was here on earth. You are exactly what he longed to be. But he himself was never able" (194).

Colette does not analyze this revelation immediately; she describes instead the rest of the afternoon, before returning to the question of her father, offhandedly, almost as an afterthought: "As for my father . . . 'You are exactly what he longed to be, and in his lifetime was never able' " (195). This second quote from Mme B represents a very slight but significant variation from the first ("he himself was never able" has become "in his lifetime was never able"). This modification, barely perceptible, nonetheless suggests that a profound identification is taking place; for the Captain apparently has new capabilities *after* his lifetime, thanks to his daughter's work. Colette does not elaborate on this observation, leaving it in its marginal, and almost parenthetical place; but she goes on to relate another anecdote, which is perhaps one of the most disturbing and powerful moments in all her autobiographical works. She begins by revealing that "the Captain" had spent a good part of his retirement (an amputee, he had ended his military career, and his political career had been a failure) locked away in his library, writing his memoirs:

I can still see, on one of the highest shelves of the library, a row of volumes, bound in boards, with black linen spines. . . . But the titles, handwritten in Gothic lettering, never tempted me, more especially since the black-rimmed labels bore no author's name. I quote from memory: *My Campaigns, The Lessons of '70, The Geodesy of Geodesies, Elegant Algebra, Marshal MacMahon Seen By a Fellow Soldier, From Village to Parliament, Zouave Songs* (in verse). . . . I forget the rest. (195)

These volumes remain unopened, in full view but neglected, until one day after the Captain's death, when his library is being converted to a bedroom. It is only at this moment that the family discovers that all these volumes, systematically entitled and arranged, are composed of blank pages: "The dozen volumes bound in boards revealed to us their secret, a secret so long disdained by us, accessible though it was. Two hundred, three hundred, one hundred fifty pages to a volume; beautiful, cream-laid paper, or thick 'foolscap' carefully trimmed, hundreds and hundreds of blank pages. Imaginary works, the mirage of a writer's career."

The plot thickens when Colette reveals that the only writing in all these "virgin volumes" is a poignant and chilling dedication to the Captain's one love, that same "Sido" who is the prime love-object for her child, the focal point in a primal triangle. "The single page lovingly completed and signed," Colette relates (197), is "the page that bore the dedication: TO MY DEAR SOUL, HER FAITHFUL HUSBAND: JULES-JOSEPH CO-LETTE." Sido herself, "out of piercing regret and the painful desire to blot out this proof of incapacity" (196), this testimony of impotence and creative sterility dedicated to her, tries to use up these "cream-laid notebooks, his invisible works" (196), but to no avail: the endless white pages prove inexhaustible ("we never saw the end of them. . . . , there were so many of these virgin pages. . . . , we never exhausted his invisible 'works' ").

In later years, Colette writes, she continued to be haunted by this "mirage," the image of all these blank pages of mute adoration, dedicated to the beloved matriarch: "At the time when I was beginning to write, I too drew on this spiritual legacy. Was that where I got my extravagant taste for writing on smooth sheets of fine paper, without the least regard for economy? I dared to cover with my large handwriting the invisible cursive script, perceptible to only one person in the world" (197). Thus the painful discovery of the ungrateful child who understands "too late" the unbearably painful secret of her father's incapacity turns out to be a source and a resource, an invisible inspiration, "like a shining tracery" (197).

Colette was, of course, to marry another creatively sterile paternal figure, who, in turn, enjoined her to do what he was unable to do, to fill the blank page with writing, which he could sign. And as ghostwriter for Willy, as well as for the paternal figure who continues to haunt her, Colette abandons her childhood name (Gabrielle, "Minet-Cheri") and is christened by Willy, her new "father," with a doubly patriarchal name, comprised of the names of father and husband. But Colette Willy, ghostwriter, of course subsequently became—and still remains—"Colette." In Lacanian terms, one could say that Colette's identity as a writer, her access to the Symbolic Order—in spite of detours and transformations—is by way of the Name-of-the-Father.

But it is the detours and transformations that make this ghost story so intriguing, and that cause us to wonder just how "the Captain"—the maimed and sterile patriarch, figure of great pathos—has contributed to his daughter's vocation, and what this might suggest about the role of the father-daughter relation in the formation of the woman artist. How can that ghost, known too little and too late, provide access to Colette's "underworld," the shadowy subtext of her own subjectivity? How may psychoanalytic theory—and particularly Lacanian theory, with its emphasis on the Father as Symbolic function rather than historical person—aid us in the exploration of "Colette" as autobiographical Subject? Conversely, might this encounter with Colette as woman and as writer, as woman writer, encourage a rereading of psychoanalytic theory concerning female subjectivity, and shed some light on the question that continues to "haunt" psychoanalysis? What does woman (as writer) want?

Screen Memories

Smokescreens

All of Colette's portraits of her father bear some family resemblance to that ghostly apparition encountered at the séance in *Sido:* for these intermittent and fleeting remembrances are veiled by mystery, "shrouded" in guilt, shaded with nostalgia. Indeed, when the Captain makes a rare appearance in *Sido* or in *My Mother's House,* the *récit* more often than not veers into the minor mode, even when the anecdote recounted is burlesque or amusing. (A case in point is the episode entitled "Father and Mme Bruneau," in which the hapless neighborwoman becomes the target of merciless sexual teasing on the part of the Captain, who offers to initiate her to the art of love for the price of "sixpence and a packet of tobacco." Yet even in this instance, the most clearly comic portrait of the Captain, an undertone of sadness persists: the one-legged Captain, confined to his home and forever barred from the exercise of his military career by his infirmity, has become a caricature, a farcical conqueror, whose "exploits" have been reduced to ribald pleasantry.)

The Captain's effusiveness, moreover, is invariably underwritten by a mysterious melancholy: "It is true," his daughter recalls, "that he often made us laugh, and that he told a good tale, embroidering recklessly when he got into the swing of it, and that melody bubbled out of him; but did I ever see him gay?" (*Sido*, 179). The Captain's very creativity, his gift of captivating an audience, is characterized as a kind of protective coloration, a smokescreen, a shield: "Wherever he went, his song preceded and protected him" (179).

Thus Colette's father is a paradox and an enigma—sad and gay, silent and sociable, hot-blooded and distant ("in our midst a man brooded bitterly" [186]). It is the Captain's sadness, and his bitterness, that constitute his mystery, especially puzzling since his relationship with Sido is characterized as on of great mutual love and joy. The Captain's false gaiety, moreover, is a screen, a decoy, for something ineffable: "Who could have believed that this baritone, still nimble with the aid of a crutch and a stick, is projecting his song like a smoke-screen in front of him, so as to detract attention from himself?" (180). His very presence has an obscure, "screened" quality; even his gaze, the color of smoke, is surrounded by mystery: Colette describes the tantalizing challenge of "that extraordinary blue-grey gaze of his, which revealed its secrets to no one, though sometimes admitting that such secrets exist" (188). Like his "smoke-screen" song, this gaze is impenetrable; and yet, like a cipher, it hints at secrets, and invites scrutiny and interpretation. Like the empty volumes in the library, like the haunting presence at the séance, the Captain's secret is tantalizingly present and yet intangible, an open book that asks to be read, and remains invisible.

Of course, for psychoanalysis, it is just this sort of sign—like the celebrated "purloined letter" of Lacan's essay on Poe, a sign present yet invisible, a clue in full view—that is at once the most interesting and the most elusive, obscured by the "screen" of unconscious desire and motivated forgetting. And it is to these tantalizing ciphers that the Captain's daughter turns in memory, in order to understand, to look behind the smokescreen, to clear the air.

Colette herself draws attention to the patchiness, the fogginess, of her recollections of her father: "I can only see my father's face vaguely and intermittently," as a "wandering, floating figure, full of gaps, obscured by clouds and only visible in patches" (177). The remembered paternal portrait is at once angelic ("obscured by clouds") and ghostly, semivisible, errant, floating. When she does succeed in fixing his memory, the experience is equally eery and uncanny, for the Captain appears frozen in time, corpselike, silent as the sphinx: "He is clear enough sitting in the big, recovered armchair. The two oval mirrors of his open pince-nez gleam on his chest, and the red line of his peculiar lower lip, like a rolled rim, protrudes a little beneath the moustache which joins his beard. In that position his is fixed forever" (177). Colette often seems to attribute the mystery surrounding her recollections of her father to a simple matter of faulty memory, the result of childhood indifference, of "Gabrielle's" failure to look behind the clouds.

Yet there is surely more to this "screened" memory than lack of information or deficient memory, particularly because these memories are such a source of torment for the adult daughter. Again, we are reminded of an important concept in psychoanalytic theory—that of "screen memories," those fragmentary and apparently innocent childhood recollections that Freud analyzes in the essay "Dichtung und Wahrheit," and reads as ciphers, signs of repressed experience.[4] Colette's recollections have many of the earmarks of classic psychoanalytic screen memory, in which the apparently insignificant and fragmentary content is problematized by the persistent and troubling quality of the images ("but now the thought of my father tortures me" [179]). The sense of filial culpability in these passages is striking indeed; or one senses rather the duplicity of the narrating voice, in which the child's indifference toward her father is doubled and underwritten by the adult's tormented curiosity, and by the melancholic and uncanny nature of those fragments of memory that persist.

For Colette, of course, the fogginess of childhood recollections of her father derives primarily from the deliberate "air of mystery" with which the Captain screens himself, his own secretive character, while in a classic Freudian screen memory the uncanniness and incompletion of the recollection result from the "screen" of repression, the motivated forgetting of the patient, rather than from any external barriers. Whatever the source of the "screen" that obscures the memory of the Captain, however, his daughter now sets herself the task of piercing the shield, dispersing the smokescreen, repiecing the fragments into a whole portrait ("So that's the real you? Now I see, I'd never understand you" [186]). This work of reconstruction and remembrance ("It takes time for the dead to assume their true shape in our thoughts" [186]), is perhaps first a kind of detective work, in which the writer functions as archeologist and as seamstress, assembling clues that have long lain unexamined, stitching them into their "true shape." But this process is also a kind of séance and autoanalysis, a work of mourning that reanimates the shades of the past in order to put them to rest.

Smoke Gets in Your Eyes

Yet the patchwork portrait is slow to emerge, hindered by the obstruction of time, the "screens" of the Captain's own enigmatic personality, and the mutual blindness of father and daughter during their time together. Colette attributes this blindness to an all-consuming love for Sido: "My attention, my fervent admiration were all for Sido and only fitfully strayed from her. . . . It was just the same with my father. His eyes dwelt on Sido" (175). Father and child, caught in the dazzling orbit of the maternal solar system, are unable to see each other, invisible in the glare of their own shared adoration. Both daughter and father, of course, to some extent choose this blindness, this indifference to the Other, who is taken for granted, considered an insignificant and marginal personage, or even an interloper.

In a telling passage, for instance, Colette relates an incident in which her mother reproaches her mate for a ribald anecdote, because of the presence of the onlooking child. The Captain retorts, "Oh the child, it doesn't matter about her" (188), and having thus summarily dismissed and excluded his daughter, proceeds to envelop himself and Sido in the smoldering and impenetrable circle of his (smoke-colored) haze ("and he would fasten on his chosen one that extraordinary, challenging, blue-grey gaze of his" [188]), a gaze that annuls the presence of all outsiders. Colette goes on to describe her father's "blindness" as an actual physical debility, or rather, to analogize the Captain's physical defect with his emotional tunnel vision, first perceived, interestingly, when the daughter is an adolescent—the age of a certain "reason" and enhanced perception (189): "I was not more than thirteen when I noticed that my father was ceasing to see, in the physical sense of the word, his Sido herself. 'Another new dress?' he would exclaim with surprise. 'Bless my soul, Madam!' " Sido protests that the dress is three years old, but the Captain has already ceased to see and to hear her, retreating to the hazy revery of days gone by: "But he was no longer listening to her. . . . He had already jealously rejoined her in some favorite spot, where she wore a chignon with Victorian side-curls, a bodice with tulle ruching and a heart-shaped opening at the neck. As he grew older he could not even bear her to look tired or ill." In this light, the Captain's "blindness" is almost a hysterical symptom, an emotional state with a physical result, a second debility that is almost another (visual) "castration," a loss of "the gift of observation and the power of comparison" (189) that reflects the loss of limb, and parallels or even partially explains that other paralysis, before the glare of the white page.

In this perspective, the Captain's love for Sido has become the cause for his emotional and artistic truncation, a curtailment of creative powers for which his physical amputation seems almost emblematic. And indeed, as Colette relates in another passage, his creative powers do decline, absorbed by the white heat of his love: at first anxious to "shine" before his love, he "little by little came to abandon even his desire to dazzle Sido" (177), *"as his love increased."* His own "dazzle," his own heat, seems to be progressively reduced to the sphere of his smoldering gaze, which not only excludes outsiders but also finally limits his own vision, even while it provides an encircling and even stifling atmosphere for the beloved object of his attention. "Her grey eyes glanced rapidly in all directions," Colette recounts. "This confusion and the vain attempt of those eyes to escape from a man's gaze, blue-grey as new-cut lead, was all that [was] revealed to me of the passion which bound Sido and the Captain throughout their lives" (192).

The Captain's passion is thus both a bond and an oppression—as piercing and inescapable as dense smoke—which at once binds and blinds both parties it engulfs. For Sido is not the only one to be oppressed by this stifling love; the Captain himself is *"reduced* now to his village and his family, his whole love being absorbed by the great love which (binds) his horizon" (181, my emphasis). Beneath the surface of perfect marital harmony, described as a kind of peaceable kingdom "where the children never fought and where beasts and men lived tranquilly together; a garden where for the space of thirty years a husband and a wife dwelt together with never a harsh word between them" (154), within this circle of perfect love, there simmers an atmosphere as restive and intense as a Racinian tragedy, within a horizon bound not only by mutual love, but by mutual evasiveness and incomprehension.

For the Captain is not the only one to suffer from the blindness of love: if he becomes increasingly incapable of seeing his family, and even his Sido herself, his mate is perhaps equally blind to the truth of the man she has married, deceived by the outward manifestations of sociability (she thought he was gay because he sang" [179]).

Ciphers

Smoke Signals

Yet if Sido is blinded by these false signs of gaiety, these "smoke-screens" of song and narrative, her daughter is less easily diverted from the truth, at least in retrospect. For her, the father's melancholic song and enigmatic gaze are signs, which not only hide but also bear witness, "admitting that secrets exist," "revealing unspoken passion." Now, as an adult, the Captain's daughter attempts to decipher these signs that haunt her memory and elicit her interpretation. Her first hypotheses concerning her father's mysterious sadness are relatively commonplace, and deal with material, tangible circumstances: the Captain's impending financial failure ("he sings in the hope that perhaps today SHE will forget to ask him if he has been able to borrow 100 louis on the security of his disabled officer's pension" [180]), and the retired officer's frustration at no longer being able to exercise his military vocation ("and now, bitterly, his spirit still soared. . . . Sido and his love for her were all that he had been able to keep" [187]). And always, accompanying and underlying these explanations of the Captain's sadness, there is the more ominous suggestion that the father's all-consuming love, rather than being a compensation for his infirmity, his bound horizon and diminishing view, is perhaps actually a source of that infirmity, that diminution. More important than his visible wound, his amputation, is perhaps his hidden wound, the wound of love.

In any case, the Captain's diversionary tactics seem to work on Sido, who listens to his song spellbound, "in spite of herself, unable to interrupt him" (179). But the adult daughter knows better, because she has come to identify profoundly with her father's secret sadness, his hidden hurt: "But I who whistle whenever I am sad, and turn the pulsations of fever, or the syllables of a name that tortures me, into endless variations on a theme, could wish that she had understood that pity is the supreme insult. My father and I have no use for pity: our nature rejects it" (179).

This remarkable passage, which is at once a reproach to the mother and an expression of identification with the father, reveals as much about the Captain's daughter as it does about the Captain himself. It suggests, moreover, that the Captain's mysterious sadness has finally less to do with financial failure, curtailed career, or underrequited love than it does with the difficulties of his other, secret vocation, shared with his daughter—the calling of writer. For in this passage language itself is described as an obsession, a feverish repetition of variations on a theme. Moreover, this passage concludes with yet another "haunting" revelation: "And now the thought of my father tortures me, because I know he possessed a virtue more precious than any facile charms: that of knowing full well why he was sad, and never revealing it" (179). For the Captain is above all a silent poet, Orpheus dismembered, torn limb from limb, a singer without tongue, a writer without pen, whose *mémoire* is paralyzed before the page; and yet, his silence—"more precious than facile charms"—is also a strength. The Captain's greatest virtue, prized and shared by the writer, his daughter, is one of simultaneous self-knowledge and dissimulation.

De-crypting the Captain

Now, years later, the daughter reveals this "precious gift"; and in so doing, she performs what is for her the writer's task par excellence, described in an earlier chapter as a kind of treasure hunt, an exhuming that is literally a discovery: "A treasure is not merely something hidden under the earth, or rocks, or the sea. . . . To me the important thing is to lay bare and to bring to light something that no human eye before mine has gazed upon" (163). In uncovering her father's secret "gift," so carefully hidden, it is precisely the operation of exposure that the writer is performing. And the father's "gift," of torment nobly and silently borne, is a virtue the daughter claims for herself, in an act of mimetic identification: "When I am alone I try to imitate that look of my father's. Sometimes I succeed fairly well, especially when I use it to face up to some hidden hurt, which proves how efficacious insult can be against something which has you in its power, and how great is the pleasure of standing up to a tyrant" (188).

What Colette admires most—and even imitates—in her father is precisely his mystery, his impenetrable gaze, his capacity for veiling a "hidden hurt" in song, in gaiety. For this quality is, for Colette, the artist's gift, the capacity to elaborate, to embroider, to veil the "bare facts." Thus the labor of the artist, in Colette's vision, is paradoxically both an exhuming or laying-bare, and a covering or cloaking—the capacity, for instance, of turning "the syllables of a name" into "endless variations on a theme" (16).

Such a vision of the writer's work, of course, is in many ways like the psychoanalytic vision of therapy, or of the process of assumption of human subjectivity by the human child. In Lacanian theory in particular, analysis is among other things a kind of mourning work, a coming to terms with one' ghosts, through the transference, which is also the encounter with one's own "wound," one's own death, in the Symbolic Order. In other words, in Lacanian theory, the Symbolic debt is transmitted from parent to child, and the (therapeutic) task of those left behind is to dig and to fathom, to lay bare the repressed "signified," which subtends the paternal metaphor, to remember the dead (father) by lifting the shroud of the unconscious, by assuming the "hidden hurt" (of castration). But the Symbolic debt is also, paradoxically, the requirement of the burial of the dead—in language, in metaphor—which entails putting the Symbolic Father to rest, in due time and with the proper work of mourning.[5]

For Freud, both of these functions—of bringing to light, and of burial or veiling—are seen as important components of the artist's or writer's labor, "the poet's secret" (discussed in "Creative Writers and Daydreaming" and in *Delusion and Dream in Jensen's 'Gradiva'*).[6] For the poet is the human subject who has access to "buried" unconscious material, and who manages to "veil" that material in artistic form. For the writer Colette, this mourning work entails the re-membering of the (castrated) father, the amputee, the reassembly of Orpheus by first discovering the "hidden hurt" in the impenetrable blue-grey gaze, and then assuming that Symbolic Debt as the motor of writing, the desire that engenders the "endless variations on a theme," which are an act of embellishment and invention. This double labor of the daughter—"undertaken" in the presence of her father's spirit—is at once a labor of endless joy and of endless torment: almost in spite of herself ("and now the thought of my father tortures me . . ."), this daughter returns to her father's "grave"—those blank pages of his memoirs—and insists on a reopening, a reworking, which is at the same time necessary and painful.

In this labor, it is the specter of her father's hand—disembodied, severed, like the lost limb—that rises up before her: "I can always see his white hands, particularly since I've begun to hold my thumb bent out awkwardly, as he did, and found my hands crumpling and rolling and destroying paper, with explosive rage, just as his hands used to do" (177). Like her father before her, Colette is "all thumbs" before the challenge of the page. And she is "haunted" by her father's incapacity, because his "hidden hurt" precedes, reflects, and signifies her own hidden hurt—the obsessive desire to write, underwritten by painful incapacity. In Lacanian terms, one could say that the daughter's torment, a sign of identification with the father, is a symptom of the Symbolic Debt passed from one generation to the next, the "debt" that is at once stigma—sign of castration, violation, or death borne by every human being—and compensation, the gift of language. Like the red ribbon worn in the Captain's lapel—a military "decoration" that both rewards his loss of limb and serves as a sign, a reminder of that diminution (187)—the wound of language is at once a "red badge of honor," a sign of humanity passed from parent to child, and a stigma, a reminder of the law (of separation, wounding, death) by which every human child accedes to the Symbolic Order. The child's assumption of the Symbolic Debt is the assumption of the torment of language as symptom and source of unassuageable desire, as tool of memory that "unearths" the past, yet enables a coming to terms with that past.

Thus the Captain's daughter is a ghostwriter who gives shape to the dead father's desire, even as she repeats his Symbolic gesture, "rolling and discarding" the white page, writing and rewriting. And in performing this creative and filial duty, in reenacting her father's desire, she seeks both to acknowledge and to soothe that "hidden hurt inflicted by some tyrant"; for that tyrant is, on some level, always herself, the guilty and negligent daughter, the parent's rival and assassin. For Colette, the writer's labor is the payment of "Gabrielle's" debt, the adult's understanding compensating for the child's crime of indifference or even of (oedipal) hostility: "It is never too late, since now I have fathomed what formerly my youth hid from me: my brilliant, cheerful father harbored the profound sadness of those who have lost a limb. We were hardly aware that one of his legs was missing, amputated just below the hip. What should we have said if we had suddenly seen him walking like everyone else?" (186–87).

The Captain's "secret," then, is finally described simply as "the sadness of those who have lost a limb"; and it is a secret so obvious as to go unobserved ("we were hardly aware . . ."). Like the empty volumes, like Lacan's "purloined letter," it is a clue in full view, overlooked by those too close to see. And this "sadness of those who have lost a limb" is of course a multivalent symptom, signifying loss of career, financial incapacity, the wound of burning love, the helplessness of the "born writer" who cannot write. But it might also signify the red badge of honor, the wound suffered by all human beings—the meaning of the oedipal drama—suffered as a condition for their entry into the Symbolic Order of humanity.

In other words, the story of the Captain's daughter may be read as an oedipal history, a struggle for subjectivity that entails a face-off with the law, and a submission to the law. As a child, Colette recalls, she used to covet her father's writing materials, "prowling, hungrily, around all these treasures of stationery" (*Earthly Paradise,* 48), and on one occasion going so far as to steal two implements from the Captain's worktable. This transgression does not go unpunished: "Not to mention the scolding, I received full in my face the glare of a small, blazing, grey eye, the eye of a rival, so fierce that I did not risk it a third time" (48). As an adult, Colette still feels that paternal *regard* upon her (from those eyes "so brilliant one can hardly endure their gaze"), the eyes of the paternal ghost encountered at the séance described in *Sido* (195). But whereas the awful glare encountered in childhood is fraternal, the gaze of a rival and an equal—a fellow member of Sido's entourage—the brilliant gaze encountered at the séance is benevolent, paternal, enjoining the daughter to do what he was unable to do "in his lifetime," to sign written pages with the name "Colette."

If this parent-daughter story is an oedipal history, then it is nonetheless a transformation from the standard, patriarchal version of psychoanalysis. Here the Subject is not Oedipus, the male-child protagonist, but Antigone, who is at once sister and daughter to Oedipus. Like Antigone, Colette is a sister who demands the proper "burial" of her sibling, with due attention and respect. But she is also the daughter companion, who guides her father Oedipus after his blinding (significantly, the Captain is described at moments in the text as being monocular, having only *one* small, blazing, grey eye [481]), his debilitation, his Symbolic castration. She thus takes on the consequences of her father's act—or, in Colette's case, his inability to act—becoming her father's eyes, his voice, his writing hand. Thanks to Colette, the white page ceases to hold the Captain captive, as she fills the page and signs it with her chosen signature, shared with the paternal ghost. Her paradoxical task is at once a laying bare of the missing limb, the clue in full view, and a clothing and compensating for the awkward excessive limb ("I've begun to hold my thumb bent awkwardly, as he did" [177]), a sign of desire. Thus Antigone will speak for and with Oedipus, telling the story of that mother beloved by them both, drawing on "that spiritual legacy" carried "like a shining tracery to that triumphant conclusion," daring to cover "with large, round handwriting the invisible cursive script" (197), which will henceforth be signed by a single feminine name, that of the daughter "Colette."

Notes

1. Colette, *Sido,* trans. Una Vincent Troubridge and Enid McLeod (New York: Farrar, Straus, and Giroux, 1953). All page numbers cited refer to this translation, published in the same volume as *My Mother's House* (note 2, below).

2. Colette, *My Mother's House,* trans. Una Vincent Troubridge and Enid McLeod (New York: Farrar, Straus, and Giroux, 1953).

3. Colette, *Earthly Paradise,* ed. Robert Phelps (New York: Farrar, Straus, and Giroux, 1966).

4. Sigmund Freud, "A Childhood Recollection from *Dichtung und Wahrheit*" in *Standard Edition of the Complete Psychological Works of Sigmund Freud,* trans. James Strachey, 24 vols. (London: Hogarth Press, 1953–74), vol. 4.

5. Freud, "Totem and Taboo," *Standard Edition,* vol. 13. For a discussion of Lacan's Symbolic Father and the Symbolic Debt, see Anthony Wilden's translation and commentary on Lacan's "The Function of Language in Psychoanalysis" in *The Language of the Self* (New York: Dell, 1968), esp. 270–71; 152; 304–5.

6. Freud, "Creative Writers and Daydreaming," *Standard Edition,* vol. 9, 143; and "Mourning and Melancholy," *Standard Edition,* vol. 14, 239.

3   *Screening the Father*
The Strategy of Obedience in Early James
Susan M. Griffin

In nearly all of Henry James's early novels, a daughter struggles with a parent over the question of a husband. Such marriage plots are the nineteenth-century woman's version of a drama of vocation; the selection of a spouse is, in effect, the choice of an identity. Drawing on this staple situation of the Victorian novel, James also follows the convention of limiting his young woman to one parent, underscoring the nature of her decision. She must choose between two persons, parent and husband; between two roles, daughter and wife. In doing so, the daughter provokes a crisis in parental authority, a crisis that threatens her own identity.

Analysis of the James family situation reveals that what structures these novels is Henry James, Jr.'s, own risky challenge to parental power. A son's attempt to discover the father's weakness is deployed in, and covered over by, the marriage plots of fictional daughters. Screened by these female strategies, Henry James can analyze both his own family drama and a larger historical crisis in parental authority. As Jackson Lears and others have argued, Victorian ambivalence about authority was acted out on the domestic scene. "On the one hand [the Victorian family] encouraged dependence and filial loyalty; on the other it promoted self-assertion and achievement."[1] Both the exercise of and the resistance to this ambiguous authority can be traced in the financial relations between Victorian parents and children, as Feinstein's analysis of the James household and

Mintz's of the Robert Louis Stevenson family have shown.[2] Mintz demonstrates that, for Stevenson, as for many other nineteenth-century middle-class children who "remained both emotionally and financially dependent upon their parents" until a relatively late age, "the quest for moral independence and self-determination became intertwined with a quest for financial independence."[3] Analogously, in the fictional Jamesian daughter's struggle for autonomy the currency of power is money: James figures the parent-child conflict in financial transactions, wills, and marriage contracts.

James's depictions of these financial proceedings unmasks its underlying sexual economy. In constructing his historical family romances, James deconstructs what we have come to recognize as the law, or language, of the father. Irigaray's *Speculum of the Other Woman* displays the fact that the law is merely a cover-up for the father's desire.[4] What James's early fictions reveal is that patriarchal law is powerful only as long as it remains unspoken. For James, to command, to make one's wishes known, is to reveal one's desire. But if the father desires, he is incomplete; he lacks. This gap in integrity and autonomy, this weakness in authority, can be masked only by a family cover-up: a paternal silence preserved by filial and maternal complicity. The authority of the father's law rests precariously on his refusal to speak and on the child's reluctance, schooled by the mother, to disobey. Mother and child act as accomplices because if the father lacks, they do too. In a patriarchal system where the woman's identity lies in her husband's, the undermining of male authority is dangerous. And, since the father locates the child's point of origin, to challenge paternal power, to uncover its gaps, is to face the possible loss of a self. Nonetheless, Henry James, Jr.'s, fictional renderings of this family romance seek to subvert the very authority that its silences and submissions support. The son plots to simultaneously mask and unmask the father weakened by desire.

Although the parents in James's early fictions clearly want to determine their daughters' fates, they are slow to force or even explicitly to demand obedience. Early in the narrative, daughters are allowed their liberty. In terms of the specific conflict about marriage and identity, this means that the parent does not overtly exercise authority—does not speak—until *after* the daughter has chosen a spouse and a self. In *Watch and Ward,* Nora's guardian Roger waits until she is deeply involved with a rival before he reveals that her filial obligations to him include marriage. In *Roderick Hudson,* it is only after her daughter openly rejects the Prince Casamassima that Mrs. Light forces Christina to marry him by laying down the law and naming her (illegitimate) father. Madame de Bellegarde in *The American* allows Claire to freely choose a fiancé, but not a husband. Similarly, Dr. Sloper in *Washington Square* refuses to interfere with Catherine's liberty before she becomes engaged. In *The Europeans,* Mr. Wentworth (the only parent who completely loses the battle for obedience)[5] also waits until after Gertrude has promised herself to Felix to express, with characteristic slowness, his disapproval. With *The Portrait of a Lady,* the pattern changes as the daughter/wife becomes two separate characters, yet even Osmond refrains from exercising his patriarchal power overtly until Isabel's loyalty to Ralph and Pansy's to Ned have been declared.[6]

This parental reluctance to speak with authority reflects the lessons of obedience that Henry James learned at home. Recent biographical and psychoanalytic studies of his siblings (Feinstein's book on William, and Strouse's and Yeazell's on Alice James) describe a familial setting in which "the struggle over vocation," which is, at base, a struggle for individuation and self-definition, is immensely complicated by Henry James, Sr.'s, refusal to be explicit and consistent about his desires for his children.[7] The cliché about the James family is that the father always told his offspring to "be," not to "do." Concealed behind that neat aphorism lies the fact that what he wanted them to "be" was *his.* By never demanding or commanding, he retained power—he could always be disappointed.

In *A Small Boy and Others,* Henry James, Jr., describes the message of his youth: "It is quite for me as if the authors of our being and guardians of our youth had virtually said to us but one thing, directed our course by but one word, though constantly repeated: Convert, convert, convert!"[8] The parent who demands this conversion is, his son makes clear, Henry James, Sr. Overtly, he directs his children to convert experience into consciousness: "Everything that should happen to us, every contact, every impression and every experience we should know, were to form our soluble stuff " (*Autobiography*, 123). However, this parental command delivers a second message: the children must give over, must convert their very selves in order to meet their parent's desires. Convert to what? The father will occasionally offer hints, but he will never say definitively, and his command is all the more powerful for its vagueness. Although Henry, Jr., recalls that "we wholesomely breathed inconsistency and ate and drank contradictions," the effect of this wholesome diet of "paradox" debilitated the James children's psychic health: they periodically took turns at nervous collapse and psychosomatic illness (*Autobiography*, 124).

Henry, Sr.'s, inconsistency was most troubling when it came to the young James' choices of vocation.[9] In *Notes of a Son and Brother*, Henry, Jr., shows how his father's conflicting messages canceled one another out, creating a silence that was not quiet. Rather than releasing his children, Henry James, Sr.'s, reserve reverberated with unstated expectations that effectively blocked all efforts at success, or even at choice:

The only thing was that our father had a wonderful way of being essentially right without being practically or, as it were, vulgarly, determinant, and that this relegation of his grounds of contention to the sphere of the non-immediate, the but indirectly urgent, from the point of view of the thing really to *do,* couldn't but often cause impatience in young breasts conscious of gifts or desires or ideals of which the very sign and warrant, the truth they were known by, was that they were susceptible of application. . . . What was marked in our father's prime uneasiness in the presence of any particular form of success we might, according to our lights as then glimmering, propose to invoke was that it bravely, or with such inward assurance, dispensed with any suggestion of an alternative. What we were to do instead was just to *be* something, something unconnected with specific doing, something free and uncommitted, something finer in short than being *that,* whatever it was, might consist of. (*Autobiography*, 267–68)

Any "that" named by the children is inadequate, not in comparison to some paternal alternative "this," but simply *because it has been named.* The child loses the battle by speaking, by being vulgarly determinant; the father wins by remaining silent, by keeping his (presumed) knowledge to himself. Henry James, Sr., here bears an uncanny resemblance to the Master, the one presumed to know, whose powerful silence Shoshana Felman traces in "The Turn of the Screw."[10] By disburdening himself of responsibility, the Master retains power: the governess must "never trouble him," must "meet all questions herself." In answering those questions, in speaking, in determining meaning, the governess, like the James children, (necessarily) fails. However, the head of the James household differs from the Master of Bly in that he is neither absent nor detached. While the Master, in refusing to read the love letters addressed to him, censors others' desire,[11] Henry James, Sr., censors himself. By not speaking, he disguises his own desire, his wish to keep his children his.

This pattern of apparent filial freedom coupled with unknowable (because inconsistent or unstated) parental expectation was experienced differently by each of the James children. In the remarks from *Notes of a Son and Brother* quoted above, Henry, Jr., is describing his father's reaction to William's decision to become a painter. Feinstein makes it clear that, as oldest son, William was the major focus of Henry, Sr.'s, threatening attention. William's long, unhealthy inability to decide on a career is notorious. Also notorious is Alice's solution to the crisis of vocation and identity: like so many of her Victorian sisters, she becomes an invalid. Alice "wins" the sibling illness competition by making "dying" her adult occupation; as Henry, Jr., observed: "her disastrous, her tragic health was in a manner the only solution for her of the practical problem of life."[12] The two youngest sons, all too clearly disposable in the eyes of their parent (Henry, Sr., sent Wilky and Bob off to fight in the Civil War while keeping his older sons safely at home), became, respectively, a bankrupt and a philandering alcoholic. Henry, Jr., set, by turns, to study painting, mathematics, and law, suffered perhaps least under his father's mixed messages about vocation. The father's focus on William left Henry somewhat freer to go his own way, and, possibly as a consequence, he knew quite early on that his vocation was to be a writer. However, his roles as witness to and participant in the family drama of vocation can be traced in his fictions of daughters' filial struggles.

Why daughters, not sons? One answer lies in the historical contexts of James's family stories—both the ones he writes and the one he lives. The daughter's drama is part of James's literary culture. As Yeazell argues, "In the tradition of the English novel it is . . . courtship that propels the plot; and the border crossing which constitutes the crisis is . . . the innocent young girl's awakening," the latter often figured, as in *Clarissa,* as the act of leaving the father's house.[13] If the young girl's sexual awakening precipitates this crisis, the father's desire to keep his daughter to himself underlies it. This desire is often given expression in the father's choice—or refusal—of a suitor.[14] By choosing his substitute, the father retains possession of the daughter. And the attempt to retain the child is precisely what the Jamesian drama of vocation is about: once a child chooses an adult identity, he or she is no longer defined by the parent. But for Henry James, Jr., showing the father's desire for the son directly is too risky. By drawing on literary convention, he can represent a culturally acceptable version of the paternal attempt to keep the child. The Victorian readers of Dickens, Eliot, and Bronte were well used to the portrayal of the *daughter's* father as a "monster of affection."[15]

The fact that such conventions were available to James indicates that his family drama is not anomalous. In his fictional explorations of his own family romance, James uncovers the forces at work in the Victorian home. The tension between what Walter Houghton calls "The Critical Spirit—and the Will to Believe" was mirrored in Victorian parents' conflicting goals for their children: what Steven Mintz identifies as "a goal of cultivating self-government through the persuasive power of various kinds of influence and an opposing goal of deference to parental authority."[16] Henry James, Sr., attempts to resolve this conflict by arguing that fathers should raise their children in an atmosphere of independence and freedom, yet at the same time provide "direction and discipline."[17] That such an ideal balance is difficult, if not impossible, to obtain is illustrated by the Jamesian parent's reluctance and inconsistency in commanding obedience. Henry James, Jr.'s, texts also hint that these Victorian plans to raise independent dependents serve a deeper (indeed, often an unconscious) strategy. If the child is left free to choose a self, but must submit to the parental authority that judges that choice as wrong, the parent retains control.

Although obedience is a topic in nearly all of James's major early fiction, two novels in particular are structured by this parent/child struggle: *Watch and Ward* and *Washington Square*.[18] In *Watch and Ward*, Roger Lawrence adopts a young orphan girl, Nora Lambert, and trains her for the vocation of wife—his wife. Growing up, Nora is not told of the duty expected of her: "Roger had no wish to cultivate in his young companion any expression of formal gratitude; for it was the very keystone of his plan that their relation should ripen into a perfect matter of course; but he watched patiently, like a wandering botanist for the first woodland violets for the year, for the shy field-flower of spontaneous affection" (*Watch and Ward*, 22).

Not only does Roger refuse to demand that Nora do as he wishes, he will not even declare himself (his marriage proposal, when it finally comes, is: "Do you love me yet?" [*Watch and Ward*, 122]). Instead he expects that Nora will spontaneously feel what he desires. When Roger's expectations for her are finally made known, Nora reacts in a way that makes the power structure of their relation clear: "The worst of the worst was, that she had been cheated of the chance to be really loyal. Why had he never told her that she wore a chain? Why, when he took her, had he not drawn up his terms and made his bargain? She would have kept it, she would have taught herself to be his wife. Duty then would have been duty; sentiment would have been sentiment" (*Watch and Ward*, 125). By expecting sentiment, rather than demanding duty, Roger has deprived Nora of the power to give in return for what she has taken, to attain a certain autonomy through *choosing* to obey. He has expected her to *be* the wife who loves him, not the woman who *does* what obligations require. By remaining silent about those expectations, the father allows the daughter's filial failure.

In *Washington Square*, Dr. Sloper describes his scrupulous deference to his daughter's autonomy—"I have not interfered, I have left you your liberty, I have remembered that you are no longer a little girl" (58)—only to immediately disapprove of her choice: "I don't like your engagement" (58). He disclaims authority even as he wields it: "I left you so much liberty. . . . You might have made a better use of it, Catherine" (*Washington Square*, 58). Like Roger Lawrence,

Austin Sloper makes sure that his demand for obedience comes after his daughter has already failed to live up to his expectations. The test (choosing a fiancé) that Catherine fails is, like Nora's, a trial of "sentiment." Although her culture has taught her that "we can't govern our affections" (*Washington Square,* 136), Catherine is nonetheless judged inferior because of her affection for Morris. She is expected to resemble the fairy-tale protagonist in "The Princess and the Pea" who proves her innate quality, not by her deliberate actions, but by the correctness of her feeling.

Expected, but not trusted, to feel like a princess, the middle-class Victorian daughter provokes her father's anxiety and challenges his financial control.[19] Although the father will not voice his demands, he does employ another medium of exchange. Wielding the currency that represents power in his society, the father transfers the struggle over the daughter's autonomy into the financial realm. Upon learning of Roger's desire, Nora runs away, resolved that "she could speak to Roger again only in perfect independence" (*Watch and Ward,* 127). However, the daughter's lack of money hinders her attempt, helping to ensure her ultimate dependence on her father/lover. Explicit in *Watch and Ward,* the father's financial effort to keep his daughter for himself is portrayed more indirectly in *Washington Square* where it takes the form of a conventional conflict over the daughter's suitors and the father's estate. Sloper initially endeavors to dismiss Morris Townsend, the only man, he is sure, who will ever propose to Catherine, by disinheriting her. Then, as his own death approaches, Sloper tries to guarantee that Morris will never replace him, first by selecting a husband for his daughter who distinctly resembles his younger self,[20] and, when that fails, by using his will (in the legal sense) to deprive Catherine of money. The father's desires are transmuted into the afterlife of the bourgeoisie: the last will and testament.[21]

This figure of the father's desire for the daughter raises an obvious question: Why is the mother excluded from these dramas of obedience? In early James fictions where the mother is present (*The American* and *Roderick Hudson*), her ability to enjoin obedience is formidable. Madame de Bellegarde's explicit statement—"My power . . . is in my children's obedience"—shows that, as with paternal authority, maternal power is not simply an external force located in the parent (*The American*, 757). When Madame de Belle-garde orders her daughter to break her engagement, Claire does so, relinquishing her choice of a spouse and an identity. Indeed, Claire goes her mother one better: by entering the convent and taking a vow of obedience, she gives up autonomy and adulthood completely. Why? Because she cannot bear to know what is revealed by the letter her dying father leaves behind: the fact and the results of his desire, his own murder at the mother's hands. Anger at his wife's plans for their daughter's marriage sends Monsieur de Bellegarde, debilitated by his sexual escapades, to the sickbed where his wife takes his life even as her gaze destroys his potency: " 'You know my lady's eyes, I think, sir," Mrs. Bread says to Newman, "it was with them she killed him; it was with the terrible strong will she put into them. It was like a frost on flowers' " (*The American*, 819). That, despite her refusal to hear this tale of killing and castration, Claire in some sense knows the story is indicated by her taking the veil as Sister Veronica. She may not read her father's accusatory letter, but she names herself after the saint whose veil is imprinted with evidence of a man's murder. When Christina Light in *Roderick Hudson* hears the castration narrative that Claire overtly refuses, when her mother reveals that her father is the poor, cowed, subservient Cavaliere, she submits to Mrs. Light's insistence on a wealthy, titled suitor. By obeying, Christina attempts to conceal her father's lack.

In both cases, the mother, who knows the father's desire, imparts, or threatens to impart, her knowledge to the daughter. The menace of this maternal speech is enough to enlist the daughter in a female conspiracy of silence. The paternal desire, which, by revealing the father's incompleteness, threatens female identity, must be hidden. Rather than accept the absence of the father's phallus, and, therefore, her own lack of an origin, Christina becomes the Princess Casamassima. By entering the society where the names, titles, and money that men inherit from one another are accepted as signs of authority, she covers herself. One might say that Mrs. Light, by naming the father, initiates her daughter into the realm of the symbolic. James, unconventionally, makes recognition of the father's, not the mother's, castration the source of this initiation.[22] Claire compensates for her suspected lack of origin differently. She refuses the initiation into the world that her mother offers in the form of Lord Deepmere. Rejecting his name and title, Claire renounces this world and relocates her origin in another. God becomes her father; Christ her bridegroom.

On the verge of becoming sexually active, both Claire and Christina encounter a kind of belated, reversed primal scene—the child discovers her parents in bed and believes that the mother is killing the father. Yet this reversal makes for an erasure, rather than an exchange, of authority. In a society where both wives' and daughters' identities are a function of the husband/father's power and position, his lack, which can only imply their own, must be concealed. The mother does not—cannot—seize a nonexistent authority. Instead of instruction in feminine power, the mother's sexual education of the daughter consists of obedience lessons.

Plotted to discover and disguise the absence of paternal authority, the stories of these two obedient daughters shed light on the novels where, in the mother's absence, the daughter obeys the father. In *Watch and Ward,* Nora finally learns of Roger's expectations by reading a letter he has written to Mrs. Keith, a woman who has earlier refused Roger's proposal of marriage and who has helped him groom Nora for wifehood. Because Nora has no money, and because her other male relatives/lovers prove doubly lacking (like her, they are without money; like Roger, they desire her), Nora ends by obeying and marrying Roger. The novel closes with Mrs. Keith's remark: "The fact is, Nora is under a very peculiar obligation to me" (*Watch and Ward,* 161). This obligation is "very peculiar" because, although Mrs. Keith performs the maternal task of initiating her into the marriage market, she is not Nora's mother. By refusing Roger, she has prompted him to write the letter that reveals his peculiarly *undivided* desire for his daughter. The mother's presence makes giving the daughter to another man feasible; the mother's absence means that the daughter must be reserved for the father.

Faced with the father's desire for her, the daughter flees. His need for her makes a mockery of her dependence on him. Resolving not to return until she has "perfect independence," Nora finds that, in her poverty, she can turn only to a series of equally inadequate males. Unable to locate a starting point for independence, she returns to the father. As Zwinger points out, when Victorian fathers control the "currency" of power, "women *have* to like men."[23] Although *Watch and Ward* reveals that Roger Lawrence, his authority and autonomy undermined by desire, possesses only the mediated power of money, at least that is the scrip of the system. By entering into a marriage contract, she will help paper over the father's lack, and thus her own.

Given the similarity of their family dramas, what permits Catherine Sloper to escape involvement in the filial cover-up that traps Nora Lawrence, to disobey by choosing her suitor over her father? Unlike Nora, Catherine can imagine herself as powerful both because she does not see her father's weakness, his desire for her, and because she has inherited money from her mother. What enables this docile daughter to say "I feel separated from my father" (*Washington Square*, 136) is not the violent scene in the Alps where Sloper reveals that he is "not a very good man" and that he "can be very hard" (*Washington Square*, 125).

Catherine simply refuses to hear this as a confession: "Such a saying as that," she thinks, "was a part of his great subtlety—men so clever as he might say anything and mean anything. And as to his being hard, that surely, in a man, was a virtue" (*Washington Square*, 126). She still believes that he possesses the phallus. Catherine *is* brought to disobey by the rather innocuous conversation that takes place on their last night in Europe, in which, she claims, her father reveals that he "despises" her. Catherine interprets this scene to mean that her father is "not very fond" of her "because he is so fond of my mother, whom we lost so long ago" (*Washington Square*, 136).

For the other Jamesian daughters, uncovering the father's desire for the mother reveals his deficiency. In contrast, the death of Catherine's mother in childbirth confronts her daughter with a more conventional primal scene: a female killed by desire. However, the mother's death is subversive in that it spares the daughter both the knowledge of her father's weakness and the need to conceal it by obeying. In dying, the first Catherine Sloper not only keeps her daughter safely ignorant of paternal desire, she also provides the financial means for leaving the father. It seems that the only way the mother can escape schooling her daughter in obedience is through death.

Catherine disobeys: she chooses Morris, rejects Sloper's choice of a spouse for her, and twice refuses her father's money. In all these ways she determines her own adult identity. But she also obeys by default: the man her father has forbidden rejects her, and she remains in her father's house, eventually taking her mother's place. Catherine ends ambiguously because her decision to "separate" from her father was based upon two mistaken assumptions about male desire. She assumes that her father does not desire her and that Morris does.[24] Having successfully veiled his desire, Sloper can retain Catherine as his possession, can to some extent determine the terms whereby she is exchanged (or in this case, not exchanged) with other men.

Morris has veiled his desire too, and the daughter is the screen. He wants Austin, not Catherine, Sloper.[25] In absence of the master of the house, Morris assumes his place, sitting in his armchair, smoking his cigars, drinking his wine, bullying his sister. When Catherine attempts to offer herself freely, rather than allowing herself to be exchanged between men, he rejects her. He does not want her without the father's money, house, inheritance—without the father.

Irigaray has argued that the patriarchal economy excludes male homosexuality precisely because it is the Archimedean point of the system: "Woman exists only as an occasion for mediation, transaction, transition, transference, between man and his fellow man, indeed between man and himself."[26] Morris's desire for Sloper, mediated through Catherine, hints at its ruthlessly repressed counterpart: the father's desire for the son. Throughout, Sloper's reaction to Morris is at once overcontrolled and violent: the older man takes an immediate dislike to the younger; he treats cruelly any woman who professes allegiance to Morris (Mrs. Montgomery, Catherine, Aunt Penniman); he claims that his rejection of Townsend is based on "a lifetime in study," and, indeed, Morris becomes Sloper's lifelong obsession (*Washington Square*, 41). The behavior is that of father-son rivalry; Sloper explicitly says that he would like to have killed Morris to make sure that the younger man will not replace him after his own death. (*Washington Square,* 171). But the father does not simply desire the son's elimination; he desires the son as well. Austin Sloper does not kill Morris Townsend. It is he, not Catherine, who continues to care about Morris, to keep him alive. The father-son power struggle is a struggle to *continue* the struggle, to sustain the relation.[27]

Washington Square tells the story of a paternal attempt to prolong the father-son conflict, but it also represents a son's efforts to do the same. Catherine Sloper mediates between two sets of clever New York men: Austin Sloper and Morris Townsend, Henry James, Sr., and Henry James, Jr. There is a kind of triple screen in *Washington Square.* The father retains power by veiling his desire for his daughter; concealed behind that obscured desire is another: the father's for the son. Finally, this father-daughter fiction is itself a protective cover for a son's ambivalent desires. In displaying Austin Sloper's desire for Catherine, the novel unmasks his paternal obsession with Morris; in writing *Washington Square,* James screens, and is therefore able to sustain, his intense preoccupation with his own father. Victorian cultural and narrative conventions offer James a way to tell his family romance. By describing the daughter's marriage plot, by using her as a fictional substitute, he can keep his father alive. Like Sloper writing and rewriting his will, James, writing and rewriting his daughters' dramas, continues the father-son struggle.

Strategies of complicity mark this struggle. Both sides work to conceal the father's desires—desires for the mother, for the daughter, for the son. To uncover this pattern in James's early fictions is not to locate sexuality as their secret center, but to recognize a plot to camouflage the absence of an original authority. Yet despite his maneuvers, James's own filial challenge to paternal law surfaces throughout these novels. His veils resemble Veronica's; they display what they have covered: the father weakened by desire. Even in the father's letters—Roger's missive to Mrs. Keith, Monsieur de Bellegarde's deathbed scrawl, Austin Sloper's will—desire uncovers itself. Like the epistles that appear within them, Henry James, Jr.'s, fictions reveal and conceal the father's lack, displaying a son's ambivalence about paternal power.

This same pattern of revelation and concealment can be traced in other James family writings. In *A Small Boy and Others,* Henry disguises the number of times his father dragged the children off to Europe from Newport: "I've covered over the fact, so overcome am I by the sense of our poor father's impulsive journeyings to and fro and of the impression of aimless vacillation which the record might make upon the reader."[28] In a letter to Henry, Jr., Mary James insists that, despite Alice's miraculous improvement in health while abroad, the daughter must sacrifice herself to the father's weakness: "Her greatest delight would be to go again and stay longer. This is not to be thought of now, but nor [*sic*] will it ever be possible during Father's life time."[29] William James's promise that his father's "words shall not suffer for being concealed" is fulfilled by the son's first book.[30] But *The Literary Remains of the Late Henry James* consists of selected *extracts* from Henry, Sr.'s, writing, plus an "introduction" by William, which takes up nearly a full third of the volume. The family drama that filters through the gaps in these texts is precisely the one hidden in so many of Henry James, Jr.'s, early fictions: rather than the autonomous origin of authority, the father is one who lacks and therefore desires. In the James household, the father's desire for the mother literally kills him. Soon after Mary James dies, Henry, Sr., starves himself to death; his last words are "There is my Mary!" As the novelist who is now, finally, Henry James says, "his support had failed" (*Autobiography,* 343).

But it will not do to end on such a solemn note. For James tells a comic version of his family drama in *The Europeans.* The general pattern is, by now, familiar. The father and the mother's substitute (the eldest daughter, Charlotte) have wanted Gertrude, the bad daughter, to marry the minister, Mr. Brand, but have not spoken "to force her" or to "arrange" the marriage (*The Europeans,* 1020). In a household where the children are disciplined by guilt, the father sees this clergyman, who is continually pushing Gertrude to confess, as the perfect husband for the "difficult" daughter (*The Europeans,* 1028). Surrounded by expectations, but allowed her liberty, Gertrude is given the opportunity to fail, and her father the chance to say, "She has not profited as we hoped" (*The Europeans,* 1028).

What enables the daughter to break out of this familiar family situation is her ability to speak freely, to voice her own desire. Near the end of the novel, there is a hilarious scene in which nearly the entire extended household pressures Mr. Wentworth to "consent." The comically priggish father is urged to give in to the fact of the daughter's desire: Gertrude declares that she wants Felix ("I know what I want; I have chosen. I am determined to marry this gentleman" [*The Europeans*, 1029]). But Mr. Wentworth responds only when the demure Charlotte speaks two words twice: "Father" and "consent" (*The Europeans*, 1031). "Her father felt her leaning more heavily upon his folded arm than she had ever done before; and this, with a certain sweet faintness in her voice, made him wonder what was the matter" (*The Europeans*, 1031).

It is a matter of desire. Ostensibly, Charlotte wants the minister Mr. Brand, but, as James's description makes clear, desire for the father's chosen substitute is actually desire for the father. She wants him to give in to her. Just as Charlotte has already replaced the mother in the household, she now replaces the problem daughter, leaving Gertrude free. Seduced, yet unable to understand the bodily language of female desire (the leaning, the sweet faintness), "the old man was left sitting there in unillumined perplexity" (*The Europeans*, 1032). Unlike so many Victorian "happy" endings, *The Europeans* closes with the daughter's separation from the father: "Gertrude left her father's house with Felix Young; they were imperturbably happy and they went far away" (*The Europeans*, 1038). Once the daughter speaks, all the father can do is listen; Mr. Wentworth "at last found himself listening for" an "echo" of Gertrude's voice (*The Europeans*, 1038). The patriarchal economy collapses when the woman voices her desire.[31] The son, by allying himself with the women, has told a story that the father cannot make his own.[32]

Notes

1. T.J. Jackson Lears, *No Place of Grace: Antimodernism and the Transformation of American Culture, 1880–1920* (New York: Pantheon, 1977), 220.

2. Howard Feinstein, *Becoming William James* (Ithaca: Cornell Uni-

versity Press, 1984), 193–97; Steven Mintz, *A Prison of Expectations: The Family in Victorian Culture* (New York: New York University Press, 1983), chap. 5, "Son and Father."

3. Mintz, *Prison*, 19, 87.

4. *Speculum of the Other Woman,* trans. Gillian C. Gill (Ithaca: Cornell University Press, 1985), 37–39.

5. Although M. Nioche in *The American* also appears to lose the battle to make his daughter obey, he, in fact, never enters the fray. As he explains to Newman, he has abdicated the role of father: "She can't obey, monsieur, since I don't command" (*Novels 1871–1880* [New York: Literary Classics of the United States, 1983], 563). Subsequent citations in the text are to this reprint of the texts of the first American book editions of *Watch and Ward, Roderick Hudson, The American, The Europeans.* I cite the second volume, *Novels 1881–86* [1985], for *Washington Square.* For clarity, individual novel titles are given with the page numbers. As M. Nioche's choice of verbs hints (she "can't," not "needn't," obey), and, as his daughter's unhappy fate on the marriage market makes clear, Noémie does not benefit from being orphaned. A powerless patriarch only makes for a devalued daughter.

6. *Confidence* (1880), generally conceded to be James's weakest full-length fiction, is the only early James novel in which the problem of obedience does not arise. Bernard interprets Mrs. Vivian's behavior as matchmaking, but we never know what pressure, if any, she exerts on her daughter Angela, who clearly chooses her own spouse. The father's complete absence from *Confidence* may explain the anomaly.

7. The phrase is Feinstein's, *Becoming, 57.* See Jean Strouse, *Alice James: A Biography* (Boston: Houghton Mifflin, 1980); Ruth Bernard Yeazell, *The Death and Letters of Alice James* (Berkeley: University of California Press, 1981).

8. *Autobiography,* ed. F.W. Dupee (1956; repr. Princeton: Princeton University Press, 1983), 123. This edition, which collects all three of James's major autobiographical works, will be hereafter cited in the text.

9. Feinstein summarizes Henry James, Sr.'s, inconsistent messages to William: "When he [William James] aspired to be an artist, a heroic figure depicted by his beloved father in glorious hues, Henry James [Sr.] was unhappy. When William reluctantly shifted toward science his father lost his enthusiasm for scientists. When William changed from science to philosophy, which his father praised as the highest degree of knowledge, his field was labeled 'technical philosophy' and judged to be inferior to his father's own spiritual doctrine" (*Becoming,* 100).

10. "Turning the Screw of Interpretation," *Yale French Studies* 55/56 (1977): 94–207.

11. Felman, "Turning," 145–46.

12. Letter to Mr. and Mrs. William James, May 28, 1894, *Henry James Letters,* ed. Leon Edel, 4 vols. (Cambridge: Harvard University Press, 1974–

84), 3:481. Both *The Death and Letters of Alice James* and *The Diary of Alice James,* ed. Leon Edel (1964; repr. Harmondsworth: Penguin Books, 1982) furnish numerous examples of Alice's claim that her business in life is dying.

13. Ruth Bernard Yeazell, "Podsnappery, Sexuality, and the English Novel," *Critical Inquiry* 9 (1982): 342.

14. On the circularity of the Victorian father's choice of his daughter's husband, see "Podsnappery," 347–48. Yeazell distinguishes between a "socially" and a "sexually" understood incest, and argues that Podsnappery exhibits the former. James's portrayals of the Victorian family shows these two incests as intertwined.

15. Diane F. Sadoff, *Monsters of Affection: Dickens, Eliot and Bronte on Fatherhood* (Baltimore: Johns Hopkins University Press, 1982). Sadoff also argues that these three writers were not anomalous: "Jane Austen, Anthony Trollope, and Elizabeth Gaskell, to name only three, wrote narratives deeply concerned with origins and paternal thematics" (3).

16. See chap. 4 of Walter E. Houghton, *The Victorian Frame of Mind, 1830–1870* (New Haven: Yale University Press, 1957); Mintz, *Prison,* 38. See also Lears, *No Place,* chap. 6, "From Patriarchy to Nirvana." The topic of authority in Victorian culture is far too broad for me to list all of the relevant scholarship here.

17. Feinstein, *Becoming,* 84–87. Feinstein's chapter, "Ideology for a Prodigal," argues that Henry, Sr., attempted to balance "independency and dependency, separation and fusion" in his social theory and his theology, as well as his childrearing.

18. Although the relations between fathers and daughters remains important in James up through *The Golden Bowl,* obedience per se is a central topic primarily in the fiction written before Henry, Sr.'s, death in 1882. The connection with James's biography is of special interest for *Watch and Ward* and *Washington Square* because James later disowned both. Not only is neither included in the New York Edition, but he always referred to *Roderick Hudson,* written five years after *Watch and Ward,* as his first novel.

19. See Lynda Zwinger's discussion in "The Fear of the Father: Dombey and Daughter," *Nineteenth-Century Fiction* 39 (1985): 420–40, of the two currencies at issue in the Victorian father-daughter war—"that of bargain and sale and speculation" vs. "the power of pure, unselfish, uncalculated (consequently infinite) love" (439), as well as the Introduction to her *Daughters, Fathers, and the Novel* (Madison: University of Wisconsin Press, forthcoming). While her conclusions about the father's power and the daughter's relation to it differ from my own, Zwinger's analysis locates a nexus of issues that I find echoed in James's early family romances.

20. John Ludlow is described as "a clever young lawyer, who, with the prospect of a great practice, and the reputation of a most agreeable man, had had the shrewdness, when he came to look about him for a wife, to

believe that she would suit him better than several younger and prettier girls" (*Washington Square,* 172). Although Sloper married a younger and prettier Catherine, he too was a "clever" young professional, who, with a knack for making his clients comfortable and the prospect of a great practice, proposed to an heiress.

21. The clutch that, to use George Eliot's phrase from *Middlemarch,* the patriach's "Dead Hand" has on the living in the form of a last will and testament is a basic premise of the eighteenth- and nineteenth-century novel.

22. Julia Kristeva argues in *About Chinese Women,* trans. Anita Barrows (London: Marion Boyars Publishers, 1977), that in order to differentiate herself from her mother, the daughter needs (the father's) language. See also Jane Gallop, chap. 8, "The Phallic Mother: Fraudian Analysis" in *The Daughter's Seduction: Feminism and Psychoanalysis* (Ithaca: Cornell University Press, 1982). Susan Rubin Suleiman, "Writing and Motherhood," in *The (M)other Tongue: Essays in Feminist Psychoanalytic Interpretation,* ed. Shirley Nelson Garner, Claire Kahane, and Madelon Sprengnether (Ithaca: Cornell University Press, 1985), explores the suggestion, which she finds in Kristeva's "Un Nouveau Type d'intellectuel: Le dissident" and "Héréthique de l'amour," that the child introduces the *mother* to the symbolic in a special way. "Motherhood, which establishes a *natural* link (the child) between woman and the social world, provides a privileged means of entry into the order of culture and of language" (367). See also Sandra M. Gilbert and Susan Gubar's recent suggestion "that the idea that language is in its essence or nature patriarchal may be a reaction-formation against the linguistic (as well as the biological) primacy of the mother" in *The War of the Words,* vol. 1 of *No Man's Land: The Place of the Woman Writer in the Twentieth Century* (New Haven: Yale University Press, 1988), 264.

23. Zwinger, "Fear," 436–40.

24. The suggestion that this father-daughter relationship is, in fact, "incestuous" has been made by a number of critics. See, for example, Richard B. Hovey, "*Washington Square:* James and 'The Deeper Psychology,'" *University of Hartford Studies in Literature* 14 (1982): 1–10, esp. n. 22, which briefly surveys the critical discussion.

25. On (male) triangulated desire, see René Girard, *Deceit, Desire, and the Novel* (Baltimore: Johns Hopkins University Press, 1965).

26. *This Sex Which Is Not One,* trans. Catherine Porter with Carolyn Burke (Ithaca: Cornell University Press, 1985), 193.

27. See Zwinger's argument that a son "ensure[s] Dombey's victory over impotence and death" whereas a daughter "stands for impotence" ("Fear," 429).

28. The remark is taken from the record that William's son, Henry, made of a conversation with his uncle on August 23, 1913. Quoted in Leon Edel, *Henry James: The Untried Years* (Philadelphia: Lippincott, 1953), 138.

29. April 27, 1873, quoted in Strouse, *Alice James,* 160.

30. Letter from William James to Henry James, Sr., December 14, 1882, *The Letters of William James,* ed. Henry James, 2 vols. (Boston: Atlantic Monthly Press, 1920), 1:220.

31. See Irigaray, *This Sex Which Is Not One,* and Toril Moi, "The Missing Mother: The Oedipal Rivalries of René Girard," *Diacritics* 12 (1982): 21–31, for the argument that (Freudian, Lacanian, Girardian) descriptions of the male economy of sexual exchange insistently deny female desire.

32. Two feminist critics, Judith Fetterley, *The Resisting Reader: A Feminist Approach to American Fiction* (Bloomington: Indiana University Press, 1978), and Joyce W. Warren, *The American Narcissus: Individualism and Women in Nineteenth-Century American Fiction* (New Brunswick: Rutgers University Press, 1984), have read James among the women, seeing him as the exception to the American male writerly tradition. For a recent criticism of James as a "sissy," see Alfred Haebegger, *Gender, Fantasy, and Realism in American Literature* (New York: Columbia University Press, 1982).

4   *Renegotiating the Oedipus*
Theseus and Hippolytos
Nancy Sorkin Rabinowitz

Greek myth offers a fruitful site for feminists trying to understand the ideology of our own society, since its material sets out in sharp and deeply affecting form the Western ideology of sexual behavior that continues to influence us even today. In particular, the power of the father in the patriarchal order is inscribed in Greek drama, with significant consequences for son and wife, as well as for us, the modern heirs to that tradition. The Greek plays—written and acted by men, and perhaps performed only for men—make abundantly clear what is more covert in later literature: that Western texts, while pretending endlessly to represent females and their desire, in fact enact male desire. The question facing us is, as Gayatri Spivak has put it, "What is man that the itinerary of his desire creates such a text?"[1] It is my claim that the desire of men for other men, especially of the father for a son, is a primary one in these plays, and a textual economy is worked out to form that relationship while excluding the sexual female.

Since Freud, the oedipal narrative has exercised a strong power over our imagination, but as Luce Irigaray notes, there are other stories: "When Freud describes and theorises, notably in *Totem and Taboo,* the murder of the Father as the foundation of the primitive tribe, he forgets one more archaic, that of the woman-mother necessitated by the establishment of a certain order in the city."[2] As in the Oedipus story the hostility of father and son is linked with a postulated desire for the mother, so the desire of father and son is linked with a hostility for the mother. Euripides' *Hippolytos* contains a false Oedipus story and under that surface an eroticized charge between father and son; the wife/mother is displaced so that these two can be alone together.

Even a bald summary of Euripides' text reveals some of its peculiarities. The goddess Aphrodite opens the play, announcing that in revenge for Hippolytos's rejection of her and the marriage bed (13–14), she has filled Phaedra with an illicit desire for her stepson.[3] Phaedra is at present silently starving herself in her chambers. When she is persuaded by her nurse to speak and to act, Phaedra sanctions the use of a drug to cure her. The nurse instead intercedes for her with Hippolytos; he replies with a misogynist diatribe that leads Phaedra to take revenge; she leaves a suicide note accusing him of rape and then hangs herself. When her husband Theseus returns and reads the note, he calls on his putative father Poseidon to kill his son with one of the three wishes granted to him; he himself condemns Hippolytos to exile. The play ends with a telling conjunction of gestures: Artemis appears *ex machina* to promise a marriage ritual in Hippolytos's honor, and father and son embrace in loving forgiveness. We might well ask why a misogynist youth is rewarded, and rewarded in these particular ways.

The *Hippolytos* would seem to be a *locus classicus* for the representation of female desire. After all, does Phaedra not die for love? In the plot that Aphrodite outlines, Phaedra loves and suffers so that Hippolytos can be punished: his refusal and her passion are coupled as necessary for the play's action. Heterosexual desire is ascribed to the woman by the goddess, myth, and playwright, with the result that in the end she suffers and punishes herself. We shall see, however, that the actual structure of desire organizing the play is the male desire for the one like himself, for legitimate heirs coined in the father's image, and for a concomitant security of meaning. Significantly, the play does not end with Aphrodite's victory, the suffering of Theseus and Hippolytos; the playwright adds a reassuring epilogue. Although I would agree with recent critics of the play that the text is about marriage,[4] it is really about marriage as an arrangement between men, in which the goal is not the relationship between husband and wife but between father and son. This relationship dominates the play's conclusion; the wife, having served the function of bringing the men together, is displaced and done in.[5]

This play has much to tell us about Greek culture and our own, for both are founded on the exclusion of women from the important sites of culture, those places where men speak together and make decisions: the Academy, the agora, the theater. The masculine orientation of Greek society, where mature women functioned only as mother of future soldiers or as manager of the household, was matched by an erotic organization as well. In this respect, there are important differences between ancient Greek society and our own. In particular, Greek society did not use the word "homosexual" and did not fear and discriminate against men who loved other men, but rather accommodated both a well-worked out system of male sexual relations with other men and marriage producing heirs.[6] Antiquity was not without homophobia, but it seems to have been reserved for practitioners of anal intercourse or for those who were not pederasts. Current scholarly acceptance of the normative position of pederasty in the culture leads me to a fresh scrutiny of father-son relations, since the lover as educator in some sense stands in place of the father. The possibility or probability of an erotic charge between father and son is denied in antiquity as it is today because it founds the social order. Although not referring to antiquity, Luce Irigaray has described it well: "The exchanges upon which patriarchal societies are based take place exclusively among men. . . . This means that the *very possibility of a sociocultural order requires homosexuality* as its organizing principle. . . . Why are homosexuals ostracized, when society postulates homosexuality? Unless it is because the *'incest' involved in homosexuality has to remain in the realm of pretense.*"[7] Homosexuality is repressed, unconscious, but seen in ritual, politics, and art—in Irigaray's "homosexuality."

While the primary antagonists in the drama are Aphrodite and Hippolytos or Aphrodite/Phaedra and Artemis/Hippolytos, Theseus is necessary to Aphrodite, and the relationship of father and son is crucial to the play's resolution. In this play, as in so many other Greek tragedies, the father is not just a father but *the father,* as function: his psychological and biological relationship to his son is paralleled by a social role. To recognize this clustering in the play, we have only to remember the position of Theseus, national hero of Athens and, like Heracles and Perseus, a monster killer. As a king, Theseus is supported by Zeus, the Olympian king, the patron of his representatives on earth; therefore Theseus in his discovery of Phaedra's note asserts that Hippolytos has shamed not only his father but also the august eye of Zeus (885). Celebrated in Athenian ritual, himself a figure for initiation, Theseus brings together the psychological and sociopolitical elements in fatherhood.

By using Theseus in her plan to take revenge on Hippolytos, Aphrodite makes of him a great sufferer. This much is clear when Artemis, hearing him groan, says "it bites you, this story?" (1313), and names him as one of the three primarily affected by the events of the play (1403–5). But does Theseus emerge as a winner or loser? As I will show, although Theseus suffers the loss of wife and son, in psychological, sociopolitical, and discursive terms, his wishes are granted.

Despite his later grief at what he has done, Theseus wants Hippolytos's death. There is ample evidence that this father is hostile to his son and that Theseus stands in relation to Hippolytos as Laius to Oedipus. As Artemis points out, Theseus causes his own suffering through his rashness and stubbornness ("too soon you hurled curses and killed your own son," 1324); he should have waited to see what divine signs would attend Hippolytos's oath (1321–23). Why does he not wait? His haste is well motivated if we consider it the result of a prior hostility to his illicit offspring. Certainly there is evidence of paternal antagonism, taken to the second generation since Theseus kills his son through the agency of his own father: "O Father Poseidon, those three curses that you once promised me, with one of them make an end of my son, may he not escape this day" (887–90). Given that Theseus has already cursed him thus, why does he doubly punish him, adding exile (a lesser sentence) to death? The excess or supplement marks psychological and dramatic overdetermination and acts also as a signifier of paternal violence.

The tone of the interaction between Hippolytos and Theseus further suggests that a history of distance lies behind the current episode; we surmise that Theseus and Hippolytos are not suddenly at odds having had a history of trust, but rather have never been "close."[8] Theseus saves his emotion for the chorus and audience, giving Hippolytos only silence, then cold generalizations from which Hippolytos must infer what is wrong. While Hippolytos calls on Theseus again and again as his father (905, 923, 983, 1041, 1348, 1362–63, 1378), Theseus never acknowledges the relationship. The two are at odds in part because of the difference between them. Theseus is fleshly and scornfully ascribes to Hippolytos the asceticism of Orpheus (953). Because Theseus is so entrenched in his own worldview, he cannot trust his son; he does not believe in his holiness any more. Rather, he blames Hippolytos for hypocrisy, for claiming great purity when he is really, so Theseus thinks, a great sinner ("You the extraordinary man who accompanies the gods? You the virtuous one, untouched by evil?" [948–49]). Theseus counters in advance an argument that men are not sexual, while women are (966–67), by asserting that he "know[s] that young men are no more secure than women when Kypris stirs up their young heart" (968–69). Hippolytos's great defense, of course, is that it is not likely that he would have touched Phaedra. First, he is not like other men—he has a "virgin soul" (1006) and no knowledge of sex except through books and pictures (1004–5). Further, he claims no interest in affairs of state, which could have led him to desire Phaedra for the position she might confer; rather, he says he prefers "Hellenic contests" (1017) to political power.

Theseus rejects these answers; everything he knows about Hippolytos is irrelevant as he reconstructs him according to his own nature and "masculinity" in general. Hippolytos cannot be tolerated as different from or other than his father. The play in this way exposes the often forgotten truth that patriarchy does not give power to all men equally. If we see Theseus as the castrating father, who is really hostile to his son, Theseus has succeeded even when he seems to have failed.

This violence satisfies Theseus's other, more conscious desires, most importantly, those for himself and his position. His lack of concern for Phaedra is striking. When he returns from his visit to the oracle and hears the women's cries, he thinks first about his father, a natural enough mistake, and then about his children ("Woe, has something stolen the life of my children?" [799]). But at no point does he think of Phaedra, and in particular, he does not grieve for what has happened to her. His subsequent mourning is mostly for himself ("Woe for my sufferings; I have suffered the greatest of evils" [817–18]; "I wish I were below earth" [836]; "you have destroyed [me], and worn me away" [839]). Finally, when he reads Phaedra's message, he is most anxious not about her fate but about his honor: "Hippolytos has dared to touch my bed, dishonoring the august eye of Zeus" (885). We can say then that Phaedra matters not for herself but for what she signifies about Theseus. In sum, the shame is not the woman's but the husband's and father's.

Theseus's social position makes his reputation especially important. His role as culture hero is alluded to in the text (34–37, 977–80) and would have been well known to an Athenian audience. It was Theseus who, with the help of Ariadne, conquered the Minotaur and fought the Amazons. Not only did he triumph over monsters and in this way imitate the cosmogonic acts of Zeus, but he was a civilizer and brought order to the road between Troezen and Athens, and founded Athens as we know it. He settled all the inhabitants of Attica in the city, making them a people, and instituted the coining of money.[9] As city-founder and representative of Zeus, Theseus must uphold his name; as he says, he must punish Hippolytos because if he did not, the monsters that he has tamed would deny him (977–80).

But since the city-founder must also establish a lineage, an underlying issue remains who will rule in Athens—the legitimate sons of Phaedra or the illegitimate son of the Amazon. The other sons are mentioned repeatedly (305–9, 421–25, 717, 799, 847, 858) and cause the plot to take shape. Concern for them leads Phaedra first to speak, and then to write her telling lie. Theseus takes as axiomatic "the enmity between bastard and legitimate" (962–63); Hippolytos mourns for his mother's birth pangs that brought forth a bastard (1082–83).[10] Theseus's defense of his honor and position in the city would require protection, even if it meant killing his son, but in this instance the son sacrificed is the illegitimate one, one who is not capable of carrying on that name in any case.

Theseus's hasty curse settles another paternity case as well, for not only does he get rid of the illegitimate son constituted as threat to his honor, but he is reassured about his own father. For, according to widely known legend, Theseus had two fathers, Aegeus and Poseidon.[11] In the text at hand, the death of Hippolytos functions to resolve Theseus's doubt in this matter. When Poseidon heeds his call and punishes Hippolytos, Theseus treats it as evidence that Poseidon is indeed his father: "then he was truly my father, since he has heard my prayers" (1169–70).

Theseus's use of his father's curse links paternity to language—Is it a sure curse? Is Poseidon his father?—in a way typical of patriarchy. Assurance that one's son is one's own means that he bears the father's name, and as Gayatri Spivak remarks, "The desire to make one's progeny represent his presence is akin to the desire to make one's words represent the full meaning of one's intention" ("Displacement," 169). The text explicitly focuses on these issues since Theseus's longing for honor and reputation, for legitimate heirs to rule Athens, to know his own father, are analogous to his desire for clear meaning. Ordinarily, words tend to have a shifting relationship to deeds, feelings, thoughts;[12] Theseus is troubled by his recognition of this problem and has the fantasy that "men should have a sure token established of their friends . . . to tell who is true and who is not, and all humans should have two voices, one just and one whatever which way, so that the one thinking unjust thoughts would be refuted by the just, and we would not be deceived" (925–26, 928–31).

The text fulfills his fantasy in two ways. First, his own word has power, granted to him by his father. Having disdained Hippolytos's demand for oaths, calling him a "magician," he becomes a magician: through the power of his father, his curse is performative and, like magic, works instantaneously.[13] We see the devastating force of paternal language. Second, he ultimately gets the voice he longs for. Although Theseus believe that Phaedra's corpse and tablet with her story give him sure proof ("clearest witness of the corpse here," 972), and is the voice giving Hippolytos the lie, he is wrong. Nonetheless, he *does* get the voice he asked for, for Artemis, a detached voice, tells him the whole story (1296–97). Even if he does not like what he hears, hearing it addresses his epistemological concern and he is no longer in doubt as to how he knows what he knows.

Thus far we have seen that Theseus's implicit and explicit desires are gratified, despite his apparent suffering at the hands of Aphrodite. To the extent that he is hostile to his son because of the latter's difference from him, he desires his death; to the extent that the son was a rival to him and his legitimate line, he is also satisfied. In the process of killing his illegitimate son, he is reassured about his own dubious paternity. Finally, as paternity is established, so is meaning made stable, for he has won sure signs from the goddess Artemis.

In the ending contrived by Euripides, he makes further gains from his losses. Let me note first that the playwright has gone to considerable lengths to create the concluding tableau of the father cradling his broken son in his arms.[14] Plays on the Phaedra/Hippolytos theme do not always end thus, and it is awkward to accomplish: the messenger says first that Hippolytos "is no longer," and then has to modify that statement to allow for his entrance (1162–63). The very awkwardness is a signal of how important it must be, and indeed is. First, the father-son pietà accomplishes the displacement of the mother (specifically, Phaedra), for the traditionally feminine gesture of cradling one's child is here performed by Theseus. Second, the appearance of Hippolytos—on the point of death, but not yet dead—makes possible the representation of both the rupture and the reunion of father and son. Hippolytos frees his father from blame and denies any claim of vengeance (1449); moreover, he wishes that Theseus might have legitimate sons as noble as he (1455). This double gesture simultaneously covers up evidence of the earlier hostility and reminds us of the question of rule implied by his illegitimacy.

In these last words Hippolytos participates in a cultural and textual tendency to support marriage by identifying the institution's problems with the female. As a bastard, Hippolytos would ordinarily be the primary sign of the instability of marriage; and as I have mentioned (above, p. 63) the text shows a persistent concern with bastardy. In fact, Theseus is responsible for this vulnerability of marriage as revealed by the illegitimacy of Hippolytos, since his excessive desire led to the rape of the Amazon and the birth of

Hippolytos, which has threatened his own legitimate line. Theseus's adventures are consistently sexual and include seductions of Phaedra's own sister Ariadne, as well as the rape of twelve-year old Helen and the attempted rape of Persephone (Plutarch 29, 30, 31).

But all of this must be muted in a play about the Athenian hero for an Athenian audience. In order to allay concern about the purity of the line, Theseus's lechery is projected onto Phaedra, in the form of maternal desire for the son. Instead of presenting men raping women who are only interested in other women (Theseus and Hippolyta), the play represents female desire as dangerous and overspilling its bounds: Phaedra's desire attacks marriage, as her desire attacks her. According to Lévi-Strauss, a universal incest taboo leads to the exchange of women between men, and so constitutes culture. The exchange of women lies at the center of marriage rules designed to mediate between extreme exogamy (bestiality) and extreme endogamy (incest), both of which are represented in the extended Hippolytos story—Phaedra's mother Pasiphae out of desire for a sacred bull gave birth of the Minotaur (a clear case of excessive exogamy) and Phaedra's desires for her adoptive son verge on the incestuous (excessive endogamy).[15] Theseus as culture hero serves as a focal point for these institutional stresses of excess in either direction. In Greek culture, and in this play, problems of illegitimacy and incest (breaking of rules for appropriate partners) seem to male eyes to come from women: the woman once exchanged may not stay so.[16] Anxiety lest female desire throw paternity into question requires monogamy as a way for men to control female sexuality.

The play *Hippolytos* confirms the father in his desire for a son just like himself, rather than the female other. It affirms that Theseus made a mistake in believing his wife's words when he should have trusted his son's. In the end the tie to the son becomes supreme. Although Theseus risked losing what he really wanted (a son) for honor (through the perishability of woman's fidelity), the son forgives him, and he achieves reunion with Hippolytos. His loss turns out to be a gain. The father's desires—to get rid of the illegitimate, to retain his honor, to consummate a relationship with a noble heir, to establish the truth through a divine voice—are satisfied.

Hippolytos, the son, goes through a similar double path, in which he is punished by the goddess and rewarded by the playwright. The play presents a double vision: he both understands and totally misunderstands what is demanded of him. While in Aphrodite's scheme Hippolytos looks for a moment like one with incestuous desires who must be punished for them, in Euripides' plot he successfully renegotiates this oedipal configuration and gains the symbolic as his kingdom: although his flesh is torn from him, he is embraced by the father. The son's filial fantasy is fulfilled: he convinces his father that he is not a rival but rather a loyal subject. And for having shown obedience to the law (after all, he did not touch the father's bed), he gains a marriage cult and songs in his honor. The ambiguity and rivalry that shadowed the father/son relationship are done away with at the play's end by Artemis. Although the price is great, he wins reconciliation with his father and continuing recognition for nobility of spirit and repression of the body.

According to Aphrodite, Hippolytos must suffer because he alone of mortals calls her "the worst of divinities" and "refuses the bed and will not touch marriage, preferring instead the company of Artemis, Phoebus' sister, Zeus' daughter" (13–15). We see him act out Aphrodite's claim by refusing to pay his respects to her altar, saying, in effect, each to his own in tastes for goddesses (104).

But what does he value in worshiping Artemis?

To you, oh Mistress, I bring this woven crown having arranged it as an adornment from your uncut meadow, where no shepherd would think to graze the flock nor does any iron come there, but only the honeybee passes through the uncut meadow in spring, and Reverence *(Aidōs)* tends it with river waters, for those to whom nothing is taught but to whom by nature it has fallen out to exercise sophrosyne always in all things, for them to harvest, for the evil it is not allowed. But oh beloved mistress, receive this band for your golden head from my pious hand. This gift is mine alone among men: I am with you and I exchange words with you, hearing your voice, though not seeing your eye. May I turn the end of my life as I began it. (73–87)

Hippolytos desires the eternal and spiritual, eschews the ephemeral and physical. On the simplest level, Hippolytos worships chastity by his reverence for Artemis; therefore, he invokes her as the "most beautiful of maidens" (66). As the play unfolds, we find that he divides women into two classes, the sexual and the chaste, represented by Aphrodite and Artemis.[17] He despises the desiring female principle, the goddess of the night, and respects his Amazon mother and patron goddess. This maidenhood, however, seems to be an existential as well as a sexual category, for Hippolytos is an absolutist: while Aphrodite implies the possibility of lip service to her, Hippolytos stresses his purity and the possibility of corruption from any contact with her. He can only greet such goddesses from afar (102) lest her "nighttime" activities rub off on him.

Moreover, in several ways his worship seems evidence that he wants to stay the same. First, he covets a form of stasis in the meadow. The meadow is twice referred to as "uncut," therefore unchanging. It does not give fruit or grain since it is not cultivated; it is not useful for animal grazing. Second, those who are with him there are perfect by nature; that is, they do not have to learn virtue, and thus they do not change. Third, his relationship with Artemis is also immune to change insofar as it is divorced from the body: he can only hear her voice. In sum, the garden of his reverence is unchanging, the object of his worship incorporeal, and he desires to end life as he began it; Hippolytos seems to avoid the physical as a sign of change and flux.[18]

The sexual is apparently absent in Hippolytos's attention to the chaste goddess, but there are signs that it is only repressed, not nonexistent. First, the meadow brings with it resonance of lovemaking (it is "par excellence a place where lovers meet").[19] The meadow is a site for eros here as well, figuring a different desire, most strongly that for Artemis, but also possibly for those of his fellows who accompany him. The prologue depicts Hippolytos as rejecting Aphrodite and what she stands for, and, because he "ever wishes to be with the maiden," (17) "falling in with company more than mortal" (19). The language used of Hippolytos's desires for Artemis has sexual connotations, which are acceptable to him because she is an absent figure. As a voice (86), Artemis does not separate him from the company of his age-mates, but rather provides them with a pretext for being together in their worship of her. Although Hippolytos is not sexually active, his companions in the hunt and the age-mates to whom alone he speaks (987) constitute his appropriate charmed circle. Hippolytos does not discount all humankind, only those who are unworthy. Those who naturally moderate themselves (*sōphronein*) can inhabit the garden (80).

Hippolytos's perspective is intimately associated with his age. His servant tries to compensate for his arrogance by reminding the goddess that Hippolytos is young (116). In his idealization of changelessness and his desire to die as he began, we also see signs of an adherence to youth and a resistance to maturity. This same inclination is echoed later in the play when he defends himself to his father by saying that he does not wish to rule the city, but far prefers contests (1016), for athletics are the province of youth, rule that of maturity.

At a central point in the play, having heard the nurse's proposition, he launches into a vitriolic diatribe against women. We hear at this point an explicit statement of his desires; this outburst leads to his downfall by making Phaedra his enemy, but the same desires are ironically fulfilled by the play's structure. Hippolytos's fantasy begins with imagery of circulation, and bespeaks his desire for a male world, but not a totally unpopulated one.[20] He opens his tirade with a cry to Zeus asking him why he "set this counterfeit coin, woman, in the light of the sun as an evil to men" (616–17). He wishes that it were possible "to buy children from the temples of the gods by giving a weight of bronze or iron or gold" (622). Male parents would be able to possess male heirs without having relationships with women. His desire for a single *Aidōs* in a garden that is never cut is appropriate to a man who reviles women as a false coin.

Hippolytos's second point is that women are oversexed. Coins circulate, but women must not, for their acting as sexual subjects would threaten the foundations of culture. Thus Hippolytos tolerates the stupid woman, "for she is at least not a harm" (638), but hates the clever one, "for Kypris engenders more evildoing in the wise; the helpless woman is restrained from lust by her short wits"

(642–44). Finally, coin, sexuality, and language come together: because of their promiscuity women should be kept inside, and even their servants should be silent beasts, so that they will not be able to converse or to take messages to the world (645–58).

Summing up what we have seen about Hippolytos, we can say that he implicitly desires youth and explicitly hates women on account of the sexuality he has (dis)placed onto them. We may hypothesize that Hippolytos's anxiety about his own position led him to imagine women as a counterfeit coin. Is he not the counterfeit, since the bastard son does not have the stamp of the legitimate? What happens to him in the course of the play? Aphrodite never wins Hippolytos's respect or even acknowledgment; rather he must obey the father ("The words of my father must be obeyed" [1184]). As a result of his filial piety, he is accepted by his father and that concern can be laid to rest. A new family based on claims of nobility is finally established, according to which Hippolytos can be legitimized. The play does not demand that he give up his misogyny or accept women; he gives up boys *in order to* enter into a socially acceptable relationship with an older man. In this he seems to identify with the other, chaste, exceptional woman.[21] His characterization of Artemis as "holy" and "virginal" (61, 66) matches his sense of himself (his virgin soul [1006] and "holiness" [1364]). He reveres Artemis for those traits that he shares. Named after his mother, the Amazon Hippolyta, he calls on her, recalling her vain labor that brought him forth; he then seems to suffer like her, for he applies the term for birth pangs to himself (1371). In the scene with Theseus, he lacks the speech that would persuade his father, even as he would have deprived the woman of speech by keeping her servants within.

Thus, it is as a woman-identified boy that he suffers. And like his mother, herself raped by Theseus, he is hurt by the power of the father, the masculine man. In his death the purely destructive power of the phallus stands revealed: "And with its very deluge and mountainous surge, the wave put forth a bull, a wild and fierce wonder; the whole earth was full of its voice shiveringly echoed, a sight revealed more than our eyes could look on. Straightaway fear seized the horses" (1210–17). The sexual symbolism of the bull cannot be missed. But what is the nature of the sexuality so inscribed? When

Poseidon comes in the form of the bull, it is adult male sexuality that arises before us.[22] The potential violence of masculine sexuality, defined as dominance, is here unleashed against a youth; this scene seems to inscribe paternal sadism against the son, leading us to interrogate again the repressed desire propelling the text.

But it is not only the bull that kills Hippolytos. It rather causes Hippolytos's horses to pull him apart by entangling him in the reins. Here is what the messenger has to say:

The master, experienced with horses, pulled on the reins. . . . The horses took the firefashioned bit in their jaws by force . . . they would not be turned, neither by the hand of the captain, nor by the horsebands, nor by the well-built chariot. . . . Until in the end he tripped up and overturned it, throwing the wheel of the chariot against the rock. All was confused . . . and the driver, unhappy man, was dragged bound in a bond hard to unravel, smashing his own head against the rocks and tearing his flesh, and crying out things terrible to hear. (1218–39)

This passage calls to mind a similar passage in Plato's *Phaedrus,* a somewhat later text, but one similarly preoccupied with relationships between men. Hippolytos is like the Platonic hero who has gone through the initiation and triumphed. In the *Phaedrus* the soul is described as tripartite, imagined as a charioteer and two horses, one chaste and one wanton. The charioteer conquers the wanton, bringing him to his knees:

But his fellow, heeding no more the driver's goad or whip leaps and dashes on . . . and when they have come close, with head down and tail stretched out he takes the bit between his teeth and shamelessly plunges on. But the driver with resentment stronger than before, like a racer recoiling from the starting rope, jerks back the bit in the mouth of the wanton horse with an even stronger pull, bespatters his railing tongue and his jaws with blood, and forcing him down on legs and haunches delivers him over to anguish.[23]

In controlling the lecherous horse distracted by the beauties of a youth, the Platonic figure gains the lofty reaches of the dialectic and philosophy. Julia Kristeva's reading of Plato underlines the sexuality inherent in that scene: "Always and without distinction love means *love of young people, love of the Good, and love of true discourse.* [Eros is] Pederast and philosopher all at once."[24] In Plato the erotic is dominated, but nonetheless represented in the process of domination; in Euripides the two moments are separated, in that an erotic

force is represented as domination (a kind of rape) and then sublimated.

If we look at the *Hippolytos* through the lens provided by Plato and
Kristeva, we can see that Hippolytos, like his father, is confirmed in
his desire for that which is like himself, for the masculine. Having
briefly survived the father's murderous wish, he is crowned by his
touch. The homoerotic content of the Platonic scene is sublimated
into philosophy; Hippolytos's homoeroticism is sublimated into
religion—philosophy and religion themselves mirror the actual all-
male spaces of the gymnasium or the city itself. Even as the Platonic
figure gains the immortal soul through his efforts, Hippolytos is
given immortality through fame. Artemis promises that he "will not
be anonymous": girls will dedicate their hair to him on the eve of
their wedding. The meadow of his Artemis worship is allowed to
remain uncut, suggesting that he does not pass puberty, but the
girls must cut their hair, symbolizing their move to womanhood.
Without his participating in the heterosexual relationship here established, cult and songs will assure his eternal reputation. In this
way he gains a name, which mortal men generally gain through
having sons to carry on the line. And in the present, he is reassured
by his father who recognizes him and accepts him: "Oimoi, what a
pious and virtuous mind" (1454). "All of Athens is deprived of a
priceless man" (1459–60). Finally, Hippolytos's cries of father are
met this time with Theseus's long-awaited response of "child"
(1456). The trial that Hippolytos goes through leads, like his father's,
to gratification. Having undergone dismemberment, he is eligible
for apotheosis.

In conclusion, let me return once again to the murder of the
woman-mother, that murder Irigaray asserts is necessary for the
"establishment of a certain order in the city." Euripides' play brings
it to pass in a number of subtle ways. First, the myth attributes
heterosexual desire to women. That desire is then seen as excessive
and uncontrollable (even monstrous in the case of Pasiphae's passion
for the bull): it is a bit, goad (39, 1300), driving Phaedra. And like
Io who wanders out of her course,[25] Phaedra turns hysteric thanks
to this visitation of the goddess of love. But her madness does not

disrupt the order for long; it soon closes in over her head. Third, in this series of strategic moves, Phaedra sentences herself to death before she even acts on her desire. The men do not kill her; the story rather requires that she kill herself, thus making the dominant male morality appear to be accepted even by its victims. Her suicide relieves Hippolytos of the blame for matricide, but it is a form of matricide nonetheless, one that serves to eliminate the figure of the passionate woman. Hippolytos's dream of a world where men can procreate without women is realized when father and son hold one another without a woman present. Both forms of eros associated with Aphrodite—destructive (525–62, 1263–82) and constructive (442–50)—converge on the two men, enacted in their embrace at the behest of Artemis. This device displaces the mortal woman and appropriates the goddess in a script for men only.

Linguistic and social order arise on the basis of this violent treatment of the feminine. As the quest for stability of heirs correlates to Theseus's longing for a truthful voice, so Phaedra's desire has its linguistic correlative. Not only does her desire work through speech and writing, but she and Hippolytos differ significantly around issues of speech and silence: he keeps his vow of silence even at his peril, while she relinquishes hers. Moreover, while he is defined by the garden that does not grow or change, with one reverence or *Aidōs* in charge of it, she regretfully acknowledges that there is confusion in the word *Aidōs,* and that the same signifier can have two referents. Since she accepts the lack of clarity that men resist, since she inscribes the death sentence on her tablet, she makes women seem the source of that which men cannot, but nonetheless wish to, control about language as well as sexuality.[26]

Legitimacy was an important concern in fifth-century Athens, as we see from the citizenship law of 451, which ruled that both mother and father had to be Athenian for offspring to be legitimate. Although that law was not enforced during the period of the Peloponnesian war, the issues it addressed did not simply disappear. This play gains some of its force from that discourse. Euripides unsettles Theseus, *the* Athenian hero par excellence, in order to resettle him more securely, having satisfactorily dealt with Hippolytos. Theseus mourns, "Glorious boundaries of Pallas and Athens you will have taken away from you such a one" (1459–60), but what would Athens have done with him had he lived? His life would have been a challenge to the lawful offspring of Theseus, but dead he can simply be the hero. Theseus's heroic deeds included the conquest of the Amazons; that city-founding gesture is secure now because his line is secure.

As the female characters (woman and goddesses) are eliminated, and as the male bond is enacted, simultaneously establishing the legitimacy of Theseus's heirs,[27] this play institutes a new marriage cult in honor of Hippolytos. Artemis's fiat normalizes what is really quite strange, a male icon worshiped by maidens, an imagined heterosexual union balanced by a staged rapprochement between men. Ceremonial cutting of hair also took place at funerals, and at the Apatouria festival of Athens, when boys and girls were registered in the deme. Construing marriage as initiation, we are face to face with the asymmetry of male and female, initiation for girls leads to heterosexual union, initiation for boys leads to the world of men. If Hippolytos is a figure for initiation, we can see new significance in the violence of the bull and horse, since at least Spartan and Cretan rituals included homosexual rape by an older lover.

The civic gains are matched for the son, who gains access to the father's power symbolically, and thus gains the discourse denied to him in their agon. Because of the power of the father, the son is constructed within a very narrow range; he must give up the youthful group of his age-mates. But if he does that, the rewards are great: a cult of his own and eternal remembrance. He is re-membered not as a man loving women, but in his forgiveness of his father. We see that the *Hippolytos* enacts the story of the destruction of (not the desire for) the mother, and the desire for (not the destruction of) the father. The heterosexual rape of Phaedra is after all a fiction; the truth of the tale is the (dominant-submissive) violence of incest repressed between father and son. Oedipus's is not the only story; the narrative of Orestes is an alternative to it, in which the attachment and affinity of father and son transcend their hostility. This is the thread leading into the labyrinth of culture as defined by the exchange of women; it will take a new Ariadne to help us find our way out.

Notes

1. "Displacement and the Discourse of Woman," in *Displacement. Derrida and After,* ed. Mark Krupnick (Bloomington: Indiana University Press, 1983), 186.

2. *Le corps-à-corps avec la mère* (Ottawa: Les éditions de la pleine lune, 1981), 16.

3. *Hippolytos,* ed. W. S. Barrett (Oxford: Oxford University Press, 1964); translations are my own.

4. There is a good deal of scholarship on this play. For a recent treatment, with good bibliography, see Froma Zeitlin, "The Power of Aphrodite: Eros and the Boundaries of the Self," in *Directions in Euripidean Criticism,* ed. Peter Burian (Durham: Duke University Press, 1985), 52–111. On marriage as thematic, see for example, Kenneth Reckford, "Phaethon, Hippolytus, and Aphrodite," *TAPA* 103 (1972): 405–32; Charles Segal, "Pentheus and Hippolytus on the Couch and on the Grid: Psychoanalytic and Structuralist Readings of Greek Tragedy," *The Classical World* 72 (1978): 138-39; also his "Solar Imagery and Tragic Heroism in Euripides' *Hippolytus,*" *Arktouros,* eds. Glen Bowersock, Walter Burkert, and Michael Putnam (New York and Berlin: de Gruyter, 1979), 151–61; Anne Pippin Burnett, "Hunt and Hearth in *Hippolytus,*" in *Greek Tragedy and Its Legacy,* eds. Martin Cropp, Elaine Fantham, and S. E. Scully (Calgary: University of Calgary Press, 1986), 167–86.

5. Eve Kosofsky Sedgwick's book, *Between Men: English Literature and Male Homosocial Desire* (New York: Columbia University Press, 1985), points out the ways in which women are necessary to facilitate relationships between men.

6. On Greek homosexuality in general and on this point, see K. J. Dover, *Greek Homosexuality* (New York: Vintage, 1980), 1, 171, passim; Bernard Sargent, *Homosexuality in Greek Myth,* trans. Arthur Goldhammer (Boston: Beacon, 1986); Hans Licht, *Sexual Life in Ancient Greece,* trans. J. H. Freese (London: Abbey Library, 1932), 445.

7. *This Sex Which Is Not One,* trans. Catherine Porter (Ithaca: Cornell University Press, 1985), 192–93.

8. Gilbert Norwood, *Essays on Euripidean Drama* (Berkeley: University of California Press, 1954), for instance, suspects that there was never any feeling between them (89). On the splitting of the father into Pittheus and Theseus, see Segal, "Pentheus," 135.

9. Plutarch, *Life of Theseus,* 8.24, 27.

10. For the point of view that the bastardy is irrelevant, see Barrett, *Hippolytos,* 363. See also Anne Rankin, "Euripides' *Hippolytos:* A Psychopathological Hero," *Arethusa* 7 (1974): 75, 78; G. M. A. Grube, *The Drama of Euripides* (London: Methuen, 1941),184; G. J. Fitzgerald, "Misconception and Hypocrisy in the *Hippolytus,*" *Ramus* 11 (1973): 27, 29.

11. See Plutarch (*Lives* 2.3), "Bacchylides," xvi, for legends.

12. The play is full of references to the search for signs or clarity: 269, 371 (Phaedra's illness is without sign), 346 *(saphōs)*, 386 *(saphēs)*, 585 *(saphes)*, 857 *(deltos . . . sēmēnai)*, 925–26 *(tekmērion saphes)*, 972 (the corpse); by contrast, because of Phaedra's and Hippolytos's vows of silence, much necessarily remains hidden. For an analysis of speech and silence in the play, see Bernard Knox, "The *Hippolytus* of Euripides," *Yale Classical Studies* 13 (1952): 3–31.

13. Knox, "*Hippolytus*," comments that Theseus's speech becomes fact.

14. Others have noted the importance of the ending, finding a humanistic comfort in it. For instance, see Knox, "*Hippolytus*," esp. 31; R. P. Winnington-Ingram, "Hippolytus: A Study in Causation," in *Entretiens sur l'antiquité classique VI: Euripide* (Geneva: Fondation Hardt, 1958), 171–97, esp. 191; Charles Segal, "The Tragedy of the *Hippolytus*," *Harvard Studies in Classical Philology* 70 (1965): 117–69, esp. 156; André Rivier, *Essai sur le tragique d'Euripide* (Paris: Diffusion de Boccard, 1975), 57–58.

15. Claude Lévi-Strauss's concept of the exchange of women, as articulated in *Elementary Structures of Kinship*, rev. ed., trans. James Bell and John von Sturmer, ed. Rodney Needham (Boston: Beacon, 1969), 60–63, 479–97, has been central to my thinking about Euripides.

16. Ann Bergren, "Language and the Female in Early Greek Thought," *Arethusa* 16 (1983): 78.

17. Anne Rankin and Jean J. Smoot, "Hippolytus as Narcissus: An Amplification," *Arethusa* 9 (1976): 37–51, consider Hippolytos with Narcissus; Sargent places Narcissus with Hyacinthus as models of the beloved (87–101).

18. Segal, "Tragedy," 139, 160.

19. J. M. Bremer, "The Meadow of Love and Two Passages in Euripides' *Hippolytus*," *Mnemosyne* 28 (1975): 279. See also J. Pigeaud, "Euripide et la connaissance de soi," *Les Etudes Classiques* 44 (1976): 3–24; Jon Corelis, "Hippolytos with the Garland: Myth, Ritual and Symbolism and Euripides' Hippolytos" (diss., Stanford University, 1978), 15, adds violence to the pattern of imagery.

20. Some of this work on Hippolytos's misogyny, as it affects Phaedra, has appeared in my essay, "Female Speech and Female Sexuality: Euripides' *Hippolytos* as Model," *Helios* 13, no. 2 (1987): 127–40.

21. On identification with the mother or woman, see Hazel Barnes, *Hippolytus of Drama and Myth* (Lincoln: University of Nebraska Press, 1960), 111; Nicole Loraux, "Le lit, la guerre," *L'Homme* 21 (1981): 37–87; Segal, "Tragedy," 141, 160; Zeitlin, "Power," 77–78, and "Playing the Other: Theater, Theatricality, and the Feminine in Greek Drama," *Representations* 11 (Summer 1985); 63–94.

22. For different discussions of the bull, see Segal, "Tragedy" and "Pentheus," as well as Zeitlin, "Power."

23. Plato, *The Collected Dialogues,* ed. Edith Hamilton, Bollingen Series, 71 (New York: Pantheon, 1961), 500.

24. *Tales of Love,* trans. Leon S. Roudiez (New York: Columbia University Press, 1987), 62.

25. Christine Clément, *The Newly Born Woman,* trans. Betsy Wing, Theory and History of Literature, vol. 24 (Minneapolis: University of Minnesota Press, 1986), 20.

26. For a development of this relationship between sexuality and language, see my "Female Speech."

27. Helene P. Foley, *Ritual Irony: Poetry and Sacrifice in Euripides* (Ithaca: Cornell University Press, 1985), views the ritual as assisting brides in their "potentially painfu! transition to marriage" (22); cf. Pietro Pucci, "Euripides' *Hippolytos:* the Monument and the Sacrifice," *Arethusa* 10 (1977): 165–95, and Corelis, "Hippolytos," 4, 84–85.

The Name of the Daughter
Identity and Incest in Evelina
Irene Fizer

I

"I hardly know myself to whom I most belong" confesses the young heroine, Evelina Anville, at a moment of crisis, uncertain as to which of her three putative fathers she should defer.[1] In Frances Burney's *Evelina; or, The History of a Young Lady's Entrance into the World* (1778) paternity is radically decentered. The father who should occupy the center of authority, Sir John Belmont, is not only absent but a notorious libertine. By taking up the rake father, Burney exposes the most disturbing contradiction of paternal privilege: though Belmont is carnal and negligent, he nonetheless retains the exclusive legal right to his daughter, Evelina. Into the literal space he leaves vacant enter paternal facsimiles: Reverend Mr. Villars, Evelina's guardian, and Lord Orville, her paternalistic suitor. Offering multiple models of paternity, Burney opens the figure of the father to comparative scrutiny. In turn, she structures an alternate patriarchal order: Belmont is replaced by Mr. Villars; Mr. Villars is replaced by Lord Orville. Yet her restructuring of patriarchy leaves no doubt about its limited impact: the lawless father Belmont cannot be redeemed; he can only be removed.

Evelina is Belmont's legitimate child, yet he has refused to acknowledge or "*properly* own her" (19). Her identity is defined by his absence; "child of a wealthy baronet, whose person she has never seen, whose character she has reason to abhor, and whose name she is forbidden to claim; [yet] entitled . . . to lawfully inherit his fortune and estate" (19). Though Evelina is an heiress, she is recognized only as a bastard daughter. Lacking a proper name, Evelina is most immediately effected on the level of language. Her letters circulate throughout the novel, yet none are authorized. Merely by putting signature to paper, Evelina commits forgery. Her own circulation within the world is equally unauthorized. The novel opens as Evelina, at seventeen, departs for the London marriage market.[2] Yet she has neither an entitlement nor an endowment with which to marry.[3] She is that most desirable of commodities, a virgin, but one who moves through society outside the jurisdiction of a legal father. Unmarked as her father's exclusive property, she becomes the subject of competing sexual exchanges among men. However, Evelina's vulnerability to sexual misappropriation does not end when she retreats from society. Within the private space of the family, she is also threatened. As long as Belmont himself refuses to properly own her, the incest taboo, which should mediate their relationship, is inoperative. For Burney, then, a restructuring of paternity is essential to secure both Evelina's legal and sexual propriety.

The crisis of paternity in *Evelina* has a single cause: Belmont cannot be challenged by the law because he stands in its place. He had eloped with Evelina's mother, Caroline Evelyn, and then deserted her after failing to gain the fortune he expected from the match, flaunting his own superiority to the law: "he infamously burnt the certificate of their marriage, and denied that they had ever been united" (15). The pregnant Caroline, reduced to the status of an unwed mother, died in childbirth. On her express instructions, her female child was to be hidden from Belmont "till some apparent change in his sentiments and conduct should announce him less improper for such a trust" (126). Indeed, when Mr. Villars considers the prospect of Evelina living alone with Belmont, the scenario is horrific; implicitly, the daughter is raped by the carnal father: "to expose her to the snares and dangers inevitably encircling a house of which the master is dissipated and unprincipled, without the guidance of a mother, or any prudent and sensible female, seemed to me no less than suffering her to stumble into some dreaded pit, when the sun was in its meridian" (126).[4]

Evelina has been raised and educated by Mr. Villars, an elderly

widower, in the rural seclusion of Berry Hill. While Mr. Villars acts
as an adoptive father, given the private nature of his agreement with
Caroline, he is not Evelina's legal guardian. Early in the novel, he
declines to pursue a paternity suit against Belmont. As he explains,
even "should the law-suit . . . be gained," Belmont cannot be compelled to recognize Evelina as his heiress: "Sir John Belmont would
still have it in his power, and, if irritated, no doubt in his inclination,
to cut off . . . [Evelina] with a shilling" (128). There is, however, an
underlying tension in Mr. Villar's refusal; he himself is reluctant to
cede his claim to Evelina. Instead, a private petition for Evelina's
acknowledgment is made to Belmont by Mr. Villar's neighbor, Lady
Howard. Belmont rejects the petition.

As a result, Evelina's acquisition of a name and an inheritance can
come only if Belmont himself summons her to a private meeting.
And it is toward this encounter that the narrative moves. Evelina
must, then, present Belmont with her claim and await his judgment.
Thus the central and irreducible conflict in the novel is set into
place: the lawless father must become the daughter's judge; his
corrupt house—the "dreaded pit"—must become her courtroom.
To circumvent this contradiction, Evelina herself distinguishes between a titular father and the real Belmont. She maintains her
filiation to her father's *name,* while refused by Belmont himself: "I
am cruelly rejected by him who has the natural claim to that dear
title; a title which to write, mention, or think of, fills my whole soul
with filial tenderness" (130). Yet given that Evelina needs Belmont's
law and yearns for his love (a reciprocal "tenderness") marks her
danger. The encounter between the rake father and the bastard
daughter is fraught with uncertainty. Will the sexually deviant father
reform his "sentiment and conduct" and acknowledge his daughter
legally, or will he persist in his art of seduction and claim her
according to his pleasure? Will the long-rejected daughter, who
wants to be taken in by the father, resist?[5]

Luce Irigaray situates her essay "The Blind Spot of an Old Dream
of Symmetry," in *Speculum of the Other Woman,* at the juncture with
which Evelina is preoccupied: the encounter between the daughter
and the father.[6] She reads Freud's conceptualization of the daughter
in order to figure the father in psychoanalytic theory. Jane Gallop,

in *The Daughter's Seduction: Psychoanalysis and Feminism,* offers an incisive rearticulation of Irigaray's essay.[7] In Freud's account of female development, the girl begins in a phallic stage, during which she overvalues her clitoris and directs her erotic feelings to her mother. She then accedes to her castrated position and redirects her desire to her father. After her experience of loss, she seeks a compensation from the father, the one who now bears the valued, phallic term. In her compensatory fantasy, she is seduced by the father, and receives from him a phallic substitute in the form of a male child. Subsequently, the daughter's erotic and maternal desires are transferred to her husband. The Freudian father thus emerges as a remote figure around whom the daughter plays out her corporeal crises. Irigaray takes Freud's reading beyond the point of the daughter's desire to the nature of the father's response. Indeed, he is the one who must give her away in marriage. She asks: How does he negotiate this exchange?

Irigaray argues that the sexually maturing daughter throws the father into conflict, as she arouses his own libidinal desires for her. He responds with a law of prohibition:

Thus, it is neither simply true, nor indeed false, to claim that the little girl fantasizes being seduced by her father, since it is equally valid to assume that the father *seduces his daughter* but that because (in most cases, though not in all) he refuses to recognize and live out his desire, *he lays down a law that prohibits him from doing so.* That said, it is his desire which . . . prescribes the force, the shape, the modes, etc., of the law he lays down or passes on, a law that reduces to the state of "fantasy" the little girl's seduced and rejected desire—a desire still faltering, barely articulate, silent perhaps, or expressed in signs or body language, a desire that must be seduced to the discourse and law of the father.[8]

By prohibiting the daughter from expressing her desire, the father safeguards his own position as a proper, legal father. The girl herself learns that she can enter language only according to the dictates of her father's discourse. In *Evelina* this encounter between father and daughter is inscribed in reverse. Evelina first enters language in the absence of her legal father Belmont and, within this unauthorized linguistic space, she produces textuality. However, as she becomes increasingly subjected to her father's law, she is gradually reduced to silence and passivity. She becomes a text to be read.

By identifying the father's response to the daughter as a law, Irigaray both engages and revises Lacan's figuring of the Freudian father. Lacanian theory distinguishes between the body of the father, his penis, and the phallus, the symbolic term with which he is invested. The symbolic father is a function of law, not reducible or equivalent to the biological father. The force of the law is carried in the name-of-the-father—through the patronymic, patrilineage, patrimony.[9] As Gallop describes the single standard with which patriarchy defines itself: "By giving up their bodies, men gain power—the power to theorize, to represent themselves, to exchange women, to reproduce themselves, and mark their offspring with their name. All these activities ignore bodily pleasure in pursuit of representation, reproduction, production."[10] However, as both Irigaray and Gallop contend, the phallus will always bear a problematic relationship to the penis within a social system where the male body is inherently privileged over the female.[11] The tacit double standard along which patriarchy actually operates allows the father to exercise his bodily pleasures outside the family, as long as he establishes his law within it. *Evelina* takes the problematic between the father's body and his law even further. Belmont exercises his illicit pleasures within as well as outside the family—he married Caroline in order to exploit her sexually rather than to continue his lineage. Yet he nonetheless retains all legal authority over Evelina. Thus, Burney's refiguring of paternity in *Evelina* reads as an attempt to eliminate the duplicitous father. Only with Belmont's removal is the sexual father finally differentiated from the legal father. The fathers who supercede Belmont—Mr. Villars and Lord Orville— are paternal in name only; they lack the body of the father.

The father's dispensation of power within the family must be read against the context of the economy of exchange. According to Lévi-Strauss's well-known terms, the institution of the incest taboo structures the change from endogamy (a closed system within which men marry the women within their group) to exogamy (an open system within which the men trade their women to men of other groups for economic benefit).[12] If one applies Lévi-Strauss's culturally variable model to patriarchy, each father must negotiate the change from endogamy to exogamy within his own family. He must repress his endogamous desire to retain control of his daughter in order to participate in exogamous exchanges with men: "the father must not desire the daughter for that threatens to remove him from the homosexual commerce in which women are exchanged between men, in the service of power relations and community for the men."[13] If he fails to release his daughter, he may jeopardize his ability to engage in further commerce. In Lévi-Strauss's model, the father retains a residual desire to keep the daughter to himself; nonetheless his need for economic and social alliance will win out. Irigaray insists on reading that moment of the father's ambivalence. She suggests an alternate scenario: through the model of psycho-analysis the analyst father can keep the hysterical daughter in inter-minable analysis and thereby legally evade the order of exchange. He can manipulate the law in order to retain the daughter and secure his own pleasure.

Belmont's profligacy throws the order of exchange into disarray. By refusing to legitimize Evelina, Belmont cannot negotiate within the economy. He forfeits his exclusive right to her and she becomes the sexual property of the male community at large. As long as Evelina does not bear his name, however, his honor within that community is guaranteed. This is a critical point as Belmont, unlike Evelina, is never compelled to live without social identity. Once, however, Bel-mont establishes his claim to Evelina, his own submission to the order of exchange is put into question. Belmont's rejection of Evelina leaves her vulnerable to the sexual abuse of other men, while his appropria-tion of her subjects her to his own violence and carnality. Burney intensifies the sexual tensions within the encounter between father and daughter by preceding this encounter with scenes of fraternal-sororal incest. J. Macartney, Belmont's bastard son, unknowingly falls in love with his sister, Miss Belmont, and his affections for Evel-ina have incestuous overtones. As such, the potentially incestuous closure between Belmont and Evelina is broken open only by the intervening presence of both Mr. Villars and Lord Orville. In turn, this triangular arrangement of paternity protects Evelina herself from an emotional fixation on one father. As her allegiances shift from one "father" to another, she is able to assert a limited but nonetheless decisive autonomy from their separate demands upon her.

II

Educated by Reverend Mr. Villars, Evelina is the personification of a proper young woman. Yet her innocence and purity are continually cast into doubt by virtue of her bastardy. Evelina enters the world with a disreputable name. She is a "little Eve"—a name that marks her both as the daughter of her unwed mother, Caroline *Eve*lyn, and of the archetypal fallen mother, Eve. She enters the world to divest herself of her matrilineage and to acquire a patrilineage, a proper name. Her own surname, "Anville," is an anagram for "Evelina." This alias, along with a fraudulent paternal history, has been concocted by Mr. Villars to cover over the fact of her illegitimacy: "I have always called her by the name of Anville, and reported in this neighborhood that her father, my intimate friend, left her to my guardianship" (19). A duplicate—and duplicitous—paternity, consisting of the foster father Villars and the fictional father Anville, must temporarily stand in for the empty place of the one, legal father. The pious Mr. Villars is willing to perpetuate this fraud, in order to protect Evelina's "blameless self [from] the odium of a title, which not all her purity can rescue from established shame and dishonour" (337).

"Bastard" is the odious "title" suppressed by Mr. Villars, and absent from the novel itself. The word itself could "contaminate" Evelina's virginal body. Evelina describes her own status with a series of euphemisms: "outcast," "orphan," "child of bounty" (367–68). As a consequence of her illegitimacy, Evelina is subject to a constant anxiety about maintaining propriety.[14] Any young woman coming out in society was expected to maintain the standards of feminine decorum: delicacy, modesty, reticence. Evelina has a more urgent task. If she is perceived as a well-bred woman, she will prove herself worthy of her birthright. She must remain pure, an empty slate, until her father imprints his name upon her. If, by contrast, she is perceived as an ill-bred woman, she will prove herself equal only to her fallen status. She may then be fated to remain unacknowledged by her father's law. Propriety is the only means with which Evelina can secure entrance into the world. However, in order to enter the world at all, she must take on an alias, an improper identity.

Without the name of the fictional "father" Anville, Evelina would be barred from society; with it, she enters on false pretenses.

Thus, her deliberate fraud can, in itself, incriminate her. In her opening letter to Mr. Villars, her dilemma is clear; if she signs her alias, she commits forgery:

> Your,
> EVELINA———
> I cannot to *you* sign *Anville,* and what other name may I claim? (24).

Before leaving for London society, Evelina must confront the profound difficulty of her situation: she will enter as an impostor. Only to Mr. Villars can she appear in her true "blankness." And, as he reminds her, she lacks the most rudimentary validation of identity: a birth certificate. In Bristol, under the scrutiny of Mrs. Beaumont, a fanatic reader of ancestry books, her falsified lineage threatens to come to light; "Mrs. Beaumont . . . distressed me by the questions she asked concerning my family,—such as whether I was related to the Anvilles in the North?—Whether some of my name did not live in Lincolnshire?" (284–85). Missing from the written law, Evelina's identity is entirely unauthorized by the patriarchy.

Yet, by this same token, Evelina becomes self-authorized. Sandra M. Gilbert and Susan Gubar have written of the daughter writer subjected to the burden of her father's prior authority.[15] Without a surname or a patrilineage, Evelina writes outside the containing limits of the father's authority. *Evelina* is, of course, structured as a correspondence between a "father," Reverend Mr. Villars, and a daughter, Evelina. However, Mr. Villars is not a legal father whose punition Evelina must fear. Rather, he is a father-confessor to whom Evelina can write without restraint. Indeed, while Mr. Villar's own letters to Evelina amount to a guidebook for female comportment, he urges Evelina to write him with "indulgence": "thank you, my best Evelina, for the minuteness of your communications; continue to me this indulgence" (55). Thus, whereas Evelina quickly learns to restrain her speech in society, in her letters she is voluble, unfettered. Moreover, she is never a passive observer of the society she moves through, and is particularly critical of male pretension and arrogance.[16] In a notable example, Evelina unreservedly expresses her dislike of Captain Mirvan—the only other natural father in the novel and to whom his own family defers: "Captain Mirvan is arrived . . . I do not like him. He seems to be surly, vulgar, and disagreeable. . . . I cannot imagine why the family is so rejoiced at his return. . . . I hope they do not think so ill of him as I do. At least, I am sure they have too much prudence to make it known" (38). Burney empowers Evelina's epistolary voice with the candor or "imprudence" of observations like these. Yet at the same time, she makes it clear that Evelina's epistolarity is empowered only so long as Evelina remains as a bastard daughter.

Evelina's writing is abruptly suspended at the end of volume 2. When her vulgar relatives, Madame Duval and the Branghtons, highjack Lord Orville's carriage in the name of "Miss Anville," she writes Orville an exculpatory letter. She is "half-frantic" that their lack of etiquette will be imputed to her and the "good opinion of Lord Orville . . . irretrievably lost" (248). Her letter of apology is the first to which she signs her surname, "Anville." Sir Clement Willoughby, the rake with designs on her, intercepts her letter and sends her a salacious response. He signs the letter: "Your grateful admirer, Orville." Two thefts are committed: Madame Duval and the Branghtons steal the carriage; Sir Clement steals Evelina's letter. However, it is Evelina who stands to be convicted. By initiating an epistolary exchange with Lord Orville, however minimally and formally, she makes an error in judgment.[17] An eligible eighteenth-century woman writing to a potential suitor on her own volition committed an act of provocation; Evelina's letter is inherently eroticized. This is what Sir Clement understands, and why his plot succeeds. In attempting to clear her name—to distinguish herself from her relatives' indecorum—Evelina herself breaches decorum. As she writes to her friend Maria Mirvan, quoting from Sir Clement's letter: "He talks of my having *commenced a correspondence* with him; and could Lord Orville indeed believe me so forward, so bold, so strangely ridiculous?" (259). The impact of the letter episode ultimately rests with the way in which it complicates the issue of Evelina's innocence. Evelina, like the deviant Sir Clement, *has* broken the law: she, too, has signed her letter with a forged name.[18]

The consequences of the letter episode are devastating: Evelina takes on the burden of guilt—"I have been my own punisher!" (264)—and subjects herself to severe self-censorship. Her voice is silenced as she flees from London to Berry Hill and collapses into a wasting sickness. She declares her intention to remain with Mr. Villars: "Never do I wish to be again separated from him" (260). However, if she would stay with him, she would either die or remain stigmatized by her illegitimacy. Thus, she must travel with Mrs. Selwyn, a wealthy widow, to Bristol Hotwells, the curative spa. With the entrance of the bold and forward Mrs. Selwyn, the highly-accomplished female satirist, Evelina' critical power is diminished. She increasingly begins to insert Mrs. Selwyn's satirical descriptions into her letters rather than to offer her own. Evelina's debilitation dramatizes the strict limit upon her ability to conduct—and finally to write—herself as a daughter unlicensed by the father.

As long as she writes in the private margin, under the name "Evelina," she is immune from punishment. The moment her writing strays into the public sphere, and she writes under the "pen name" of Evelina Anville, she is immediately censored. Her letter to Lord Orville marks the beginning of the end of her writing. In Bristol, she is acknowledged by Belmont, and married to Orville. Taken to the restorative waters of Bristol, she is purified of her bastardy and forgery. Already restrained in public, she is effectively silenced in private: after producing a profusion of letters as an illegitimate daughter, she writes only one letter as Evelina Belmont and one short note as Lady Orville. The bastard daughter produces writing but she is ultimately criminalized; diseased; and threatened with death, a fatal silencing. The legitimate daughter is proper, silent, but free of contagion. Thus, Burney liberates the writing of her female narrator from the father only as a temporary strategy, and she justifies the closure of Evelina's writing as the necessary price for the acquisition of a proper identity.

Before Evelina is legitimized, however, her imposture reaches an extreme point. Her arrival in Bristol is seconded by the arrival of Miss Belmont, "only daughter and heiress of Sir John Belmont" (316), onto the marriage market. A long-standing deception is subsequently revealed: Evelina's first nurse, Dame Green, had presented her own fatherless infant, Polly, to Belmont as his daughter by Caroline. The fraud has succeeded because of Belmont's libertinism: unable to identify his children with any real certainty, he accepted the girl as his own. The duplicity of the father leads to a radical splitting of the daughter's identity. The real and the fictitious Miss Belmonts meet in Bristol but their positions are misaligned. Evelina is "bewildered" by her own "contrareity" (316): she watches from the side, at an assembly, as Miss Belmont commands the center of attention and dances with Lord Orville. Evelina's own identity is suddenly and completely nullified: she becomes both the impostor "Miss Anville", and the fraudulent "Miss Belmont." Yet Polly Green's presence serves, in the end, a compensatory function. When Evelina is acknowledged as Belmont's true daughter, her own criminality shifts to Polly Green. She is further cleansed of her own association with bastardy and fraud as the lower-class Polly is indicted—in Mrs. Selwyn's words—as the "little imposter" (378).

However, Polly does threaten to undermine Belmont's patriarchal and class authority. He fears the disapprobation of his ruling-class male community for attempting to exchange the "bantling of . . . [a] wash-woman" (378) into its ranks. He thereby insists that Polly's true identity remain concealed, and he removes her from the market by marrying her to his bastard son, Macartney. As Mrs. Selwyn observes: "I, who know the world, can see that half . . . his prodigious delicacy for the little usurper is the mere result of self-interest, for while *her* affairs are husht up, Sir John's, you know, are kept from being brought further to light" (378). It is in this sense that Belmont is finally punished for his profligacy: he must adulterate his own bloodline to protect his position within the economy of exchange. Burney redeems—elevates—Belmont's illegitimate progeny at his expense.

III

Evelina's body is subjected not only to disease, but to continual sexual assault.[19] As Lord Orville notes: "this young lady seems to be peculiarly situated; she is very young, very inexperienced, yet appears to be left totally to her own direction. She does not, I believe, see the dangers to which she is exposed" (346). Evelina is conspicuous as a beautiful but unattended and naive young woman. Men insinuate themselves upon her, exploiting the absence of a mediating, male guardian in her life. As a bastard, she has neither a reputable family name nor a dowry—terms that would establish her exchange value in the marriage market. Her status thus becomes material; she is the sum total of her beauty, her body. She has use value alone—sexual availability.[20] Sir Clement, who plots to "trap" Evelina as his mistress, assesses her as a "a girl of obscure birth, whose only dowry is her beauty, and who is evidently in a state of dependency" (347).[21] As yet unclaimed by her father, Evelina is taken to be a readily available commodity. Worse, as an unescorted young woman, she is taken to be sexually willing.

Burney underscores her heroine's susceptibility to assault with scenes in which Evelina is abandoned, separated from, or left behind by her guardians. Finding herself alone in ballrooms and assemblies, Evelina is harangued and pursued by men. At first, inexperienced in the rules of the dance, she is uncertain how to control men's access to her. She eventually learns how to manipulate etiquette within these enclosed spaces to reject such advances. Etiquette, however, is of no consequence when she finds herself alone in public spaces and is literally seized. Her visit to Vauxhall is particularly harrowing. Mr. Smith, a member of her own party, first endeavors "to attach himself" to her with such "impertinent freedom" that she is "quite sickened" (193). He believes that Evelina's bastardy allows him to importune her even as she refuses his marriage proposals. Subsequently separated from him, Evelina is diverted into the dark alleys of the park and encircled by a "large party of gentlemen" (192) who grab her and block her path. When yet another party of gentlemen surrounds her, Sir Clement suddenly appears and intervenes. Yet he "rescues" Evelina only to divert her into another dark alley, where he attempts to molest her in turn. Evelina is passed from man to man like a common property, in a scene that has the gruesome charge of a gang rape. Her sexual "fall" is inscribed as a perversely upward movement: she is traded from the lower-bour-geois Smith, to the higher-class gentlemen, to the baronet Sir Clement. And, in the end, the men of highest rank sort out their superior proprietary rights to her. One of the gentlemen refuses to relax his grip on Evelina and cede her to Sir Clement: "in a passionate manner [he] vowed he would not give me up, for that he had the first right to me, and would support it" (196).

Evelina's fear about being misperceived as a common woman is fully objectified in the Marybone Gardens scene. Divided from her company after a fireworks display, she is seized by an officer who conscripts her into his sexual "service": "a young officer, marching fiercely up to me, said, 'You are a sweet pretty creature, and I enlist you in my service'; and, then, with great violence, he seized my hand. . . . I screamed aloud with fear" (233). The solitary Evelina is assaulted even by a representative of the law. Terrorized, she asks for protection from two nearby prostitutes, who exert their own hold upon her, pinning her between them. While caught in this contaminating "frame," Evelina is spotted by the omnipresent Lord Orville. Orville is Evelina's appointed suitor in the novel precisely because he discerns her intrinsic worth; he alone sees *through* her body. Yet even Lord Orville must pay Evelina a visit, after seeing her with the prostitutes, to settle his own "incertitude" (240)—to renegotiate her fallen value. The Marybone scene serves to mark Evelina's similarity to the whores, rather than her dissimilarity from them. The distinction between the high-born woman and the fallen woman has become blurred. As an illegitimate daughter, Evelina is also a woman without a family; who circulates alone in the city; whose value accords solely with her body; who is potentially available to any male "buyer."

As Irigaray argues, a woman is always "no more than a vehicle for relations among men."[22] With a proper name, Evelina would be exchanged once as a sexual property between her father and a suitor. Without a proper name, she is exchanged as a sexual property among many men. Burney indicates the impossibility of a woman's status as male property by structuring an implicit parallel between Sir Clement and Belmont. Belmont, like Sir Clement, is a proven libertine: he may claim Evelina as his own, "saving" her from the assault of other men, and then molest her in private. As such, Evelina is threatened by sexual misappropriation up until the moment, in

Bristol, when she is *married* to Lord Orville: the lecherous and inebriated Lord Merton gropes at her; Sir Clement tears at her clothes; but, more disturbingly, Belmont himself repeatedly places his hands upon her. Only when Evelina becomes the exclusive property of the proper Lord Orville is her body protected from further transaction.

Thus, the assaults upon Evelina in public have a disettling, private equivalent. Without a name to mark her identity, Evelina must present Belmont with the evidence of her body. Caroline Evelyn had secured the one hope for her daughter's paternal recognition on her physical traits. As her deathbed letter to Belmont reads: "Should'st thou, in the features of this deserted innocent, trace the resemblance of the wretched Caroline. . . . Wilt thou not, Belmont, wilt thou not therefore renounce it?" (339).[23] Mr. Villars has substantiated that Evelina is indeed her mother's double: "without any other certificate of your birth, that which you carry in your countenance, as it could not be effected by artifice, so it cannot admit of a doubt" (337). For Evelina, uninscribed in law, her body alone can certify lineage. Thus, within as well as outside the family, Evelina's perceived value is corporeal. Her body is a text to which her father must acknowledge authorship—upon which he must imprint his name. In acknowledging Evelina as his daughter, Belmont will concomitantly confess to his crimes against her mother. Evelina herself cannot convict Belmont: he must reform himself.[24] Thus, Belmont's institution of Evelina's birthright and his self-recrimination are contingent upon an act of perception, and an act of assignation. He must read Evelina's body correctly and then assign her his proper name.

Evelina is "staged" for Belmont's view. She is hidden by Mrs. Selwyn within an inner apartment and then suddenly revealed to her father. Evelina herself cannot bear to look at Belmont. She instinctively covers her face and collapses: "an involuntary scream escaped me, and covering my face with my hands, I sunk on the floor" (372). Evelina hides her face—the very bodily evidence she has come to display—in a defensive gesture against Belmont's view. If he rejects her, he will destroy her true identity. Evelina expires under the power of her father's gaze but he, in an ostensible act of recognition, revives her, lifts her up:

"My God! does Caroline Evelyn still live! . . . if my sight has not blasted thee—lift up thy head, thou image of my long-lost Caroline! . . . Yes, yes," cried he, looking earnestly into my face, "I see, I see, thou art her child! she lives—she breathes—she is present to my view!—Oh God, that she indeed lived!—Go, child, go," added he, wildly starting, and pushing me from him, "take her away Madam—I cannot bear to look at her!" And then, breaking hastily from me, he rushed out of the room . . . [and] with a violence almost frantic, he ran up stairs (372–73).

Belmont confirms Evelina's resemblance to Caroline—"never was a likeness more striking!—the eye, —the face,—the form[!]" (385). Yet, his violent and frantic reaction to her cannot be explained fully as an admission of guilt about his past. In fact, this is the explanation he himself gives for his actions. Clearly, his word is unreliable. Evelina's presence is disturbing to Belmont for another reason altogether.

Evelina has come before Belmont to receive the name "Belmont." Taking account of the names Belmont actually assigns her, a highly irregular pattern emerges. In this initial encounter between father and daughter, Belmont never calls Evelina by her own name. Without this assignation of legitimacy, Belmont's relationship to his daughter remains unregulated by law. Instead he refers to Evelina by her mother's name. Moreover, he names her not "Caroline Belmont," his wife, but "Caroline Evelyn," the virginal and sexually eligible daughter of Mr. Evelyn. She is the exact duplicate of the young woman Belmont had sexually exploited and then discarded. How, then, will Belmont renegotiate his relationship with "Caroline Evelyn"? Will he retake her as his bride? If his sexual desire is revived, it will prove equally fatal to Evelina, as it will now be incestuous. Yet Belmont portrays *himself* as Evelina's victim. During their second meeting, he flies into yet another "frantic fury" and accuses her directly of stripping him of authority: "starting suddenly, with a sternness, which at once surprised and frightened me, 'Child,' cried he, 'hast thou yet sufficiently humbled thy father?—if thou has, be contented with this proof of my weakness, and no longer force thyself into my presence!' " (383). Belmont acknowledges Evelina's threat to his patriarchal power: her body, as the site of his focalized view, may arouse his libidinal desire, rather than his legitimate interest.

The father's unlawful view of his daughter dismantles his symbolic authority. Her presence causes him to abandon the law, and discloses what the law keeps under cover—his desire for her. As Gallop writes:

The Father's law is a counterphobic mechanism. He must protect himself from his desire for the daughter. . . . The law of the father protects him and patriarchy from the potential havoc of the daughter's desirability. Were she recognized as desirable in her specificity as daughter . . . there would be a second sexual economy. . . . The father gives his daughter his law and protects himself from her desire for his body, protects himself from his body. For it is only the law—and not the body—which constitutes him as patriarch.[25]

The encounter between Belmont and Evelina occurs within the endogamous "second, sexual economy." Confronted with Evelina's body, Belmont must sublimate his own. To stave off the threat of incestuous desire, he imposes a self-defensive law of prohibition. In order to institute himself as a patriarch, and refute his identity as an improper father, he must give Evelina his law. Determined to put himself at a safe remove from her, he bars a second meeting; Evelina is categorically "banished [from] his sight" (379). Within his terms, their relationship must remain strictly legal, their corporal contact entirely foreclosed. As Lynda Boose analyzes the father's response to the sexually mature daughter: "For the father, whose unbidden desires no longer hide themselves . . . the assertion of new emotional and physical distance from the daughter serves as a defense against conscious recognition. In trying not to be the incestuous father, he instead becomes the rejecting one who turns away from his daughter."[26] After Belmont banishes Evelina, he issues an inheritance of £30,000 "in the name of Evelina Belmont" (378). At this point, he has structured his legal relationship with his daughter. In public, Belmont becomes an upstanding father whom Evelina can now call, without conscious conflict, "the noblest of men" (387): he settles her inheritance; sends her money for a trousseau; marries her to Lord Orville; and marries Miss Belmont to Macartney. However, Belmont's institution of law takes place outside the confines of his house. In private—beneath the cover of the law—he is irresolute.

On account of Evelina's fervent requests, Belmont agrees to a final meeting with her. She seeks a private bestowal of his paternity. Daughter and father play out a disordered scene: Belmont resists the law; Evelina supplicates before it. Belmont persists in withholding the name "Evelina." He places his daughter near a window, to view her face more closely, and calls her by her mother's name: "Poor, unhappy Caroline!" (383). And with this, he again banishes Evelina from his sight. Rather than complying, Evelina requests to be recognized by him, in person, not as his former bride, but as his daughter: " 'Oh, go, go!' cried he, passionately . . . 'leave me,—and forever!' 'I will, I will!' cried I, greatly terrified; and I moved hastily towards the door: yet stopping when I reached it, and, almost involuntarily, dropping on my knees, 'Vouchsafe,' cried I, 'Oh, sir, vouchsafe but once to bless your daughter, and her sight shall never more offend you!' " (383). Once more Belmont ritualistically lifts up Evelina but, in so doing, pronounces her name for the first time: "rise, Evelina" (384).

Nonetheless, the father's recognition of his daughter remains unsound. When Evelina hands Belmont her mother's letter, he becomes disoriented. Kneeling before her, he begs her as "the representative of my departed wife, [to] speak to me in her name!" (385–86). Evelina must resist her father's order and rearticulate the terms of "father" and "daughter" that he persists in withholding. She refuses to become the corporal embodiment of her mother, and compels her father to follow the law: " 'Oh rise, rise, my beloved father,' cried I, 'I cannot bear to see you thus; reverse not the law of nature, rise yourself and bless your kneeling daughter!' " (386). Ostensibly, by "bending thus lowly" (385) before Evelina, Belmont is ceding to her power of punishment or forgiveness. But the figuring of an empowered daughter does not hold. Rather, at this moment when Belmont has assigned Evelina a *double* identity—she is both his bride "Caroline Evelyn" and his daughter "Evelina"—he maintains an overriding dispensation of power. He has, at once, a sexual-marital claim and a legal-paternal claim to her. And the fact that Belmont has not remarried adds further tension to this moment. Belmont is unable to own Evelina without simultaneously perceiving her as Caroline. He can resolve his doubled ownership of Evelina only by exchanging her—he gives her to Lord Orville and makes it clear that he will never meet with her again:

"Adieu, my child—be not angry—I cannot stay with thee,—oh Evelina! thy countenance is a dagger to my heart!—just so, thy mother looked,— just so—" Tears and sighs seemed to choak him!—and waving his hand, he would have left me,—but, clinging to him, "Oh, Sir," cried I, "will you so soon abandon me?—am I again an orphan?—oh my dear, my long-lost father, leave me not, I beseech you!" . . . "You know not what you ask," cried he . . . suffer me, then, to leave you. . . . Lord Orville has behaved nobly;—I believe he will make thee happy." [386]

With these closing words, Belmont sublimates his desire to retain sexual control of the daughter for the greater benefit of economic control: "If the father were to desire his daughter he could no longer exchange her, no longer possess her in the economy by which true, masterful possession is the right to exchange."[27]

Belmont's institution of the law has instigated, rather than dispelled, the issue of incest. Meeting his daughter, Belmont cannot keep his violent passions under control. His two meetings with Evelina are characterized by his aggression and physicality toward her: he brutally rages at her, shoves her, and twice embraces her. Evelina herself characterizes her father's touch as violent. However much she seeks her father's embrace, her encounters with him correlate to her molestations by men in public. The law of the father, as the prohibition against incest, cannot become a reliable decree as long as it is linked up in this way with the father's body. Pointedly, even Belmont's tears do not sufficiently purify his corrupt body, nor do they sufficiently neutralize his excessive charge of masculinity. (Evelina, by contrast, "almost drowned in tears" [386] at her father's departure, is cleansed of her bastardy; these are the true Bristol "waters" in which she immerses herself.) Only the father's strict separation from his daughter will act to differentiate securely his law from his desire. Belmont's legal language itself is unreliable, marked by incompletions—slashes and broken words. He professes his own redemption. Burney, however, does not take him at his word and restore him as paterfamilias. Instead, she forcefully removes him. Belmont appears in the novel only long enough to give Evelina a name and an inheritance, and then to give her away. That

Belmont's long-awaited appearance in the novel is conspicuously circumscribed points to the impossibility of reconciling his duplicity.

Belmont's removal secures Evelina herself from her desire for him. As the chronically devalued daughter, Evelina yearns to receive not only proof of her birth, but also proof of her father's love. "The only redemption of her value as a girl would be to seduce the father, to draw from him the mark, if not the admission of some interest."[28] Evelina's reaction to Belmont is intense: she clings to him, begs him not to leave her. However, Burney structures the encounter between Belmont and Evelina so as to mitigate Evelina's emotional need for her father: when Evelina meets Belmont she is already betrothed to Lord Orville. Her libidinal feelings are shifting from father to fiancé. She even asks Orville to accompany her to her final meeting with Belmont; Orville defers, in principle, to Belmont's authority by leaving Evelina on his threshold: "I besought Lord Orville to accompany me; but he feared the displeasure of Sir John, who had desired to see me alone. He led, me, however, to the head of the stairs" (383). Assured of Lord Orville's love Evelina needs Belmont's law alone—the entitlement and endowment that will authorize her marriage. Thus, in the final scene with Belmont, Evelina's desire for a loving father is deferred. Her status as Belmont's daughter is markedly brief.

At the close of her penultimate letter to Mr. Villars, Evelina fills in the blank space of her signature:

> Now then therefore, for the first—and probably the last time I shall ever own the name, permit me to sign myself,
> >Most dear Sir,
> >Your gratefully affectionate,
> >EVELINA BELMONT. (404)

This final arbiter of legitimacy, the name-of-the-father, which Evelina has sought throughout the course of the novel, is no sooner acquired than renounced, as she takes it on the day before her wedding. Evelina's filial love is swiftly redirected away from Belmont and toward her "fathers" in name only: Lord Orville and Reverend Villars. The similarity in their names serves to mark their shared paternal qualities: Lord Orville is the "golden" ("or"/aurum) version of Mr. Villars.

Lord Orville's willingness to marry Evelina before she is legally acknowledged contravenes the order of exchange: he accepts her intrinsic virtue as a sufficient "dowry."[29] (Although his perception of her "true" value ultimately accords with her economic value.) There is an implicit logic behind this structure of plot. By becoming the first man to *"properly* own" Evelina, Lord Orville supercedes Belmont's natural paternal right to her. He is an intervening figure who blocks the possibility that Belmont will assert an overpossessive claim to Evelina—that he might refuse to exchange her. As such, an implicit contrast is suggested between the scene of Evelina's engagement and the scene of her paternal acknowledgement. Lord Orville asks for Evelina's hand by kneeling before her, and he remains in this posture. When Belmont kneels before Evelina, in the scene that follows, the gesture reads as a perversion of betrothal. Evelina can readily refuse her father's "hand"—imploring him to get off his knees—because she is already another man's intended bride. Moreover, inasmuch as Evelina will be forever separated from Belmont, Lord Orville is a compensating figure, providing her with the legal paternity she is once again without. By merging so closely two forms of union—that of Belmont and Evelina, and that of Evelina and Lord Orville—*Evelina* blurs the distinction between patrimony and matrimony. Belmont, the spouselike father, is a tremendously dissettling figure, who assigns Evelina an improper name and whose love for her is adulterated with desire. Lord Orville, the paternalistic husband, is a fulfilling figure who grants Evelina a proper name and professes his "disinterested desire" for her (369).

Before their betrothal in Bristol, Lord Orville and Evelina assign each other familial names. Moreover, they already live within the same house. As Evelina cheerfully writes to Mr. Villars: "Here I am, my dear Sir, under the same roof, and inmate of the same house, as Lord Orville!" (294) Orville urges Evelina to "think of me as if I were indeed your *brother"* and "takes every opportunity of calling [her] . . . his *sister"* (315). He is also quick to assume a paternal title to her. When he asks for her hand and she admits to her fatherlessness, he responds with a surge of proprietary desire: "suffer me then

. . . to hasten the time when that shall no longer admit a doubt!—
when your grateful Orville shall call you all his own!" Evelina's
illegitimacy allows Lord Orville to indulge his own authority. An
engaged man ordinarily must live out a period of submission, deferring to the father's prior claim to the daughter. Orville himself never
holds the inferior claim to Evelina.

In her turn, Evelina confesses that "as a sister I love . . . him"
(315). But, in her most exalted praise, she compares Lord Orville to
her beloved adoptive father, Mr. Villars: "I sometimes imagine that
when his youth is flown, his vivacity abated, and his life devoted to
the retirement, he will perhaps resemble him whom I most love and
honor" (72); "Oh Sir! was there ever such another man as Lord
Orville?—Yes, *one* other now resides at Berry Hill!" (320). Evelina
seeks a husband who will be like a father to her, and she will love
him best when he has been fully desexualized, his "vivacity abated."
Her acceptance of Lord Orville's proposal is concomitant with her
collapse into passivity: " 'Oh my Lord,' cried I, 'your generosity
overpowers me!' And I wept like an infant. For now that all my
hopes of being acknowledged [by my father] seemed finally crushed,
I felt the nobleness of his disinterested attachment so forcibly, that
I could scarce breathe under the weight of gratitude that oppressed
me. 'You little know what an outcast you have honoured with your
choice!—a child of bounty,—an orphan from infancy' " (367–68).
She becomes Lord Orville's weeping "infant" and "child," gratefully
submitting to his paternal authority, which Belmont has as yet
denied her. These familial terms of father/daughter and brother/
sister carry a dual significance. On the one hand, they annul the
erotic nature of Orville and Evelina's marriage: it becomes a legal
contract between a protector and his charge, rather than a pairing
of impassioned lovers. On the other hand, the terms are inherently
erotic; they safely fulfill the libidinal wishes of the family romance
through marriage.

Lord Orville's muted masculinity feminizes him. Evelina compli-
ments him for "so feminine his delicacy" (261).[30] In Bristol, he is
distinguished from the rakes who are proposing a joust to determine
the most "potent" phaeton. A telling comment comes from Mr.
Coverley: "why, my Lord Orville is as careful,—egad, as careful as

an old woman! Why, I'd drive a one-horse cart against My Lord's phaeton for a hundred guineas!' " (288). Or, as Mrs. Selwyn flatters Orville: "in an age so daring, you alone should be such a coward as to forbear to frighten women" (283). Orville lacks literal armature: a phaeton, a sword. He is marked by the absence of a penis. Yet this neutralization of Lord Orville's sexuality does not obviate his power. He, in fact, "wins" the proposed race by deferring it as too "dangerous" an idea, "to make the ladies easy" (287). Lord Orville articulates the word of law, the rule of decorum, the prohibition against excess. Identified throughout the novel by his exacting conduct—Lord Orville comes above all to stand as the decisive representative of the law. Thus he is more qualified to take the place of the father than Belmont himself. Where the elder Belmont is described "not [like] an old man, but, on the contrary, strong and able" (227), the 26-year-old Lord Orville is described as aged and sedentary. Where Belmont is defined through the language of the body, Orville is defined by the language of rationality, a "philosophic coldness" (46). Belmont is the duplicitous father who simultaneously wields a penis and the law. Lord Orville, by contrast, wields the phallic law but is corporally neutral.

Lord Orville must be neutralized to an extreme in order to become the proper suitor within a novel where "suitors" are opportunists, protorapists, or drunken lechers. Moreover, he must be neutralized to an extreme in order to become the proper father within a novel where the natural father is physically, legally, and sexually abusive. By making Orville so anomalous, Burney leaves little doubt about the true state of patriarchy: Orville is the single exceptional man within an utterly debased male community (save for the dying Mr. Villars). Nor does Burney's elevation of Orville signal a future reordering of the patriarchy. As Mrs. Selwyn notes: "there must have been some mistake in the birth of that young man; he was, undoubtedly, designed for the last age" (282). Orville's time is already past.

The novel ends without playing out its final ritual of exchange between Lord Orville and Mr. Villars. Lord Orville proposes to Evelina a postwedding plan that includes Mr. Villars: "instead of my immediately accompanying him to Lincolnshire, we should, first, pass a month, at *my native Berry Hill*. This was, indeed, a grateful proposal to me, and I listened to it with undisguised pleasure" (379). Lord Orville's conduct toward Evelina is controlling to an extreme—he monitors her movements and speaks for her: "allow me, my Evelina, to say *we,* and permit me [to speak] in your name as well as my own" (382). By underscoring Orville's willingness to "share" Evelina with Mr. Villars, Burney seeks to offset the potential tyranny of this perfect husband who claims Evelina as "all his own" (404). Mr. Villars, however, unlike Belmont, cannot compete with Orville's legal proprietorship of Evelina.

As such, Evelina's own affections remain focused on both men. She writes a brief note to Mr. Villars before her arrival: "I have time for no more; the chaise now awaits which is to conduct me to dear Berry Hill, and to the arms of the best of men" (406). The plural "men" leaves the distinction between Evelina's adoptive father and her new husband unmarked. She seems to be writing concurrently of her reunion with Mr. Villars (their expected embrace) and of her wedding night with Lord Orville (which they will spend in her childhood room). Before the moment of her loss of virginity, she belongs to both "fathers." Following social order, Evelina has transferred her allegiance from her legal father to her husband. Having completed this required transference, Evelina can, at least momentarily, maintain her extralegal tie with Mr. Villars.

Evelina has identified the nature of Mr. Villar's paternity by comparing him to Belmont: "Oh, Sir . . . You *commit me to my real parent,*—Ah, Guardian, Friend, Protector of my youth!—by whom my helpless infancy was cherished, my mind formed, my very life preserved,—*you* are the Parent my heart acknowledges, and to you do I vow eternal duty, gratitude, and affection" (350). Paternity here is not a matter of bloodline: the father who rears the daughter, rather than the inseminating father, is her true parent. Belmont assigns Evelina her social identity, but Mr. Villars is her actual creator—the formulator of her inner identity. Evelina, in turn, can name Mr. Villars "my *more* than father" (130) as he takes on an additional, nurturing role as a mother for her.[31]

However, Mr. Villars's femininity, unlike that of Lord Orville, is unenforced by law. His private guardianship of Evelina has no external jurisdiction. His authority, like that of a mother, is bounded in domesticity. Indeed, because of this domestic limit, his prior guardianships in the Evelyn family—of Evelina's grandfather, Mr. Evelyn, and of her mother, Caroline—were unmitigated failures. Both the father and the daughter placed into Mr. Villar's care married disastrously. Mr. Villars's influence in their lives ended as soon as they reached maturity and left his home. Evelina, likewise, leaves Mr. Villar's home when she comes of age. They communicate only by frequently delayed letters. As he well knows, he would be unable to prevent Evelina's replaying of her mother's sad history: "Thus it has happened that the education of the father, daughter, and granddaughter, has devolved on me. What infinite misery the two first caused me! Should the fate of the dear survivor [Evelina] be equally adverse, how wretched will be the end of my cares—the end of my days!" (16). Mr. Villars's failure as a *legislating* father is a measure of his lack of the name-of-the-father. Unable to institute law, he cannot control the sexuality of "his" family. Hence, Belmont's carnal paternity is countered directly against Mr. Villars's maternal paternity—the first is excessive, the second deficient.

Yet despite his lack of paternal authority, Mr. Villars does exert his own possessive claim to Evelina. He seeks to retain her in Berry Hill, and, when she leaves, to urge her return. He admits that "she does not, even for a moment, quit my sight, without exciting apprehensions and terrors which almost overpower me" (16). Mr. Villars's fears for Evelina's security are not misplaced, on account of her illegitimacy, but he risks immobilizing her. As the novel opens, Lady Howard is urging him to allow Evelina to visit her home. When he defers the invitation for months, on account of his own ill health, she must petition him again. (Where she must petition Belmont to acknowledge Evelina, she must petition Mr. Villars to let her go.) Lady Howard politely chides Mr. Villars for his control of the girl: "I cannot wonder that you sought to monopolize her. Neither ought you, at finding it impossible" (21).

Similarly, Mrs. Selwyn must convince the reluctant Mr. Villars to allow the debilitated Evelina to travel to Bristol Hotwells. Thus, each time Evelina leaves Berry Hill, she leaves a place of disease. When Mr. Villars learns that Evelina is living with Lord Orville in

Bristol, he commands her to return to him. He is certain that their domestic intimacy will soon turn to sexual intimacy: "Awake, then, my dear, my deluded child, awake to the sense of your danger. You must quit him! . . . his society is death to your future tranquility!" (309). Evelina apologetically but emphatically declines to return to Berry Hill, claiming to be "overpowered" (323) by Mrs. Selwyn. It is only her protracted distance from Mr. Villars that allows her to place her own needs above his desires. As Mrs. Selwyn has reminded her, Belmont soon will arrive from Paris and may settle her birthright. Thus, just as the force of Lord Orville is necessary to separate Belmont from Evelina, the combined influence of Lady Howard and Mrs. Selwyn is necessary to separate Mr. Villars from her. The father's claim to the daughter in *Evelina* is always excessive. If Evelina had returned to Berry Hill, Mr. Villars would neither have pursued the petition with Belmont, nor allowed her to meet with Lord Orville. He would again have had her all to himself. Thus, where Belmont's house is a site of carnality, Mr. Villars's house is a site of stagnation. Evelina must leave both houses to enter the truly proper site: Lord Orville's elevated country seat.

Mr. Villars's possession of Evelina is imbued with a subtle eroticism. He had given Caroline an oath that he would allow Evelina to wed only a duplicate of himself: "I solemnly plighted my faith, *That her child, if it lived, should know no father, but myself, or her acknowledged husband*" (125). There is an obvious reverse implication to this oath—that Mr. Villars himself, living alone with Evelina, is like a husband to her. However, Burney precisely defines the terms of his intimacy with Evelina. As a widowed clergyman, "weak and aged" (405), Mr. Villars is emasculated. He refers continually to Evelina's body but only as a receptacle to which he will turn in death: "my fondest wish is now bounded in the desire of bestowing her on one who may be sensible of her worth, and then sinking to eternal rest in her arms" (15); "[may I receive] the ultimate consolation of . . . closing these joy-streaming eyes in her presence, and breathing my last faint signs in her loved arms!" (405). Mr. Villars's embrace of Evelina will bring him that long-awaited apotheosis, death in the arms of his daughter. While the erotization of this embrace is palpable, it poses no sexual threat to the beloved Evelina.

Occurring at the moment of the father's death, it cannot go further. Mr. Villars's desire will be fulfilled and he will then properly give over the act of sexual consummation to the legal husband.

Thus, at the close of the novel, Evelina's anticipated embrace with both Mr. Villars and Lord Orville allows for an intense bond between father and daughter but without the accompanying threat of incest.[32] In order for such a fulfilling intimacy to be possible, the duplicity posed by Belmont between the father's proper name and his improper body must be canceled out. Lord Orville and Mr. Villars are fathers only in name; they are both disembodied. Yet, even according to Burney's revised terms, what is the price the daughter must pay for propriety? To gain both the father's protection and love, must Evelina retreat into silence and seclusion?[33] Her withdrawal from society is rationalized by the degree to which she has been subjected to sexual assault when outside the rule of the family. However, her retreat into domesticity cannot completely close off the profound tensions generated in the novel by the figure of the debased father. Burney ends *Evelina* by affirming family law, but she has made it clear that the family itself can become the most treacherous enclosure for the daughter.

Notes

1. Fanny Burney, *Evelina; or, The History of a Young Lady's Entrance into the World* (1778; repr. New York: Oxford University Press, 1968), 353. All future references are to this edition and are cited by page number.

2. See Lawrence Stone, *The Family, Sex and Marriage in England, 1500–1800* (New York: Harper and Row, 1977), for a history of marriage in eighteenth-century England.

3. Mr. Villars will give Evelina a small inheritance, which *may* enable her to marry a man within the community of Berry Hill. Also, her grandmother, Madame Duval, offers her a dowry if she consents to marry the lout Branghton. However, neither of these potential marriages would rectify the central problem of her illegitimacy: Evelina would remain a devalued woman.

4. Mr. Villars's scenario, although imagined, accurately depicts Belmont's household in Paris. Belmont negligently leaves his daughter Miss Belmont in the care of an old, female servant. She falls into the "dreaded pit" of a corrupt familial sexuality when her brother Macartney enters the

house and they begin an incestuous affair. It is important to remember that if Belmont *had* claimed Evelina as an infant, she would have been in Miss Belmont's place.

5. Margaret Anne Doody, although referring to Burney's dramas in the following passage from *Frances Burney: The Life in the Works* (New Brunswick: Rutgers University Press, 1988), provides an illuminating historical context within which to read *Evelina:* "If the Restoration drama had been largely interested in relations between fathers and sons, eighteenth-century serious dramas were much occupied with relations between fathers and daughters. The late Georgian period seems addicted to the pleasures of the father-daughter relationship. Officially, it is always presented as pure and holy, with the strength of heterosexual love yet delightfully innocent. Under the insistent innocence, however, emotional incest is never far away" (184).

6. Luce Irigaray, "The Blind Spot of an Old Dream of Symmetry," in *Speculum of the Other Woman,* trans. Gillian C. Gill (Ithaca: Cornell University Press, 1985), 13–129.

7. Jane Gallop, *The Daughter's Seduction: Feminism and Psychoanalysis* (Ithaca: Cornell University Press, 1982), 56–79.

8. Irigaray, "The Blind Spot," 38.

9. See Jacques Lacan, *Speech and Language in Psychoanalysis,* trans. with notes and commentary by Anthony Wilden (Baltimore: Johns Hopkins University Press, 1968), esp. 270–84; and also Juliet Mitchell and Jacqueline Rose, *Feminine Sexuality: Jacques Lacan and the école freudienne* (New York: Norton, 1982), esp. 38–44 and 55–57.

10. Gallop, *Daughter's Seduction,* 67.

11. As Gallop writes in *The Daughter's Seduction:* "Certainly the signifier 'phallus' functions in distinction from 'penis,' but it must also always refer to penis. . . . Lacanians would perhaps wish to polarize the two views into an opposition. . . . But as long as the attribute of power is a phallus which refers to and can be confused . . . with a penis, this confusion will support a structure in which it seems reasonable that men have power and women do not" (96–97).

12. Claude Lévi-Strauss, *The Elementary Structures of Kinship,* trans. James Harle Bell and John Richard von Sturmer (Boston: Beacon, 1969).

13. Gallop, *Daughter's Seduction,* 76. See also Gayle Rubin, "The Traffic in Women: Notes on the 'Political Economy' of Sex," in *Toward an Anthropology of Women,* ed. Rayna Reiter (New York: Monthly Review Press, 1975), 157–210.

14. For a discussion of Evelina's fears about acting in society, apart from her fears about revealing her illegitimacy, see Patricia Meyer Spacks, *Imagining a Self: Autobiography and Novel in Eighteenth-Century England* (Cambridge: Harvard University Press, 1976), chapter 2, "Dynamics of

Fear: Fanny Burney." Spacks also analyzes Evelina's response to her lack of paternity: "Evelina makes quite explicit her desire . . . to find a lover or husband to fill the same role as father or guardian. She assumes the utter propriety of remaining as much as possible a child: ignorant, innocent, fearful, and irresponsible" (178).

15. Sandra M. Gilbert and Susan Gubar, *The Madwoman in the Attic: The Woman Writer and the Nineteenth-Century Literary Imagination* (New Haven: Yale University Press, 1979), esp. chapter 2, "Infection in the Sentence: The Woman Writer and the Anxiety of Authorship."

16. For analyses of Evelina's narrative voice, see John J. Richetti, "Voice and Gender in Eighteenth-Century Fiction: Haywood to Burney," *Studies in the Novel,* 19/3 (1987): 263–72; and Judith Lowder Newton, *Women, Power, and Subversion: Social Strategies in British Fiction, 1778–1860* (Athens: University of Georgia Press, 1981), 42–44.

17. See Edward A. Bloom's explanatory note in *Evelina:* "It was bad form for eligible young people, not publicly engaged, to correspond" (418). In turn, the romantic fantasy Evelina has nurtured about Lord Orville is shattered when she receives the forged letter: the paragon of morality is "revealed" as yet another duplicitous male figure, a common seducer. Orville is, however, quickly reestablished as a singular figure of law in Bristol.

18. One is reminded here that Evelina herself "steals" Lord Orville's name and that he forgives her for this "crime." At a ridotto early in the novel, she implicitly makes use of his name in order to refuse the request of a man who is pestering her to dance. When her "theft" is publicly revealed, she bursts into tears of shame and distress. In a prelude to their marriage, Lord Orville responds by granting her his name: "[he] immediately led me to a seat, and said, in a low voice, 'Be not distressed, I beseech you; I shall ever think my name honored by your making use of it' " (47).

19. Newton, in *Women, Power, and Subversion,* writes of Evelina's subjection to male assault and control with extraordinary insight. However, Newton does not reflect upon the way in which Evelina's bastardy exacerbates her susceptibility to such assault.

20. See Luce Irigaray's discussion of woman's exchange and use value in "Women on the Market," in *This Sex Which Is Not One,* trans. Catherine Porter with Carolyn Burke (Ithaca: Cornell University Press, 1985).

21. As Margaret Doody writes in *Frances Burney:* "The social destiny of such an attractive, well-bred female bastard would seem inevitably to be some upper-class man's kept mistress, as Sir Clement Willoughby implicitly believes" (40).

22. Irigaray, "Women on the Market," 186.

23. The irresolution of Belmont's identity is brought out particularly well in the opening paragraph of Caroline's letter. She cannot find the term with which to inscribe the salutation: "I address myself to Sir John Belmont

... Yet in what terms,—oh most cruel of men!—can the lost Caroline address you, and not address you in vain? . . . Shall I call you by the loved, the respected title of husband?—No, you disclaim it!—the father of my infant?—No, you doom it to infamy!—the lover who rescued me from a forced marriage?—No, you have yourself betrayed me!" (338).

24. Mary Poovey, in "Fathers and Daughters: The Trauma of Growing up Female," *Women and Literature*, 2 (1982): 39–58, offers the only other sustained reading of the encounter between Belmont and Evelina. She reads the scene differently than I, arguing that "Evelina serves as the agent for both humbling and punishing her father [by] speaking in the 'name' and with the face of her mother" (46). Her remarks on the incestuous implications of the scene are cogent but very brief. I am nonetheless indebted to her reading.

25. Gallop, *The Daughter's Seduction*, 76–77. Also see Gallop for a suggestion of the alternate ways Belmont could have perceived Evelina—within Freudian terms—as either a "son" or a "mother."

26. Lynda E. Boose, "The Father's House and the Daughter in It: The Structures of Western Culture's Daughter-Father Relationship," in *Daughters and Fathers,* ed. Lynda E. Boose and Betty S. Flowers (Baltimore: Johns Hopkins University Press, 1989), 36.

27. Gallop, *The Daughter's Seduction*, 76.

28. Irigaray, "Blind Spot," 106.

29. Burney later inserts a "confession" by Lord Orville that he "fully intended" to investigate Evelina's background—to ascertain whether or not she was indeed a bastard and, moreover, whether or not she was indeed connected to the prostitutes in Marybone: "When I expressed my amazement that he could honour with his choice a girl who seemed so infinitely, in *every* respect, beneath his alliance, he frankly owned, that he had fully intended making more minute enquiries into my family and connections, and particularly concerning *those people* he saw with me in Marybone, before he acknowledged his prepossesion in my favour, but the suddenness of my intended journey, and the uncertainty of seeing me again, put him quite off his guard, and 'divesting him of prudence, left him nothing but love' " (389).

30. Susan Staves noted, in *"Evelina;* or Female Difficulties," *Modern Philology,* 73 (1976), that "Fanny Burney sympathized with the general eighteenth-century desire to feminize the masculine ideal. . . . The boldness, activity, independence, and aggressive sexuality which had been earlier associated with masculinity were all objects of incessant attack" (372–73).

31. The complex issue of maternity and female guardianship in *Evelina* deserves a separate and detailed treatment.

32. For a reading of the broader family themes in *Evelina,* see Toby A. Olshin, " 'To Whom I Most Belong': The Role of Family in *Evelina,"* *Eighteenth-Century Life,* 6/1 (1980): 29–42.

33. Kristina Straub, in *Divided Fictions: Fanny Burney and Feminine Strategy* (Lexington: University Press of Kentucky, 1987), offers a powerful model for reading Burney's writing as an inscription, but never a revision, of social and cultural contradictions. Thus, within the terms of my own argument, Burney inscribes a profoundly disturbing reality: the daughter must submit herself dutifully to a father who can readily abuse her. Yet, at the same time, Burney finally repositions Evelina under the authority of a father, rather than seeking an alternative to filial subordination.

6   *The Naked Father in Toni Morrison's* The Bluest Eye

Vanessa D. Dickerson

In Toni Morrison's *The Bluest Eye* (1970), the nine-year-old narrator Claudia McTeer and her ten-year-old sister Frieda lie in bed one night and peer at their naked father who "pass[es] the open door of [their] room":

> We had lain there wide-eyed. He stopped and looked in, trying to see in the dark room whether we were really asleep or was it his imagination that opened eyes were looking at him? Apparently he convinced himself that we were sleeping. He moved away, confident that his little girls would not lie open-eyed like that, staring, staring. When he had moved on, the dark took only him away, not his nakedness. That stayed in the room with us. Friendly-like. (60)

These lines are busy with meaning. On the one hand, they point up the father's insistence on the innocence of his daughters. On the other hand, they intimate the vulnerability of McTeer himself: the lines suggest that for the father the gaze of his daughters would constitute some exposure or violation of his self. Incredulous and suspicious, the father resists the reality of the incident; silent and wide-eyed, the girls grant the significance of the encounter as they acknowledge a difference between a "him" that the darkness takes away, removes, or obscures, and a "nakedness" that is "friendly-like."

Understandably, McTeer refuses to see the open-eyed presence of his daughters because their gaze is an assertion of female selfhood, which threatens the personal power of McTeer. By looking at "him" the girls show a curiosity and a boldness, which the patriarch Noah found so presumptuous and disrespectful as to warrant anathema

(Gen. 10:18–29). By denying the gaze of his daughters, McTeer, like this biblical figure, both restricts Frieda and Claudia's access to and understanding of a masculine self that is rendered awesome because it is remote and obscure, and also limits the knowledge, growth, and empowerment of the girls themselves by disallowing the part of his daughters that may be curious about sexuality. While McTeer refuses to acknowledge this dimension of his girls, the daughters perceive two sides to the father—the "him" or self that is in the shadows—that is, the self that the dark obscures, the self they cannot see or know directly—and the nakedness of a physical self revealed, a self they can see and interpret as familiar, if not intimate, companionable, if not congenial, knowable, if not open: "friendly-like."

The phrase "friendly-like" takes the relationship between McTeer and his daughters out of the realm where the father is the "big and strong" (7) parent who acts as the lawgiver and the benevolent keeper of his biological charges to a place where the children feel they are not confronting a seemingly infallible, inscrutable other, but rather an adult they recognize as vulnerable, warm, primal, accessible. Frieda and Claudia construe the nakedness of their father as "friendly-like" because when he is naked he is less dignified and distant, less concealed, less adulterated, more natural. Cloaked by the darkness, McTeer symbolically adds one more layer to the personal, social, psychological complexities that already separate child and adult. To put it another way, the clothed adult is a complicated, often formidable—if not intimidating text for which the child lacks the analytical skills. "Adults," announces Claudia who perceives grown-ups as enigmatic and obscure, "do not talk to us—they give us directions. They issue orders without providing information" (12). Claudia describes the father who denies the possibility that his daughters would stare at his nakedness, the shadowy father who insists that he remain unseen, unknown, hidden. But she also admits, "The edge, the curl, the thrust of their emotion is always clear to Frieda and me. We do not, cannot, know the meanings of all their words, for we are nine and ten years old. So we watch their faces, their hands, their feet, and listen for the truth in timbre" (16). Naked, the body becomes a primer that the child can more easily decipher.

In *The Bluest Eye*, the children, those readers of the truth in adult hands, faces, feet, and voices, also give us the key we need to understand the most provocative father in the novel, Cholly Breedlove, who rapes his eleven-year-old daughter Pecola at the height of "lust and despair," states of genitals and of mind engendered in his own unneat primerless childhood. Toni Morrison writes in awe of a character she herself finds it difficult to fathom: "The pieces of Cholly's life could become coherent only in the head of a musician. Only those who talk their talk through the fold of curved metal, or the touch of black-and-white rectangles and taut shins and strings echoing from wooden corridors, could give true form to his life" (125).[1] It is not only this jazz musician of Morrison's specification, but also the more primal musician of her suggestion, the child, that can give us the clues needed to piece together the episodes of Cholly's being. Indeed, the explanation for Cholly's tender rape lies fittingly enough in the afterschool chant of "uncorrigival" (56) black schoolboys who taunt Pecola one day after school. "Black e mo Black e mo," they incant, "Ya daddy sleeps nekked" (55).

While these boys provide the key to Cholly's unstorybooklike improvised fatherhood, the girls—Pecola, Maureen, Frieda and Claudia—pick up the reference to nakedness that the boys so quickly drop and worry it until it begins to yield meaning. It is Frieda and Claudia's frank and shameless encounter with their own father's nakedness that enables us to define the truth of Cholly's nakedness. The scene in which McTeer stands naked before his daughters introduces, as we have seen, the figure of two fathers—one, the "him" that passes into the darkness, is obscure, distant, dignified, jealous of his power, a lawgiver; the other, the father with the "friendly-like" nakedness that remains before the girls and the reader, is warm, exposed, spontaneous, physical. Unlike Claudia and Frieda's father, who survives, Morrison suggests, because he is able to be the obscured and the naked father, Pecola's father, even more the victim of unpropitious personal, social, and economic conditions, is cast out. He lives the life of the naked father. In a society controlled by traditional white patriarchs, Cholly, denied the opportunity to protect, provide, and command, becomes not just confused and frustrated, but desperately extreme in his spontaneity, passions, physicality, weaknesses—his nakedness. In *The Bluest Eye*, Morrison portrays the conditions under which a naked father such as Cholly is created and shows how such a nontraditional father operating in a traditional Dick-and-Jane society ruins himself and his own.

Cholly Breedlove's childhood is vexed by bitter-sweet exposure and overexposure. When he is only a helpless four-day-old, his mother compromises his existence when she leaves him on a junk heap, "Down in the rim of a tire under a soft black Georgia sky" (105). The ugliness of the junk heap is not mitigated by the soft black Georgia sky, rather the two are juxtaposed forever like the ebony and ivory of a keyboard in Cholly's life. Fifteen years later, when Cholly has his first sexual experience, he suffers a more blatant exposure that undercuts the ecstacy of the moment. Heady with the "thunderous beauty of [Aunt Jimmy's] funeral" and the "exultation" of the funeral banquet (113), Cholly, who has set out with a small group of youths to a wild vineyard, finds himself alone and about to experience his first sexual encounter with one Darlene. However, just as Cholly, astride Darlene, feels "an explosion threaten" (116), two white men out coon hunting interrupt the lovemaking with their eyes, lamps, flashlights, and laughter.

> "Hee hee hee heeeee." The snicker was a long asthmatic cough.
> The other raced the flashlight all over Cholly and Darlene.
> "Get on wid it, nigger," said the flashlight one.
> "Sir?" said Cholly, trying to find a buttonhole.
> "I said, get on wid it. An' make it good, nigger, make it good." (117)

As the "flashlight [makes] a moon on his behind" (117), Cholly, having lost the thrust of his desire, fakes "with a violence born of helplessness" (117) the moves of intercourse. The two white men have spotlighted Cholly's nakedness, vulnerability, and powerlessness, and in doing so have put a junk heap beneath his soft Georgia sky. The dissonance is jarring as the pleasurable excitement of co-ition collides with the painful make-believe of coition performed for two white men, as love slides into hate. Cholly feels deeply the degradation of having this very private act of affirming his manhood turned into a sideshow, into the spectacle of two animals rutting in the woods.

Unable to shield Darlene or himself from the snickering, gun-toting, coon hunting, white men, Cholly transfers his hatred to the weakest player in "the drama" (117), the one who lies beneath him literally and figuratively: "He hated her. He almost wished he could do it—hard, long, and painfully, he hated her so much. The flash-light wormed its way into his guts and turned the sweet taste of muscadine into rotten fetid bile. He stared at Darlene's hands cover-ing her face in the moon and lamplight. They looked like baby claws" (117).

This hatred is no more or less than the inversion of Cholly's desire to protect Darlene from exposure. But since he "had not been able to protect, to spare, to cover [her] from the round moon glow of the flashlight" (119), he opts to save something of himself by hating Darlene. Since hating the hunters "would have destroyed him" (119), he must degrade and reduce Darlene. She has proffered him a thing as fruity as muscadine, but under the light of the white men her gift has soured. The pitiful hands she uses to cover her face so that she cannot see or be seen become "claws," but significantly those of a small, helpless baby.

This reference to Darlene's babylike helplessness recalls Cholly's own helplessness as an abandoned infant at the same time that it points up his inability to protect not only Darlene but himself from the violation of the white man. In fact Cholly's hatred of Darlene is also self-hatred. For in her he senses the dawning of his own parental nakedness. That is, unable to protect, to fight, to hide, Cholly cannot manifest the patriarchal prowess, benevolence, or obscurity (after all, his backside is literally exposed) that is tradition-ally associated with maleness and manhood. Like Darlene he is accessible, weak, and naked. And to be thus naked is to share not only the tenderness and the plight of the female, but also to share a role traditionally assigned to her. The naked male is feminized, if not humanized.[2]

It follows, then, that Cholly, revolted by his identification with the femininity of nakedness, goes in search of his father. What Cholly finds strips him of any illusions he entertains about a relation-ship with that parent. He does see in his parent his own eyes, mouth, and head; however, instead of a man as tall as the black father who had broken open the watermelon at the July picnic, he finds a man shorter than himself and going bald at that. Instead of a man as sympathetic as Blue, one who is willing to share the heart of life with his son just as Blue had shared the heart of the watermelon, instead of the dignified, firm, but benevolent patriarch, he finds a man impatient, insensitive, unapproachable, and hard. The father made present is flawed and alien, the bastardization of the inscrutable father, the diametrical opposite of the naked father.

In the wake of these painful discoveries, Cholly reveals how tender and vulnerable he really is when "he soil[s] himself like a baby," goes down to the river where, "finding the deepest shadow under the pier . . . [he] crouched in it [the river] behind one of the posts . . . [and] remained knotted there in the fetal position, paralyzed, his fist covering his eyes, for a long time" (124). The fetal position and the paralysis of this scene recall Cholly the infant deserted on the junk heap and Cholly the teenager momentarily paralyzed by the flashlight of the white men. Smelling himself just as he had smelled the white men in the woods, just as he had "inhaled a rife and stimulating man smell" (121) among the black gamblers, young Breedlove "takes off his pants, underwear, socks, and shoes" and washes all but these last in the river" (125).

Having thus regressed, Cholly lets his thoughts return to one of the first females who helped define his passage from childhood to manhood:

Suddenly he thought of his Aunt Jimmy, her asafetida bag, her four gold teeth, and the purple rag she wore around her head. With a longing that almost split him open, he thought of her handing him a bit of smoked hock out of her dish. He remembered just how she held it—clumsy-like, in three fingers, but with so much affection. No words, just picking up a bit of meat and holding it out to him. And then the tears rushed down his cheeks to make a bouquet under his chin. (125)

Up to this point, Cholly's feelings for Aunt Jimmy have been as confused as those he later has for Darlene. Aunt Jimmy has saved Cholly from death on a junk heap; however, Cholly has wondered whether it "would have been just as well to have died" (105) on that junk heap. Some of Cholly's ambivalent feelings about his mother-aunt are mirrored in the character of the aunt as Morrison presents her. For example, Aunt Jimmy subsumes the manly role of the rescuer and provider as well as the womanly role of the nurturer. The feminine role of nurturer finally characterizes the aunt for Cholly (he is nearly split open with a recognition of love when he remembers her "just picking up a bit of meat and holding it out to him"); as her androcentric name suggests, she has not only been aunt and mother to Cholly, but also Jimmy and father.

Aunt Jimmy, then, embodies both a remoteness, firmness, and maleness, and a tenderness, weakness, and femaleness that Cholly finds difficult to accept. When Cholly smells the old asafetida bag that Aunt Jimmy wears to ward off sickness and infirmity, when he sees the purple rag (not kerchief) she uses to cover and protect her hair, and when he is made to sleep with her for warmth in the winter, he has mixed feelings of pity and revulsion about the smell of that asafetida bag, about the sight of that purple rag, and finally about the sight of Aunt Jimmy's nakedness, of her old, wrinkled breast sagging in her nightgown (105). Cholly has misgivings about the vulnerability these things ultimately signal.

The pity Cholly has felt for his Aunt Jimmy intimates an identification with the aunt. And it becomes clear elsewhere in the novel that the experiences of a maturer Cholly will bear some resemblance to those of all the Aunt Jimmy's of Cholly's childhood. For like these old black women he too "had grown, [e]dging into life from the back door" (109). He too had taken orders from the white men. And he too had knelt by the riverbank. But the difference between Cholly and these old black women is indeed "all the difference there was" (110). Listening to the chatter of these old women, hearing the lullaby of their grief (110), the child Cholly can at best only revision the thing that most strikingly sets him apart from them and validates his man-life. "In a dream his penis changed into a long hickory stick, and the hands caressing it were the hands of M'Dear" (110). This childhood dream identifies Cholly's penis as the one thing that does not allow him, like the old black women, to "walk the roads of Mississippi, the lanes of Georgia, the fields of Alabama unmolested" (110). His penis marks a manhood that the Southern white man openly and continually flouts or denies. In this way Cholly's penis is simultaneously his rod of affliction and of self-validation. The transformation of Cholly's penis into a hickory stick that M'Dear caresses also points to another association that will in part help account for Cholly's rape of Pecola. For the hickory stick that M'Dear carries when Cholly first sees her is used "not for support but for communication" (108). The dream suggests, then, that Cholly will use his stick-penis to communicate.

From start to finish, Cholly's communications and relations with women are problematic. Aunt Jimmy's love for Cholly, clumsy and unspoken, is nevertheless and eventually communicated. Cholly, however, never manages to express clearly to Aunt Jimmy what he feels. Dead, she can never receive the bouquet of tears that token his love for and loss of her. Similarly, after the trauma Cholly and Darlene both experience under the glare of the white man's flashlight, Cholly's communications with Darlene are strangled when he turns to her: "We got to get girl. Come on!" (118). Cholly's confusion and fear of vulnerability coupled with the growing desire to move from adolescence to manhood further qualify Cholly's relations with the female as he opts, if not for the role of the traditional male who is firm, in control, a protector of women, then for the "strong black devil" (106) who is defiant, daring, bad, a user of women.

In a rite de passage with three unnamed prostitutes, Cholly proves himself the mighty disposer of women, a male reminiscent of the "woman-killer" Blue, whom Cholly had so admired and yet had found an unapproachable father figure (119). In the encounter with the prostitutes, an event that quickly follows Cholly's memories of his dead aunt, Cholly puts aside the weakness, tears, and love he begins to feel by the Georgia riverside for the kind of power and obscurity that sex in a brothel affords him. Here, Cholly takes back "aimlessly" (125) a manhood from women who remain unnamed because they are dwarfed by Cholly's need to affirm his male self. In the transaction, these women are used to satisfy his hunger. And yet what Cholly receives from this incident, Morrison suggests, is equivocal in value as he does not get anything as substantial as Aunt Jimmy's smoked hock or even Darlene's grapes. From the prostitute he takes "lemonade in a Mason jar," "slick sweet water" (125).

Having received this unsubstantial libation from a Mason jar, Cholly sets out on the road to a godlike freedom too extreme to result in good for himself or others. The man Pauline meets and marries has experienced a freedom that ultimately accentuates his nakedness:

Only a musician would sense, know, without even knowing that he knew, that Cholly was free. Dangerously free. Free to feel whatever he felt—fear, guilt, shame, love, grief, pity. Free to be tender or violent, to whistle or weep. Free to sleep in doorways or between the white sheets of a singing woman. Free to take a job, free to leave it. He could go to jail and not feel imprisoned, for he had already seen the furtiveness in the eyes of his jailer, free to say, "No, suh," and smile, for he had already killed three white men. Free to take a woman's insults, for his body had already conquered hers. Free even to knock her in the head, for he had already cradled that head in his arms. Free to be gentle when she was sick, or mop her floor, for she knew what and where his maleness was. He was free to drink himself into a silly helplessness, for he had already been a gandy dancer, done thirty days on a chain gang, and picked a woman's bullet out of the calf of his leg. He was free to live his fantasies, and free to die, the how and the when of which held no interest for him. In those days, Cholly was truly free. Abandoned in a junk heap by his mother, rejected for a crap game by his father, there was nothing more to lose. He was alone with his own perceptions and appetites, and they alone interested him. (125–26)

The "godlike" freedom that reveals itself in these lines is neither the genuine nor the conventional thing. The force here represented is not that of a lawgiving, unbending, inscrutable godlike Yaweh. Cholly's acts tend to invert those of the patriarchy. For Cholly, the law becomes lawlessness; firmness can quickly turn to meanness, order passes into confusion. The freedom posited in these lines is one of contradiction, of paradox, of extremity, of heavenly tenderness and hellacious murder. Cholly's liberation is here exposed as a liberation of detachment and worthlessness: "there was nothing more to lose." Having no real power, no real possessions, no relationship, Cholly is naked. Having no real power, Cholly is subjected to prison, insults, bullets, and rejection. Having no real possessions, he is cut adrift as he moves from one place to another. Having no real relationship, he is "alone with his own appetites and perceptions."

As we have seen, Cholly's appetites and perceptions have in the course of his move from childhood to manhood shifted from smoked hock to slick sweet water, from love to sex. In his marriage to Pauline, Cholly tries to have the smoked hock, the love, the traditional Dick-and-Jane idea. He even tries to realize that which can more firmly establish the male's place in a patriarchal society—fatherhood. However, "having no idea of how to raise children, and having never watched any parent raise himself, he could not even comprehend what such a relationship should be. Had he been interested in accumulation of things, he could have thought of them as his material heirs; had he needed to prove himself to some nameless 'others,' he could have wanted them to excel in his own image and for his own sake" (126–27). The problem is that as a father Cholly has been stripped by his past of the possibilities of material accumulation and of social standing. Poor and black, renting a storefront because of a poverty that "was traditional and stultifying" (31), Cholly Breedlove and his family cannot indulge the "hunger for property, and for ownership" (18) that drives other blacks like the Peals, the Geraldines, and the McTeers (18). Cholly's modest attempts to buy his family and himself some of life's amenities are thwarted by whites who, in control of money and materials, take advantage of the helplessness and powerlessness visited upon black men in American society who, like Cholly, suffer deprivation of the goods and experiences by which manhood is signified.[3] Thus when Cholly buys a new sofa that is delivered to his house with split fabric, it becomes, as the delivery man tells Cholly, "Tough shit, buddy. *Your* tough shit" (32).

The "joylessness" (32) of paying for something that is damaged marks a social impotence that is accentuated by the presentation of other fathers in the novel. The white male in Morrison's novel, for example, usually realizes the idea of the powerful but somewhat distant if not inscrutable provider. Morrison encourages this notion of remoteness and obscurity with her purposefully brief representations of the white fathers in the novel. At most the reader learns that these patresfamilias have money, which equals power, or they have possessions, land, and servants, which also amount to power and control. Though these often unnamed white men tend not to be physically present in the novel (and we can never know them or even McTeer as intimately as we do Cholly), their presence is very definitely felt as the heads of households of "power, praise, and luxury" (101). As the Dick-and-Jane text with its own brief mention of the father suggests, these obscure figures are the ideal patriarchs, the father against which society measures Cholly. At the top of a hierarchy of color and money is Mr. Fisher, a well-to-do white father who commands a household in which Pauline finds "beauty, order, cleanliness and praise" (101). At the very bottom is Cholly, a poor renting black father whose household is characterized by ugliness, cold, and strife. The distance between this naked black father and the white ideal of fatherhood looms insurmountable.

While Cholly in no way resembles the white patresfamilias in the novel, Morrison's multiple imaging of black fatherhood shows that he is both unlike and like his black contemporaries especially in his relations with his daughter. Cholly is most unlike the father of "the high-yellow dream child" (52), Maureen Peal. A black approxima-tion of Mr. Fisher, Mr. Peal is able to secure the financial well-being of his daughter. According to the McTeer girls, Maureen "was rich . . . as rich as the richest of the white girls, swaddled in comfort and care" (52). The fine patent-leather shoes, fluffy sweaters, brown velvet coat trimmed in white rabbit fur, kelly-green knee socks, and money with which Peal outfits his daughter help reinforce, if not foster, her sense of self-esteem and beauty: "I *am* cute! And you ugly!" she screams to "the three black girls [Claudia, Frieda, and Pecola] on the curbside, two with their coats draped over their heads, the collars framing the eyebrows like nuns' habits, black garters showing where they bit the tops of brown stockings that barely covered the knees" (61).

Pecola is finally the strongest foil to the confident daughter of Mr. Peal. For Cholly Breedlove has neither genetically nor financially created a doll-like child, a storybook Jane, or a Polly Fisher. In one of her most unconfident and vulnerable moments, Cholly's daughter, a representative of his fatherly accomplishments, stands in a "dirty torn dress, the plaits sticking out on her head, hair matted where the plaits had come undone, the muddy shoes with the wad of gum peeping out from between the cheap soles, the soiled socks, one of which has been walked down with the heel of the shoe . . . a safety pin holding the hem of the dress up" (75).

The McTeer girls are not without slack in their own worn stockings (54); however, Morrison suggests that though their father shares some of Cholly's weaknesses, his is not so starkly impotent or naked. We can never know McTeer as well as we know Cholly. The circumstances of his childhood and his entry into manhood are not given; Morrison textually obscures and reveals McTeer. For us, then, as well as for his children, a side of him remains in shadow. We glimpse him only when we hear of his nakedness and again when he turns the lecherous boarder, Mr. Henry, out of his house for making lewd advances to Frieda (80).

Yet one of the most sustained though oblique commentaries on Cholly's fatherhood comes through the portrayal of McTeer in a poetic interlude that commences the section of the novel called "Winter." Here Claudia McTeer pays tribute to a father who, like Cholly, cannot swaddle his girls in luxury, but a father, who unlike Cholly, is not so naked as to turn physically his frustration at his condition upon his daughters. Claudia writes:

My daddy's face is a study. Winter moves into it and presides there. His eyes become a cliff of snow threatening to avalanche; his eyebrows bend like black limbs of leafless trees. His skin takes on the pale, cheerless yellow of winter sun; for a jaw he has the edges of a snowbound field dotted with stubble; his high forehead is the frozen sweep of the Erie, hiding currents of gelid thought that eddy in darkness. Wolf killer turned hawk fighter, he worked night and day to keep one from the door and the other from under the windowsills. Vulcan guarding the flames, he gives us instructions about which doors to keep closed or opened for proper distribution of heat, lays kindling by, discusses qualities of coal, and teaches us how to rake, feed, and bank the fire. And he will not unrazor his lips until Spring. (52)

The first part of this tribute to McTeer describes a parental figure reminiscent of the white patriarchs whom Cholly can never be or emulate. With skin that "takes on the pale, cheerless yellow of winter sun," father McTeer is identified not only with the coldness and whiteness of a season, but also with the remoteness of the traditional white father. A cheerless face given to "avalanche" and "currents of gelid thought" requires study, as it is formidable, grim, and reticent—the face of the stern, unreadable "him" obscured by the dark.

As Claudia continues the description of her daddy, and that cold parent warms up, as it were, with images of heat that lead toward a spring, the father depicted comes to resemble Cholly especially as he assumes the role and blackness of the Vulcan. Vulcan, the lame keeper of the flames, is a more human and frail form than the wintry one Claudia first pictures. In his blackness and vulnerability, Vulcan is also a figure closer to the black devil with which Cholly had identified as a youth.[4] Nevertheless, as the description progresses, it becomes clear that even as a Vulcanlike figure, McTeer's warmth, his nakedness is still governed by the wintriness of the obscured parent we hear of in the opening lines. He never completely exposes himself to his daughters as Cholly finally does. When McTeer opens up enough to talk to his offspring, he teaches, directs, and instructs them about the blackness of coal and about warmth, and thus remains the lawgiver and the supervisor. In other words, the unrazored slash in McTeer's face becomes a mouth as he moves from the role of wintry, remote patriarch to the role of the communicative, less aloof, father who is not so almighty and invincible as not to worry "night and day" about food, shelter, and warmth. And in his difficulties, his troubles, and his nakedness, McTeer is able to remain distant enough to give what comfort and care he can to his children in a way that is not so extreme as to devastate them. He has that degree of nakedness that his daughters need to feel loved and secure instead of defiled and brutalized.

McTeer does what Cholly Breedlove has not, can not: "Wolf killer turned hawk fighter, he [McTeer] worked night and day to keep one from the door and the other from under the windowsills." This is to say that McTeer has kept hunger from the door and the cold from the windowsills. Cholly, so repeatedly unmanned by a society and by personal relationships that have allowed him comparatively no respect, no money, no voice, has been worsted in the struggle of the father to provide care and comfort. He has suffered a defeat that negates his ability to act conventionally—that is, within a patriarchal circle of commerce. Therefore instead of "guarding the flames" Cholly does not bother to fetch the coal his wife needs to warm the house and prepare the food. Rather, he burns down the house and puts his family outdoors. Finally when spring comes and Cholly unrazors his mouth—that is, when he tries to speak to his child—he rapes her.[5]

The actual rape (which is preceded by a rush of seemingly contradictory emotions) is the culmination of Cholly's own deflowered life, his own weakness and powerlessness, his own nakedness. Without money, without authority, without dominion, without education, Cholly looks at the hunched back of his child and perceives in the "clear statement of her misery . . . an accusation" (127). Here is the same accusation with its accompanying guilt, pity, and revulsion that Cholly felt when, caught with his pants down, he could not shield Darlene. "He wanted to break her neck [Pecola's, as presumably he had Darlene's]—but tenderly. Guilt and impotence rose in a bilious duet. What could he do for her—ever? What give her? What say to her? What could a burned-out black man say to the hunched back of his eleven-year-old daughter?" (127) As Cholly casts about for something to lay hold of that will confirm his manhood and his fatherhood, it is apparent that he has a strong desire to communicate with his child, to relieve her of the burden of unhappiness; however, he feels stripped and exposed as he so often has been in the past.

When Cholly, "reeling drunk" (127), sees his young, helpless, hopeless daughter, he sees in her the focal point for poignant feelings predominant in childhood events, such as the picnic with Blue and his encounter with his father. But more important, he experiences feelings codified in his relationship with the significant females in his life. Cholly's mixed feelings for Aunt Jimmy, his interrupted experiment with Darlene, his marriage to Pauline, and presumably his knowledge of his rejecting mother generate varying degrees and combinations of the "revulsion, guilt, pity, then love" (127) that lead up to Cholly's violation of Pecola. The questions that run through Cholly's mind before he crawls "on all fours" toward his daughter are questions that pertain to all the women who have cared for Cholly Breedlove. "How dare she love him? Hadn't she any sense at all? What was he supposed to do about that? Return it? How? What could his calloused hand produce to make her smile? What of his knowledge of the world and of life could be useful to her? What could his heavy arms and befuddled brain accomplish that would earn him his own respect, that would in turn allow him to accept her love?" (127).

Pecola at this point is not just Cholly's offspring, she is Cholly's everywoman. She is the woman who can open her legs and thereby testify to Cholly's manhood, and yet when he cannot protect that same woman that he himself is victimizing, she becomes the one who undercuts that testimony; she is implicated in the degradation and the denial of his manhood. She is a human baby with claws. Cholly's ambivalence, contradiction, and befuddlement are underscored in questions that reveal an almost indignant desire to help and to please his child and a simultaneously anxious need to aggrandize himself (to "earn him his own respect" and allow him to accept her love?).

Cholly, of course, answers these questions, which lay bare his feelings of worthlessness and degradation, by offering (for the rape is, in his mind, both a violation and a gift, a tender fuck) the knowledge and the power that is naturally his, the knowledge and the power that has ever been begrudgingly and mythically granted the black male, that of sexuality. And in the wake of Cholly's carnal gift to his daughter is the wholesale carnage of his life and hers, of their potential and hope. Pecola, despairing of a white "heavenly, heavenly Father" (141) who will grant her the bluest eyes, unwittingly sacrifices an old dog Bob at the altar of another of the black fathers imaged in the novel Soaphead Church.[6] Pecola loses her baby and her sanity. Even the marigolds that Claudia and Frieda superstitiously plant to insure the life of Pecola's baby die. Cholly's "touch was fatal," writes Claudia, "and the something he gave her filled the matrix of her [Pecola's] agony with death" (159).

Claudia goes on to explain that Cholly had really loved Pecola, loved her enough to be the only one "to give something of himself to her." Cholly is not the obscured paterfamilias who hides himself from his daughter. Unlike the partially naked McTeer who denies the gaze of his daughters, Cholly bares himself: he gives Pecola complete access to his masculine self. However, while Cholly thus acknowledges the sexual side and power of his daughter, his nakedness is not "friendly-like," because it is finally unmitigated by any reference to others or to a reachable, sociable idea of fatherhood. Unleashed in its social meaning, friendly nakedness becomes fiendish in the havoc wreaked upon the child. The gift Cholly gives his daughter is poisoned by the starkness of Cholly's very self, which has been warped by personal experience, social and economic conditions and circumstances that have stripped him of the capacity to share in a tradition inimical to that self. As Claudia puts it, "Love is never any better than the lover," and "the love of a free man is never safe. There is no gift for the beloved. The lover alone possesses his gift of love. The loved one is shorn, neutralized, frozen in the glow of the lover's inward eye" (159–60).

Shorn, and neutralized, himself, Cholly's love for his child is the love not only of a man who is free, but also of one who is so naked he is consequently dispossessed. And in the extreme nakedness of abandonment, degradation, poverty, and confusion there is no friendliness for children; there is only the waste and barrenness of aborted fatherhood. With its worship of whiteness, maleness, and power, and its high valuation of land, wealth, and acquisitions, with its hatred and exclusion of blackness and its fierce disdain of femaleness, frailty, and want, Western society has warped black fatherhood and consequently sacrificed the children.

The magic, the miracle of Morrison's novel is the survival, if not the transcendence, of a black father like McTeer who, in spite of the stress of being a black man in a white paternalistic culture, is able to foster in his children a feeling of security and a good sense of self. The saddest reality in the novel is the naked father like Cholly who, distressed unto madness by his total segregation from purportedly godly ideals of manhood and fatherhood, raises children who cannot see, and so deny the value and beauty of their selves and wish for the bluest eye.

Notes

1. In her analysis of *The Bluest Eye,* Barbara Christian notes the musical qualities of the novel's form (*Black Women Novelists: The Development of a Tradition, 1892–1976* [Westport: Greenwood, 1980], 138–53).

2. The ways in which Cholly's humanity is undercut are worth noting. Mrs. McTeer straightaway refers to Cholly as "that old Dog Breedlove" (Toni Morrison, *The Bluest Eye* [New York: Washington Square Press, 1970], 17). Claudia explains, "Cholly Breedlove, then, a renting black, having

put his family outdoors, had catapulted himself beyond the reaches of human consideration. He had joined the animals; was, indeed, an old dog, a snake, a ratty nigger" (19). Later on we find Cholly sniffing the air like an animal to identify the scents of white men and the black gamblers (116, 121). And finally before he rapes his daughter, he gets down on all fours and crawls toward her like an animal.

3. Susan Willis (*Specifying: Black Women Writing, The American Experience* [Madison: University of Wisconsin Press, 1987]) offers an interesting insight into the ways in which black men have maintained themselves when she writes, "Historically, gambling and bootlegging have afforded black men the opportunity to deal in a money economy without being employed by the economy" (12). When Cholly finds his father, that parent is gambling. When Cholly moves north with Pauline he quickly finds work in the steel mills of Lorain, Ohio. By the end of the novel Cholly has succumbed to the bootleggers, if he has not become one. Frieda notes that he is "always drunk" (*Bluest Eye*, 81), and he dies in a workhouse.

4. According to Thomas Bulfinch (*Mythology*, abbr. Edmund Fuller [New York: Dell, 1959]), in one account of the titans, Vulcan (Hephaestos), son of Jupiter and Juno, was born lame; Juno, dissatisfied with Vulcan's deformity, flung him out of the heavens. In another account, Vulcan's lameness results from his fall.

This reference to Vulcan links McTeer with Cholly. Though a crippled potentate, Vulcan was also the celestial artist. Morrison hints at Cholly as a frustrated artist of sorts when she insists that his psyche and life are the stuff of jazz musicians. Vulcan, in his smithy with all its attendant blackness and heat, is also reminiscent of the devil in his workshop. The devil is, of course, a figure with which young Cholly at one point openly identifies. Significantly, Cholly's understanding of the devil is not traditional or conventional. Cholly's devil is that opposite of the patriarchal devil. "He wondered if God looked like that [the black father at the picnic]. No, God was a nice old white man, with long white hair, flowing white beard, and little blue eyes that looked sad when people died and mean when they were bad" (106). Cholly's devil is a strong black man, caring and accessible. The black devil-father wants, as Cholly sees it, to split open the world (watermelon) and give its red guts (sustenance, good things) to the blacks who need it. Quite the opposite of the obscured, distant father, the devil-father stands so close that Cholly "felt goose pimples popping along his [own] arms and neck" (106). Cholly here is describing a version of the naked father. As Cholly in his own nakedness performs apparently devilish acts in the novel, it becomes clear that in the weakness and vulnerability of the naked father is also included the idea of the fallen father. This is to say that the naked father is fallen in the sense that he has fallen away from the white patriarchal idea, and fallen in the sense that acts in which he engages mark his weakness, his powerlessness to resist temptation, his sin, and finally fallen in the sense that he is pushed away or dispossessed. A tabular schema of this assertion follows:

1st father—"obscured"	2nd father—"naked"
Yaweh	devil
inscrutable	exposed
powerful	weak (or fallen)

5. In his *Fingering the Jagged Grain: Tradition and Form in Recent Black Fiction* (Athens: University of Georgia Press, 1985), Keith Byerman writes that Cholly attempts to deal with "self-hatred and oppression by becoming as evil as possible. . . .Behind this 'bad-nigger' persona lies a history of distortions of principal relationships and rituals of life." In various ways society has so conditioned and controlled Cholly, Byerman perceptively observes, that the effect has been one of "denying him a socially acceptable means of expressing authentic human emotion." Byerman goes on to note that Cholly "is incapable of appropriate fatherly behavior because he has had no parents" (187–89). I contend that this want only partly accounts for Cholly's inappropriate behavior. What Cholly needs most is covering and the protection that may come out of love, consistency, sustenance, and equality in any significant personal and social relationships. For indeed, such covering provides the space, the time, and the wherewithal to integrate and affirm a culturally constructed self.

6. Mr. Henry, but especially Elihue Micah Whitcomb, alias Soaphead Church, are part of Morrison's device of multiple imaging. These two characters are not biological fathers per se, rather they are father figures. Mr. Henry, a fatherly figure who lives with the McTeers, is soon cast out of that household when he gets too friendly with Frieda McTeer. Soaphead Church, whose attentions to Pecola are not physical, though they are very damaging, emerges as a more interesting fatherlike character. A self-appointed instrument of God (138), a type of Father Divine who had "dallied with the priesthood in the Anglican Church" (130), Soaphead Church, as his name suggests, is a pseudo-father whose relations with "his daughters"—that is, the young black girls who visit him—connect him to Cholly Breedlove. Morrison deliberately and carefully links Soaphead to Cholly to drive home further her point about how Western standards of fatherhood or fatherliness can be distorted or perverted in black fathers who live in a society that has historically, socially, and economically pushed them toward complete vulnerability. In his letter to the "heavenly, heavenly Father" of white patriarchy, Soaphead essentially locates his weakness and the beginning of his trouble in the history of his West Indian family, which has sought to whiten itself:

We in this colony took as our own the most dramatic, and the most obvious, of our white masters' characteristics, which were, of course, their worst. In retaining the identity of our race, we held fast to those characteristics most gratifying to sustain and least troublesome to maintain. Consequently we were not royal but snobbish, not aristocratic but class-conscious; we believed authority was cruelty to our inferiors, and education was being at school. We mistook violence for passion, indolence for leisure, and thought recklessness was freedom. We raised our children and reared our crops; we let infants grow, and property develop. Our manhood was defined by acquisitions. Our womanhood by acquiescence. And the smell of your fruit and the labor of your days we abhorred. (140)

In trying not only to be white, but also to adopt the white standards, the Whitcombs are falsified and weakened.

Soaphead's father, a bad version of the white Yawehlike paterfamilias inflicts upon young Elihue not only "the precision of his [the father's] justice and the control of his violence" (133), but also "his theories of education, discipline, and the good life" (133). But "for all his exposure" to the fathers of "the Western world"—Christ, Hamlet, Gibbon, Othello, Dante—Soaphead only learns "the fine art of self-deception" and hatred (133). These two inculcations help lead Elihue to, among other things, his preference for little girls, the members of humanity whom he finds "least offensive" because they "were usually manageable and frequently seductive" (132). The little girls are just as vulnerable as he, if not more so, and so he identifies with these children in his sick way.

Soaphead Church himself is every bit as destructive as Cholly Breedlove when he insists that he felt that he was being "playful" and "friendly" when he "touched their [the little girls'] sturdy little tits and bit them—just a little" (142). Soaphead's characterization of his deeds as "playful" is his perverted rendering of the lines in the Dick-and-Jane primer: "See Father. He is big and strong. Father, will you play with Jane? Father is smiling. Smile, Father, smile" (7). A bogus parent, Soaphead is neither big nor strong, though magical powers are attributed to him. Were he a little boy, his actions may possibly be construed as innocent exploratory play; however, the play of this "father" is not, as he declares, innocent. His play is abuse and victimization. Soaphead's description of his actions as "friendly" is not the "friendly-*like*" (my italics) warmth and nurturing that Claudia and Frieda sense in the presence of their naked father who denies, as it were, the tacit and full-blown realization of "friendly" (that is, unlike Cholly and Soaphead, McTeer dismisses the possibility of ever physically manifesting friendliness to his daughters).

Like Cholly, this false father Church gives to Pecola a gift no better than himself. The parallels between Cholly and Soaphead are telling. The caresser of little girls, Soaphead never touches Pecola. Instead, like a fairy godfather, he grants her wish for the bluest eyes. While he, a self-deceived and deceiving father figure, passively gives Pecola a lie that leads her to madness. Cholly Breedlove, a more confused than deceived father, violently gives Pecola his physical self, a gift that has propelled her not only toward Soaphead's gift of insanity, but also toward exile and death.

Finally, Soaphead voices an important indictment against white patriarchy and how it has excluded and injured black lives when he writes:

You said, "Suffer little children to come unto me, and harm them not." Did you forget about the children? Yes. You forgot. You let them go wanting, sit on road shoulders, crying next to their dead mothers. I've seen them charred, lame, halt. You forgot, Lord. You forgot how and when to be God.

That's why I changed the little black girl's eyes for her, and I didn't touch her; not a finger did I lay on her. . . . I did what You did not, could not, would not do: I looked at that ugly little black girl, and I loved her. I played You. And it was a very good show! (143)

The truth here is that Yaweh has not been kind to the children, especially to the daughters like Pecola who have black fathers in white society who cannot recreate Yaweh in themselves, cannot manage a mite of the power to protect, provide, and comfort. In Soaphead's cry for the children is a cry interestingly enough for both Cholly and for Soaphead himself. For both these men are in some sense reduced to children; that is, in as far as their manhood has been denied or undercut in society, they remain children who have urges to "play" in particular with those who are at least as weak and exposed as they are—the little girls.

Part II   *Oedipal Hermeneutics*

Framing Lolita

Is There a Woman in the Text?
Linda Kauffman

Lolita is about love . . . not about sex, but about love. Almost every page sets forth some explicit erotic emotion or some overt erotic action and still it is not about sex. It is about love. This makes it unique in my experience of contemporary novels.

Lionel Trilling[1]

For unwary readers like Trilling, Humbert Humbert's narrative is a Nabokovian trap, for one can celebrate Humbert's role as lover only by minimizing his role as father. Yet paradoxically, only Humbert's role as father makes it possible to be Lolita's lover, since it gives him unmonitored access to the girl by designating him her legal "guardian." Trilling is right to notice the overt erotic activity on every page, but wrong to conclude that the novel is about love, not sex. *Lolita* is not about love, but about incest, which is a betrayal of trust, a violation of love. How have critics managed so consistently to confuse love with incest in the novel? My aim here is to show how—through a variety of narrative strategies—the inscription of the father's body in the text obliterates the daughter's.

Literature as Social Change or Aesthetic Bliss

The first strategy involves the frame within which Humbert's narrative is placed between John Ray's foreword and Nabokov's afterword. John Ray, Jr., is the psychologist who reads Humbert's narrative for the message, the general lesson, the ethical impact: this cautionary tale "should," he pompously dictates, "make all of us—parents, social workers, educators—apply ourselves with still greater vigilance and vision to the task of bringing up a better generation in a safer world."[2] Yet everything conspires against Ray's exhortation. The issue of child abuse is obscured by Ray's professional self-advertisement, his pompous literary allusions, and his high-blown literary style. Nabokov not only parodies such seeming erudition through Ray's preface but pokes fun at readers who so simply correlate art with life. For " 'old-fashioned' readers who wish to follow the destinies of the 'real' people beyond the 'true' story" (6), we learn in the preface what became of both Humbert and Lolita after Humbert ceased writing: he died of a heart attack and she died in childbirth. But readers curious about such matters belong at the bottom of the class, along with other dreary moralists, Freudians, and feminists who may murmur against the brutality of Lolita's treatment. As parody then, the foreword acts as an injunction against the kind of reading that foregrounds social issues like child abuse.

Such readers will always miss the appeal of "aesthetic bliss," which Nabokov proposes as the appropriate response in "his" afterword: "After doing my impersonation of suave John Ray . . . any comments coming straight from me may strike one—may strike me, in fact—as an impersonation of Vladimir Nabokov talking about his own book. . . . I am neither a reader nor a writer of didactic fiction, and, despite John Ray's assertion, *Lolita* has no moral in tow. For me a work of fiction exists only insofar as it affords me what I shall bluntly call aesthetic bliss" (286).

Here, then, is the second strategy that explains why incest is overlooked: critics take Nabokov at his word. His wry disclaimer effectively throws sand in our eyes, for the fact is that the afterword is as thoroughly cunning an impersonation as John Ray's foreword. The "end," in other words, is as much a part of the fiction as the beginning. The afterword is a sham because it simply extends the Humbertian aesthetic manifesto, a detail that credulous readers fail to notice. The artifice of self-referential textuality extends through Nabokov's afterword: it is a trap for readers who pride themselves on their sophistication and their ability to distance themselves from "real life." It contributes as much to the text by way of irony and distortion as the spurious index at the end of *Pale Fire*.[3] Foreword and afterword are mirror images—distortions, displacements, impersonations that seduce us into reading Humbert's narrative in a way that minimizes the viewpoint of a bruised child and foregrounds Humbert's obsession with his own body.

Foreword and afterword each direct us toward monologic readings that are mutually exclusive. The choice between John Ray's foreword (to use literature to make a better world) and Nabokov's afterword (literature as self-referential artifice) involves irreconcilable differences, and since Ray is the butt of parody, readers will go to any length to avoid being identified with him. Parody thus acts as an injunction against a certain mode of referential reading.

The challenge for feminist criticism is thus to read against the text by resisting the father's seductions. Is it possible in a double movement to analyze the horror of incest by reinscribing the material body of the child Lolita in the text and simultaneously to undermine the representational fallacy by situating the text dialogically in relation to other texts? It is in the interest of feminist criticism to expose the representational fallacy, since the most sexist critical statements come from critics who take the novel as a representation of real life.

Trilling, for instance, paradoxically begins by citing Humbert's "ferocity . . . his open brutality to women." Yet, Trilling continues: "Perhaps [Humbert's] depravity is the easier to accept when we learn that he deals with a Lolita who is not innocent, and who seems to have very few emotions to be violated; and I suppose we *naturally* incline to be lenient towards a rapist—legally and by intention H.H. is that— who eventually feels a deathless devotion to his victim!" (14).

Trilling does not find rape and incest shocking; what shocks him is how few contemporary novels are about love, but *Lolita* is one of them, despite the fact that Humbert's greed is, as Trilling notes, "ape-like."

One might expect that critics who read the novel as a representation of real life would pay more attention to Lolita, but few have imagined what her victimization is like. Instead, they identify with the sensations Humbert records about his body by uncritically adopting his viewpoint. Thomas Molnar is representative:

The central question the reader ought to ask of himself is whether he feels pity for the girl. Our ethical ideal would require that we look at Lolita as a sacrificial lamb, that we become in imagination, her knight-protector. Yet this is impossible for two reasons. One is very simple: before yielding to Humbert, the girl has had a nasty little affair with a nasty little thirteen-year-old. . . . Besides, she is a spoiled sub-teenager with a foul mouth, a self-offered target for lechers. . . . throughout, she remains an object perhaps even to herself.[4]

Molnar indicts Lolita for being a tease who "asks for it," and who deserves what she gets since she is spoiled, foul, "damaged goods." Both Trilling and Molnar castigate Lolita for being unknowable. Despite his will to power, it is Humbert who never knows Lolita; he even confesses that there are depths in her inaccessible to him (259). Humbert is, moreover, a notoriously unreliable narrator who lies to psychiatrists, deceives two wives, and otherwise takes elaborate precautions to avoid detection. In view of his unreliability, it is doubtful his claim that Lolita seduced him is true; more importantly, it is unverifiable, and credulous critics who read the novel as a reflection of life thus end up merely reifying codes that can be traced directly from literature, codes that—from the courtly love tradition to *Clarissa* to modern cinema—first idealize and then degrade the female by blaming her for her own victimization.

The opposite approach to the novel as self-referential artifice is, however, no more enlightened. Take Alfred Appel, who describes the novel as a "springboard for parody," adding: "Humbert's terrible demands *notwithstanding,* Lolita is as insensitive as children are to their *actual* parents; *sexuality aside,* she demands anxious parental placation in a too typically American way, and affords Nabokov an ideal opportunity to comment on the Teen and Subteen Tyranny."[5]

Such passages are ruptures in the critical stance that self-referentiality demands; when it comes to women, such critics seem to forget that their main point is that the novel is *not* realistic! In a now famous statement, Appel goes on to assert: "By creating a reality which is a fiction, but a fiction that is able to mock the reader, the author has demonstrated the fiction of 'reality,' and the reader who accepts these implications may even have experienced a change in consciousness" (120).

But before one can analyze a fiction that mocks the reader, or results in a change in consciousness, one needs to examine the kind of reader one has in mind. Humbert is not only an avid writer, he is an avid reader: of motel registers, class rolls, road signs, comics, even movie posters. His reading of Lolita is the model on which male critics rely—whether they read self-referentially or mimetically. And that is the source of their blindness: they fail to notice that Humbert is not only a notoriously unreliable narrator but that he is an unreliable reader too. If he were not, he would have solved the mystery of Quilty's identity. As it happens, he never does solve it; Lolita has to tell him. Like his heart, his powers of perception and his eyes are "hysterical, unreliable organ[s]." A voyeur, he wants to see but not be seen.

Despite his unreliability, feminist readers have the choice of either participating in their own "immasculation" by endorsing aesthetic bliss, or of demonstrating their humorlessness and frigidity. Judith Fetterly defines "immasculation" as the process by which "the female reader is co-opted into participation in an experience from which she is explicitly excluded; she is asked to identify with a selfhood that defines itself in opposition to her; she is required to identify against herself."[6] Consider the famous scene of Lolita on the couch with Humbert while he surreptitiously masturbates and enjoins the reader to respond:

I want my learned readers to participate in the scene I am about to replay: I want them to examine its every detail and see for themselves how . . . chaste, the whole wine-sweet event is. . . . What had begun as a delicious distension of my innermost roots became a glowing tingle . . . not found elsewhere in conscious life. . . . Lolita had been safely solipsized. Suspended on the brink of that voluptuous abyss (a nicety of physiological equipoise comparable to certain techniques in the arts). . . . I crushed out against her left buttock the last throb of the longest ecstasy man or monster had ever known. (57–58)

This is a scene where the father's body is the site and the source of not only aesthetic bliss but literal orgasm; both come at the same time—if, that is, the reader is male. Lolita, however, is not just "solipsized" but annihilated, as Humbert reveals while congratulating himself in the next scene:

What I had madly possessed was not she, but *my own creation*, another fanciful Lolita—*perhaps, more real* than Lolita; overlapping, encasing her; floating between me and her, and having no will, no consciousness—indeed no life of her own. The child knew nothing. I had done nothing to her. And nothing prevented me from repeating a performance that affected her as little as if she were a photographical image rippling upon a screen and I a humble hunchback abusing myself in the dark. (59, emphasis added)

Thus physical as well as aesthetic jouissance for Humbert requires psychic anesthesia or annihilation for Lolita. "Reader! Bruder!," Humbert exclaims, "I shall not exist if you do not imagine me" (119).

What the text mimes, then, is a bundle of relations between men, as clarified not only in the passage above but in the responses of critics like Trilling and Molnar. The incest taboo, as Lévi-Strauss reveals, has nothing to do with protecting the girl, and everything to do with ensuring that she functions as an object of exchange between men: "it is the supreme rule of the gift . . . which allows [the incest taboo's] nature to be understood."[7] The scene in which Humbert masturbates with Lolita on his lap is a good example of how the text makes what is male seem universal. As Patrocinio Schweickart explains in discussing the implied authorial contract:

For the male reader, the text serves as the meeting ground of the personal and the universal . . . the male reader is invited to feel his *difference* (concretely, from the *girl*) and to equate that with the universal. Relevant here is Lévi-Strauss's theory that woman functions as currency exchanged between men. The woman in the text converts the text into a woman, and the circulation of this text/woman becomes the central ritual that establishes the bond between the author and his male readers.[8]

The bond and that identifiction with the male body help to explain further how incest can be mistaken for love. From the opening words, Humbert's body is a palpable presence: "Lolita, light of my life, fire of my loins. My sin, my soul. Lo-lee-ta: the tip of the tongue taking a trip of three steps down the palate to tap, at three, on the teeth" (11). "Lolita" is a word; Humbert is flesh: loins, tongue, palate, teeth. Humbert's obsession with his body is infantile; it is he who is marked by a preoedipal fascination with his own bowels, his digestion, his heartburn, his headaches, his blood pressure—and of course, his penis—that "pentapod monster" that feels like a "thousand eyes wide open in my eyed blood" (41). As he masturbates, he "entered a plane of being where nothing mattered, save the infusion of joy brewed within my body" (57). Thus, while exploiting his role as legal guardian to enforce the Law of the Father, Humbert also reverses it. He turns oedipalization inside out, just as his "only grudge against nature was that I could not turn my Lolita inside out and apply voracious lips to her young matrix, her unknown heart, her nacreous liver, the seagrapes of her lungs, her comely twin kidneys" (151). She is the *fèmme morcélée* par excellence. The incestuous father-as-his-own child: he feasts on the female body, sucking Lolita's flat breasts and "brown rose." In Lacanian terms, "Lolita" is little more than a signifier in Humbert's image-repertoire, and Humbert's revealing allusion to her heart being "unknown" highlights how illusory his project (and his projections) are.[9] Her sole functions are in reflect and satisfy the body of the father. Initially, she has no reality for him except as the incarnation of his childhood love, Annabel Leigh; Lolita is little more than a replication of a photographic still. He wishes he had filmed her; he longs to have a frozen moment permanently on celluoid, since he could not hold her still in life. She is thus the object of his appropriation, and he not only appropriates her, but projects onto her his desire and his neuroses. Significantly, she only serves as a simulacrum when her nicknames—Lolita, Lo, Lola, Dolly—are used, for her legal name, Dolores, points too directly toward another representation—Our Lady of Sorrows—and thus to a higher law than man's. An abyss lies between the "Lolita" who is a purely imaginary project of Humbert's desire, and the "Dolores" whose legal guardian is the source of her suffering.

Nabokov's Authors

John Ray's foreword and Nabokov's afterword are diametrically opposed monologic readings. By exposing the weaknesses in such readings, one discovers what feminist criticism stands to gain by dismantling the representational fallacy. I should like to propose a dialogic reading, one that is both feminist and intertextual; one that releases the female body both from its anesthesia and from

Humbert's solipsism while simultaneously highlighting textual artifice. Nabokov, I would argue, is not writing in either the one mode
or the other: he is writing a book that elides the female by framing
the narrative through Humbert's angle of vision. He then comments
indirectly on that framing device by references not to "real life" but
to other literary texts. That the novel is an exercise in intertextuality,
however, does not mitigate the horror of Lolita's treatment. Instead,
it reinforces it. Among the multiple levels of intertexuality operating
in the novel, four in particular deserve mention because they suggest
the myriad ways in which the novel allegorizes woman: the major
poems in the courtly love tradition; certain stories and poems of
Edgar Allan Poe; Henry James's *The Turn of the Screw;* and Charles
Dickens's *Bleak House.*

Lolita is, among other things, a compendium of definitions of
woman, in texts ranging from *Know Your Own Daughter* and *The
Little Mermaid* to *Carmen* and *Le roman de la rose.* As in the courtly
love tradition, Humbert moves from adoration to disillusionment
when the beloved fails to measure up to his code of perfection. Like
the knights who celebrated the chastity of the lady and the difficulty
of their endeavors, Humbert boasts of his difficulties when he
masturbates with Lolita on his lap. In contrast to his idealized
"lady," "real" women are miserly, envious, fickle, loudmouthed,
drunkards (like Rita, the drunk with whom Humbert lives after
Lolita flees), or slaves to their bellies (like Valeria, the "brainless
baba" who is Humbert's first wife). As he reveals when he insists
that Lolita has no will or life of her own, Humbert denies not just
what is womanly in Lolita—he denies what is human.[10] That is why
he must insist that nymphets are demonic, and it is the myth of
demonic children that ties the novel to James's *Turn of the Screw.*

Nabokov confesses, "My feelings towards James are rather complicated. I really dislike him intensely but now and then the figure
in the phrase, the *turn* of the epithet, the *screw* of an absurd adverb,
cause me a kind of electric tingle, as if some current of his was also
passing through my own blood."[11] James said that he devised the
tale as a trap to catch the "jaded, the disillusioned, the fastidious"
reader—in other words, the reader who is beyond sentimentality.[12]
Similarly, sophisticated readers of *Lolita,* avid to align themselves

with "aesthetic bliss," fall into precisely the same trap by ignoring the pathos of Lolita's predicament. James said his subject was "the helpless plasticity of childhood: that *was* my little tragedy."[13] For Nabokov as for James, "plasticity" is the medium that creates aesthetic bliss. But plasticity has other connotations: to mold, to form, to freeze, to fix. The governess in *The Turn of the Screw* tries to arrest the children's development; the desire to fix things indeed is one of her motives for writing her retrospective narrative. She wants to frame time itself, just as Humbert desires "to fix the perilous magic of nymphets." In both texts—indeed throughout Poe and Dickens as well as James—how and what you see depends on the frame: James's governess and Humbert Humbert both resort to fancy prose styles to frame a murder.[14] "Aesthetic bliss" is a frameup. In both the governess's narrative and in Humbert's, silence, exile, and cunning lie in that gap between past and present, and determine what inflection will be given to the murder of childhood. As Poe asks in *Lenore*, "How *shall* the ritual then be read?—the requiem how be sung/By you—by yours, the evil eye—by yours the slanderous tongue/That did to death the innocence that died and died so young?"[15]

To recognize that violence, one must first defuse the charge that any lament for the murder of Lolita's childhood is sheer sentimentality, a willful misreading of a novel meant to parody such attitudes. Lecturing at Cornell, Nabokov himself defused the charge, noting that Dickens's *Bleak House* deals "mainly with the misery of little ones, with the pathos of childhood—and Dickens is at his best in these matters."[16] Nabokov emphasizes the astonishing number of children in the novel—he counts over thirty—and says that "one of the novel's most striking themes" is "their troubles, insecurity, humble joys . . . but mainly their misery" (65). Their parents are either "frauds or freaks" (69). And then he says something that will surprise contemporary readers:

I should not like to hear the charge of sentimentality made against this strain that runs through *Bleak House*. I want to submit that people who denounce the sentimental are generally unaware of what sentiment is. . . . Dickens's great art should not be mistaken for a cockney version of the seat of emotion—it is the real thing, keen, subtle, specialized compassion, with

a grading and merging of melting shades, with the very accent of profound
pity in the words uttered, and with an artist's choice of the most visible,
most audible, most tangible epithets. (86–87)

His allusion to "grading and merging of melting shades, with
the very accent of profound pity," echo a poignant and revealing
sentence about Lolita's temperament—that temperament to which
critics like Trilling and Molnar claim no reader has access. After he
overhears Lolita commenting that "what is so dreadful about dying
is that you are completely on your own," Humbert realizes that
"Behind the awful juvenile clichés, there was in her a garden and a
twilight, and a palace gate—dim and adorable regions which happened to be lucidly and absolutely forbidden to me, in my polluted
rags and miserable convulsions, . . . living as we did, she and I, in
a world of total evil" (259).

In his lecture on *Bleak House,* Nabokov goes on to contrast
Skimpole, who *represents* a child, with the real children in the novel
who are overburdened with adult cares and duties, like Charley—
the little girl who supports all her little brothers and sisters. Dickens
writes: "She might have been a child, playing at washing, and
imitating a poor workingwoman." And Nabokov observes, "Skimpole is a vile parody of a child, whereas this little girl is a pathetic
imitator of an adult woman" (86). The same is true of Humbert;
like Skimpole, he imitates a child. It is Humbert, after all, who
wants to play forever in his "pubescent park, in my mossy garden.
Let them play around me forever. Never grow up" (22). It is Humbert who talks baby talk to Lolita—never she to him.[17]

Lolita, conversely, is forced to imitate adult womanhood by performing "wifely" duties before she gets her coffee. In the very act
of trying to fix her forever in childhood, Humbert not only stunts
her growth but makes her old before her time. Her fate is presaged
by Humbert's transactions with the whore Monique; he is briefly
attracted to her nymphet qualities, but she grows less juvenile, more
womanly overnight: only for a minute does "a delinquent nymphet
[shine] through the matter-of-fact young whore" (24). From the
moment he first masturbates on the couch, Humbert proceeds to
turn Lolita into a whore, calling her vagina a "new white purse,"
and priding himself upon having left it "intact." By the time they

reach the Enchanted Hunters Motel, he has begun paying her with pennies and dimes.

Father-daughter incest, as Judith Lewis Herman points out, is a relationship of prostitution: "The father, in effect, forces the daughter to pay with her body for affection and care which should be freely given. In so doing, he destroys the protective bond between parent and child and initiates his daughter into prostitution. This is the reality of incest from the point of view of the victim."[18] The victim's viewpoint in *Lolita* is elided, for eventually Humbert bribes her to perform, reporting the fact as a "definite drop in Lolita's morals" (167). The fact that she ups the ante from fifteen cents to four dollars has been seen by misogynist critics as a sign that she was a whore all along. Humbert once again reveals his obsession with his own body and once again astutely sizes up readers' allegiances when he exclaims: "O Reader . . . imagine me, on the very rack of joy noisily emitting dimes and great big silver dollars like some sonorous, jingly and wholly demented machine vomiting riches; and in the margin of that leaping epilepsy she would firmly clutch a handful of coins in her little fist" (168).

Humbert implicitly assumes that his [male?] readers will identify solely with his sexuality and sensibility. Since he presents himself as a schlemiel, the comic urge to identify with him is an almost irresistible temptation. The hilarity, however, is considerably undercut when we realize that Lolita is trying to accumulate enough money to run away—an escape Humbert thwarts by periodically ransacking her room and robbing her.

Materialist critiques of the novel could focus on the rampant consumerism of American society in 1955, since Lolita is the ideal consumer: naive, spoiled, totally hooked on the gadgets of modern life, a true believer in the promises of Madison Avenue. Yet a materialist-*feminist* perspective enables one to see something that has not been noted before: Lolita is as much the object consumed by Humbert as she is the product of her culture. And if she is "hooked," he is the one who turns her into a hooker. She is the object of both his conspicuous consumption and concupiscence, as his voracious desire to devour her heart, liver, lungs, and kidneys demonstrates. When he sees a dismembered mannikin in a department store, Humbert comments that "it's a good symbol for some-thing," and "Dolly Haze" (one of Lolita's many nicknames) comes more and more to resemble those mute, inanimate dolls on whose bodies consumer wares are hung. By the time of their final reunion in Gray Star, she has been so thoroughly prostituted that she assumes Humbert will only give her her own inheritance if she accompanies him to a motel.

What is most stunning about Ray's preface is that, despite his alleged interest in "reality," he says none of these things. He never once names incest; instead he refers to it as that "special experience," and insists that " 'offensive' is frequently but a synonym for 'unusual' " (7). While ostensibly reading Humbert's narrative as a "case history" and unctuously referring to its "ethical impact," he notes that if Humbert had undergone psychiatric treatment, "there would have been no disaster; but then, neither would there have been this book" (7). The statement has disturbing implications, for it reveals an utter disregard for Lolita's suffering. Ray effaces her entirely; "Lolita" is merely the title of a narrative by which he is "entranced." By thus focusing solely on Humbert's "supreme misery," Ray becomes Humbert's dupe. In charting Humbert's quest, he replicates his crime. Is Lolita anywhere to be found in the text?

Is There a Woman in the Text?

What effect does incest have on Lolita? The first act of coitus is rendered so poetically as to camouflage what is being described; importantly, it is one of the few passages depicting the sensations of Lolita's body rather than Humbert's. He describes it *as if* it were a painting: "a slave child trying to climb a column of onyx . . . a fire opal dissolving within a ripple-ringed pool, a last throb, a last dab of color, stinging red, smarting pink, a sigh, a wincing child" (124). Aesthetic form distances us from Lolita's pain, diverting our attention from content: Lolita is enslaved, bleeding, and in such pain that she cannot sit because Humbert has torn something inside her. Humbert's aesthetic response, however, cannot completely disguise the fact that with this act, Lolita's aborted childhood is left behind forever: she learns that her mother is dead and realizes that she has nowhere else to go. In contrast to conventional criticism, which divides the first part of the novel from the second part in terms of such dichotomies as illusion/reality or dream/nightmare, these framing devices always elide Lolita herself. Whether part one focuses on Humbert's body and part two on his misery, Humbert remains the focus: his suffering, his sensations, his sex and sensibility. The crucial dichotomy involves the shift in Humbert's role from Charlotte's lover to Lolita's father, from lodger to legal guardian. Perhaps the novel's most profound paradox is that Humbert cannot violate Lolita sexually until he receives society's legal sanction by being designated her stepfather.

John Ray's foreword is a parody of responses that might lead the reader to inquire about the relation of fictional representations of incest to clinical analyses. And for that reason, it acts as an injunction, prohibiting the reader from inquiring into "reality." But readers who defy that prohibition discover that the novel is an uncannily accurate representation of father-daughter incest. Not surprisingly, the clinical literature reveals that stepfathers are guilty of incest as often as natural fathers are. The overwhelming majority of children experience no pleasure in the act; even later in life, as mature women they are seldom able to enjoy sexual relations.[19] The fact that Lolita similarly feels nothing for Humbert is repeatedly presented as a black mark against her: "Never," Humbert confesses, "did she vibrate under my touch," and for this "crime" he dubs her "My Frigid Princess." As he realizes , "she was ready to turn away from [me] with something akin to plain repulsion" (152). But her response is not akin to repulsion, it *is* repulsion, and the difference is one of Humbert's characteristic strategies of evasion. Elsewhere, he describes their existence as a "parody of incest," but the incest is literal, not parodic. Nabokov's framing device parodies Ray's reading of the novel as a case history, but he also ensures that we only think of one kind of case—that of obsessional love. The fact that he never mentions incest is no accident. Parody, which prohibits inquiry into "real cases," also prohibits us from asking, "Whose case is it anyway?"

Humbert's jealousy, his tyranny inside the home balanced by his ineffectuality and obsequiousness outside it, the threats of reform school or punishment if Lolita reports him—are all patterns of incest documented clinically as well as textually. To enjoy not Lolita but his fantasies, Humbert decides to "Ignore what I could not help perceiving, the fact that I was to her not a boy friend, not a glamour man, not a pal, not even a person at all, but just two eyes and a foot of engorged brawn" (258). Humbert exaggerates the size of his penis, but to Lolita he must seem enormous, given the disparity in their physical proportions. The allusion to his eyes is revealing, for Humbert voyeuristically measures every aspect of Lolita's physical development. "Has she already been initiated by mother nature to the Mystery of the Menarche?" he wonders (45).

Critics usually cite Humbert's obsessive scrutiny of Lolita's body as evidence that the novel is a love story; instead, such obsessions are typical of father-daughter incest, signs not of overpowering love but of domination. Humbert spies on Lolita, monitors her every movement, subjects her to endless inquisitions about her where-abouts, her girlfriends, and potential boy friends in a pattern common to incest. The father tyrannically controls the daughter's ac-tions, is insanely jealous of boys, and strives to isolate her as much as possible from the rest of the world.[20] The only time Humbert plays the role of the father is when he subjects Lolita to parental interrogations: Why has she missed two piano lessons? Who is she talking to when she disappears for twenty-eight minutes? His avidity to learn the names of all her schoolmates and acquaintances culmi-nates in the crucial question he asks her in Gray Star: "Where is he? . . . Come, his name?" (273). His dominant mode of discourse and of parenting is inquisitorial.[21]

Thus critics who condemn Lolita as wanton misunderstand the significance of Humbert's compulsion, for in philosophical terms it is he who is wanton, rather than Lolita. As Harry K. Frankfurt explains, free will involves the freedom to have the will one wants. Those, like Humbert, who lack such freedom, are "wanton": "The essential characteristic of a wanton is that he does not care about his will. His desires move him to do certain things, without its being true of him either that he wants to be moved by those desires or that he prefers to be moved by other desires."[22] Humbert's sexual craving compels him to abuse Lolita, and while he insists that he does not want to be moved by such desires, he is never able to cease violating her sexually or psychically.

His mania for making Lolita reveal herself and respond to him demonstrates that she is not—nor was she ever—"safely solipsized." The word he uses most frequently to describe his violation of her is "operation," but an operation in which Lolita is anesthetized neither psychically nor physically: "The operation was over, all over, and she was weeping . . . a salutory storm of sobs after one of the fits of moodiness that had become so frequent with her in the course of that otherwise admirable year!" (154). Her "sobs in the night,— every night, every night" (160), the moodiness that Humbert finds unfathomable, her powerlessness to escape him when she says, "Oh no, not again!"—all point to a despair that surpasses his powers of description, or so he claims. But from *The Sorrows to Young Werther* (1774) to *The Turn of the Screw* (1898), guilty narrators have taken refuge in the ineffable: whatever they want to evade they claim is impossible to describe. The ineffable—like the inevitable (nick-named "McFate" by Humbert)—is invariably an evasion. In one such passage, Humbert says that Lolita has "a look I cannot exactly describe—an expression of helplessness so perfect that it seemed to grade into one of rather comfortable inanity just because this was the very limit of injustice and frustration" (258).

Does such a statement imply that Humbert finally perceives the enormity of his crimes against Lolita? Not until Humbert is entrapped by Quilty does he begin to comprehend his injustice, for as Thoreau said, "How much more eloquently and effectively he can combat injustice who has experienced a little in his own person."[23] Quilty "succeeded in thoroughly enmeshing me and my thrashing anguish in his demoniacal game. With infinite skill, he swayed and staggered, and regained an impossible balance, always leaving me with . . . betrayal, fury, desolation, horror and hate" (227). Quilty is the doppelganger, the figure traditionally presented not just as a double but as a brother, with whom one has the usual rivalry of siblings, according to Freud. As doppelganger, Quilty is the figure onto whom Humbert projects his guilt in an attempt to evade responsibility for the crime of incest. Freud suggests that the aim of the incest taboo is not to protect female children but to control male sexual rivalry. Lolita functions as the object of exchange between Quilty and Humbert, who are mirror images, locked in a Girardian triangle of mimetic desire.[24] Each wants what the other wants: "[Quilty's] condition," says Humbert, "infected me" (271).[25] In pursuing Lolita, Humbert plays three roles: avenging father, jealous lover, and rival scholar. The latter role torments him most, for as Humbert embarks on his "cryptogrammic paper chase," he is indignant that Quilty "challenged my scholarship" in motel registers across the country; furious that Quilty's anagrams "ejaculate in my face" (228). While that is an experience Lolita surely shared in Humbert's hands, Lolita's perspective has no place in this confrontation of rivals. (That, indeed, is the problem with Girard's theory of mimetic desire: the female is always lost in translation.)[26]

In "The Springboard of Parody," Appel compares Lolita to Poe's "William Wilson," another "first-person confession by a pseudonymous narrator who "fled in vain" from the Double who pursued him from school to school; like those doubles, "Humbert and Quilty are rivals in scholarship rather than love" (125). In their final confrontation, Humbert can no longer distinguish his own body from Quilty's: "I rolled over him. We rolled over me. They rolled over him. We rolled over us." Humbert describes the struggle as a "silent, soft, formless tussle on the part of two literati" (272). This competition between two second-rate talents disguises the fact that even if they had been first-rate, their struggle would have been equally senseless, since it fails to undo the crimes against Lolita. Aesthetic bliss is not a criterion that compensates for those crimes; instead it is a dead-end, meager consolation for the murder of Lolita's childhood. Conventional readings based on sin, confession, and redemption argue that Humbert exacts revenge because Quilty broke Lolita's heart. But Humbert's vengeance is more egotistic: Quilty outauthored him. He turned Humbert into a character in his script, which is precisely what Humbert does to Lolita. Armed with the tattered totemic photograph of his childhood love, Annabel Leigh, he "reincarnates" her image and superimposes it on Lolita. In his avid pursuit of immortality through art, he studies Poe's dictum that the death of a beautiful woman is "the most poetical topic in the world—and . . . that the lips best suited for such topic are those of a bereaved lover."[27]

Indeed, even in his last scene with Lolita, Humbert continues to interrogate her as if she were his legal possession, to interpret her as if she were a frozen image, a blank page. He is still talking at her. When she says that she would sooner go back to Quilty than leave now with Humbert, he writes: "She groped for words. I supplied them mentally ("He broke my heart. You merely broke my life)" (254).[28] The narrative we read is an exercise in what Humbert calls "poetical justice"—but it is so only for himself, not for Lolita—although he never points this out. He writes simultaneously to set the record straight, to settle the score, and to make certain that the last word is his. But like all his other attempts to possess, to control, to fix, and to frame—this one too reveals his sterility and his impotence, for while he has the last word on Quilty, John Ray has the last word on him. ("For better or worse it is the commentator who has the last word," says Kinbote in *Pale Fire*."[29] Humbert appropriates visibility, vulnerability, carnality for himself, and in so doing, he evacuates Lolita's body, turning it into a projective site for his neuroses and his narrative.

Humbert's notoriously poor circulation finally leads to coronary thrombosis; his heart, like his narrative, is unreliable. His heart prompts him to declare that he has fallen in love forever, but, he adds, "The word 'forever' referred only to my own passion, to eternal Lolita *as reflected* in my blood" (67, emphasis added). His is a closed circulatory system, solipsistic and narcissistic. He fathers nobody. Lolita only exists insofar as she can reflect him, magnifying his stature. "The refuge of art" for Humbert is the mirror of castration for Lolita, a polarity clearly exposed in her tennis game. Humbert appreciates it aesthetically: "her form was, indeed, an absolutely perfect imitation of absolutely top-notch tennis . . . it had . . . beauty, directness, youth, a classical purity of trajectory" (211). But her form lacks—as does she herself—feeling, force, conviction, for she has no will to win. Sex with Humbert has taught her too well merely to mime, without enthusiasm.

By thus inscribing the female body in the text, rather than consigning it to the hazy and dolorous realm of abstract male desire, or letting it circulate as the currency of exchange between male rivals, one discovers that Lolita is not a photographic image, or a still life, or a freeze frame preserved on film, but a damaged child. This is what Humbert's own humiliation at the hands of Quilty enables him finally to perceive: the "semi-animated, subhuman trickster who had sodomized my darling" (269) turns out to be not Quilty but himself. Quilty quite correctly maintains that he saved Lolita "from a beastly pervert" and that he, Quilty, is "not responsible for the rapes of others" (271).

The crucial distinction is between Humbert the focus, trapped in chronological time, and Humbert the voice,[30] writing from prison, composing his death sentences: "Had not something within her been broken by me—*not that I realized it then!*—she would have had on the top of her perfect form the will to win" (212). If in part one his sole obsession is with his lust, he is in part two still utterly self-absorbed: his guilt and his misery are his themes: "*my* heart and *my* beard, and *my* putrefaction" (258). Humbert challenges the reader to prove to him that "in the infinite run it does not matter a jot that a North American girl-child named Dolores Haze had been deprived of her childhood by a maniac . . . (and if it can, then life is a joke), I see nothing for the treatment of my misery but the melancholy and very local palliative of articulate art" (258).

The thirty-five year sentence he imposes on himself for rape lets him off the hook for other murders besides Quilty's: Lolita's death in childbirth, and her stillborn baby's demise, are anticipated as early as the first act of intercourse with Humbert when he feels "as if I were sitting with the small ghost of somebody I had just killed" (129). "Palliative," moreover, is yet another of Nabokov's Jamesian traps for the reader, for it can mean either to "lessen the pain without curing," or "to make appear less serious or offensive." Humbert is guilty on both counts, and while he takes refuge in the sham lyricism of articulating his shame, for Lolita, the rest is silence.

Is there, then, a woman in this text—and in what sense is that question meant? For Shoshana Felman, it is allegorical: "The allegorical question 'She? Who?' will thus remain unanswered. The text, nonetheless, will play out the question to its logical end, so as to show in what way it *precludes* any answer, in what way the question is set as a trap. The very lack of the answer will then write itself as a different question, through which the original question will find itself dislocated, radically shifted and transformed."[31]

The feminist critic can expose the lack, the trap, and the frameup by reading symptomatically. She can dismantle the misogyny of traditional critical assessments of Lolita's wantonness by analyzing the precise nature of Humbert's craving. A feminist perspective thus shifts suspicion from Lolita to Humbert, for his organs—"heart," penis, eyes—expose his hysteria, treachery, and delusions. As Patrocinio Schwiekart explains, feminist criticism must pay attention to material realities in order to effect social change: "Feminist criticism . . . is a mode of *praxis*. The point is not merely to interpret literature in various ways; the point is to *change the world*" (39). But feminist theory must also focus on language and signification, not just on what is being represented, but on the manifest and latent mechanisms of representation. On the one hand, feminist criticism must inscribe the female body in the text and on the other hand show how that textual body is *fabricated*—in both senses of the word as a fiction and as a construct. One can inscribe Lolita's viewpoint and simultaneoulsy stress its verisimilitude—as opposed to its *veracity*: "Is it possible," Nabokov asks, "to imagine in its full reality the life of another, to live it oneself and transfer it intact onto paper? I doubt it . . . it can only be the verisimilar, and not the verifiable truth, that the mind perceives. . . . What we call art is, in essence, truth's picture window: one has to know how to frame it, that's all."[32]

Framed between Ray's foreword and Nabokov's spurious afterword, Humbert's narrative fixes our attention on love as the vehicle for artistic immortality. Paradoxically, the more he mocks his own prose style, the more we notice its beauty and endorse the Humbertian aesthetic manifesto of "aesthetic bliss." Since Ray's foreword is a parody of case histories, we forget that "representation *does* bear a relation to something which we can know previously existed."[33] In *Lolita*, the incestuous father's jealousy, tyranny, voracity, and possessiveness are both verisimilar and clinically verifiable. By seeing how the framing of *Lolita* elides the issue of father-daughter incest, one shifts and transforms the questions, revealing how the father's sexuality is superimposed upon the daughter's body. The answer to the question, "Is there a woman in this text?" is no. But there was a female, one whose body was the source of crimes and puns, framed unsettlingly between the horror of incest and aesthetic jouissance, between material reality and postrepresentation, between pathos and parody. Like *Lolita*'s stillborn child, that body was not a woman's—it was a girl's.

Notes

1. Lionel Trilling, "The Last Lover: Vladimir Nabokov's *Lolita*," *Encounter* 11 (October 1958): 9–19, hereinafter cited parenthetically in the text.

2. Vladimir Nabokov, *Lolita* (1955); repr. New York: Berkeley Books, 1977), 7, hereinafter cited parenthetically in the text.

3. The afterword, "On a book entitled *Lolita*," dated November 12, 1956, is appended to every edition except the first, including over twenty-five translations. There are many precedents for discussing afterwords or appendices—some written many years later—as "integral" parts of novels: William Faulkner's *The Sound and the Fury* and *Absalom, Absalom!* come to mind. No afterword, however, can be relied upon as an answer to questions raised in a novel; instead it makes the questions more problematic, as Nabokov's afterword to *Lolita* demonstrates.

4. Thomas Molnar, "Matter-of-Fact Confession of a Non-Penitent," *Chronicles of Culture* 2 (January–February 1978): 11–13.

5. Alfred Appel, Jr., "*Lolita:* The Springboard of Parody" in *Nabokov: The Man and His Work,* ed. L.S. Dembo (Madison: University of Wisconsin Press, 1967), 121, emphasis added; hereinafter cited parenthetically in the text.

6. Judith Fetterly, *The Resisting Reader: A Feminist Approach to American Fiction* (Bloomington: Indiana University Press, 1978), xii.

7. Claude Lévi-Strauss, *The Elementary Structures of Kinship* (1949; repr. Boston: Beacon, 1969), 115.

8. Patrocinio Schweickart, "Reading Ourselves: Toward a Feminist Theory of Reading" in *Gender and Reading: Essays on Readers, Texts, and Contexts,* eds. Elizabeth A. Flynn and Patrocinio P. Schweickart (Baltimore: Johns Hopkins University Press, 1985), 31–62, hereinafter cited parenthetically in the text.

9. Jacques Lacan, *Ecrits: A Selection,* trans. Alan Sheridan (New York: Norton, 1977). See especially chap. 1 on the mirror stage.

10. Frederick W. Shilstone, "The Courtly Misogynist: Humbert Humbert in *Lolita,*" *Studies in the Humanities* 8 (June 1980): 5–10.

11. Appel, "An Interview with Vladimir Nabokov," in Dembo, *Nabokov,* 19–44, emphasis added.

12. Henry James, *The Art of the Novel,* introd. Richard P. Blackmur (New York: Scribner's, 1934), 172. For a discussion of the tale as an elegiac reaccentuation of sentimental fiction, see Linda Kauffman, *Discourses of Desire: Gender, Genre, and Epistolary Fictions* (Ithaca: Cornell University Press, 1986), chap. 5.

13. Henry James to Dr. Louis Waldstein, October 21, 1898, in *The Turn of the Screw,* ed. Robert Kimbrough (New York: Norton, 1966), 110.

14. For evidence that James's governess murders Miles, see Kauffman, *Discourses,* chap. 5.

15. Edgar Allan Poe, "Lenore," in *Poetry and Tales* (New York: Library of America, 1934), 69.

16. Vladimir Nabokov, *Lectures on Literature,* ed. Fredson Bowers, introd. John Updike (New York: Harcourt Brace Jovanovich, 1980), 83, hereinafter cited parenthetically in the text.

17. See James R. Pinnells, "The Speech Ritual as an Element of Structure in Nabokov's *Lolita,*" *Dalhousie Review* 60 (Winter 1980–81): 605–21. Pinnells points out that in the speech rituals in *Lolita,* two realities come in conflict: average reality and Humbert's solipsism. Lolita is seldom allowed to speak in her own voice, but when she does, she effectively shatters Humbert's fantasies and exposes his lies, distortions, and duplicity. The best example of Pinnels' thesis is the scene at the Enchanted Hunters Motel, when Humbert speaks euphemistically about fathers and daughters sharing hotel rooms: "Two people sharing one room, inevitably enter into a kind—how shall I say—a kind—" "The word is incest," said Lo (110–11).

18. Judith Lewis Herman, *Father-Daughter Incest* (Cambridge: Harvard University Press, 1981), 4.

19. Herman, *Incest,* chaps. 5–7.

20. Herman, *Incest,* chap. 5.

21. Pinnells, "Speech Ritual," 612, 618.

22. Harry K. Frankfurt, "Freedom of the Will and the Concept of a Person," in *Free Will,* ed. Gary Watson (New York: Oxford University Press, 1982), 81–95.

23. Henry David Thoreau, *Civil Disobedience,* 1849 (repr. in *The American Tradition in Literature,* eds. Sculley Bradley et al. [New York: Random House, 1956], 744).

24. See René Girard, *Deceit, Desire, and the Novel: Self and Other in Literary Structure,* trans. Yvonne Freccero (Baltimore: Johns Hopkins University Press, 1965).

25. In *Totem and Taboo,* trans. James Strachey (London: Routledge and Kegan Paul, 1950), Freud states: "anyone who has violated a taboo becomes

taboo himself because he possesses the dangerous quality of tempting others to follow his example: why should he be allowed to do what is forbidden to others? Thus he is truly contagious in that every example encourages imitation, and for that reason he himself must be shunned.

"But a person who has not violated any taboo may yet be permanently or temporarily taboo because he is in a state which possesses the quality of arousing forbidden desires in others and of awakening a conflict of ambivalence in them" (32).

26. For feminist critiques of mimetic desire and male rivalry, see Michelle Richman, "Eroticism in the Patriarchal Order," *Diacritics* 6 (1976): 46–53; Mary Jacobus, "Is there a Woman in this Text?," *New Literary History* 14 (Autumn 1982): 117–42; and Toril Moi, "The Missing Mother: The Oedipal Rivalries of René Girard," *Diacritics* 12 (Summer 1982): 21–31.

27. Edgar Allan Poe, "The Philosophy of Composition," in *Essays and Reviews* (New York: Library of America, 1984), 19.

28. Clinical case studies help to explain Quilty's appeal for Lolita: incest victims tend to overvalue and idealize men, to seek out men who resemble their fathers (men who are older, or married, or indifferent to them), thereby compulsively reenacting the familiar pattern of exploitation and debasement. See Herman, *Incest*, chap. 2.

29. Vladimir Nabokov, *Pale Fire* (1962; repr. New York: Berkeley Books, 1977), 12.

30. On temporal differences between narrative focus and voice, see Gérard Genette, *Narrative Discourse: An Essay in Method,* trans. Jane E. Lewin (Ithaca: Cornell University Press, 1980), 180–83, 206–7, 255.

31. Shoshana Felman, "Women and Madness: The Critical Phallacy," *Diacritics* 4 (Winter 1975): 2–10.

32. Vladimir Nabokoff-Sirine, "Pouchkine ou le vrai et le vraisemblable," *La Nouvelle Revue Française* 48 (1937): 362–78, trans. Dale Peterson "Nabokov's Invitation: Literature as Execution," *PMLA* 96 (October 1981): 824–36.

33. Michèle Barrett, "Ideology and the Cultural Production of Gender" in *Feminist Criticism and Social Change: Sex, Class, and Race in Literature and Culture,* eds. Judith Newton and Deborah Rosenfelt (London: Methuen, 1985), 70.

8 "Maybe Freedom Lies in Hating"
Miscegenation and the Oedipal Conflict
Heather Hathaway

"I dearly loved my master, son," she said.
"You should have hated him," I said.
"He gave me several sons," she said, "and because I loved my sons I learned to love their father though I hated him too."
"I too have become acquainted with ambivalence," I said. . . ."Maybe freedom lies in hating."

Ralph Ellison, *Invisible Man*

Plagued by a history of prejudice, interracial relations in the United States are turbulent and disturbing. Blacks have hated whites; whites have hated blacks—but this is not the "freedom to hate" of which Ellison speaks in *Invisible Man*. Ellison addresses an issue of even greater complexity: that of black/white relations within the family structure, or miscegenation. Rooted in the Latin words *miscere,* meaning "to mix," and *genus,* meaning "race," miscegenation describes the cohabitation or marriage between persons of different races. In miscegenous relationships, kinship and race rhetoric overlap and conflict. While it is important to know who *you* are when I choose you as a spouse, it is equally and sometimes more important to know who *I* am in order to be sure of our consanguineal and racial compatibility. The choice of a mate is affected by both the incest taboo and the rules governing exogamy, those customary or legal injunctions that prohibit marriage outside a specific group, clan, or race. Miscegenous parent/child relationships are equally intricate. Mixed blood provokes a simultaneous confirmation and denial of kinship bonds: the very life of a mulatto offspring confirms a blood tie, yet the exogamy taboo against acknowledging this tie prohibits that same relationship. Miscegenation creates, yet destroys, the family.

Mulatto literature, focusing on the children of miscegenous relationships, provides a channel through which to study interracial relations bound within consanguinity. The peculiar relation between race and kin that such writing addresses, particularly in its depiction of plantation societies, offers, according to Simone Vauthier, the most "suitable setting for the staging of 'realistic' incestuous dramas, since, if bastardy is a common enough phenomenon, in no modern society has the silence of the father been to the same extent a factor in the development and structuration of the social organism."[1] The role of the father in mulatto literature is particularly intriguing since it involves both the problems that accompany the coupling of incest and miscegenation, as well as the intricacies of the "traditional" oedipal triangle. The desire to kill the father for sleeping with the mother is intensified by the rejection of the "black" son by the "white" father because of racial "impurities." The violation of identity caused by miscegenation exacerbates oedipal motivations.[2]

Both Charles Chesnutt's pre-Freudian short story entitled "The Sheriff's Children" (1889) and Langston Hughes's post-Freudian tale entitled "Father and Son" (1934)[3] bind miscegenation and incest via the oedipal complex. A reconstructive feminist reading of these texts enables us to explore how the characters and plots designed by Chesnutt and Hughes work toward reforming the image of "the father" into a tangible and conquerable figure. It will reveal how both mulatto protagonists, in literally destroying invisible patriarchal symbols, essentially redefine their own fathers as visible, vulnerable, and undeniably carnal human beings. In both tales the white father begins as an abstraction; his detached position symbolizes the oppressive legality on which interracial kinship and social structures are based. Compelled by motives jointly rooted in the oedipal complex and a history of subjugation, both protagonists challenge the role of "the father" to the point where he can no longer function only in the abstract. Confrontation by the son insists upon recognition from and subsequent redefinition of "the father." Finally, a reexamination of these plots will lead to a deeper understanding of how, using the Freudian models on which the stories were unknowingly and knowingly constructed, interracial unions have often oppressed not just women but their children as well.

In most cases, male mulattoes are represented in literature as violent, dynamic, and vengeful, while female mulattoes "tragically" reject their ambiguous relationship to family and race through suicide. Judith Berzon, in *Neither White Nor Black: The Mulatto in American Fiction,*[4] provides numerous examples of mulatto characters in fiction and classifies them along gender lines. Her generalization that there are "almost no male suicides" is disproved, however, by the two tales discussed here. In both cases, the "militant" male mulattoes choose death over a life with no name, no lineage, no home. Charles Chesnutt's "The Sheriff's Children" tells the story of a mulatto taken prisoner for his suspected murder of a white community leader, Captain Walker. A vengeance-seeking white mob surrounds the jail in which the mulatto is being held and demands his release. The sheriff, firmly committed to his civic duty, refuses the mob entry but provokes their gunfire. During the battle the prisoner seizes the sheriff's weapon and reveals his identity as the man's son. Just as the mulatto appears willing to murder his father, the sheriff's white daughter, Polly, enters and shoots but does not kill her half brother. The sheriff then bandages the mulatto's wound, returns him to his cell, and spends a harrowing night contemplating his own conflicting obligations as father and civil servant. Resolving to assist this black child whom he unconscionably betrayed by selling into slavery, the sheriff decides to use his influence to secure the acquittal of the mulatto. But the law-enforcer is too late in acknowledging his progeny—the mulatto has committed suicide in the night.

Langston Hughes's "Father and Son" describes a similar confrontation. Bert, the mulatto son of a plantation owner named Colonel Norwood, returns home for the summer after having been sent away for six years because he called his father "papa" in front of guests. A rebellious twenty-year-old, Bert is determined to claim his birthright as the colonel's son. Continually violating codes required of blacks on the plantation, he moves freely through the front door of the house despite the colonel's orders that no blacks enter, exit, or even cross the front porch. Bert offers to shake hands with his father and he identifies himself as a Norwood to both tenants and townspeople. Tension between father and son mounts all summer until finally a dispute between Bert and a white postal clerk provokes hostility from the colonel's friends and results in a climactic confrontation between parent and child. Norwood threatens to kill Bert, but the son murders the father first. He attempts escape with the help of his mother, Cora, but is trapped by a lynch mob and chooses to take his own life rather than to die at their hands.

Both Chesnutt's and Hughes's tales illustrate the complexities of oedipal relationships when race intervenes. Both pose a black son against a white father, and in so doing, set the stage for a conflict not only between father and son but also between consanguinity and race.[5] Freud's *Totem and Taboo* illuminates the relationships between incest and miscegenation, progenitor and progeny, black and white, as it reveals how social taboos add to the explosiveness of the oedipal triangle. Among the primary objectives of taboo are the "guarding [of] chief acts of life—birth, initiation, marriage and sexual functions, and the like, against interference" and the "securing of unborn infants and young children"—the securing of kin—"who stand in a specially sympathetic relation with one or both parents, from the consequences of certain actions." Violation of a taboo results in the "taboo itself [taking] vengeance."[6]

The mulatto son of the sheriff, and Bert, the mulatto in "Father and Son," are personifications of the taboo violation between their black mothers and white fathers, and as such "stand in a specially sympathetic relation with both parents," belonging fully to the race of neither. The sheriff's son's intended and Bert's actual murder of their fathers represent, in part, "taboos taking vengeance" for white men's "interference" in "chief acts of life." The white fathers violate rights of birth and initiation by denying their paternity; they violate

Western laws of marriage and sexuality by refusing both to acknowledge and wed the mothers of their children.

Both Chesnutt's and Hughes's mulatto sons become "taboo" themselves as products of taboo liaisons; similarly, the two are "taboo*ed*" by both black and white society. This inference is difficult to document in "The Sheriff's Children" because the mulatto son is in jail and may be "taboo*ed*" for his potential criminality as well as for his mixed blood. In "Father and Son," however, Bert is carefully placed in situations where he is ostracized by blacks and whites alike. Whites are afraid of his cataclysmic temper; blacks and other mulattoes, most specifically his brother Willie who has opted for a black identity, are afraid "with a fear worse than physical . . . of the things that happen around Bert" (113). In systems of taboo, the practice of "transference" results in an individual who has "transgressed one of these prohibitions" becoming in turn prohibited himself, "as though the whole of the dangerous charge had been transferred over to him. This power is attached to all 'special' individuals, such as kings, priests, or new born babies."[7] Bert, as a personification of the miscegenation taboo violated by his parents, has essentially "transgressed the prohibition" simply by being, and thus becomes comparably prohibited. As the "new born baby" of a black/white liaison, the "dangerous charge" has been "transferred over to him": the taboo and the "taboo*ed*" become one. Visibly representing an infraction of rules prohibiting miscegenation, Bert, as the taboo object, "takes vengeance" upon his father. But as "taboo*ed*" by the social transference of prohibitions, he must also die himself.

The oedipal components of incest expressed in miscegenous relationships are illustrated in "The Sheriff's Children" by the very fact that the mulatto has *not* killed Captain Walker, the man of whose murder he is originally accused. If the mulatto's motivations for homicide were merely the destruction or avenging of white power structures, he would have murdered the captain or any other white man, for that matter. But he seeks only the life of his father. The speech delivered by the sheriff to the angry mob foreshadows the central issue of the story: " 'All right, boys, talk away. You are all strangers to me, and I don't know what business you can have.' The sheriff did not think it necessary to recognize anybody in particular on such an occasion; the question of identity sometimes comes up in the investigation of these extra-judicial executions" (74). As Robert Bone argues, the mulatto son is actually the "stranger" and the one whom the sheriff has never thought it "necessary to recognize." The question of "identity" plagues the father's conscience, and his decision, though tardy, to free his son is actually an "extra-judicial" activity in that it violates his civic duty as sheriff.[8]

Prior to the patricide attempts, the mulatto is alternately referred to as "the nigger," "the negro," and "the prisoner" by the sheriff, the lynchers, and the narrator. Only once, in a nonspecific description of Captain Walker's murder related by the narrator, is the term "mulatto" applied (63). At the point of confrontation between the sheriff and his son, however, the words "mulatto" and "prisoner" are those predominantly used to describe the son. This juxtaposition semantically reflects the peculiar position of the mulatto as imprisoned by black and white society. Because of his simultaneous "sameness" and "otherness," he is neither wholly rejected nor wholly accepted by either group. Furthermore, the introduction of "mulatto" at the point of oedipal conflict emphasizes the kinship ties between father and son.

The following dialogue between the "prisoner" and the sheriff reflects the complexity of their relationship as father to son, as black to white:

"Good God!" [the sheriff] gasped, "you would not murder your own father?"

"My father?" replied the mulatto, "it were well enough for me to claim the relationship, but it comes with poor grace from you to ask anything by reason of it. What father's duty have you ever performed for me? Did you give me protection . . . freedom . . . [or] money? . . . *You* sold *me* to the rice swamps."

"I at least gave you the life you cling to," murmured the sheriff.

"Life?" said the prisoner, with a sarcastic laugh. "What kind of life? You gave me your own blood, your own features. . . . You gave me a white man's spirit, and you made me a slave, and crushed it out. . . . I owe you nothing . . . and it would be no more than justice if I should avenge upon you my mother's wrongs and my own. But I still hate to shoot you." (84–87 passim)

The issues involve not solely transgressions of kinship systems in the rejection of son by father and lifelong denial of paternity, and not solely offenses against race in the enslavement of blacks by whites. Rather, they involve simultaneous violations of *both* kin and race through the selling into slavery of son by father; the reckless passing on and entrapment of a "white" spirit in a "black" body in a society that "despise[s] . . . scorn[s] . . . and set[s] aside" (86) biracial individuals; and finally, the essential uxoricide of the black mother by the white father.

But the mulatto prisoner is unsuccessful in his patricide attempt; he is preempted by his half sister, Polly. Allusions to Greek myth in Chesnutt's tale expose oedipal elements intrinsic to miscegenation as the intervention of race adds a new dimension to the older, traditional equations. Polly (whose name echoes Polynices), is also involved in an oedipal relationship with the sheriff. Recalling the devotion that Antigone feels for Oedipus her father/brother, Polly displays comparable adoration for the sheriff, her father/husband. I refer to him as such because of the telling descriptions of the interaction between Polly and the sheriff throughout the story that imply a relationship reminiscent of one between husband and wife rather than between father and daughter. Significantly, there is no mother—black or white—present in the sheriff's family. In a traditional triangle the mulatto son is allied with the maternal line, and in this miscegenous trio that alliance is even stronger because of mother and son's shared and socially stigmatizing color. Thus Polly, in attempting to kill her mixed-blooded brother, symbolically seeks vengeance upon the entire maternal line with whom she is in contest for the father.

Resembling Oedipus's need for redemption, the sheriff is overcome by conscience as he tries to envision a way to "in some degree, atone for his crime against this son of his—against society—against God" (93). But Oedipus atones only for crimes against "society" and "God"—for the social crime of incest and the divine crime of murder. The sheriff, as the white miscegenator who is aware of the existence of his mulatto son, must atone for an additional crime against his child—the denial of paternity, and therefore of the son's identity. The intervention of race adds a more personal dimension to the traditional equation since the two figures in conflict, "white" father and "black" son, are both alive and both conscious of their relationship.

Finally, just as Antigone buries her brother in defiance of Creon's edict, the sheriff is tempted to value claims of kinship over the order of the polis when he considers letting "the prisoner" escape. But in the end civic duty (white law) overrules personal rectitude (paternal responsibility), and though the sheriff has developed a plan to absolve himself of some guilt, the forces of atonement are never put into action, because the mulatto son has chosen death over a life with "no name, no father, no mother" (92).

Hughes's "Father and Son" discloses other oedipal elements common to miscegenation. In Sophocles, the verbalization of incest increases the horror that surrounds it. Though the act itself is taboo, vengeance need not be taken until Oedipus's murder of his father, marriage to his mother, and fathering of his sisters are acknowledged through speech. Only the actual recognition and expression of these "sins" set the forces of punishment in motion. A similar pattern underscores "Father and Son." The white father, Norwood, continually abdicates his responsibilities as parent by referring to his children as "your" kids, as "Cora's brats," as "yellow-bastards." The "sin" for which Bert first gets subjugated by his father (at an age of great Freudian significance, not surprisingly) is that of verbally acknowledging his own ancestry. He calls his father "papa" in front of guests, and receives a slap that "made him see stars and darkness. . . . As though he were brushing a fly out of the way, the Colonel had knocked him down under the feet of the horses" (116).

Norwood's punishment of Bert conversely provokes the son to reassert his identity as the colonel's child. Early in life Bert realizes that his playmates "were named after their fathers, whereas he . . . bore the mother's name, Lewis. He was Bert Lewis—not Bert Norwood" (115). Bert strongly identifies with his mother as mutual victim as he grows to understand that his father's denial of paternity is crucial to the maintenance of the entire oppressive, Southern social structure. Vauthier explains: "if black, which is non-white, can look non-black, nay white, then the opposition white/

non-white shows up as problematical. . . . The social structure insofar as it determines status according to race, i.e. color, is
jeopardized. . . . The place of the white individual within the race-
based social scheme and hence his very identity are threatened by
the mere existence of a white Negro."[9]

Bert's recognition of this incites him to assert his heritage rebel-
liously, in defiance of both familial and socially imposed diminutions
of his ancestry, of his very identity. He challenges Norwood's denial
of paternity as well as the entire paternalistic structure every time
he enters through the front door, every time he offers to shake
hands with or speak to his father, every time he refers to Norwood
as his "old man." Most blatantly, Bert asserts that he is a "Norwood"; he takes his father's name. As Mr. Higgins, the postal clerk,
describes to Norwood: "He said last week, standin' out on my
corner, he wasn't *all* nigger no how; said his name was Norwood—
not Lewis, like the rest of Cora's family; said your plantation would
be his when you passed out—and all that kind o' stuff, boasting to
the niggers listening about you being his father" (123).

Motivated by similar rebelliousness the mulatto son in "The Sheriff's Children" is shocked when the sheriff refers to himself, at last,
as the mulatto's father: "My father?" replied the mulatto. . . . "What
father's duty have you ever performed for me? Did you ever *give me
your name?*" (85, emphasis mine). In an inversion of Freud's discussion about certain societal practices of changing names after death
to avoid vengeance,[10] never *giving* the name in the first place acknowledges neither the life nor the taboo violation.

Both fictionally and historically slaves and mulattoes have been
stereotyped as having no origins, implying the denial of any birthright to blacks by the entire social system of slavery. The black
"pickaninnies" in Dion Boucicault's 1861 drama, "The Octoroon,"
for example, are described as children who have no heritage: "dem
black tings never was born at all; dey swarmed one mornin' on a
sassafras tree in the swamp" (3). A similar conversation occurs
between Topsy and Miss Ophelia in *Uncle Tom's Cabin or, Life
Among the Lowly.* In response to Ophelia's question, "Who was your
mother?," Topsy replies, "Never had none! . . . Never was born!
. . . never had no mother, nor father, nor nothin" (355–56). Lines of

descent are obscured in the case of blacks—and by conjecture—mulattoes especially.[11] According to Vauthier, "the planter may scatter his seed indiscriminately; as long as he refuses to acknowledge his off-spring, he can keep his blood-line pure and his dynastic order working."[12] She goes on to explain that by "refusing to acknowledge his slave son, the father fails to transmit with his surname what Lacan calls the Name-of-the-Father—[that is], the universal law that prohibits incest."[13] Failure to transmit the Name-of-the-Father not only obscures kinship lines, complicating relationships of affinity and consanguinity, but it is precisely what opens the door for a reenactment of the oedipal drama.

Both Chesnutt's and Hughes's mulattoes breach the "silence of the father," crucial to the maintenance of a paternalistic society, as they challenge denials of filiation by attempting to enact the oedipal goal. Additionally, as nameless mulatto children, Bert and the sheriff's son stand outside the law prohibiting incest. Their status as taboo objects is amplified by their existence beyond the circle of taboo liaisons; they are neither black nor white—they are both. This biracial pariah identity psychically allies these mulatto children with the mother who, as a black woman in Southern plantation society, represents a similar taboo against which white men must guard themselves under the rules governing exogamy.

Ambivalence is a crucial factor in both systems of taboo and the oedipal complex,[14] and provides another link between miscegenation and incest. At the same time that we revere, adore, or admire a leader or ruler, we are also seized by latent hostility and anger at this leader/father's superiority and power over us. We both love and hate our enemies; simultaneously we seek and fear vengeance upon them. Norwood is clearly ambivalent about Bert. Upon his son's arrival at the plantation, Norwood schemes to stay in the library for a number of minutes in an effort to avoid appearing anxious to see his child: "Colonel Norwood never would have admitted, even to himself, that he was standing in his doorway waiting for this half-Negro son to come home. But in truth that is what he was doing. . . . Not once [since being sent away to school] had [Bert] been allowed to come back to Big House Plantation. The Colonel had said then that never did he want to see the boy. But in truth, he did" (106). Norwood acknowledges the similarities in their appearance and temperament with a modicum of pride: "This boy had been . . . the most beautiful of the lot, the brightest and the baddest of the Colonel's five children . . . Handsome and mischievous, [and] favoring too much the Colonel in his ways" (106). The sheriff in "The Sheriff's Children" is equally torn between love and hatred for his offspring. "He knew whose passions coursed beneath that swarthy skin and burned in the black eyes opposite his own. He saw in this mulatto . . . he, himself" (86). The paradoxes implied in hating their sons' "otherness" and loving their "sameness" results in Norwood's inability to kill his son and in the sheriff's compulsion to "atone" for his "sin." Both are bound by a responsibility to kin.

Obviously, however, the same is not true for the mulatto progeny. As Werner Sollors has noted, the oedipal triangle requires "the unmarried son [to] confront the father who possesses the mother [in order] to approach the riddle of his own existence."[15] This tension is expressed in the dialogues between the fathers and the sons that directly precede the shots of death in both stories. The sheriff's son screams in rage: "you gave me a black mother. Poor wretch! She died under the lash, because she had enough womanhood to call her soul her own. . . . I should avenge upon you my mother's wrongs and my own" (86, 87).

Bert expresses similar sentiments in the dynamic scene preceding his murder of Norwood. The colonel demands from Bert an explanation for his behavior in town, warning him to "talk right." When Bert asks what he means by "talk[ing] right," the Colonel snaps:

"I mean talk like a nigger should to a white man."
"Oh, but I'm not a nigger, Colonel Norwood," Bert said, "I'm your son."
The old man frowned at the boy in front of him. "Cora's son," he said.
"Fatherless?" Bert asked.
"Bastard," the old man said. . . . "You black bastard."
"I've heard that before." Bert just stood there. "You're talking about my mother." (pp. 126–27)

In the 1928 dramatic version of the tale entitled "Mulatto" the oedipal tension over the mother is even more apparent:

ROBERT: . . . I'm your son.
NORWOOD: (Testily) You're Cora's boy.

ROBERT: Women don't have children by themselves.
NORWOOD: Nigger women don't know the fathers. You're a bastard. . . .
ROBERT: . . . (Slowly) You're talking about my mother.
NORWOOD: I'm talking about Cora, yes. Her children are bastards.
ROBERT: (Quickly) And you're their father. (Angrily) How come I look like you if you're not my father? . . . You had no right to raise that cane today when I was standing at the door of this house where *you* live, while *I* have to sleep in a shack down the road with the field hands. (Slowly) But my mother sleeps with you.
NORWOOD: You don't like it?
ROBERT: No, I don't like it.
NORWOOD: What can you do about it?
ROBERT: (After a pause) I'd like to kill all the white men in the world.[16]

Both Bert and the sheriff's son hate their fathers *because* they sleep with (or "kill") their mothers. But this is not merely oedipally motivated. In the traditional oedipal triangle the son hates the father who possesses the mother in marriage; when miscegenation becomes a factor under the economy of slavery, the desire for retaliation magnifies: the son must avenge both figurative and literal possession of mother by father. In miscegenous oedipal plots the son is allied with his mother because both are defined as "black" while the father is placed in a different social category. Lines of filiation are affected insofar as oedipal ambitions are fulfilled through the son's greater social similarity to the maternal line. Thus in both tales the mothers, viewed as mutually tabooed and victimized figures by their mulatto sons, are absolved of blame. For the mulattoes, interracial sex is not the ultimate evil; rather, the rejection of parental and spousal responsibility by the socially dominant, white, male miscegenator is the crime that cannot be excused. As Bert cries in Hughes's 1949 operatic rendition of the same story, *The Barrier,* "not in Georgia nor anywhere else/Should a man deny his son," for such a denial is an offense against both son and mother.

By murdering his father, Bert transfers his hatred to "all the white men in Georgia" on whom he wants to wreak similar vengeance, fusing what Vauthier describes in a different context as "the Oedipal fantasies of [patricide] and the dream of social redress."[17] The mulatto son's desire "to kill all the white men in the world" expresses his attempt to prohibit not only miscegenation and incest, but also to destroy the entire social system of slavery based on the literal possession of one human being by another. The death of both the sheriff and Norwood—indeed, the imagined death of all white men—would mean the death of unrecognized consanguinity through miscegenation and the complications that result from it. More significantly, it would mean the death both of the white, male, rule—of law—as well as of the racist patriarchal order that denies its own paternity. Most interestingly, the murder of white father by black son dismantles the alliance between "the father" as lawmaker, as governor, as ruler, by transforming *him* into the vulnerable, victimized role that the mother and son once occupied. The obfuscation of kinship lines through incest and miscegenation is transformed into a symbolic destruction of an entire social system through the fulfillment of oedipal ambitions.

On one level, Charles Chesnutt's "The Sheriff's Children" and Langston Hughes's "Father and Son" help to reveal the complexities that result from a superimposition of race on an already elaborate oedipal triangle by disclosing the additional tensions that exist when black and white, son and lover, leader and enemy are all embodied within the same consanguineal bond. Racial differences between father and son, given the history of tension between black and white in America, create both an additional barrier between parent and child as well as an additional motivation for oedipal desires to kill the father. Justifying the violation of race by creating an artificial familial construct through a paternalistic interpretation of slavery, Southern society simultaneously built into its culture the opportunity for systematic denial of those consanguine bonds that actually did exist. Desiring straightforward acts of racial segregation and white paternalism, the South was paradoxically a land of amalgamation, fundamentally rooted in the denial of paternity.

On another level, the characters created by Chesnutt and Hughes foreshadow the goals of many contemporary feminist writers. By confronting and killing the literal and figurative fathers of a patriarchal familial and social structure, these mulatto men essentially attack the image of "the father" as one who is detached and intangible—as one who is the abstraction of law and power. In this sense at least, these two black male writers can be considered allies of all women who strive to attain the social ideal of equality.

Notes

This paper grew out of a seminar entitled "Kinship and Literature" led by Werner Sollors in the fall of 1986 at Harvard University. I am greatly indebted to Professor Sollors for his inspiration, encouragement, and wisdom, as well as for generously providing me with a copy of his article, " 'Never Was Born': The Mulatto, An American Tragedy?," which has since been published in the *Massachusetts Review*, 27:293–316.

1. Simone Vauthier, *"Textualité et Stereotypes:* Of African Queens and Afro-American Princes and Princesses: Miscegenation in *Old Hepsy," Publications du Conseil Scientifique de la Sorbonne Nouvelle*, Paris, 3 (1980): 91.

2. It is interesting to note that few if any narratives address this issue from the opposite perspective: a "black" father and a "white" son. The absence of such reversed tales indicates the degree and direction of racism in this country.

3. Unless otherwise stated, excerpts by Charles W. Chesnutt are quoted from "The Sheriff's Children," contained in *The Wife of His Youth and Other Stories of the Color Line* (Boston: 1899; repr. Ann Arbor: University of Michigan Press, 1968). Excerpts by Langston Hughes are quoted from *Something in Common and Other Stories* (New York: Hill and Wang, First American Century Series edition, 1963). Subsequent references will be cited in the text.

4. Judith Berzon, *Neither White Nor Black: The Mulatto in American Fiction* (New York: New York University Press, 1978) 74.

5. Werner Sollors, " 'Never Was Born' ": The Mulatto, An American Tragedy?," *Massachusetts Review* 27:306. The presence of the father in the story itself, which thereby allows him an active role in the drama, is in contrast to Dion Boucicault's 1861 play entitled "The Octoroon" (Miami: Mnemosyne Publishing, first Mnemosyne reprinting from a copy in the Fisk University Library Negro Collection, 1969) and another of Chesnutt's stories concerning mulattoes entitled "Her Virginia Mammy" (also contained in *The Wife of His Youth and Other Stories of the Color Line*). Here, the "sinning" white fathers, Mr. Peyton and Mr. Stafford, are conveniently freed from taking responsibility for their paternity through death. Again, the gender difference between the "tragic" and "militant" mulatto is suggested, since both these tales involve a mulatto heroine. The absence of the

father precludes interaction, which in some ways forces "tragic" responses on the part of the mulatto because there is no white paternal figure to confront directly with the issue of patrimony.

6. Sigmund Freud, *Totem and Taboo: Some Points of Agreement between the Mental Lives of Savages and Neurotics* (1913; transl. James Strachey, New York: Norton, 1950), 19, 20.

7. Freud, *Totem and Taboo*, 22.

8. Robert Bone, *Down Home: A History of Afro-American Short Fiction from Its Beginnings to the End of the Harlem Renaissance* (New York: Putnam's, 1975), 96–97.

9. Vauthier, "Textualité," 88–89 passim.

10. Freud, *Totem and Taboo*, 54–57.

11. For a more detailed discussion of mulatto genealogies in literature, see Werner Sollors's article cited in note 5 of this chapter. For a large-scale attempt to show the status of slaves in general as "never [having been] born," see Orlando Patterson, *Slavery and Social Death: A Comparative Study* (Cambridge: Harvard University Press, 1982).

12. Vauthier, "Textualité," 84.

13. Vauthier, "Textualité," 90.

14. Freud, *Totem and Taboo*, 29–30, 157.

15. Sollors, *Massachusetts Review* 27:308.

16. Arthur P. Davis explains in his classic essay, "The Tragic Mulatto Theme in Six Works of Langston Hughes" (*Phylon* 16 [1955], 195–204, reprinted in *Five Black Writers,* ed. Donald B. Gibson [New York: New York University Press, 1970]), that Hughes developed the mulatto theme in a variety of genres including poetry, drama, and opera. The play entitled "Mulatto" is contained in *Five Plays by Langston Hughes,* ed. Webster Smalley (Bloomington: Indiana University Press, First Midland Book edition, 1968), 1–37. This excerpt is found on pages 23–24.

17. Vauthier, "Textualité," 90.

9 The Humiliation of Elizabeth Bennet

Susan Fraiman

I belong to a generation of American feminist critics taught to read by Sandra Gilbert and Susan Gubar. *The Madwoman in the Attic* (1979) both focused our regard on women writers of the nineteenth century and formed in us invaluable habits of attention. It alerted us to eccentric characters, figures off to the side, to the lunatic fringe. We learned to see certain transients—required by the plot to move on before things can work out—as feminist doubles for the author as well as heroine. Bertha Mason in *Jane Eyre* and Lady Catherine de Bourgh in *Pride and Prejudice,* unexemplary as they are expendable, register nonetheless the screams and tantrums of Charlotte Brontë's and Jane Austen's own rage. These marginal women voice anger and defiance that split open ostensibly decorous texts.

I want, in keeping with this tradition, to stress the accents of defiance in *Pride and Prejudice,* but I locate these less at the edges than at the very center of the book; my argument concerns the much-admired Elizabeth Bennet and the two major men in her life, Mr. Bennet and Mr. Darcy. I read *Pride and Prejudice* as the ceding of Mr. Bennet's paternity to Mr. Darcy, with a consequent loss of clout for Elizabeth. Austen's novel documents the collapse of an initially enabling father into a father figure who, in keeping with his excessive social authority, tends to be rather disabling. As Elizabeth passes from Bennet to Darcy, her authorial powers wane: she goes from shaping judgments to being shaped by them. I want to look at Elizabeth's gradual devaluation, her humiliation, in terms of this double father.[1] Austen, I believe, stands back from her decline, ironizing both the onset of marriage and the father-daughter relation. She shows us a form of violence against women that is not hidden away in the attic, displaced onto some secondary figure, but downstairs in the drawing room involving the heroine herself.

Elizabeth's first father is a reclusive man and seemingly ineffectual; beside the rigid figure of *Northanger Abbey*'s General Tilney, Mr. Bennet may well appear flimsy. But the general (his love of new gadgets notwithstanding) is an old-fashioned father whose authoritarian style was all but outmoded by the end of the eighteenth century.[2] Mr. Bennet is not really a bad father—just a modern one, in the manner of Locke's influential text on education. Smooth-browed advocate of instruction over discipline and reason over force, he typifies the Lockean father. As Jay Fliegelman points out, however, Locke's concern "is not with circumscribing paternal authority, but with rendering it more effective by making it noncoercive."[3] Mr. Bennet, apparently benign to the point of irresponsibility, may seem to wield nothing sharper than his sarcasm. But what he actually wields is the covert power of the Lockean patriarch, all the more effective for its subtlety.

This aloof, unseen power of Mr. Bennet's suggests to me, for several reasons, the peculiar power of an author. His disposition is emphatically literary. Taking refuge from the world in his library, Mr. Bennet prefers the inner to the outer life, books to people. He asks two things only: the free use of his understanding and his room—precisely those things Virginia Woolf associates with the privilege of the male writer, the privation of the female. Most important, among women whose solace is news, he keeps the upper hand by withholding information. Mr. Bennet is a creator of suspense. In the opening scene, for example, he refuses to visit the new bachelor in town, deliberately frustrating Mrs. Bennet's expectation and desire. Actually, "he had always intended to visit him, though to the last always assuring his wife that he should not go; and till the evening after the visit was paid, she had no knowledge of it."[4] Mr. Bennet relishes the power to contain her pleasure and finally, with his dénouement, to relieve and enrapture her.

But the suspense is not over. Elizabeth's father is, even then, as stingy with physical description as some fathers are with pocket money. He controls his family by being not tight-fisted but tight-lipped, and in this he resembles Austen herself. George Lewes first noted the remarkable paucity of concrete details in Austen, her reluctance to tell us what people, their clothes, their houses or gardens look like.[5] If female readers flocked to Richardson for Pamela's meticulous descriptions of what she packed in her trunk, they must surely have been frustrated by Austen's reticence here.[6] So Mr. Bennet only follows Austen when, secretive about Bingley's person and estate, he keeps the ladies in the dark. Their curiosity is finally gratified by another, less plain-styled father, Sir William Lucas, whose report they receive "second-hand" from Lady Lucas. Much as women talk in this novel, the flow of important words (of "intelligence") is regulated largely by men. In this verbal economy, women get the trickle-down of news.

When Mr. Collins proposes to Elizabeth, Mr. Bennet again con-trives to keep his audience hanging. Pretending to support his wife, he hides until the last moment his real intention of contradicting her. After a stern prologue he continues: "An unhappy alternative is before you, Elizabeth. From this day you must be a stranger to one of your parents.—Your mother will never see you again if you do *not* marry Mr. Collins, and I will never see you again if you *do*" (112). Not only this particular manipulation but indeed the entire scene goes to show the efficacy of paternal words. Throughout his proposal, to Elizabeth's distress and our amusement, Mr. Collins completely ignores her many impassioned refusals. He discounts what she says as "merely words of course" (108); even his dim, self-mired mind perceives that a lady's word carries no definitive weight. Mr. Collins accuses Elizabeth of wishing to increase his love "by suspense, according to the usual practice of elegant females" (108). Yet creating suspense is exactly what Elizabeth, rhetorically unrelia-ble, cannot do. She has no choice but "to apply to her father, whose negative might be uttered in such a manner as must be decisive" (109). Mr. Bennet's power resides, as I say, in his authorial preroga-tive: his right to have the last word.

Though Mr. Bennet uses this right to disparage and disappoint his wife, regarding his daughter he uses it rather to praise, protect, apparently to enable her. Like many heroines in women's fiction (think of Emma Woodhouse or Maggie Tulliver) Elizabeth has a special relationship to her father. She is immediately distinguished as a family member and as a character by his preference for her and hers for him. The entail notwithstanding, she is in many respects his heir. To her he bequeaths his ironic distance from the world, the habit of studying and appraising those around him, the role of social critic. In this role, father and daughter together scan Mr. Collins's letter, dismissing man and letter with a few, skeptical words. Mr. Bennet enables Elizabeth by sharing with her his authorial mandate, which is Austen's own: to frame a moral discourse and judge characters accordingly. Through her father, Elizabeth gains provisional access to certain authorial powers.

But Mr. Bennet also shares with her, illogically enough, his disdain for women; he respects Elizabeth only because she is unlike other girls. This puts his exceptional daughter in an awkward position—bonding with her father means breaking with her mother, even reneging on femaleness altogether. Elizabeth is less a daughter than a surrogate son. Like a son, by giving up the mother and giving in to the father, she reaps the spoils of maleness. We can understand her, alternatively, in terms of Freud's scheme for girls. Freud contends that girls first turn to the father because they want a penis like his. They envy, as Karen Horney explained, the social power this organ signifies under patriarchy.[7] To complete their oedipal task, however, girls must shift from wanting a penis for themselves to wanting a man who has one; ceasing to identify with the powerful father, they must accept instead their own "castration."[8] In these terms the cocky Elizabeth we first encounter is charmingly arrested in the early phase of male-identification. We can see her, then, in one of two ways: as an honorary boy who has completed his oedipal task, or as a backward, wayward girl who refuses to complete hers.

The point is, first, that whatever discursive acuity Elizabeth has derives from an alliance and identification with her father. As the Mr. Collins scene demonstrates, the force of her words is highly contingent. Elizabeth's authority is vicarious, second-hand; like a woman writing under a male pseudonym, her credibility depends on the father's signature. In addition, however enabling, Mr. Bennet is essentially ambivalent toward Elizabeth. "They have none of them much to recommend them," he says of his daughters in chapter 1. "They are all silly and ignorant like other girls; but Lizzy has something more of quickness than her sisters" (5). Insisting that all of his daughters are silly and ignorant, that none of them have much to recommend them, Mr. Bennet blithely classes Elizabeth with "other girls," even as he appears to distinguish her from them. So we find, already in the opening scene, a tension between Elizabeth's "masculine" alacrity and the slow-witted "femininity" threatening to claim her. Mr. Bennet's double vision of her suggests right away the basic ambiguity of Austen's father-daughter relationship, coded not only diachronically in the Mr. Bennet-Mr. Darcy sequence, but also synchronically in Mr. Bennet's duplicity regarding Elizabeth.

For in Austen the male-bonding between father and daughter is set up to collapse. Eventually the economic reality asserts itself, the axiom of the famous first line held up to a mirror and read backward: a single woman not in possession of a good fortune must be in want of a husband. Sooner or later what Adrienne Rich calls "compulsory heterosexuality" (conspiracy of economic need and the ideology of romance) forces Elizabeth out of the library, into the ballroom, and finally up to the altar.[9] The father's business in this ritual is to give the daughter away. If Mr. Bennet is enabling up to a point, the marriage ceremony requires him to objectify his daughter and hand her over. He not only withdraws his protection and empowerment, but also gives away (reveals) her true "castrated" gender, her incapacity for action in a phallocentric society. This ceremony—posing father as giver, daughter as gift—underlies and ultimately belies the father-daughter relationship in *Pride and Prejudice*.

So Elizabeth's gradual falling out with her father, which means forfeiting her authorial status, is built into the institution of marriage. Austen makes it quite clear that Mr. Bennet neglects Lydia, failing to protect her from ruinous male designs. Yet, is not the father's letting go of the daughter precisely what the wedding ritual requires?[10] Mr. Bennet's profligacy with Lydia is simply a starker form of his cheerful readiness to give away any and all of his daughters. "I will send a few lines by you," he tells his wife, "to assure [Bingley] of my hearty consent to his marrying which ever he chuses of the girls" (4). Exposing a pattern intrinsic to the nuptial plot, Mr. Bennet's abandonment of Lydia provides a crude paradigm for Elizabeth's milder estrangement from her father and for the literal distance between father and heroine in *Northanger Abbey* and *Mansfield Park.*[11] Bennet, by retiring as Elizabeth's champion, is not ineffectual as a father, but correct.

In his discussion of marriage and the incest taboo, Lévi-Strauss proposes that the exchange of women among kin groups serves, like the exchange of money or words, to negotiate relationships among men. Women are, in effect, a kind of currency whose circulation binds and organizes male society.[12] It seems to me that *Pride and Prejudice* offers a similar anthropology. Here, too, marriage betrays the tie between father and daughter in favor of ties among men. I have the idea that Elizabeth's economic imperative is not the only motive for her marriage, that the fathers have an agenda of their own, involving considerations of class.

Mr. Bennet's class interest in a Bennet-Darcy match is fairly obvious and similar to Elizabeth's own. He may laugh at Mrs. Bennet's schemes, but the fact remains that a liaison to aristocracy will benefit him significantly. And in spite of his philosophic detachment, Mr. Bennet is not without a streak of pragmatism—after all, he has always intended to visit Mr. Bingley. Nor is he unimpressed by wealth and rank. He is frankly delighted that Darcy has used his money and influence to straighten out the Lydia-Wickham affair. "So much the better," he exults. "It will save me a world of trouble and economy" (377). Sounding even, for a moment, strangely like Mr. Collins, he consents to Elizabeth's marriage with little of his habitual irony. "I have given him my consent," he tells her. "He is the kind of man, indeed, to whom I should never dare refuse any thing, which he condescended to ask" (376).

Though Mr. Darcy's class interests may seem to rule against a connection to the Bennets, they too are subtly at work here. In her remarks on eighteenth-century marriage, Mary Poovey notes that Cinderella matches frequently allayed not only middle-class status anxiety, but also the financial anxiety increasingly rife among the well-born.[13] Cinderella's family may be obscure, but her share in merchant profits is attractive to a prince who is poor. Austen does not fully represent, until *Persuasion*'s Sir Walter Elliot, the material as well as moral impoverishment of the landed class in her day. Yet as early as *Sense and Sensibility* (1811) she gives us Willoughby who, unsure of his aristocratic heritage, leaves Marianne for a certain Miss Grey with fifty thousand pounds. Of course in *Pride and Prejudice* cash flows the other way: Darcy has it and Elizabeth needs it. But a decline in aristocratic welfare is nevertheless suggested by the sickly Miss De Bourgh. It may well be the enfeeblement of his own class that encourages Darcy to look below him for a wife with greater stamina. As a figure for the ambitious bourgeoisie, Elizabeth pumps richer, more robust blood into the collapsing veins of the nobility, even as she boosts the social standing of her relatives in trade. Most important, however—to the patriarchs of both classes— she eases tensions between them. By neutralizing class antagonism, she promotes the political stability on which industrial prosperity depends.[14]

I turn, now, to the handing of Elizabeth from Bennet to Darcy, which is prefigured by a scene on the Lucas dance floor. Here Sir William Lucas stands in for Mr. Bennet, jockeying for power with Mr. Darcy, who has the upper hand. Sir William begins to despair, when suddenly he is "struck with the notion of doing a very gallant thing" (26). Laying claim to Elizabeth, he offers her up to Darcy as "a very desirable partner." Sir William understands that gift-giving can be an "idiom of competition." As anthropologist Gayle Rubin explains, there is power in creating indebtedness.[15] We imagine the three of them: Elizabeth between the two men, her hand held aloft by Lucas, Lucas eager to deposit it, Darcy "not unwilling to receive it" (26). The fathers' device here is synecdoche. Elizabeth is reduced to a *hand*, extended in friendship or hostility, the means of fraternal intercourse. Suddenly, however, Elizabeth pulls back. With startling resolution she withdraws herself from the debt nexus. Indeed, throughout much of the novel Elizabeth resists the conventional grammar of exchange. She would not only extract herself as object but, contesting the fathers' right to control the action, insert herself as subject. Saboteur, Elizabeth threatens to wreck the marriage syntax. Needless to say, this makes for one of the stormier courtships in nineteenth-century fiction.

It was, as I have noted, Lévi-Strauss who first saw marriage as a triangulated moment, a woman exchanged between two (groups of) men. Gayle Rubin went on to identify this kind of traffic, its organization of a sex-gender system, as the basis for female subordination. But the immediate model for my placing such an exchange at the heart of *Pride and Prejudice* is provided by Eve Sedgwick; her recent book, *Between Men,* examines the way men bond across the bodies of women in a range of English texts.[16] Her mapping of "male homosocial desire" posits, however, an essentially passive female term. It imagines a triangle that is stable and uncontested; even women who begin active and ambitious, once drawn into the space between two men, fall automatically still. What I have tried to suggest above is that Elizabeth does not readily accept a merely pivotal role. The book stretches out because she puts up a fight before acceding (and never entirely) to the fathers' homosocial plot. The site of her resistance, as well as her compromise, is language.

This brings us to Mr. Darcy—a father by virtue of his age, class, and a paternalism extending to friends and dependents alike. A man given to long letters and polysyllables, a man with an excellent library and even hand, Darcy may also be seen as an aspiring authorial figure. If Bennet sets out to create suspense, Darcy hankers to resolve it. Their relation is one of literary rivals, with Elizabeth the prize. The complication is Elizabeth's own formidable way with words. As surrogate son, father's heir, Elizabeth is herself a contender for the authorial position. Instead of rewarding Darcy for his accession, she competes with him for it. In these terms, Elizabeth's and Darcy's matching of wits is more than flirtation—it is a struggle for control of the text. There are two heated and definitive moments in this struggle: Elizabeth's refusal of Darcy's first proposal and the day after, when he delivers his letter.

Chapter 11 of the second volume finds Elizabeth alone at the Collins's house in Kent. Concerned sister and conscientious reader, she is studying Jane's letters. Suddenly Darcy bursts in and blurts out a proposal, more an admission of weakness than a confession of love. The chapter closes by resuming Elizabeth's internal dialogue, "the tumult of her mind" (193) after Darcy's departure. But have we, throughout this chapter, been anywhere *but* in Elizabeth's mind? By all rights this should be Darcy's scene, his say. In fact, we get relatively few of his actual words. His amatory discourse is quickly taken over by a narrator who represents the scene, renders Darcy's language, from Elizabeth's point of view: "His sense of her inferiority . . . [was] dwelt on with a warmth which . . . was very unlikely to recommend his suit" (189). The text of Darcy's proposal is completely glossed, and glossed over, by her interpretation of it. Of Elizabeth's refusal, by contrast, Austen gives us every unmediated word, a direct quotation four times as long as that permitted Darcy. This sets the pattern for what follows. Every time Darcy opens his mouth, he is superseded by a speech of greater length and vehemence. She answers his question—Why is he so rudely rejected?—with a tougher question of her own: "I might as well enquire . . . why with so evident a design of offending and insulting me, you chose to tell me that you liked me against your will, against your reason, and even against your character? Was not this some excuse for incivility, if I *was* uncivil?" (190). Conceding nothing, she accuses him at some length of everything: of breaking Jane's heart and unmaking Wickham's fortune, of earning and continually confirming her own dislike. She betters his scorn for her family by scorning him. "I have every reason in the world to think ill of you" (191), she asserts. Her language, her feelings, her judgments overwhelm his and put them to shame. They drive him to platitude, apology, and hasty retreat. This rhetorical round leaves Elizabeth clear victor.

The following day, however, she is obsessed by Darcy: "It was impossible to think of any thing else" (195). She receives his letter. As the man has crowded out all other thoughts, so now his letter crowds out all other words, monopolizing the narrative for the next seven pages. Longer than the entire preceding chapter, it completely dispels Elizabeth's inspired performance of the day before. If Darcy was not "master enough" of himself then, he regains his mastery now. He takes back his story and, in a play for literary hegemony (to be author and critic both), tells us how to read him. The letter is a defense of his judgment, its impartiality and authority. About Jane he insists: "My investigations and decisions are not usually influenced by my hopes or fears.—I did not believe her to be indifferent because I wished it;—I believed it on impartial conviction" (197). As for Wickham, the letter documents Darcy's early suspicions and the events that proved him right. It further demonstrates the power of Darcy's moral discourse over others. Bingley has "a stronger dependence on [Darcy's] judgment than on his own" (199). Georgiana, fearing her brother's disapproval, decides not to elope after all.[17]

Only after Darcy's unabridged epistle do we get Elizabeth's response to it. She reads "with an eagerness which hardly left her power of comprehension, and from impatience of knowing what the next sentence might bring, was incapable of attending to the sense of the one before her eyes" (204). Darcy's letter saps her power to comprehend, disables her attention. It addresses her as reader only to *indispose* her as reader. At first Elizabeth protests: "This must be false! This cannot be! This must be the grossest falsehood!" (204). She rushes through the letter and puts it away forever. But the text, unrelenting, demands to be taken out, read and reread. Against the broad chest of Darcy's logic, Elizabeth beats the ineffectual fists of her own. Putting down the paper, she "weighed every circumstance with what she meant to be impartiality . . . but with little success" (205). Her interruptions, procrastinations, do nothing to stop the inexorable drive of Darcy's narrative to its foregone conclusion. In what Roland Barthes might call its "processive haste," it sweeps away Elizabeth's objections and has its way with her.[18]

In its second sentence, the letter disclaims "any intention of paining" (196). It apologizes for wounding, yet proceeds all too knowingly to wound. There is indeed a disturbing insistence on its hurtfulness, a certain pleasurable recurrence to the violence of its effect. "Here again I shall give you pain" (200), the writer unhesitatingly announces. But now Darcy's determination to inflict seems matched by Elizabeth's to be afflicted. They coincide in their enthusiasm for her humiliation: " 'How despicably have I acted!' she cried.—'I, who have prided myself on my discernment!—I, who have valued myself on my abilities! who have often disdained the generous candour of my sister, and gratified my vanity, in useless or blameable distrust.—How humiliating is this discovery!—Yet, how just a humiliation!' " (208). Vindicating Darcy's judgment and debasing Elizabeth's, disqualifying her interpretation of things in favor of his, the letter leaves her "depressed beyond any thing she had ever known before" (209).

This is the point, the dead center, on which the whole book turns. Darcy's botched proposal marks the nadir of his career, after which, launched by his letter, he rises up from infamy in an arc that approaches apotheosis. In the ensuing chapters he turns deus ex machina, exerting an implausible power to set everything straight—a power Mr. Bennet conspicuously lacks. It is Darcy who arranges for three lucky couples to be, each, the happiest couple in the world. Like the authorial persona of *Northanger Abbey,* Darcy herds us all to "perfect felicity." The nature of his unseen influence is precisely authorial. Darcy's letter proves his textual prowess. At this point he succeeds Mr. Bennet as controlling literary figure and displaces Elizabeth as her father's scion. From now on the pen, as *Persuasion's* Anne Elliot might say, is in his hands.

Soon after receiving Darcy's letter, Elizabeth meets up with Kitty and Lydia. Officer-crazy as ever, Lydia gushes on about Brighton and her plans to join the regiment there for its summer encampment. This first reference to Brighton unfolds into an unexpectedly earnest seduction plot that might seem more at home in a novel by Richardson or Burney. It is latent, however, in Lydia's very character, throwback to those too sentimental heroines so mercilessly parodied by Austen's juvenilia. That such a plot should surface now, seize center page and, brash as its heroine, hold the spotlight for more than seven chapters, is by no means accidental. The Lydia-Wickham imbroglio creates, for one thing, a situation before which Mr. Bennet will prove inadequate, Mr. Darcy heroic. Elizabeth first doubts her father regarding his decision to let Lydia go to Brighton, and she blames her father bitterly for the subsequent scandal. For Mr. Darcy, by contrast, the calamity is a chance to prove his nobility both of heart and of purse, his desire to rectify and his power to do so. The Lydia plot therefore accomplishes Elizabeth's separation from her father and her reattachment to another. It works a changing of the paternal guard.

By showcasing Darcy, the upstart plot that seems to delay and even briefly to replace Elizabeth's and Darcy's courtship serves actually to advance it. Yet there is another reason that Lydia's story, a classic case of seduction, moves into the foreground at this moment. It fills the curious gap between Elizabeth's first, private softening and her final, public surrender. I would argue that, at this juncture, Elizabeth's narrative is displaced onto that of her sister. Lydia's seduction registers an emotional drama—of coercion, capitulation, and lamentation—missing from but underlying Elizabeth's story proper. Of course Elizabeth is a foil for Lydia, one sister's wisdom held up to the other's folly. Yet there remains a sense in which their positions are scandalously similar. At one point, in response to Lydia's rudeness, Elizabeth admits, "However incapable of such coarseness of *expression* herself, the coarseness of the *sentiment* was little other than her own breast had formerly harbored" (220). And perhaps this is more generally the case: that Elizabeth and Lydia differ more in *style* than in substance. In other words, far from being an alternative plot, Lydia's is, albeit in cruder terms, a parallel one. Like the interpolated tales in that protonovel *Don Quixote*, Lydia's tale works less to distract from the central narrative than to distill its meaning. It does not defer Elizabeth's progress toward marriage so much as code the seduction and surrender on which her marriage relies.

We leave Elizabeth at the end of volume 2, chapter 13, completely, under Darcy's influence. "She could think only of her letter" (209). As the next chapter explains, "Mr. Darcy's letter, she was in a fair way of soon knowing by heart" (212). The unusual syntax here is succinct indication of the new order—Mr. Darcy and his text come pointedly before Elizabeth, would-be subject. The narrator continues, "When she remembered the style of his address, she was still full of indignation; but when she considered how unjustly she had condemned and upbraided him, her anger was turned against herself" (212). Elizabeth's reversal here, the introversion of her anger, is again revealing. Her initial judgment of Darcy is now recanted as unjust, its accusation redirected against herself.

When we first meet Elizabeth, daughter of a social critic resembling Austen herself, she is proud of her ability to know things deeply and to judge them knowingly. Yet by the end of the novel she claims only to be high-spirited. Sorry to have refused Darcy, she longs to be schooled by his better judgment: "By her ease and liveliness, his mind might have been softened, his manners improved, and from his judgment, information, and knowledge of the world, she must have received benefit of greater importance" (312). It should not surprise us to find, in an Austen novel, that judgment, information, and knowledge rate higher than ease and liveliness. While these are all Austen's professional virtues, the former are fundamental to her moral lexicon.[19] (Thus her impatience with Jane's dumb neutrality.) What may surprise and sadden us, however, is that a heroine who began so competent to judge should end up so critically disabled, so reliant for judgment on somebody else. Not that Elizabeth lapses into sheer Lydiacy. Just that by the closing chapters her eye is less bold, her tongue less sharp, the angularity—distinguishing her from the rest of her more comfortably curvaceous sex—less acute.

According to one critical truism, *Pride and Prejudice* achieves a kind of bilateral disarmament: Elizabeth gives up her prejudice, while Darcy relinquishes his pride.[20] I am arguing, however, that Darcy woos away not Elizabeth's "prejudice," but her judgment entire. While Darcy defends the impartiality of his opinion, Elizabeth confesses the partiality and thus worthlessness of hers. His representation of the world is taken to be objective, raised to the level of universality; hers is taken to be subjective—*prejudiced*—and dismissed. True, Elizabeth was wrong about Wickham. But was she really that wrong about Darcy? He may warm up a bit, and his integrity is rightly affirmed, yet the fact remains that he is hardly less arrogant than Elizabeth at first supposed. Her comment to Fitzwilliam can stand: "I do not know any body who seems more to enjoy the power of doing what he likes than Mr. Darcy" (183).

And is Darcy's own record of accuracy much better? His judgment of Jane is just as mistaken, and as partial, as Elizabeth's of Wickham. Yet his credibility remains intact. Finally admitting to having misinterpreted Jane, Darcy explains that he was corrected not by Elizabeth, but by his own subsequent observations (371). On the basis of his new appraisal he readvises the ever-pliant Bingley. His error, far from disqualifying him to judge, only qualifies him to judge again. Elizabeth's error, on the other hand, is irreparably discrediting. What happens in *Pride and Prejudice* is not that an essentially prejudiced character finally sees the error of her ways. Rather, a character initially presented as reliable, who gains our and Austen's respect precisely for her clear-sightedness, is ultimately represented as prejudiced. The real drama lies not in the heroine's "awakening" to her true identity, but in the text's reidentification of her.

If Elizabeth does not overcome her "prejudice," neither does Darcy abandon his pride. Early in the book Elizabeth declares, "I could easily forgive *his* pride, if he had not mortified *mine*" (20). Yet by the last volume her feelings have changed considerably: "They owed the restoration of Lydia, her character, every thing to him. Oh! how heartily did she grieve over every ungracious sensation she had ever encouraged, every saucy speech she had ever directed towards him. For herself she was humbled; but she was proud of him" (326–27). Elizabeth and Darcy begin skeptical of each other, proud of themselves, and they reach a connubial consensus that is altogether different: at last both are skeptical of her, both proud of him.

But wait. Does not Darcy make a pretty speech to his bride confessing, "By you, I was properly humbled" (369)? Here it is useful to see how the text itself defines "pride," and how this definition relates to Mr. Darcy. The bookish Mary—another figure for Austen, if a self-mocking one—distinguishes "pride" from "vanity": "Pride relates more to our opinion of ourselves, vanity to what we would have others think of us" (20). As for Darcy, Charlotte Lucas suggests that his pride is excusable: "One cannot wonder that so very fine a young man, with family, fortune, every thing in his favor, should think highly of himself. If I may so express it, he has a *right* to be proud" (20). A younger Lucas puts it more bluntly: "If I were as rich as Mr. Darcy . . . I should not care how proud I was. I would keep a pack of foxhounds, and drink a bottle of wine every day" (20). The practical Lucases have a point. Darcy's richness gives him if not a "right," then a careless readiness to be proud. A man in his social position need not consider any opinion but his own. Darcy is proud because he does not have to be vain—others' opinions do not affect him. His pride, we might say, comes with the territory. It is less a psychological attribute than a social one, and as such it is only heightened by Darcy's enhanced status—as husband, hero, and authorial figure—in *Pride and Prejudice's* last act.

Of course we continue to admire Elizabeth. She may care for Darcy's regard, but she is not so utterly enslaved by it as Miss Bingley. She may hesitate to laugh at Darcy, but she does show Georgiana that a wife may take (some) liberties. We admire her because she is not Charlotte, because she is not Lydia. I am insisting, however, that Elizabeth is a better friend to Charlotte, a closer sister to Lydia—that her story runs more parallel to theirs—than previous readings have indicated. The three women live in the same town, share the same gossip, attend the same balls—why, as some critics have claimed, should Elizabeth alone be above the social decree?[21] There are, in Elizabeth's marriage, elements both of crass practicality and of coercion. Elizabeth is appalled by Charlotte's pragmatism, and yet, choosing Darcy over Wickham, she is herself beguiled by the entrepreneurial marriage plot.[22] If she is embarrassed by her personal connection to Lydia, she is also implicated by the formal intersection of their plots: in the course of the novel she loses not her virginity but her authority.

Elizabeth marries a decent man and a large estate, but at a certain cost. Though she may stretch the marriage contract, it binds her nonetheless to a paternalistic noble whose extensive power is explicitly ambiguous: "How much of pleasure *or pain* it was in his power to bestow!—How much of good *or evil* must be done by him!" (250–51, emphasis added). If Mr. Bennet embodies the post-Enlightenment, modified patriarch, Mr. Darcy harks back to an earlier type—before fathers were curbed by Lockean principles, before aristocrats began to feel the crunch. Darcy disempowers Elizabeth if only because of the positions they each occupy in the social schema: because he is a Darcy and she is a Bennet, because he is a man and she is his wife. If Mr. Bennet permits Elizabeth to fill the role of "son," she marries another father figure only to revert, in terms of privilege, to "daughter."

In *Pride and Prejudice,* Austen shows us an intelligent girl largely in the grasp of a complex mechanism whose interests are not hers. She does this, I think, less in resignation than in protest; here, as in *Northanger Abbey,* Austen is concerned to ironize girls and novels that hasten to the altar for conclusive happiness.[23] I should stress, however, that my purpose in outlining a trajectory of humiliation has been not to displace but to complexify the reading that takes for granted connubial bliss. We can experience the ending as euphoric (most readers do) and still recognize those aspects of the novel working strenuously against this. I want, as Gilbert and Gubar suggest, to appreciate the doubleness that characterizes the work of nineteenth-century women writers, the tension between conventionality and subversion. This tension is, on the one hand, produced by an author who knows what she is doing, whose art is a deliberate shaping, whose ironic tendencies were manifest at fifteen. To ignore any such intentionality is to slight Austen's mastery. But the ideological slipperiness of *Pride and Prejudice* is, on the other hand, finally a matter of the text's own logic, its own legibility. Beyond any fully conscious intention on Austen's part, a pattern of duplicity is at work in the narrative itself, with a consistency amounting to design.

As I have argued, part of this novel's design is to reveal a system of homosocial relations underlying the institution of heterosexuality. Anticipating Claude Lévi-Strauss, Gayle Rubin, and Eve Sedgwick, it recognizes in marriage a displacement of the father-daughter bond by a bond between fathers. Elizabeth's humiliation has everything to do with transactions between various fathers that take place behind her back, over her head, and apart from, if not against, her will. I want to close by offering some further support for this view.

By the end of the book, Mr. Bennet's paternal role has been assumed by his brother-in-law, Mr. Gardiner. Mr. Gardiner, though "gentleman*like,*" is not technically a gentleman. Living by trade "and within view of his own warehouses" (139), he represents, more than Mr. Bennet, the rising middle class. No wonder Elizabeth fears that Darcy will rebuff him, unkind as Darcy has been toward her bourgeois relations. She is quite unprepared for Darcy's civility to Gardiner, and for the apparent power of fishing to overcome class differences. Perhaps their shared fondness for Elizabeth, their lengthy haggle over Lydia, as well as their equal passion for trout, serve to reinforce the social/economic advantages of a Darcy-Gardiner alliance. They become, in any case, suggestively close. The very last paragraph of the novel informs us that: "With the Gardiners, they were always on the most intimate terms. Darcy, as well as Elizabeth, really loved them; and they were both ever sensible of the warmest gratitude towards the persons who, by bringing her into Derbyshire, had been the means of uniting them" (388).

At first this seems a peculiarly insignificant note on which to end. On second glance it appears to confirm the notion I have had: that just as the Gardiners have been the means of uniting Darcy and Elizabeth, so Elizabeth has been the means of uniting Mr. Darcy and Mr. Gardiner. *Pride and Prejudice* attains a satisfying unity not only between a man and a woman, but also between two men. Austen's novel accomplishes an intercourse not merely personal, but social—as much a marriage of two classes as a marriage of true minds.

Notes

1. My title and my argument are a turn on Mark Schorer's "The Humiliation of Emma Woodhouse" (1959), in *Jane Austen: A Collection of Critical Essays,* ed. Ian Watt (Englewood Cliffs, N.J.: Prentice-Hall, 1963), 98–111. Here he remarks: "The diminution of Emma in the social scene, her reduction to her proper place . . . is very beautiful" (102).

2. See Lawrence Stone, *The Family, Sex and Marriage in England: 1500–1800* (New York: Harper and Row, 1977), 239–58.

3. Jay Fliegelman, *Prodigals and Pilgrims: The American Revolution Against Patriarchal Authority* (Cambridge: Cambridge University Press, 1982), 13. See Beth Kowaleski-Wallace's discussion of the Lockean father in "Milton's Daughters: The Education of Eighteenth-Century Women Writers," *Feminist Studies* 12, no. 2 (1986): 275–95.

4. Jane Austen, *Pride and Prejudice* (1813), ed. R. W. Chapman, 3rd edition (Oxford: Oxford University Press, 1932), 6. Future references are to this edition.

5. Lewes's observation is cited by Judith O'Neill in her introduction to *Critics on Jane Austen: Readings in Literary Criticism,* ed. Judith O'Neill (London: George Allen, 1970), 8.

6. See Ian Watt, *The Rise of the Novel* (Berkeley: University of California Press, 1957), 153.

7. Karen Horney, "The Flight from Womanhood: The Masculinity Complex in Women as Viewed by Men and by Women" (1926), in *Psychoanalysis and Women,* ed. Jean Baker Miller (New York: Penguin Books, 1973), 19.

8. For a useful recapitulation of Freud on fathers and daughters, see Nancy Chodorow, *The Reproduction of Mothering: Psychoanalysis and the Sociology of Gender* (Berkeley: University of California Press, 1978), 94, 114–16.

9. Adrienne Rich, "Compulsory Heterosexuality and Lesbian Existence" (1980), in *Powers of Desire: The Politics of Sexuality,* eds. Ann Snitow, Christine Stansell, and Sharon Thompson (New York: Monthly Review, 1983), 177–205.

10. See, for example, Lynda E. Boose, "The Father and the Bride in Shakespeare," *PMLA* 97, no. 3 (1982): 325–47. According to Boose, King Lear's faux pas is his unwillingness to release Cordelia—he "casts her away not to let her go but to prevent her from going" (333)—thereby obstructing the ritual process of her marriage to France.

11. In these terms, Emma's conclusion may have certain advantages for its heroine. It is true that Emma defers to Knightley's worldview much as Elizabeth does to Darcy's. But remaining under her father's roof may preserve some of the authority she has had, in his household and the community, as Mr. Woodhouse's daughter.

12. Claude Lévi-Strauss, *The Elementary Structures of Kinship* (1949) (Boston: Beacon, 1969), 61.

13. Mary Poovey, *The Proper Lady and the Woman Writer: Ideology as Style in the Works of Mary Wollstonecraft, Mary Shelley, and Jane Austen* (Chicago: University of Chicago Press, 1984), 11.

14. See Terry Eagleton, *The Rape of Clarissa: Writing, Sexuality and Class Struggle in Samuel Richardson* (Minneapolis: University of Minnesota Press, 1982), 15.

15. Gayle Rubin, "The Traffic in Women: Notes on the 'Political Economy' of Sex," in *Toward an Anthropology of Women,* ed. Rayna R. Reiter (New York: Monthly Review, 1975), 172.

16. Eve Kosofsky Sedgwick, *Between Men: English Literature and Male Homosocial Desire* (New York: Columbia University Press, 1985).

17. Georgiana's position as "daughter" in relation to Darcy contributes to our sense of him as "paternal," as does his fatherly advice to Bingley.

18. Roland Barthes, *The Pleasure of the Text,* trans. Richard Miller (New York: Hill and Wang, 1975), 12.

19. See Austen's famous defense of the novel as a "work in which the greatest powers of the mind are displayed . . . the most thorough knowledge of human nature . . . the liveliest effusions of wit and humour" (*Northanger Abbey*, 1818, ed. R. W. Chapman, 3rd edition [Oxford: Oxford University Press, 1933], 38).

20. John Halperin's recent biography, *The Life of Jane Austen* (Baltimore: Johns Hopkins University Press, 1984) is notably complacent toward this formulation: "It is unnecessary to rehearse again the process by which Darcy's pride is humbled and Elizabeth's prejudice exposed—'*your* defect is a propensity to hate every body,' she tells him early in the novel; 'And ıyours . . . is wilfully to misunderstand them,' he replies" (70).

21. I have in mind D. W. Harding and Marvin Mudrick, old guard of Austen criticism's "subversive school" (as opposed to Alistair Duckworth, Marilyn Butler, et al., who see Austen as a social conservative): D. W. Harding, "Regulated Hatred: An Aspect of the Work of Jane Austen," *Scrutiny* 8 (1940): 346–62; Marvin Mudrick, *Jane Austen: Irony as Defense and Discovery* (Princeton: Princeton University Press, 1952); Alistair M. Duckworth, *The Improvement of the Estate: A Study of Jane Austen's Novels* (Baltimore: Johns Hopkins University Press, 1971); Marilyn Butler, *Jane Austen and the War of Ideas* (Oxford: Clarendon Press, 1975). While I am taking Harding's and Mudrick's side, I disagree with their view that Austen challenges her society by allowing Elizabeth somehow to transcend it, that Elizabeth represents the "free individual." *Pride and Prejudice* is not, in my opinion, about the heroine's independence of the social context; it is about her inextricability from it.

22. See Karen Newman, "Can This Marriage Be Saved: Jane Austen Makes Sense of an Ending," *ELH* 50, no. 4 (1983): 693–710. Newman points out that critics as early as Sir Walter Scott have noticed Elizabeth's fascination with Pemberly: "Austen is at pains from early in the novel to show us Elizabeth's response to Darcy's wealth" (698). It is interesting that Hollywood, of venal habits and puritanical tastes, should recognize and be uneasy with Elizabeth's suspicious position as Austen wrote it. In the 1940 film version of *Pride and Prejudice*, Lady Catherine threatens to cut Darcy out of her will if he goes ahead and marries a Bennet. Elizabeth proves her romantic integrity by vowing to marry him anyway. Needless to say, Austen conspicuously chose *not* to test Elizabeth in such a manner.

23. In *The Madwoman in the Attic: The Woman Writer and the Nineteenth-Century Literary Imagination* (New Haven: Yale University Press, 1979), Gilbert and Gubar refer us to Lloyd W. Brown (*Bits of Ivory: Narrative Techniques in Jane Austen's Fiction* [Baton Rouge: Louisiana State Press, 1973]) for "the most sustained discussion of Austen's ironic undercutting of her own endings" (667). Karen Newman also sees the happy ending in Austen as parodic: despite its comic effect, there remain "unresolved

contradictions between romantic and materialistic notions of marriage" (695). The idea of a fairy-tale union is falsified by Austen's clairvoyance about why women need to marry. My reading accords a good deal with Newman's, though I am less confident than she that Austen's heroines manage nevertheless to "live powerfully within the limits imposed by ideology" (705).

10   ## "Dying Between Two Laws"

Girl Heroines, Their Gods, and Their Fathers in Uncle Tom's Cabin *and the* Elsie Dinsmore *Series*

Helena Michie

To write about Harriet Beecher Stowe's *Uncle Tom's Cabin* and Martha Finley's series for children, the *Elsie Dinsmore* books—and especially to write about them in relation to each other—is to invoke the specter of the wilderness outside the American canon.[1] *Uncle Tom's Cabin* is precariously perched between the canon and the wilderness; the *Elsie* books, unknown except for a faint infamy that depends largely on the psychopathology of one scene from the first book,[2] have no place even in the more capacious and responsive canon of the late 1980s. What brings *Uncle Tom's Cabin* and the *Elsie* books together in this reading is precisely what makes *Uncle Tom's* inclusion in the canon so problematical: like the *Elsie* books it depends on the emotional effect generated by the attenuated death scenes of an angelic girl-heroine; like the *Elsie* books it can and has been read as manipulative, melodramatic, and sentimental. In fact, little Eva's death scene has become, for detractors of the novel, a synecdoche for its nonliterariness, a code word for all that is wrong in this novel and "sentimental fiction" in general.[3]

The sentimental, of course, occupies a vexed and gendered space in American literary criticism. Even defenses of the sentimental novel typically begin with preemptive apologies or confessions.[4] I would argue that critical unease with sentimentality has to do precisely with *dis*ease, with an alignment of the sentimental with the body, its disturbances (illness, pain, hunger), and its excesses (tears, fevers, tantrums). Bodily anxiety has even infected critical language about the genre: Herbert Ross Brown begins his classic study of the domestic novel by invoking its "feverish sentiment," while Hannah Webster Foster attests to the communicable nature of that fever by warning that "An American novel is such a moral, sentimental thing, that it is enough to give one the vapors to read one."[5] The roots of the term "sentiment," in "sensation or physical feeling," betray the connection between sentimentality and the corporeal. In American literature at least the sentimental is additionally gendered female; it is women writers who reproduce fevers in their characters and produce vapors in their readers. In *Uncle Tom,* the *Elsie* books, and countless other novels by women of the period, it is the woman or the little girl whose deathbed we as readers are invited—or forced—to attend.

It is easy to slip into a reading of *Uncle Tom's Cabin* and the *Elsie Dinsmore* series in which Eva and Elsie represent the body and, by extension, a constellation of melodramatic and sentimental impulses that privilege the body over the word, the corporeal over the literary. Reducing the two heroines to the body, however, ignores their complex and vital relation to verbal structures: the "Little Eva" subplot in *Uncle Tom* and Elsie's apparent death in *Elsie's Holidays* have as much to do with promises, contracts, quotations, and laws as they do with disease. Although their dying bodies are rendered visually by the texts in which they appear, and although characters and readers alike repeatedly focus on Eva and Elsie's faces and bodies, both heroines deal explicitly and sagaciously in words. Eva's body, feeble and transparent as it is, mediates painfully between two predominantly verbal structures: the law of God and the law of the land; Elsie's, equally frail, mediates between the law of the two figures she repeatedly contrasts as her earthly and heavenly fathers.

Both *Uncle Tom's Cabin* and the *Elsie* books link the verbal and the paternal by their insistence on the importance of law: Eva struggles to change the law of the land by converting her father to Christianity and thus to abolition, while Elsie works to convert her authoritarian and secular father to the higher law of Christianity. Both seek desperately, through the pathos of their bodies and the power of their words, to align the laws of their earthly and heavenly fathers. Despite the Lacanian resonance of the connection between the father and the law, the relations between father and daughter in these texts are not simply oedipal. Each girl has two competing fathers who embody two competing laws; each comes to a sense of identity and power by constructing and manipulating the struggle between them for the daughter's love and obedience.

This chapter focuses on the relationships between the two dying girl-heroines of *Uncle Tom's Cabin* and the *Elsie* series with their fathers and with paternal law as a way into the vexed issue of the novels' relation to language. While *Uncle Tom's Cabin* has recently been the subject of much critical scrutiny and the *Elsie* books have almost never been seriously considered from a literary point of view, both suffer from a criticism of bodily anxiety that dismisses their often complex and deeply political renderings of the relation between language and power. While the *Elsie* series is psychodynamically rawer—Elsie and her father, for instance, repeatedly exchange "burning kisses"—it, like *Uncle Tom's Cabin,* makes a series of astute political and psychological assumptions in figuring moral change as an oedipal battle over words. While the *Elsie* books are more openly fantastical—Elsie is mysteriously resurrected after appearing to die in the second book of the series—both participate in a fantasy of female potency that unites body and word in the struggle against the earthly father and the power he represents.

The *Elsie* series is structured by a series of encounters between fathers and daughters; Elsie's own life is shaped by three frequently competing father figures: God, her "real" father, and her husband, Mr. Travilla, who is her father's contemporary and best friend. The first two books, which take Elsie through the middle years of childhood, dramatically pit her moral but irreligious father against God. As the series opens Elsie already "belongs" to Jesus, taking advantage of his "precious promise" to be "a father to the fatherless." She has never seen her biological father, who has avoided her as the inadvertent cause of her mother's death in childbirth. Horace Dinsmore's entry upon the textual scene and into Elsie's life is marked by a series of injunctions and proscriptions. In the psychodynamically charged ethics of the series, they constitute the authority and position of "father." Almost from his first encounter with Elsie, Dinsmore begins the work of regulating her diet, her dress, her lessons, and her associates. His rules—most of which center on the regulation and deployment of his daughter's body—quite literally become Elsie's law: Dinsmore himself repeatedly compares his commands and the system of authority in which they are enmeshed to "the laws of the Medes and the Persians which altereth not."[6]

The verbal structure of Dinsmore's authority over Elsie is revealed in the self-referential nature of many of his rules. One of Dinsmore's first commands to Elsie is really a metacommand: that she not question anything he tells her to do. Each injunction must be taken literally; there is no room for Elsie to speculate upon the reason or the origin of the law. When, for example, Elsie asks her father whether she can play jack-stones after he has explicitly forbidden her to, he locks her in a closet. Elsie has only asked a second time because she thinks her father's objection to the game is that it is played on the floor; she wants to know whether he will let her play it on the table. It is only after her punishment in the closet that he decides to give any explanation: his dislike of Elsie sitting on the floor is only one reason why he forbids jack-stones; it also enlarges the knuckles of the hands.

In any case, the reason is not, from the point of view of Elsie's obligation to him, important. He insists on the principle of perfect obedience: "It is very strange . . . that you cannot learn not to ask to do what I have forbidden. I shall have to punish you every time you do it; for you *must* learn that no *means no,* and that you are never to coax or tease after papa has once said it. I love my little girl very dearly, and want to do all I can to make her happy, but I must have her entirely submissive and obedient to me" (*Elsie's Holidays,* 23).

Dinsmore's insistence on the power of his word to represent and to shape reality, his axiomatic "no means no," is also a warning to Elsie that she has no interpretive power within the closed system that is his law. Dinsmore's refusal to allow his daughter the freedom to interpret stands in direct contrast to Elsie's Protestant biblical hermeneutics, which allow—indeed command—all persons to read and interpret the Bible for themselves. God's law, then, despite its severity, gives Elsie a power and a freedom denied to her within the system of rules produced and articulated by her earthly father.

For Dinsmore paternal law is an expression of paternal love; many of his rules—including the one forbidding Elsie to play jack-stones—are framed as attempts to protect against the disfigurement of his daughter's body. The legal trope of protection allows Dinsmore a benign rhetorical space in which he can safely articulate impulses of appropriation, sadism, and desire. Perhaps the most vivid and complex example of Dinsmore's problematic use of protectionism is in his remarkable dialogue with Lucy Carrington, a young friend of Elsie's, who asks Elsie to give her one of her curls as a memento. Dinsmore interrupts the conversation between the two girls to say: "No, Miss Lucy . . . you can't have one of my curls; I can't spare it" (*Elsie's Holidays,* ii). When Lucy responds that she has asked for one of Elsie's curls, he becomes quite arch: " 'I beg your pardon, Miss Lucy, if my ears deceived me . . . but I was quite certain I heard you asking for one of my curls. Perhaps, though, you are not aware that my curls grow on two heads . . . Elsie doesn't own any . . . they all belong to me. I let her wear them, to be sure, but that is all; she has no right to give them away' " (*Elsie's Holidays,* ii).

In declaring his ownership of Elsie's curls, Dinsmore is not only referring to the legal fiction that makes Elsie's body his; he is actually inhabiting her body, breaking down and rendering permeable the physical barriers between himself and his daughter. This attempt to control Elsie by—legally speaking—penetrating her body, is particularly ironic here, since his injunction against Elsie's cutting off her curls is aimed at preserving the wholeness of her body and her beauty. While it is irresistible to read the curl Miltonically and to see in Dinsmore's anxieties about the dissemination of his daughter's body and attempt to preserve and somehow to possess her virginity, what concerns me here is the power of what Lacan would call the legal fiction of paternity to contain, transform, and to appropriate the female body. Dinsmore is quite aware of the fictional—that is to say, legal—nature of his claim to have curls that grow on two heads; the absurdity of such a contention in a man so strictly truthful and so rarely playful only underscores the power of a system of laws that makes that claim true and actionable.

Despite Elsie's almost pathological submissiveness to her father's law, his authority over her body extends only to what Elsie defines for herself as "earthly" matters. Elsie also lives under the jurisdiction of another law, another, more powerful Father, whose capitalized name betrays a disruptive textual and psychological presence. At two crucial points in the first two books Elsie refuses to obey her father by doing what she considers to be breaking the Sabbath. The first, infamous, piano episode, where Elsie refuses to play a secular song to her father on Sunday, ends with her falling off the piano stool, striking her head on the bench, and bloodying her curls. The second, far more prolonged, conflict that extends almost the whole length of *Elsie's Holidays at Rose-lands*, begins, also on a Sunday, with Elsie's refusal to read a certain book to her sick father. This time Dinsmore is determined to "break her will"; after threatening her with his own death, he "banishes" her "from his arms," cuts off her mail, sends her permanently to her room, takes away her beloved Mammy and all her reading material except her school books and her mother's Bible, leaves her behind while he travels indefinitely in the North, and, finally, threatens to send her to a convent.

Dinsmore's punishments take a dramatic toll on Elsie's physical health; she grows visibly paler and thinner until she collapses into delirium under the specter of enforced Catholicism. From the beginning of her conflict with her father, characters within the novel and readers of it are invited by Elsie's vivid decline to gaze at her body and to read its symptoms. Not surprisingly, Dinsmore combats the pathos of Elsie's body against the strength of his own word; he casts each punishment as a contract from which he cannot go back. Elsie's body also tempts him with the susceptibility of his own. When he leaves her to go North, Elsie's agony and her physicality tempt him to give way, but he cannot:

"Papa, dear, *dear* papa, kiss me once before you go; just *once*, papa; perhaps you may never come back—perhaps I may die. Oh, papa, papa! will you

go away without kissing me?—me, your own little daughter that you used
to love so dearly? Oh, papa, my heart will break!"

His own eyes filled with tears, and he stooped as if to give her the coveted
caress, but hastily drawing back again, said with much of his accustomed
sternness—

"No, Elsie, I cannot break my word; and if you are determined to break
your own heart and mine by your stubbornness, on your own head be the
consequences." (*Elsie's Holidays*, 113)

Elsie's repeated demands for kisses, for the language of the body
as a substitute for and a contravention of her father's word, have
been successful up to this point; some of the most passionate scenes
in the book come from this contradiction between the letter and
the body when Dinsmore, moved out of his sternness, embraces
Elsie only to push her away again. Just before the scene quoted
above, however, Dinsmore outlawed his own caresses, bringing his
own body under the jurisdiction of his word. Dismore's use of the
verb "break" first for his word and then for both his and Elsie's
hearts, betrays Dinsmore's need for the body and the word to
operate under the same (linguistic) law: that law he inscribes so
painfully on his daughter's body and his own.

One could make a compelling argument here that the conflict
between Elsie and her father is a conflict *between* the body and the
law. In this reading, Elsie becomes an embodiment of Christian
law, her life an imitation rather than an interpretation of Christ. At
the end of the conflict, when Elsie—apparently—dies of the brain
fever she has contracted, we can see her "corpse" as an empty and
poignant trace of the female body sacrificed to paternal rule. While
Elsie's body, its absent and then barely present pulse, are indeed at
the center of the scene that perpetrates Dinsmore's conversion, we
cannot afford to ignore the presence, at the "deathbed," of two
documents: Elsie's last letter to her father, and her Bible.

Elsie's letter, containing, among other things, her will and one
of her curls, is a remarkably articulate production for an eight-year-
old who is suffering from hallucinations, and who, earlier in the
book, worried about disgracing her father with her poor punctua-
tion and spelling. Finley makes no attempt at realism in the grammar
of this letter; it is written as it were in the grammar of the law
that will ultimately produce Dinsmore's conversion—in a language

whose power lies in its source beyond the grave. The letter, a powerful defense of Elsie's apparent "willfulness," also acts as a will; in bequeathing her mother's Bible to her father and begging him to read it, Elsie both expresses her will for the first time, and makes it one with God's. The curl acts as a sign that madness and death have put her beyond the law of her earthly father (she claims later that she did not know what she was doing when she cut it off), while the letter and the Bible assert her allegiance to a law more powerful than any Dinsmore can command.

Curl, letter, will, and Bible conjoin the power of the verbal and of the corporeal and make Elsie's death into a spectacle of the word as well as of the body. Elsie's illness forces Dinsmore to study the book by whose authority she lived and died: "he could not at first trust himself even to look at the little volume that had been so constantly in his darling's hands, that it seemed almost a part of herself. . . . Hour after hour he sat there reading that little book; at first interested only because of its associations with her . . . but at length beginning to feel the importance of its teachings" (*Elsie's Holidays,* 163). The metonymic relation between body and book compels Dinsmore to study God's word. Elsie's body leads him to the word; it is necessary but not sufficient in Dinsmore's abandonment of his own law in favor of God's.

If the apparently binary conflict between body and law can be complicated by a careful reading of the relationship between Elsie's body and textuality, the opposition between earthly and heavenly fathers can also be elaborated by an addition of a third, complicating, term. Elsie's twin powers of embodiment and interpretation can be read back upon a figure seemingly repressed by the narrative of *Elsie's Holidays:* she is, significantly, another Elsie, Horace's dead wife and Elsie's mother. Elsie is heiress not only to her mother's fortune, but to her face, her figure, and her Bible. Elsie's access to God occurs literally through her mother's body and her mother's word; in embodying Christ she also embodies her mother, and in reading his word she reads her mother's Bible.

Elsie's similarity to her mother might help to explain Dinsmore's resistance to his daughter's piety. Dinsmore married the first Elsie against the wishes of his father who used all the tricks of melodrama, including intercepting their letters and planting false information, to make the two lovers believe that they had deserted each other. Horace's gullibility and his subsequent neglect of his wife, the text suggests, had as much to do with her death as Elsie's birth. His daughter's face and piety, so closely reminiscent of his dead wife's, must have reminded Dinsmore of a time when his word was *not* law, when he was forced to obey the law of his own father. It is fitting that the oedipal rivalry between Horace and his father should be transferred and transcribed onto the heavenly father whose law was infinitely more powerful than the rules of either father or son. In replicating the maternal body and the maternal discourse, Elsie must have reminded Horace of his sexual and legal failures—his inability, for example, to make the legal fiction of his marriage into an emotional reality. The metaphoric chain, which allows Elsie to stand for her mother and both of them to stand for God, is, as we shall see in the discussion of *Uncle Tom's Cabin,* in keeping with a nineteenth-century tradition that recast God in a maternal mold; the battle between heavenly and earthly fathers in the *Elsie* series is also a battle between father and mother, father and daughter.

It is not easy to decide, at the end of *Elsie's Holidays,* who has "won" the battle for power between Elsie and her father. While one can easily read Elsie's "death" as a fantasy of female revenge, her survival, strangely enough, mitigates that victory. Although Dinsmore apologizes for what he calls the "abuse" of his "authority," it is quite clear that, after his conversion, it is he who interprets biblical passages for himself and his daughter, he who asserts his authority to interpret the word. Perhaps more importantly, after Elsie's recovery, he reappropriates Elsie's Bible—which she has apparently reclaimed during her recovery—by asking for it as a Christmas present. For the first time, the series records what might be read as an ungenerous hesitation on Elsie's part:

A slight shade had come over the little girl's face, and she sat for a moment apparently deep in thought; then, looking up lovingly into his face, she replied, "I love it very much, papa, and I don't know whether any other Bible could ever seem *quite* the same to me—it was mamma's, you know— and it has been with me in all my troubles, and I don't think I would be quite willing to give it to anybody else; but I am glad to give it to you, my own dear, dear, papa!" and she threw her arms around his neck. (*Elsie's Holidays,* 204)

In Dinsmore's crucial demand—carefully framed this time as a request because, as he puts it, "I like to feel that you have some rights of property"—Elsie's earthly father literally appropriates the words of both mother and heavenly father. Elsie must be content with a new Bible, unmarked by the story of her own and her mother's bitter experiences. The new Bible represents a sort of second New Testament in which Elsie as redeemer has initiated a world in which the law of the heavenly and earthly father are one, but in which she has no authoritative place.

If we look for the sources of Elsie's power after her father's conversion, they seem to lie, appropriately enough, in her corporeal and verbal fecundity—in her relation to her own maternity. Elsie's physical fertility is obsessively documented by the series: she has eight children, innumerable grandchildren, and any number of acquaintances whom she appropriates as family. She is also an inveterate producer of stories; not only are there twenty-eight books that bear her name in their titles, but almost all the books depict her as a teller of stories from the Bible, from American history, or from her own life. Interestingly, the story she is most frequently asked to tell is the story of *Elsie's Holidays at Roselands.*

Most important of Elsie's reproductive feats is the replication—with benign modifications—of her father. In an inverted creation fantasy that might rival Adam's, Elsie seems consistently to be producing fathers. As a child, abandoned by Dinsmore, she created a heavenly father in his image; when her father banished her from him during their religious conflict she renewed her acquaintance with a paternal God. Finally, after an abortive relationship with a fortune hunter from whom Dinsmore rescued her, she chose as her husband her father's best friend. Lacan, in explaining how the oedipal conflict could flourish even in the absence of a literal father, coined the term "paternal metaphor" to describe the ever-present psychic *position* of "father." Elsie, in her repeated production of names and faces to fill this otherwise empty position, has harnessed the power of the paternal metaphor.

While the few other critics of the *Elsie* series tend to see her marriage to Travilla as the ultimate capitulation to Dinsmore, I prefer to see it as the imaginative act of revenge and subversion of someone who has relatively few options to exercise. By choosing ıher father's best friend as her husband, Elsie both forestalls her father's ability to object to this evidence of her sexuality and establishes herself as more important to Travilla than Dinsmore can ever be. She can also, from the safety of the paternal idiom, celebrate the eroticism of her union with Travilla; when, for instance, Dinsmore looks displeased when Elsie returns from her honeymoon calling her husband by his first name, Elsie responds with a magnificent sadism by contending both that Travilla "ordered" her to do so, and that he declared it was the only command he would ever give her. Elsie speaks simultaneously here from her father's emotional lexicon of command, and from an eroticized lexicon of persuasion and intimacy; she can do all this because the structuring paternal metaphor is well in place. Elsie is allowed to marry Travilla because he is like a father, but the very difference in their ages makes the use of his first name a sign of the erotic, a sign that he is not really Elsie's father.

Travilla, of course, does not escape punishment in the series. During the honeymoon, he is shot at by the man whom Elsie almost married, relatively early in the marriage he is shot and almost killed by his infant son, and five books into the series he dies of an undiagnosed and painful disease. It is easy to see Travilla's purpose in the *Elsie* books as a necessary but uninteresting participant in the creation of generations of Elsies; it is Elsie's name, and not Travilla's, that survives not only as part of the title of each book in the series, but also in the endless grandchildren, great-grandchildren, nieces and half-relations named Elsie with whom the series is increasingly populated. It is also possible to work out Travilla's death as a displacement of oedipal rage; if she cannot destroy either her earthly or heavenly fathers, if she cannot rid herself of their law(s), Elsie— or at any rate, Finley—can revenge herself on the man with no law: the husband who cannot issue a command. After Travilla's death Elsie returns almost completely to her father's house; with the help of Travilla, Elsie can make sure she returns as a namer of generations.

Elsie's reproductive and metaphoric facility, which allows for the almost infinite repetition of paternal relationships and the production of little Elsies throughout the series, is both verbal and corporeal in origin. Although Elsie never gets to "tell her story" in the familiar feminist sense of the term, she is clearly the principle of generation and reiteration upon which the series is based. Elsie's name supercedes Dinsmore's as the series continues; after the series-opening *Elsie Dinsmore,* only Elsie's "Christian" name appears in any book title. After the fourth book she becomes, of course, Elsie Travilla, with the power to name her first child after herself. Although Elsie consistently maintains that she will obey her father all her life, and although she continues to love and revere him throughout the series, it is the name she and her mother share that she carries with her as her story unfolds. If, in dying in the second book she might seem to have had the last word, in dying and then living again, the last word joins the living body that will carry Elsie triumphantly through the rest of the series into heaven.

There is, of course, an almost eerie series of parallels between Elsie and Eva. Eva is also a figure of embodiment; she has the face and form not of her own but of St. Clare's pious and beautiful mother. Like Elsie, Eva draws her spiritual authority from a heavenly father, who in turn seems to impregnate her child's body with spiritual meaning; we gaze at Eva's body for the symptoms of truth and illness it offers, just as we do with Elsie's. Elsie and Eva actually look alike, from their childlike white-robed forms to their golden brown curls; even more importantly, their reiterative bodily gestures—their continual occupation of their father's knees, their cutting off of their curls as deathbed legacies—mark them as corporeal/incorporeal doubles.

There are, of course, also important structural differences, most of which can be accounted for by the different generic and political ambitions of the novels. As children's books, the *Elsie* novels can operate more flamboyantly as fantasy; paradoxically, of course, the very code "children's book" allows them, allows Elsie, an eroticism denied heroines in mainstream women's literature. It is only, strangely enough, in a children's book that a dying angel can survive and grow up.

The genre of the *Elsie* books also protects them from the political; Eva's life and death invoke a new level of law, a movement out of the family and into the question of slavery. Finley manages to repress almost all political conflict over slavery, even while dealing with great emotion and specificity with the events of the Civil War, which is represented merely as a struggle between the Union and the South over secession. Elsie, her father, and husband, who are all Unionists, spend the duration of the war with their immediate families in Europe: news of the war comes in family letters and is registered as a series of family deaths. Even when the slavery issue is briefly raised with reference to Elsie and Dinsmore's plantations, it is settled immediately by the decision of all the slaves to remain. The wages paid to the slaves, as Elsie points out, do not make a dent in her fortune. Throughout the rest of the series the plantation structure— depicted predictably in a series of familial metaphors—remains intact.

The domestic idiom is equally capacious but very different in the appropriately named *Uncle Tom's Cabin*. Stowe's remark that she is addressing herself to an audience of mothers *as* a mother is of course quite famous; the lexicon of family is equally powerful within the novel that begins its presentation of the evils of slavery by depicting its effects on the black family, continues by working out the question of slavery in the white community through the relationship between Eva and her father, and ends with a series of improbable family reunions among runaway blacks in Canada. There is, however, an important difference between the way the family and the world connect in *Uncle Tom* and the *Elsie* series; structurally, the *Elsie* books reproduce the family as a barrier against the world. If the family gets larger and larger as the series progresses, it is to provide Finley with a safe space of fantasy in which marriages, deaths, and subplots can occur. By the end of the series weddings of four hundred persons are still "family gatherings"; an entire fictional world of characters protected by Elsie's name and money has been created by a collaboration between Finley and her heroine.

The family idiom in *Uncle Tom's Cabin*, on the other hand, allows precisely for the movement of Stowe and Eva into the political space usually constituted as being *outside* the family. Stowe's metaphor of motherhood allows her a safe and feminine entrance into political concerns; Eva's declaration that she would rather live on a big plantation down South than a farm in Vermont, because the community of a plantation "makes so many more round you to love," makes her critique of slavery into a matter of private rather than public relations. The fact that these distinctions are in no way valid and that Eva in her living and dying and Stowe in her writing are doing deeply political work does not mean that the code of the domestic is not necessary and expedient.

The site of fatherhood within the familial idiom bears the weight of many of the structural differences between the *Elsie* books and *Uncle Tom's Cabin*. While in the *Elsie* books the earthly father wrests the law of the heavenly father from the maternal and the feminine to align himself with it and its powers, the father in *Uncle Tom* is not strong enough for the task. St. Clare's position vis-à-vis the law is far more complex than Dinsmore's; he repeatedly refuses to command or to punish his slaves, producing for himself and his family a model of the lawless domestic scene. St. Clare's charm lies, of course, in his continued abrogation of phallic power. His words, unlike Dinsmore's, are not meant to carry meaning; he is half proud that he can make speeches without taking action. In contrasting himself with his brother Alfred, he speaks slightingly but with great charm of his own inconsistency: "(Alfred) has the better of me, I grant,—for he really does something; his life is a logical result of his opinions, and mine is a contemptible *non sequitur*" (252). By describing himself in syntactical terms, St. Clare speaks to the heart of his apparent powerlessness; he depicts himself not only as a speaker of random and inconsequential words, but as a word spoken at random. This double denial of agency would seem to remove him twice from the law.

The paradox of St. Clare's position is, of course, that his very lawlessness is a form of complicity with the law that permits slavery; he must learn through Eva and Ophelia that, as a man of wealth and position, his words have power. Although St. Clare wants to put off signing Topsy over to Ophelia, his sister forces him to act with New England promptness, warning that St. Clare might die or fail before he carries through his purpose. Ophelia's lectures are not, however, sufficient to get St. Clare to go through the legalities of granting Tom his freedom before St. Clare dies. Ultimately, it is not St. Clare's unwillingness to put Eva's wishes into practice, but a misapprehension of his own relation to the law that denies Tom his chance to return to his family.

Unlike her brother, Ophelia understands the law and its relation to the human body; when she asks that Topsy be "given" to her, she knows she must use the law in order to subvert it:

"There, now, she's yours, body and soul," said St. Clare, handing the paper.

"No more mine than she was before," said Miss Ophelia.

"Nobody but God has a right to give her to me; but I can protect her now."

"Well, she's yours by a fiction of the law, then," said St. Clare, as he turned back into the parlor, and sat down to his paper. (333)

The phrase "fiction of the law" is vital here because it describes the relation of masters to their slaves and fathers to their children. Both relations depend on the name of the father and on the law of the land; the proof of fatherhood, like the proof of ownership, is in the law and not in the body. In this scene the fictional nature of ownership is figured in the paper that St. Clare signs; fictional or not, the paper has the power of law and of public discourse. As St. Clare closes this interaction with Ophelia by turning to his newspaper, we must recognize a connection between the two papers; when St. Clare is killed going to buy a newspaper to discover "the news of the day" (he is in this case also trying to avoid a legal contract—the freeing of Uncle Tom), we must see that the issue of putting words into public circulation is a fraught one for St. Clare and the novel. As much as he might try to hide behind his own idiosyncratic speech, as much as he may refuse to be "pinned down," the knife that will do the fatal pinning is waiting to freeze him into a political position. The fact that it is the wrong political position, and one in which he does not believe, is due to his own misunderstanding of his legal and paternal authority. He dies a slave-owner because he blinds himself to the power of that position.

We should be prepared for Stowe's position on the power of the word by the life and death of "little" Eva. Unlike Elsie, Eva does not start off as a repository of scripture; she fumbles for words to describe the problems of slavery and can only fall back on the language of her own body: "it sinks into my heart." Eva's relationship with the quasi-literate Uncle Tom gives her, ironically, her first sustained contact with the word. As Eva explains their arrangement: "Yes, he sings for me, and I read to him in my Bible; and he explains what it means, you know" (203). Tom, who can find significant passages in his own Bible only by marking with his own system of pencillings, turns Eva into a student of the word. It is no wonder that on her deathbed she frames the problems of slavery in terms of reading. "You must be Christians," she tells the assembled slaves at her bedside:

"You must remember that each one of you can become angels, and be angels forever. . . . If you want to be Christians Jesus will help you. You must pray to him; you must read"—

The child checked herself, looked piteously at them, and said, sorrowfully,—

"Oh, dear! you, *can't* read,—poor souls!' and she hid her face in the pillow and sobbed. (311)

Access to God's word becomes, for Eva, the crucial right denied to slaves. She fears that after her death there will be no one to read the Bible to Mammy and the others, and that they will be cut off from the word. The partial solution of this problem in the novel lies once again in the power of embodiment; in remembering Eva, the slaves retain some kind of contact with the word. Like her grandmother, who, according to St. Clare "was the direct embodiment and personification of the New Testament" (243–44), the memory of Eva is enough to begin the work of inspiration.

Despite the famed sentimentality of the novel's attitude toward Eva, however, it is not enough for the slaves or her father to remember *her;* Topsy, who will later become a missionary, and St. Clare both are left books by Eva: St. Clare, like Horace Dinsmore, studies his daughter's Bible after her death, while Topsy keeps a small book of daily lessons from the Bible in her bosom along with one of Eva's curls. Once again, we see the familiar configuration of book and curl, word and body, at work upon the soul to be converted.

Eva, of course, leaves her father yet another gift from beyond the grave in the shape of Uncle Tom who insists he will not claim his freedom until his master has given himself to Christ. Since Eva does really die, and cannot, like Elsie, leave her father the legacy of herself, she must make do with an eloquent substitute. Tom, like Eva, insists on the literalness of biblical promises and rejects what the novel clearly sees as the sophistries of overfigurative readings or intellectual nit-picking; armed with the biblical assurance that the truth is "hid from the wise and prudent, and revealed unto babes," Tom resists the power of St. Clare's superior learning and repeatedly invokes the authority of his own beliefs. In learning the literalness of the law, St. Clare begins to accept the power of all words and learns the lesson Horace Dinsmore has understood from the beginning.

Like Dinsmore, however, St. Clare must learn to humble himself before the Word; to do this he must adopt the position of his slave, his daughter, and his mother toward it. This "position" is fittingly literal: he sits where Eva used to sit and reads to Tom from the same passages Eva used to read. In occupying the space of the literal, he begins to inhabit the place of what Luce Irigaray would call the "feminine," that place of weakness and perspective outside the dominant culture. The "feminine" is, of course, according to Irigaray, also the place of other marginalized persons recast in what she feels to be the culture's central idiom of gender. Interestingly, before his conversion experience, St. Clare has misunderstood the gender alignment of words, the word, and the literal. He calls his own hesitation about taking action "womanish." What he does not understand, and what the structure of the book explains for him, is that while the gentleness of his character is feminine, his early repression of the literal, simple truth is not.

In moving toward the word of God, St. Clare moves toward his mother and daughter who have for him always embodied the word of God. They reach him, however, as Elsie reaches her father, through the word as well as through the body. On the last night of his life, St. Clare shows Ophelia a book that once belonged to his mother. It is not the Bible, but a notebook in which she arranged a series of songs from Mozart's *Requiem*. In singing his mother's songs, St. Clare begins to represent and to embody his mother; in reading her arrangements, he acknowledges and celebrates her power over words and signs. We do not need St. Clare's last word, his euphoric "Mother!" to know that the return to God is a return to the body and the word of the woman who bore him. Like Elsie, and like Elsie's mother, Grace, Mrs. St. Clare has triumphant powers of physical and spiritual self-replication: by the end of the novel both father and daughter join in reproducing the image of the mother.

It would be easy, without the benefit of comparison with Elsie's resurrection, to misunderstand the cynicism at work in the deaths of the father and daughter. Despite the drama of Eva's death and its emotional effectiveness within the community of the plantation, her conversion of her father—if it is in fact a real conversion—does not "take": he dies before he can act. Unlike Elsie, Eva really does die; unlike Horace Dinsmore, Augustine St. Clare does not construct an earthly paradise. Elsie's survival is both the ultimate concession to "low" literary tastes and the ultimate triumph of subversive female fantasy; Eva's death is simultaneously a gesture of melodrama and realism. Elsie and Dinsmore survive, ultimately, because they can create a private world into which the world only intrudes to be absorbed; Eva and St. Clare die because the stakes are larger and more public. Elsie's real survival lies not even so much in the fact that there are so many Elsie novels, but in the constant requests of her children and grandchildren to retell the story of her illness—to retell, in fact, the story of *Elsie's Holidays*. If Eva survives, it is in books, plays, and pamphlets by authors other than Stowe who were provoked or inspired by her apparent death in *Uncle Tom's Cabin*.

Notes

1. I use the metaphor of the wilderness here in three senses and in relation to three issues in feminist criticism. First, as Elaine Showalter suggested several years ago, feminist criticism is itself in a sort of wilderness, a "no-

man's land," alternately looking for and rejecting "directions." Second, as Annette Kolodny points out in *The Lay Of The Land,* the wilderness has historically been associated with female sexuality by male authors of the American canon and of the concept of "America." The third sense of wilderness brings us back to Showalter via certain French feminists who see women's writing as taking place in a "wild-zone" outside the restraints of patriarchy. See Elaine Showalter, "Feminist Criticism in the Wilderness," in *Writing and Sexual Difference,* ed. Elizabeth Abel (Chicago: University of Chicago Press, 1982), 9–10, 28–29); Annette Kolodny, *The Lay of the Land: Metaphor as Experience and History in American Life and Letters* (Chapel Hill: University of North Carolina Press, 1975) chap. 1; Monique Wittig, *Les Guerilleres,* trans. David le Vay (New York: Avon, 1973).

2. Nina Baym's *Guide to Fiction by and about Women in America 1820–1870* (Ithaca: Cornell University Press, 1978), 296, mentions the *Elsie* books only once in the context of the scene where Elsie's father tries to force her to play secular piano music on the Sabbath. When Elsie refuses, her father punishes her by making her sit on the piano stool until she submits. After sitting motionless for hours, Elsie grows faint, falls off the piano stool, strikes her head, and bloodies her curls. Her father clasps her in his arms and forgives her. Criticism of the *Elsie* series tends to depend heavily on amazed and parodic plot summary. The most serious published piece of criticism to date is Janet E. Brown, "The Saga of Elsie Dinsmore: A Study in Nineteenth Century Sensibility," *Buffalo Studies* 17, no. 3 (July 1945): 127. I am indebted for elements of my present Lacanian reading of the *Elsie* books to discussions with and the unpublished work of Marla Harris.

3. See, for example, Thomas F. Gossett, *Uncle Tom's Cabin and American Culture* (Dallas: Southern Methodist University Press, 1985), ix. Gossett defends his interest in the novel by claiming that while it is "sentimental" about "the devotion of a father to his almost angelic child," it is "not at all sentimental about political and social institutions."

4. Nina Baym, for example, admits: "I confess frankly that although I found much to interest me in these books, I have not unearthed a forgotten Jane Austen or George Eliot, or hit upon even one novel I would propose to set alongside *The Scarlet Letter*" (Baym, 14).

5. Herbert Ross Brown, *The Sentimental Novel in America* (New York: Pageant Books, 1959), 59. Foster is quoted as an epigraph to the book on p. 1. Although, as Nina Baym makes clear in her *Novels, Readers, and Reviewers* (Ithaca: Cornell University Press, 1984): "sentimental fiction" was a term applied only to a relatively small and specific genre, twentieth-century critics have tended to use the term more loosely. It is our contemporary critical accounts of sentiment and the sentimental that interest me most here.

6. Martha Finley, *Elsie's Holidays at Roselands* (New York: M.A. Donohue, n. d.), 151.

Part III *Beyond the Figure of the Father*

II ## Creation by the Father's Fiat

Paternal Narrative, Sexual Anxiety, and the Deauthorizing Designs of Absalom, Absalom!
Joseph A. Boone

Death of the Father would deprive literature of many of its pleasures. If there is no longer a Father, why tell stories? Doesn't every narrative lead back to Oedipus?

Roland Barthes, *The Pleasure of the Text*

You do not do, you do not do
Any more, black shoe

. . .

Daddy, Daddy, you bastard, I'm through

Sylvia Plath, "Daddy"

There was an old woman who lived in a shoe
She had so many children she didn't know what to do

Mother Goose rhyme

Is the Oedipus story, the doomed plot of fathers and their progeny, really paradigmatic of all narrative? Is every story, as Roland Barthes suggests, a "staging of the (absent, hidden, hypostatized) father" calculated to whet our appetite "to know, to learn the origin and end," after the manner of Oedipus? Much recent and influential theorizing about narrative has assumed as much, from Peter Brooks's psychoanalytically based analysis of narrative authority in terms of failed fathers to Teresa de Lauretis's feminist argument that all stories construct their acting subjects as masculine—that is, as mirrors of Oedipus questing for answers to riddles through a text-space inexorably gendered feminine.[1] It seems to me that we should not only begin questioning the assumed universality of the oedipal scenario as the basis of all narrative, but also pause to ask whether any "origin," be it Oedipus or other, is really descriptive of the possible desires that fictions may engender. Might not it be, as Susan Stanford Friedman has recently suggested, that "the concept of all narrative as necessarily Oedipal is a plot *against* narrative," perhaps a plot of the father himself? Some feminist critics have indeed begun to propose alternatives to the father's plot by turning to lyric modes of structuration, Chodorovian theories of preoedipal bonding between mother and daughter, and female morphological models to describe a female-based textual erotics distinguishing women writers from Madame de Lafayette and George Eliot to Kate Chopin and Virginia Woolf.[2] But what would happen, I keep wondering, were we to scrutinize father-centered fictions in the same way, scratching the surface of Oedipus to see what lies beneath? Might there be ways in which even paternal fictions deauthorize their proclaimed originary power? And how absolute is the assertion (pace de Lauretis) that the female position in such plots can never serve as their motive desire or shaping force but only as a marker of their limits?

These are questions I should like to begin exploring by turning to William Faulkner's *Absalom, Absalom!* (1936), a modernist classic in which the power of the father—as lawgiver, as namer, as literal and figurative "author" of being—is immediate and near to overwhelming. Set in the strife-torn American South in the decades surrounding the Civil War, the legend of Thomas Sutpen emerging from the text's multiple narrative voices would seem, at first glance, to raise to the status of heroic myth the will-to-power of a father whose driving obsession is that of generation, of *producing* generations, as an exercise of his patriarchal privilege as name-bearer and at the expense—or neglect—of the women who actually bear his namesakes. Sutpen's determined effort to produce a male dynasty that will immortalize his name and confirm his status, however, hides a much more pressing psychological imperative, one related to his society's construction of manhood: for Sutpen uses his children as a means of imposing his ego on the external world, recreating its otherness in his own image. He thus unconsciously practices what Luce Irigaray has identified as a specular "logic of the same,"[3] striving to confirm his autonomy, power, and superiority as a man by creating sons who will mirror his desires back to him.

By envisioning himself as the autonomous creator of his own dynasty, moreover, Sutpen effectually treats his family as a text, subject to his authorial whims and control. What interests me is the fact that this family text, this paternal design, proves inherently self-subverting; it not only unravels itself, but it does so in ways that exceed the generational rebelliousness (especially of sons against fathers) that critics like Peter Brooks have taught us to expect in examples of "oedipally plotted" narrative. In fact, the frayed designs of the father in *Absalom, Absalom!* should begin to make us suspicious of the way in which our cultural institutions have forced a duplicitous, indeed disastrous, link between the materials of male procreativity and our metaphors of narrativity. For the story that Faulkner finally tells, once we read through and into the various lacunae punctuating this multilayered text, ends up being less a demonstration of the ubiquity of the father than of the threats to paternal ubiquity that make the father's story an impossibility from its very inception. Indeed, Sutpen's self-proclaimed authority reveals itself to be less an abstract universal and more a highly ambiguous construction, one founded on a profound anxiety about the meaning of masculinity itself—an anxiety suffusing his all-too-tangible identity as a man, as a sexual being, and as a father for whom the status of paternity must always be ambivalent rather than assured.

And this is an anxious narrative, indeed, if the sheer frustration that it provokes in many of its readers is any reliable indication. However much one may praise Faulkner's achievement, one can hardly deny the extreme perversity, the downright irritability at times, of his narrative method: readers inevitably find themselves trapped in a labyrinth of repeating stories and proliferating interpretations that remain frustratingly incomplete, unresolvable, and partial. Admittedly, all stories by definition provoke some degree of anxiety, temporarily frustrating us with detours and digressions in order to heighten our anticipation of their resolutions. *Absalom, Absalom!*, however, plays out this tendency to an extreme that points us back to the anxieties and frustrations embedded in its specific representation of paternal authority. And the primary source of Sutpen's anxiety involves precisely the repressed elements of his plot, all those visible signifiers of otherness, of nonmaleness—female sexuality, racial difference, latent homosexuality, daughter-texts—that his dynastic scheme has been constructed to subdue and contain. But despite such efforts at containment, these subversive elements *do* escape the father's plotting, threatening to wreck its transcendent designs and thus call the invisible, hypostatized authority upon which Sutpen's male identity rests into question.

For the critic in search of Oedipus, for the reader interested in issues of race and gender, the result is profoundly important. For these "escaped" strands of narrative reconstitute, reorder, our perception of where we have been and what we (might mistakenly think we) have been reading: that which confronts us is no longer "simply" an oedipal retelling, for Sutpen's paternal design has been deauthorized, shown to be illusive even in its origin. Out of such rereadings, of not only this but other novels, a much more real and vulnerable father, stripped of his guises and abstractions, his powerful absences and preordained plots, may hopefully emerge— one whose material presence immediately problematizes the cultural ethos that constructs fatherhood as a doomed heroic narrative, and one whose story, always "other" than his self-representation would have us believe, calls forth our sympathy rather than fear.

Those readers of *Absalom, Absalom!* left frustrated by Faulkner's elliptical narration may take some comfort in the fact that the novel's narrators find themselves left in equal states of frustration, seemingly fated to repeat a story that refuses to die. This makes for a particularly masochistic erotics of the text, as it were, both in regard to the tellers and to the sexually anxious narrative that is the subject of their protracted telling. But what, exactly, are the investments of Rosa Coldfield, Mr. Compson, and his son Quentin (abetted by his Harvard roommate Shreve) in retelling this already-told legend, and what can their proliferating interpretations of Sutpen's life tell us, in turn, about the self-subverting "plot of the father" being enacted in this novel? Quite a bit, I should like to suggest, once we look at their urge to narrate in light of Freud's conjectures about the human compulsion to repeat repressed or traumatic psychic materials as a means of exorcizing the tyranny of the past. For at least to Rosa, Mr. Compson, and Quentin, the myth of Sutpen is not simply a fascinating source of endless speculation but a specific threat to be expunged. Thus each of their retellings becomes, in a real sense, a fight to master a story that threatens to master them. For Sutpen represents to these narrators, as he does within his own plot, an authority figure whose interdiction, like that of all fathers, appears irrevocable. In the psychodrama of narrative transference that ensues, therefore, Rosa, Mr. Compson, and Quentin weave their tales to ward off what they intuitively sense to be the castrating power of this demonic, now absent, but still ever-powerful father.

On the other hand, their narrations simultaneously reveal an investment in *not* mastering this story, in letting it continue without end. At least subconsciously, that is, all three tellers repeat (and listen to and then repeat again) Sutpen's story as a way of putting their own lives on hold, of postponing a confrontation with present-day reality. Examining their compulsion to repeat in this light, we can see how intimately their roles as narrators are linked to the psychosexual anxieties that motor Faulkner's entire enterprise. The example of Rosa is the most complex, a point to which I will return, but in terms of Faulkner's initial representation of her "lonely thwarted old female flesh embattled for forty-three years in the old insult"[4] of virginity, her narration is presented as the garrulous outpouring of a spinster's "impotent yet indomitable frustration" (7); talk has become the only way of wreaking vengeance upon the "long-dead object" (7) of her hatred, Sutpen, for having jilted her those forty-three years before, as well as an erotic substitute for the life that she claims has ended in that past moment. The world-weary Mr. Compson, on the other hand, uses the saga of Sutpen's dynasty as a pretext for indulging in decadent fantasies of desire that allow him to avoid the reality of his own dynasty's decline and his impotence to do anything about it. For Quentin, too, the sexual and textual are inextricably, and masochistically, linked: relaying the incestuous triangle formed by Sutpen's progeny to Shreve allows him to participate verbally in the very desires that he also harbors yet fears to initiate.[5] Internalizing his inaction as a failure of manhood, Quentin, like Rosa and his father, turns to the erotics of narrating as a substitute for the erotic fulfillment that is missing in life.

What are the anxieties hidden within Sutpen's story, then, that so powerfully summon forth the thwarted, indeed doomed, narrative desires of these storytellers? To begin to answer this question, we need to look more closely at Sutpen's desire to be the omniscient, omnipotent author of his personal history, for he often treats his life as if it were a plot-in-progress, a narrative design that already exists as a Platonic whole in his mind: "You see, I had a design in my mind" (263), he will repeatedly explain to General Compson, his one confidant and Quentin's grandfather, in the two episodes in chapter 7 when we get the story in his own words. And as far as this self-nominated maker of "designs" is concerned, the plan or blueprint he has conceived merely awaits physical realization or consummation. The operative words here, however, are "physical" and "consummation," since Sutpen's plan depends on issuing forth a dynasty of sons who will immortalize his name. He wishes to become the author, that is, of nothing less than a paternal plot, an explanatory myth of origins and endings that will at once give his identity retrospective significance and proleptic authority. "You see, I had a design," his confession to General Compson continues, "To accomplish it I should require money, a house, a family, slaves . . . [and] incidentally, of course, a wife" (263).

Likewise, the Sutpen legend inherited and embellished by Jefferson's community of tellers powerfully attests to the stakes involved in Sutpen's self-assumed status as sole author of his familial design. In Rosa's estimation, for example, Sutpen is a consummate if demonic master artist who orchestrates his godlike arrival into Jefferson as high mythic drama, willing the plantation Sutpen's Hundred out of swampland, marrying into respectability, begetting his family. The biblical allusions that Rosa uses to describe Sutpen's enterprise only accentuate his self-appointed role as archetypal, disembodied Father-Creator; not only does he summon a world into being "out of the soundless Nothing . . . like the oldentime *Be*

Light" (9), but he remains, like the unspeakable divinity of Jehovah, "not articulated in this world" (171), and, like the original patriarch Adam, the sole "namer" of his progeny and possessions: "He named them all himself: all his own get and all the get of his wild niggers . . . naming with his own mouth his own ironic fecundity" (61–62).

Underlying the authorial control that Sutpen exerts over his design is the wish "to make his position impregnable" (15), and, ironically, the only means to the abstract ideal of impregnability is by the very *real* sexual act of impregnation. Hence Sutpen's creative enterprise—even before it involves marriage to Ellen Coldfield—is repeatedly embued in phallic imagery. Hyperbolically described as a "thunderclap" orgiastically "abrupt[ing]" upon the scene (8), he claims his "virgin" land (40) in an act of archetypally masculine aggression, "overrun[ning] the astonished earth" in a "conquest" that is as violent as it is an act of possession (8). Analogously, he penetrates the Coldfield sanctum to claim his virgin bride "with the abruptness of a tornado" that wreaks "irrevocable and incalculable damage" (23) and is gone. Always "project[ing] himself ahead," as if "in some fierce dynamic rigidity of impatience" (159) to consummate his design, Sutpen effectually masquerades as the phallus; even the terms of his decline and death remain recalcitrantly phallic. Repudiated by his one legitimate son, Henry, he sets out to father an illegitimate one, his attitude likened to "an old worn-out cannon which realizes that it can deliver just one more fierce shot" (181), and that "next time there might not be enough powder for . . . a full-sized load" (279).

As all this exaggerated phallicism would seem to indicate, the male act of impregnation is fraught with more anxiety and uncertainty than Sutpen would care to acknowledge; until the symbolic father proves he also has a body, that the word can indeed be made flesh, he leaves his dream of an "impregnable" position open to challenge. Thus, when his final plot to sire a male heir by Milly Jones misfires, as it were, it is appropriate that Sutpen meets his death in an act of symbolic castration, felled by the scythe that Milly's incensed grandfather raises against him: one thwarted Bearer of the Phallus topples another in an act of now meaningless conquest.

Plainly, it is neither old-fashioned lust nor dewy-eyed sentimentality that prompts Sutpen's phallic aggressiveness. A much more abstract, narcissistic desire motivates his monomaniacal urge to procreate. For Sutpen primarily, essentially, conceives of his "family plot" as an extension of his own ego, a blueprint for imposing and imprinting his identity on all his surroundings. Paternity, like the godly power of naming, becomes a way of subsuming one's anxieties about authority by rendering one's possessions miniature, hence inferior and less threatening versions of oneself. Given such an overwhelming narcissistic imperative, the authority of fatherhood inevitably becomes sadistic, for Sutpen's entire sense of himself rests on the psychic, when not physical, violation and penetration of the identities of all his dependents—whether his wife, children, slaves, or, on a textual level, the narrators and readers who inherit his story. Sutpen's anxious desire for complete mastery over his story, his paternal text, however, turns on a very ambiguous relation to the Southern caste system he purports to uphold. Only at the novel's midpoint do we learn, via his retrospective explanation to General Compson, that Sutpen's entire design springs from humiliations undergone as an adolescent, turned away from the front door of *his* master's plantation as poor white trash by a "monkey-dressed butler nigger" (231). In effect, the rest of Sutpen's life is "spent"—and here sexual, social, and psychological levels of meaning interpenetrate— in a series of violent entries to make up for this one barred threshold; class, race, and gender come together in a devastating illumination of the anxieties underpinning this father's desire for an identity based on disembodied authority rather than the all-too-embodied inferiority he has felt as a youth. Designed to cover over the vulnerability briefly exposed in this incident, Sutpen's paternal plot thus turns out to be in large part a compensatory narrative, one that tries not merely to explain his origins, but to explain *away* his origins by means of his more successful ends.[6]

All this may have begun to sound like the stuff of a classically oedipal narrative—the father who was once an ashamed son begets sons who in turn rebel against him—until we look more closely at the narratological implications of Sutpen's attempt to give shape to the plot of his own life. For as an artist, Sutpen is so fixated on the final product—establishing a genealogy that will immortalize his single-handed rise to an "impregnable" position of authority—that he forgets the necessary "middle" that constitutes the very substance of narrative plot, the living "middle" that is always, necessarily, transgressive, a deviation from the straight line that in linking the beginning and end would obviate the need for "story." In narrative terms, that is, Sutpen neglects metonymy, the flow of event that is the means to an end, in favor of metaphor, the illumination conferred by the end itself. And this oversight critically dooms Sutpen's esthetic design, precisely because, like all plots of the father, life is *not*, in the final measure, a written text, however much patriarchy may treat it as such; Sutpen's story will have no final illumination until it is over, leaving him quite literally unable to predict its "meaning."[7]

Hence, by definition lacking the retrospective vision of a completed whole, Sutpen is actually too involved in the making of his history to be either the removed, omniscient author he impersonates or the all-powerful abstraction whose disembodied law he would have his subjects obey without question. Nor is Sutpen's premature determination of his "ends" his only oversight. He also fails to see that the very goal, the fixed metaphor, toward which he drives is itself contrary to the stasis he desires. For the very achievement of a genealogy of Sutpens-in-perpetuity, far from being final, must necessarily remain metonymic, depending on a continuing line of generations that must occur *in*, not out of, time. Sutpen's desire to summon into creative being the "fixed goal in his mind" (53), whose static meaning he has already determined, will always escape his impositions since he, a living man, cannot freeze life into a final shape before it has ended.

Most obvious among the transgressive elements disturbing the synchronic reading of the "end" that Sutpen attempts to impose on the narrative "middle" of his paternal plot are, of course, his children. Male and female, black and white—the straight and pure line of patronymic descent that Sutpen means to create deviates rather wildly from his Platonic intentions. The case of his two sons is particularly telling in this regard. Sutpen's legitimate heir Henry quite simply repudiates his birthright, choosing fraternity with his illegitimate half brother Charles Bon over fealty to his father. Forcing a break in Sutpen's design by depriving him of his heir, Henry effectually abandons the family text, and he returns only to die and bring the House of Sutpen to an apocalyptic close more final than any of Sutpen's projected ends. However, as the very fact of Henry's return home at the end of his life suggests, his revolt against Sutpen's command has really never ceased, nor have his acts of defiance entirely escaped the Law of the Father. Eventually murdering Charles, the beloved brother for whom he has repudiated his inheritance, Henry in fact executes "the office of the outraged father's pistol-hand" (179), perversely fulfilling Sutpen's desire while thwarting his own. In the vicious circle of patriarchal logic in which Henry finds himself trapped (doomed to rebel against, yet serve, his father), we have the most unadulterated evidence of a strand of oedipal narrative at work in Faulkner's text: according to classic Freudian theory, sons wish to replace the father but do so by acceding to the father's law, learning to wield the same phallic power. Yet the fact is that Henry does not *simply* become Sutpen or, for that matter, the phallus. Self-exiled to an unknown plot, a figurative no-man's-land outside the text where he exists as a non-Sutpen, he comes to emblematize an element of difference, or indifference, that Sutpen's design cannot control; refusing the rules of male procreativity (as far as we know he sires no heirs) *and* creativity (by becoming a creative absence in Faulkner's text), Henry in his small way reveals the "outraged father's pistol-hand" to be no more than an "outrage": a victimizing authority whose only law is violent coercion of the self.

If the son Henry repudiates his father, in a chiasmic reversal the father Sutpen has already repudiated his firstborn son, Charles Bon, for "not [being] adjunctive or incremental to the design which I had in mind" (240)—the consequence of Sutpen's belated discovery that Eulalia Bon, his first wife, is partially black. As the taint that Sutpen's plot attempts to void, Bon thus represents a kind of return of the "textually repressed" when he appears at the door of Sutpen's Hundred as Henry's best friend. And the repressed in Sutpen's design, the already written that cannot be erased, is not only this son's blackness. It is also Sutpen's own unconscious, governed, as we have already seen, by a pathology of lack and need that reaches back to that fateful day when he was denied access to his master's plantation and made so painfully aware of his own economic and social inferiority in a white man's world of power. Thus, it is ironically appropriate that the specter of the "boy symbol . . . on the outside of a white door" (261) makes its return in the very body of Sutpen's illegitimate son, knocking (as Sutpen once did) at a plantation door that is now Sutpen's; and this event, significantly, introduces an element of repetition into the father's fiction of progress that subverts its desired linearity. The successful transcendence of origins for which Sutpen has plotted so long and hard cannot, after all, cover over its narrative beginnings in a boy's specific, anxiety-striken crisis of identity.

The self-defeating nature of authority derived from such ambiguous origins is exposed by Sutpen's reaction to this unwonted reminder of the past; for in refusing to acknowledge his kinship to Bon, the mirror-image of his youth, Sutpen denies, in a literal as well as figurative sense, his own flesh and blood. As such, Bon's return begins to disrupt Sutpen's plot. But at the same time, Sutpen's threatening presence deprives Bon's life of any narrative shape other than that of inactive passivity. For Bon desperately *needs* that very acknowledgment of origins that his father's plot attempts to suppress; as long as Sutpen withholds his recognition, Bon lacks the retrospective ordering perspective that would allow the rest of his life to assume an intentional or meaningful pattern.

Sutpen thus exerts a stultifying, castrating effect on both his sons. He has "unmanned" Henry by condemning him to serve as his unwilling "pistol-hand," and he condemns Charles Bon to a life of hopelessly masochistic waiting, textually evoked in the "feminine" imagery used to describe him.[8] But in so victimizing his sons, Sutpen also dooms his own plot, which, as we have seen, depends on male heirs, and thereby provides a clue to the self-subverting nature of his sexual and paternal authority. For, ultimately, the stymied desires of Henry for autonomy and of Bon for recognition stand less as proof of Sutpen's incontrovertible power than as signifiers of the profound anxieties underlying his phallic identity—anxieties given narrative figuration as plot excrescences, "castrations" or "feminizations" of the parent plot, formed by sons whose sin is only imperfectly to reflect the father's image.

While the conflict of sons and fathers in our culture will always be oedipal to some degree, I have begun to suggest how the "deviant" narrative energies generated by this conflict—which I have just described as plot excrescences—begin to deauthorize the story of the father in its very origin. If we turn from a consideration of Henry and Bon as sons to their role as siblings, linked with their sister Judith in an incestuous triangle, the text reveals an even more powerfully transgressive permutation of antipaternal narrative. The intense affinity of Henry and Judith early establishes incest as a brother-sister attraction. But it is the introduction of Bon (not yet known to be their half brother) into the Henry-Judith dyad that makes possible "the pure and perfect incest" (96) that Mr. Compson attributes to Henry in one of the novel's most famous passages. For by plotting the engagement of his best friend Bon to his sister, Henry makes possible a doubly satisfying displacement of his own incestuous desire. Not only does it allow him to possess Judith "in the person of the brother-in-law, the man whom he would be if he could become, metamorphose into, the lover, the husband"; but it also allows him the homoerotic satisfaction, via Judith's mediation, of uniting with the object of his worshipful infatuation, Bon, "by whom he would be despoiled, choose for despoiler, if he could become, metamorphose into the sister, the mistress, the bride" (96). The incestuous parameters of this configuration are not confined to Henry and Judith, once we become aware that Bon is also Sutpen's son: the subsequent engagement of Bon and Judith, as well as the attraction between the half brothers, also become literally incestuous possibilities.

Which is to say that the incestuous, as nearly all of Faulkner's critics have acknowledged, forms an extremely powerful undertow in Sutpen's paternal plot. To what degree the structure of incest supports an oedipal reading of this novel is another question. John Irwin has most prominently linked the two patterns as refractions of the same wish, a move facilitated by his Freudian reading of the oedipal triangle of mother-son-father, wherein the brother's desire for the sister becomes a displacement of an original desire for the mother.[9] But in the world of *Absalom, Absalom!*, Ellen Coldfield, Henry's mother, is strikingly absent as an object of desire, for Henry or anyone else, and Charles's mother, Eulalia Bon, only has textual life insofar as she is a projection of the narrators' fantasies of her. What Henry and Bon seek in incestuous union with Judith has very little to do with a return to the maternal womb and much more to do with their ambivalent relations to their father and to each other.

In fact, all three of the incestuous variations formed by these siblings covertly work to block Sutpen's design. For example, if we turn to the violation of the incest taboo incipient in Henry and Judith's closeness, and look at it from an anthropological rather than psychoanalytic perspective, it becomes clear that their endogamic exclusivity undermines Sutpen's need for those external family alliances (such as he has sought by marrying into Coldfield respectability) that will strengthen his dynasty and better its chances for survival. The incestuous union of Bon and Judith, on the other hand, threatens to adulterate the racial purity of the central family line with the impermissable taint of negro blood.[10] And, third, the pairing of Henry and Bon would strike the biggest blow of all to Sutpen's design by its nonreproductive nature; their union threatens no line of descent at all. As a thematic element of this text, then, sibling incest stands in direct opposition to the plot of the father. It is also worth observing that one of the threats of incest, structurally speaking, is that it augurs a continual return of the same, hence a break in temporal and genealogical progression. Thus, what I earlier called the narrative perversity of this novel—its nonchronological ordering, its doublings of character and narrative levels, its repetitions and continual loopings back in time—can be seen as a structural analogue of this thematically represented incestuous impulse, working equally to frustrate the straightforward progress upon which Sutpen's dynastic narrative model depends.[11] What, then, does it finally mean that Sutpen's design depends on progeny whose desires subvert that plan? Most simply put, all of these children become tangible emblems of Sutpen's worst fears about otherness: whether in the form of femaleness (as in Judith's case), blackness (as in Bon's), or latent homosexuality (as in Henry's), these siblings in their myriad incestuous alignments return to the surface of Sutpen's text precisely those repressions upon which its construction of masculine power, racial superiority, and (hetero)sexual procreativity have depended.

The anxieties that gender, race, and sexuality create for Sutpen's phallic identity become all the clearer once we recognize the extent to which the world of this novel is structured by a complex network of male bonding. Designed to confirm men's power through their exchange of women, the male homosocial bond, as Eve Kosofsky Sedgwick has shown, simultaneously generates men's deepest anxieties about their manhood precisely at that point where culturally fostered comaraderie between men becomes barely distinguishable from sexual intimacy.[12] Male identity within patriarchy—no less Southern patriarchy—depends, that is, on a very fine, often ambiguous line separating the acceptable from the unacceptable, the "real" man from the sexual suspect. And this is the very boundary on which Henry and Bon's relationship dangerously hovers. There are the obvious explanations, of course, including blood-affinity, for their bonding—Henry sees in Bon the sophisticated and worldly mentor figure he would like to become, Bon sees in Henry confirmation of his paternal origins (*"He has my brow my skull my jaw my hands"* [314]). But "love" is the quality that Faulkner's narrators continually invoke to describe the youths' mutual attraction; and, as we have seen above, one of the functions, perhaps *the* primary function, of the sibling incest triangle is to bond Henry and Bon over the body of Judith, in a homoerotic union whose structure is also ineluctably homosocial: "it was not Judith who was the object of Bon's love or of Henry's solicitude. She was just the blank shape, the empty vessel in which each of them strove to preserve . . . what each conceived the other to believe him to be—the man and the youth, seducer and seduced, who had known one another, seduced and been seduced, victimized in turn each by the other" (120). Given the novel's title, critics have understandably made much of Faulkner's use of the Absalom-Tamar-Ammon biblical analogue to elucidate its incest triangles.[13] But if we dig behind this analogue to the preceding generation of Absalom's father, David, we will uncover another, almost equally applicable, archetype—"the love that passeth understanding" shared by the youthful David and Jonathan.

And this archetype, presenting homoerotic male comradeship in its most idealized and disembodied form, can be seen at work in the way the various narrators (especially the men) re-create Henry's love for Bon, poeticizing the tragic division that comes between the two youths while relegating Judith, the "blank" page on which the story of their division is written, to the background.

The tragedy, however, is not simply that Henry and Bon fall out in the end. It is that from the very beginning of their friendship they are only able to conceive of their mutual desires within the homosocial and consequently heterosexual terms provided by the father's law, in which "the similarity of gender" looms as an "insurmountable barrier" (95), a final and hopeless intervention, to realized love. Given this cultural repression of the homoerotic, along with the paternal anxieties about masculinity that it inevitably reproduces, it is ironically fitting that the act of murder serves as their final, and only, consummation. The gunshot that Henry fires at Bon, "heard only by its echo" (153), becomes an ironically apt metaphor for a sexual climax that never occurs, itself only "heard" in the narrative via its reverberating absence. With this image, we return, circuitously, to the militaristic metaphor—the nearly exhausted "cannon" with its one good last load— used to describe Sutpen's procreative imperialism. But whereas the father's rusty weapon invoked the act of sexual intercourse as unfeeling violence, the firing of Henry the son's pistol connotes an act of anguished violence deprived even of the sex: all that is left is an empty, unanswered erotic charge.

The homosocial structure that turns love into murder also suffuses and disturbs the historical, psychological, and narrative levels of Sutpen's dynastic plot. Historically speaking, if Henry and Bon can be seen as fraternal soul mates at war, so too the Civil War from its inception was viewed in familial terms as the struggle of brother against brother—a struggle, moreover, fought over the figuratively female body of the mother country herself. Second, in psychological terms, *Absalom, Absalom!* includes a terrifyingly visceral primal scene in which the act of parental copulation to which the young child is exposed is replaced, significantly, by an emblem of the homosocial, exclusively male, network of power that governs Sutpen's world. For I would argue that the set piece serving as the climax of the very first chapter, the wrestling spectacle that Ellen discovers her children furtively watching from the barn loft, forms this text's most authentic equivalent of Freud's famed "two-backed" beast—only this vision is not of mother and father, but of two naked men locked in an embrace, a public display, that is actually a deadly struggle for "supremacy, domination" (29). Nor are the wrestlers "the two black beasts she had expected to see but instead a white one and a black one . . . her husband and the father of her children standing there naked and panting and bloody and the negro just fallen evidently" (29).

Here, finally, is the father's uncovered, carnal body. And here, too, is the David and Jonathan archetype stripped of its ideality, caught in a violent embrace that not only embodies the underlying structure and fate of men's relationships in patriarchal society but that also encodes, quite visibly, the ugly truth of hierarchical relations in the American South: white triumphing over black. That the father *forces* Henry to watch this overtly public display of male competition, that the mother's entrance into the tableau virtually makes no difference ("I don't expect you to understand it . . . because you are a woman" [30]), powerfully suggests that exposure to the homosocial paradigm—not simply heterosexual coitus—has become *the* affective experience in the formation of male identity in the world of this novel, as well as in the creation of its oedipal plots.[14]

The same might also be said of the oedipal myth itself, once we look at the story of the father that precedes, in narrative time, the drama of discovery that Sophocles records. For the fact is that the curse leading King Laius to abandon his son Oedipus in the first place originates in a crime that is at once homosocial *and* homosexual in nature: it is none other than Laius's violation of his brotherly bond with a neighboring king (Pelops) by raping that ruler's son (Chrysipus) that precipitates the curse of the House of Laius, a curse carried out by *his* son's enactment of the "oedipal drama" of incest and patricide. Faulkner's text may thus be said unconsciously to supplement Freud's paradigmatic scenario of male identity development by restoring to the oedipal myth its hidden pre-text, its suppressed origin, in homosocial violence.

The complicities of male bonding infiltrate *Absalom, Absalom!* on yet a third level, that of its narrative retelling. For Quentin and his roommate Shreve, the novel's final narrators, participate in a creative intercourse of words that intimately bonds them, via Sutpen's story, in a "marriage of speaking and hearing . . . in order to overpass to love" (316): an act of imaginative union that nonetheless, as we shall see, also becomes a shouting match, a battle for mastery not only over this story but over each other, a frustrated dialogue that ends in an ejaculation of love-hate ("*I dont hate it,* he thought, panting in the cold air . . . *I dont. I dont!* [378]) as abrupt as the gunshot at the gate of Sutpen's Hundred beyond which Henry and Bon, unable to "pass" (133), stop forever.

As all these instances of male bonding begin to indicate, the place allotted to women in Sutpen's construction of his family text, even more than that of wayward or unclaimed sons, is extremely peripheral.[15] Yet the very inconsequentiality of the roles accorded women in Sutpen's plan, like its other suppressed elements, becomes a potent sign and symptom of those very anxieties that fuel the plot of the father in the first place. For beneath the flowery encomiums adorning ante- and postbellum rhetoric about women, its representations of the Southern belle reveal a profound misogyny and fear of female sexuality. A case in point is the fundamentally contradictory attitude underlying the eroticized images that Mr. Compson, for one, uses to describe women—on the one hand, as empty "vessels" (108, 119–20) waiting to be filled, on the other, as parasitic "vampires" (67, 86) actively draining life from others: he who bases his power on the phallus as an instrument of penetration stands, in his worst nightmares, to be penetrated, sucked dry. And if men like Mr. Compson or Sutpen—and perhaps Faulkner himself—see women as endangering their own potency, it is precisely because female sexuality harbors the one element—the bodily ability to reproduce—that men's ostensible power and designs can never completely control. Women's sexuality has an authority, a creative fiat, to which all the father's fictions of authority in the world can only presume, can only possess by way of metaphor.

The most striking textual manifestation of the male anxieties engendered by female sexuality in *Absalom, Absalom!*, I would suggest, involves the absence of mothers throughout the *entire* novel. Both in Sutpen's plot and in the text as a whole, motherhood is by and large an invisible state. Those mothers represented in any depth are literally disembodied male projections (such as Mr. Compson's evocation of Ellen or Shreve's fiction of Eulalia Bon). Other mothers—Sutpen's, Clytie's, Ellen and Rosa's, Milly Jones's, Jim Bond's, even Quentin's—are simply stricken from the text, often without explanation. Two such revealing lacunae involve Mrs. Coldfield, who literally drops out of the picture during her daughter Ellen's wedding in chapter 2, and the "coal black and ape-like woman" (205) that Bon's son Charles Etienne brings home as his wife, who disappears from the postwar narration without a trace once she has served her primary function in the plot by giving birth to a son, Jim Bond.[16]

As the example of Charles Etienne's wife also indicates, the lack of mothers in this text is complemented by the quite visible, disruptive rise of black sons. For the one realized dynasty in the novel, the legacy of all Sutpen's procreative efforts, is the genealogy that stretches from his repudiated son, Charles Bon, to his great-grandson Jim Bond, a genealogy that is at once male (which, after all, is Sutpen's dream) *and* characterized by an exponential rise in degree of blackness (the nightmarish opposite of his dream). Once again, an aspect of the otherness—here, the taint of racial otherness—that Sutpen has attempted to exclude from his design redounds upon his authorial control, and, once again, the outcome points to the unresolved anxieties of identity that work to unravel this father's plot from its inception. For Sutpen's greatest fear has always been an adulteration of the family plot by those extraneous narratives—the story of mothers and daughters, half-caste sons, "unmanly" men—that stand outside, hence threaten the hegemony, of his desired identity as all-powerful, white patriarch. It is fitting, then, that a woman—Eulalia Bon—is made the culprit responsible for introducing the strain of negro blood that upsets Sutpen's projected ends by "defiling" the family line; in the novel's complex symbology, femaleness, and particularly female sexuality, is often equated with an equatorial darkness personified by the black races.[17]

Indeed, the specific challenge that the pairing of fecundity and racial otherness poses to white male identity, thus to the sanctity of Sutpen's plan, forms the novel's closing statement, as Shreve taunts Quentin about the horror that the very idea of Sutpen's black heirs hold for the Southern imagination: "I think that in time the Jim Bonds are going to conquer the western hemisphere. Of course it won't be quite in our time and of course as they spread toward the poles they will *bleach out again* like the rabbits and the birds do, so they won't show up so sharp against the snow. But it will still be Bond; and so in a few thousand years, I who regard you will also have sprung from the loins of African kings" (378, emphasis added). Shreve's vision is not simply that the black race (like metonymy run wild) will conquer the world, but more precisely that whiteness will cease to be a marker of difference, the absolute metaphor of achieved ends, once the various races eventually mix *under the guise of* whiteness. For the Southern aristocracy, then, the great fear is the threat of nondifferentiation, of the collapse of the boundaries and polarities that allow for the repression and subjugation of otherness constitutive of (in this case) white male identity. And these boundaries, as the psychoanalyst Jessica Benjamin has shown, have everything to do with the male child's desire to repudiate the powerful maternal connection in order to establish his separate sense of self.[18]

If Sutpen's paternal masterplot cannot successfully do away with his black descendants, neither can it totally neutralize the covertly transgressive presence of his two daughters, Judith and Clytie. Unlike their white and black counterparts in Henry and Bon, these half sisters seem doomed to inhabit the background of Sutpen's family text, ever-present but useless in furthering his patronymic designs (both remain childless) except as the dutiful keepers of his house. Their joint impassivity, however, should not be construed as unconditional passivity: they may keep his house, but they do not necessarily keep to his plot.[19] Judith, for instance, at first glance appears totally identified with her father, yet of all the Sutpens it is she who most actively concerns herself with preserving a written record that will allow for the handing down, even to strangers, of the suppressed stories underlying the official history of the family's rise and fall. Thus, Judith passes Bon's crucial letter to her on to General Compson's wife, in an act of female-to-female transmission that makes possible Mr. Compson's retelling of these events to his son Quentin forty-five years later: the transmission of father-to-son, the ostensible basis for this (and all oedipal) narrative, depends on at least one prior transaction that is an exchange between women rather than men.[20]

Like Judith, Clytie also proves a covertly destabilizing force in Sutpen's design. "Free yet incapable of freedom," she is the embodiment of the "perverse and inscrutable paradox" (156) of slavery: at once too proud to think of herself as chattel yet never questioning the fact that Sutpen is her absolute master. Yet this unacknowledged daughter is also "the presiding augur of [Sutpen's] disaster" (256), who with the murderous fury of her classical namesake Clytemnestra brings destruction onto the House of her father, setting fire to Sutpen's Hundred rather than cede to Rosa her guardianship of the dying Henry. As in Judith's passing on to Mrs. Compson of Bon's letter, it is once again an act of transmission between women— what one might call Rosa's telepathic decoding of the secret Clytie has kept hidden at Sutpen's Hundred—that has enabled this story from its beginnings. Authorial fiat, it would seem, does not lie entirely in the hands of the father.

Which returns us, at long last, to Rosa Coldfield—a surrogate "daughter" of Sutpen's text—and to a reconsideration of the role she plays in the making and unmaking of the father's story. I have already mentioned how Rosa's "outraged recapitulation" (8) of the Sutpen legend may initially strike one as a spinster's "impotent" act of revenge, the perverted child, as it were, of her years of sexual frustration and emotional sterility. But there is another, much more actively subversive side to Rosa's role as narrator that I should like us to consider—one that is productive, indeed potent, rather than powerless or self-defeating. Established at the very beginning of chapter 1 as Yoknapatawpha County's "poetess laureate," Rosa is the only published writer, however open to question the quality of her writings may be, among the novel's narrators, "issuing . . .

poems, ode, eulogy, and epitaph, out of some . . . implacable unre-
serve of undefeat" (11). One might also take note of the fact that she
begins writing only when her neurotic, Yankee-sympathizing father
nails himself in the attic during the war—becoming, as indeed,
Henry Sutpen hidden in *his* attic will also become a half century
later, a *male* version of the madwoman in the attic, Gilbert and
Gubar's figure for the woman writer's angry double. Even more
importantly, Rosa's authorial status is reflected in the fact that she
is the narrator who initiates this text by summoning Quentin to her
house, first to listen to her tale and then to serve as her witness
on the revelatory night-trip to Sutpen's Hundred where Henry is
discovered: without Rosa, there would be, to put it simply, no
novel for us to read.[21]

Nor is Rosa's garrulous narrative style, elongated by seemingly
endless and frustrating repetitions, only an emblem of the speaker's
sexual unfulfillment or her passive entrapment in a long-dead past,
however much both may be contributing factors. Rather, I would
suggest, the technique of deferral and postponement that marks her
retelling may be a sign of her subversive if partial power *over* Sutpen's
text and its desired climaxes. At the beginning of this discussion, I
suggested that Sutpen's story itself refuses to die, exacting its revenge on its auditors by dooming them to perpetual frustration.
But in Rosa's case, we can also reverse this proposition to state that
it is *she* who refuses to let Sutpen's story die. In effect, by using her
role as narrator to keep the unruly plot-in-process, the transgressive
narrative "middle" that Sutpen would rather ignore, alive and anxiously disruptive, Rosa rebels against what I have already characterized as his compulsive desire for metaphor, for the completed goal
or design. If oedipal narrative is an explanatory myth of beginnings
and endings, the search for the "proper" narrative death that will
bestow retrospective meaning on the irregularities and deviations
of the individual's life-career, then Rosa's refusal to lay the myth of
Sutpen to rest de-oedipalizes, in a real sense, its power; rewriting
Sutpen's deeds as undying and communal legend, she "unstrings"—
to use Susan Winnett's memorable metaphor—the oedipal logic of
a "masterplot that wants to have told us in advance where it is that
we should take our pleasures and what must inevitably come of

them."[22] Rosa emphatically takes her pleasures elsewhere, as we can see in the metonymic play of the "middle" to which her "outraged recapitulation" of "undefeat" gives vent, and in so doing her narrative retelling clears space for our illuminated rereading of the self-subverting forces, the plot excrescences, generated by Sutpen's textual enterprise. In the war between Sutpen's formidable will-to-power and her own authorial stratagems, Rosa finally succeeds in turning the castrating power of the father against itself: the psychic wounds he has inflicted on his progeny redound posthumously to rend his own suddenly vulnerable narrative.[23]

The primary recipient of the narrative transmission that Rosa initiates and at least symbolically closes, of course, is Quentin Compson. "Maybe someday you will remember this," she tells him, "and write about it" (10). The fictional improvisation that he and his college roommate Shreve weave from the "rag-tag and bob-ends of old tales and talking" (303), forming the reader's most immediate link to the recorded events of the novel, becomes another retelling that, like Rosa's, will not let Sutpen's story die easily. Yet if Rosa's habits of deferral amount to a covert counterplot against the father, the boys' obsessive reliving of his history indicates that what cannot "die" for each of them primarily involves the unresolved anxieties of masculine identity that have driven Sutpen to his doom. For Quentin especially, the anxieties of sexual and creative generation that have beset Sutpen's design now become his own personal nightmare: *"Yes, we are both Father. Or maybe Father and I are both Shreve, maybe it took Father and me both to make Shreve or Shreve and me both to make Father or maybe Thomas Sutpen to make all of us"* (261–62). In other words, because both Quentin and Shreve *are* sons, the Harvard-bred, male inheritors of the dominant culture (and not dispossessed daughters like Rosa, Judith, or Clytie), they cannot escape the crises of authority and conflicts of identity embedded in the story that they retell.

One can see this truth, first of all, in the way their creative dialogue begins to repeat the pattern—and contradictions—of homosocial bonding characterizing the world of Sutpen and his progeny, as their "marriage" of words is transformed into a struggle for mastery ("Wait, I tell you! . . . I am telling [it]" [277]); their very intimacy has become the grounds for an increasingly anxious contest of male one-upmanship. Second, at least for Quentin, storytelling only enmeshes him more disastrously in the self-subverting struggle of fathers and sons, as he attempts to make himself the primary narrator of the events that his father has told him, indeed to become his father's superior in knowledge by telling the story better than his progenitor.[24] Finally, even the lacunae in Quentin and Shreve's fiction refer us back to tremendous anxieties of identity motivating Sutpen's desire to establish a dynasty in his own image. For the questions that remain unanswered in *Absalom, Absalom!*—Is miscegenation really the key to Sutpen's repudiation of Bon? How does Bon learn (if ever) that he is black? What does the dying Henry reveal to Quentin?—all turn on questions of white male identity, of which the only explanations are those *created* by the boys. The fundamental uncertainty of the status of such "fictionalized" explanations—upon which not only the novel's "mystery" but Sutpen's otherwise inexplicable repudiation of his sons rests—thus self-reflexively points to the uncertainties lying at the core of phallic identity itself.

An emblem for the anxiety produced by such uncertainties exists in the climactic moments of the novel. When Quentin finally confronts the dying Henry at Sutpen's Hundred, a much-discussed gap in narration occurs, as the two engage in a surreal, italicized dialogue consisting of a short series of repetitive phrases that eventually move full circle without confirming anything; this elliptical conversation, as Peter Brooks has noted, "seems to constitute a kind of hollow structure, a concave mirror or black hole at the center of the narrative."[25] And this fear of empty centers, of dark "holes" and gaps into which all meanings tumble and out of which nothing certain emerges—imagery powerfully evocative of female sexuality in our culture—is very much, and on very many levels, what the anxieties haunting *Absalom, Absalom!* (and often its critics) are all about.

For years critics have pointed out how Faulkner's foregrounding of issues of intelligibility within this text have made it a quintessential example of novelistic self-reflexivity; the fundamental uninterpretability of this anxiety-producing text, I would add, has everything to do with its interrogation of the grounds on which all plots of the father erect their dubious beginnings. For underneath those masterful designs, *Absalom, Absalom!* reveals a story not of the power of the father, but of how one man's sexual anxieties dismantle the very notion of his transcendent, abstract authority. Oedipus, however empowered by our society or its myth-making processes, is finally and nonetheless a vulnerable man caught in the middle of a story that he has indeed helped create but cannot control—caught, as it were, with his pants down, his fallacies exposed, his repressive efforts showing for the ineffectual cover-up they are. Moreover, as Shreve's prophecies on the last page warn of Sutpen's dynastic dreams, there is always the nigger who gets away: all those fractious, marginal excrescences of plot, all those emblems of "nonmaleness," of otherness, that refuse to mirror the father or confine their desires to his preformulated masterplot. Thus Shreve says of any and all attempts to give a balanced, tidy explanation of Sutpen's failure: "Which is all right, it's fine; it clears the whole ledger, you can tear all the pages out and burn them, except for one thing. And do you know what that is? . . . You've got one nigger left" (378). Escaping the shapers of dynastic and narrative designs by their very exclusion, these trangressive elements remain, then, to unravel the ends whereby the father would explain his origins and to return the reader to the obsessions that remain in play, despite the paternal effort to repress difference, in the midst of a story doomed by its very premises never to end.

Notes

I should like to acknowledge a debt of gratitude to the students in the graduate course, "The Psychology of Sex and Self," where I first taught this novel in 1985. I am particularly grateful for the contributions of Deirdre d'Albertis and Elizabeth Young, whose seminar papers I cite below.

1. Barthes, *The Pleasure of the Text,* trans. Richard Miller (New York: Hill and Wang, 1975), 10, 47; Brooks, *Reading for the Plot: Design and Intention in Narrative* (New York: Knopf, 1984), esp. chap. 3; Teresa de Lauretis, *Alice Doesn't: Feminism, Semiotics, Cinema* (Bloomington: Indiana University Press, 1984), esp. chap. 5.

2. Friedman, "Lyric Subversions of Narrative in Women's Writing: Virginia Woolf and the Tyranny of Plot," forthcoming in *Reading Narrative: Form, Ethics and Ideology*, ed. James Phelan (Columbus: Ohio State University Press, 1989). In what is perhaps the most important feminist reworking of oedipal models since de Lauretis, Susan B. Winnett extracts a female-based morphological model of narrative desire from Mary Shelley's *Frankenstein* and George Eliot's *Romola* in order to counter the male assumptions of sexual pleasure and response girding traditional Freudian-based structures, in "Coming Unstrung: Women, Men, Narrative, and (the) Principles of Pleasure" (forthcoming). For alternative narrative models based on the mother-daughter relations, see, among many others, Marianne Hirsch, "A Mother's Discourse: Incorporation and Repetition in *La Princesse de Clèves*," *Yale French Studies* 62 (1982): 63–87, and Elizabeth Abel, "(E)merging Identities: The Dynamics of Female Friendship in Contemporary Fiction by Women," *Signs: A Journal of Women in Culture and Society* 6 (1981): 413–35.

3. Irigaray, *Speculum de l'autre femme* (Paris: Minuit, 1974).

4. Faulkner, *Absalom, Absalom!* (1936; repr. New York: Vintage, 1972), 14. All further references to this work appear in the text.

5. Quentin's unmentioned incestuous feelings for his sister Caddy can be derived from an intertextual reading of *Absalom, Absalom!* with *The Sound and the Fury* (1929). See John T. Irwin's influential reading of the two novels as companion texts in *Doubling and Incest/Repetition and Revenge: A Speculative Reading of Faulkner* (Baltimore: Johns Hopkins University Press, 1975).

6. Brooks, *Reading for the Plot*, 300, also uses the phrase "compensatory plot" to describe Sutpen's design; what I find fascinating about so many of Brooks's insightful points, as my frequent citations begin to indicate, is the degree to which, if taken another step, these very arguments could be used to deauthorize the fairly exclusively masculine oedipal model that his reading attempts to establish for the novel.

7. Brooks, *Reading*, 301, puts it well when he notes that "Sutpen attempts to write the history of the House of Sutpen prospectively, whereas history is evidently always retrospective. . . . One cannot postulate the authority and outcome of a genealogy in its origin." Or, as one of my students, Deirdre d'Albertis noted in a seminar paper, Sutpen is "doomed to fail" because one cannot demand "an end in the midst of [one's] middle. . . . The violation of time which enables Sutpen to impose narrative selection on his life can be sustained only in such moments of isolated telling, not in the organization of his own 'work in progress' or unfinished existence" (in " 'The Web of the Text': Narrative Strategies in Faulkner's *Absalom, Absalom!*" [1985]).

8. Bon's worldly sophistication and sensuality, as filtered through Mr. Compson's jaded fin de siècle projections, becomes "a little femininely

flamboyant" (110), the seductive charm of an "indolent esoteric hothouse bloom" (97). His feminized sexuality is repeatedly evoked in Mr. Compson's mental image of the student lounging around his quarters in flowered dressing gowns and "the outlandish and almost feminine garments of his sybaritic privacy" (96).

9. Irwin, *Doubling,* 43 (here Irwin is reading Freud through Otto Rank) and 88–90.

10. Sutpen, of course, is not bothered by issues of racial purity when he beds any of his slaves, such as Clytie's mother.

11. See also Patricia Tobin's discussion of incest and narrative repetition in *Time and the Novel: The Genealogical Perspective* (Princeton: Princeton University Press, 1978), 107–32, and Brooks, *Reading,* 109, on literary incest-as the threat of a narrative "short circuit."

12. Sedgwick, *Between Men: English Literature and Male Homosocial Desire* (New York: Columbia University Press, 1985), 1–5.

13. See 2 Samuel 13. Absalom, son of King David, kills his brother Ammon for raping their sister Tamar.

14. It should be added that this exposure to the homosocial paradigm may be primary in female development as well; unknown to Sutpen, Judith and Clytie also witness the scene and, unlike the sickened Henry, remain ominously unmoved.

15. Lévi-Strauss's observation in *The Elementary Structures of Kinship* (Boston: Beacon, 1969), 115, that women serve as items of exchange between men, thereby solidifying a male network of power, is reflected in the mediating function of women in this novel: Sutpen accepts Eulalia Bon from her father in exchange for saving his plantation on Haiti during the slave uprising; Ellen Coldfield is the prize of his demonic dealings with her father ("whose daughters he might even have won at cards" [20]); Milly is the understood price her grandfather Wash Jones pays for the privilege of drinking scuppernong wine with the master. "So it was no story about women," Mr. Compson says of the life-story Sutpen confesses to his father the general, "and certainly not about love" (248).

16. Sutpen's mother, for instance, is accorded only one sentence, where she is described as "a fine wearying woman" who died in her son's youth (223); Clytie's mother is presumably one of the two nameless slave women Sutpen has brought with him from Haiti; Milly's mother is mentioned for the first time in the chronology that ends in novel. In the chapter of a work-in-progress of which this article is a much reduced and edited part, I examine in greater depth the case of Mrs. Coldfield (Ellen and Rosa's mother) and of Jim Bond's mother. The disappearance of both women provides a glaring example of a degree of textual repression so extreme that it creates outright inconsistencies and "loose ends" in Faulkner's otherwise scrupulously woven narrative design.

17. The equation of gender and race implicit in Freud's (in)famous characterization of female sexuality as a dark continent is echoed in Faulkner's text. For Sutpen describes the island of Haiti, where he encounters female sexuality for the first time in the form of Eulalia Bon, with her shadowy racial heritage, as "a dark inscrutable continent from which the black blood, the black bones and flesh and thinking and remembering and hopes and desires, was ravished by violence" (250). I am grateful to Elizabeth Young for bringing this connection to light in her seminar paper, "Gender and Anxiety in William Faulkner's *Absalom, Absalom!*" (1985).

18. Benjamin persuasively argues that sons who have passed through the oedipal crisis into an awareness of gender difference experience a need for separation and differentiation from the mother much more extreme than that experienced by daughters. To establish a separate sense of their maleness, men are propelled to embrace an ethos of solipsistic individuality, based on such absolute ego-boundaries that a profound sense of inner alienation ensues. This in turn leads to violent attempts to break out of egoistic enclosure through domination, possession, and control of other selves—the very methods by which Sutpen attempts to effect his plot and impose his identity on the world around him. See "Master and Slave: The Fantasy of Erotic Domination," in *Powers of Desire: The Politics of Sexuality,* eds. Snitow, Stansell, and Thompson (New York: Monthly Review, 1983), 281–82.

19. In this light, it is worth noting that Judith and Clytie, along with Rosa, form an all-female "triumvirate" whose combined strength keeps Sutpen's plantation running throughout the last months of the war. Without men ("No, it did not even require the first day of the life we were to lead together to show us we did not need [Sutpen], had not the need for any man" [154]), the three women weave a narrative for their lives shaped to *their own desires*—"we now existed in an apathy which was almost peace" (155). This is, significantly, a story without designs, or what Rosa identities as the "furious desire" and "mad intention" (154) fueling Sutpen's monomaniacal impulse to climax and completion.

20. This is not to ignore the importance of the complementary "man-to-man" transmissions between Sutpen and General Compson (whose subject, appropriately, is a father-son narrative), passed on to Mr. Compson and thence to Quentin; my point is that this male chain of narrative transactions often depends on unrecognized female exchanges, which not only make possible the father-son story that the men want to tell, but keeps alive the counteroedipal strands of plot I am interested in excavating. Moreover, Judith's effort to make a mark, a protesting counterstatement, does not stop with her passing on of Bon's letter to General Compson's wife. For, as Deirdre d'Albertis, "The Web of the Text," has brilliantly shown, Judith constructs her own textual equivalent of Sutpen's family plot, and even

hides it out in the open, in her arrangement of the family graveplot upon the successive deaths of Ellen, Sutpen, Bon, and Charles Etienne. Within this demarcated plot of land, Judith places the various tombstones so that Sutpen is surrounded with the denied, disruptive elements of *his* plot; then, to complete *her* counterplot, she orders her headstone from her deathbed, which is tellingly placed "at the opposite end of the enclosure, *as far from the other four* as the enclosure could permit" (210, emphasis added). Symbolically fulfilling the role of her biblical namesake, the Judith who beheads, castrates, the patriarchal oppressor, by so encompassing Sutpen's grave, Judith thus also leaves behind a silent testimonial to the marginal position that, as an expendable daughter, she has always occupied in his plot.

21. On the subversive centrality of Rosa's narrative role, see Linda Kauffman, "A Lover's Discourse in *Absalom, Absalom!*," *Modern Fiction Studies* 29 (1983): 183–200, and Robert Con Davis, "The Symbolic Father in Yoknapatawpha County," *The Journal of Narrative Technique* 10 (1980): 39–55. Davis sees Rosa as the Lacanian "Other" of the symbolic father, attesting to "the repressed experience that lies within paternal structures"—namely, the "feminine"; Rosa thus "emerges as the dominant figure in this paternal fiction, over and above . . . the males the novel seems to be about" (39).

22. Winnett, "Coming Unstrung," 38. What Winnett says apropos Eliot's *Romola* about the communal genesis of legend as a counter to the intentions of oedipal plotting has equal significance for the counternarratives established by *Absalom*'s community of tellers: "legend tells a story that is over. Its significance has been established not by its protagonist, but by the community whose retelling of the story has become the sole measure of its importance. . . . The narrative significance of a life history lies ultimately in the hands (ears, mouths, pens) of others; however we attempt to shape this plot in terms of our sense of its retrospective significance, the retelling of the tale is always beyond our control" (32–33).

23. Given the fact that hidden origins and proleptic endings are the essential cornerstones of Sutpen's masterplot, it is fascinating to note how Rosa usurps control over both the beginning and end of the novel that tells his story. Not only does she regulate the text's opening—without her summons to Quentin, as we have seen, there would be no novel per se—but by making Quentin her companion, her witness, on the revelatory night-trip to Sutpen's Hundred, where Henry is discovered, she also summons into being the final event of the Sutpen family plot—the fire, set by Clytie, that burns down the house, destroys its last white descendant, and sends Rosa "to bed because it was finished now, there was nothing left. . . . And so she died" (376). These are simultaneously the penultimate events narrated by the two boys, and within a page of the mention of her death, the novel ends. It is as if the literal "story" must cease when Rosa is no

longer alive to keep it going. Thus, even in death Rosa continues to usurp Sutpen's desire for metaphoric finality, preempting his "proper" end by "breaking off" the account of *his* story where and when *she* desires.

24. I am indebted to Michele Whelan for making a similar point in class. Much of Irwin's argument also has to do with Quentin's contradiction-ridden attempts to master his father through the fantasy of a reversal of generations (*Doubling,* 68–76).

25. Brooks, *Reading,* 306.

12   *(Re)Reading Faulkner as*
        Father and Daughter of
        His Own Text
        Minrose C. Gwin

What contemporary readers may find most mysterious and provocative about Faulkner's narrative is the way it produces itself out
of what Barbara Johnson might call its own "difference within."[1]
Difference is by its very nature a slippery and elusive term. I would
suggest that it may be an appropriate way of describing the unsettling *fluctuations* of language and meaning that keep such works as
The Sound and the Fury and *Absalom, Absalom!* always so hauntingly
beyond our grasp. Where does this "difference within" come from?
In a strangely symbiotic way it seems both to generate and be
generated by certain irresolvable contradictions that splinter the
identity of the literary text in which they occur. This splintering
often makes Faulkner's writing seem to speak against itself, creating
a relationship of interior otherness somewhat like that between the
conscious and the unconscious mind. Such a text suggests, by its
own example, that identity is not one thing but rather many; and
that those many, and their *own* differences within, may indeed
necessitate a rethinking of the whole notion of *character*.

This process of difference may occur at the various levels of
language, narrative structure, character, story; in Faulkner's greatest moments it seems to encompass them all and dissolve boundaries between them. As I converse with some of Faulkner's most
compelling and problematic fiction, I am listening to the ways

in which his stories and his characters speak against themselves, how they come to tell their own subversive stories and so create spaces in Faulkner's texts where things break down and meaning ruptures—spaces where difference finds a voice. For it is in these spaces, if it is anywhere, that the mystery and power of Faulkner move and breathe. It is there that the play of meaning achieves its highest velocity, spinning Faulkner's texts out into infinite patterns of production, and so creating their unending energies.

It is possible, I believe, to read this element of difference within Faulkner's narrative process as being connected to what Luce Irigaray would call a feminine economy. This is an endlessly productive force linked to woman's sexuality and maternity. It is an economy of spending, one that puts into question other economies that rely on a balance of give and take.[2] This feminine difference of Faulkner's texts has the effect of dissolving boundaries—particularly those between author and character; sometimes, I would suggest, those between text and reader. As feminist reader conversing with male author, I am listening for Faulkner's feminine voices as they rise from within what I will describe as the bisexual spaces of difference that layer his narrative. Within these spaces I am attempting to read female characters in new ways, as they themselves seem to create a tension within Faulkner's art by undercutting and subverting patriarchy—the law of the father—by playing creatively on and within its margins.

Faulkner thus creates a symbolic order of father-author only to allow its disruption—often by a female character's own voice of difference within the patriarchal text. In this sense Faulkner becomes father and daughter of his own text: he authorizes the text's meaning and then relinquishes that authority in favor of difference and play. He thereby frees his art to speak and reproduce its own difference from itself in ceaseless variance—to go, as it were, *somewhere else*. It is impossible to know how this process came about. Yet Faulkner himself seems to have had a sense not only that all of his works "failed" to say what they were meant to, but that those "failures," as we see in his comments on *The Sound and the Fury,* his "finest failure," were indeed to be valued *to the extent* that they were failures.[3]

I am appropriating the father-daughter model as a trope for linking sexual difference to narrative process because its dynamics permit us to read Faulkner in several directions at once and hence to enter those spaces of difference with which we hope to converse. Let me be clear that, in part, I am thinking metaphorically in a traditional Lacanian sense of the father's associations with power and authority, symbolization and repression. In this sense the daughter is *of* the father because she is created by him; yet she is also, because of her femininity, his difference within—that which subverts the authority of the word by disallowing a univocality that would silence the process of difference at work within language and narrative.

In a sense, then, I am deposing the paternal metaphor through which Robert Con Davis, John Irwin, André Bleikasten, and other critics link psychoanalysis to narration because I am reading the daughter as much more than a linguistic or cultural construct in Faulkner's texts. I am reading her as female subject, as woman who speaks difference from the position of subject, as she who can *say* desire, loss, absence, and so who can draw us into the *processes* of productivity in Faulkner's texts—those processes that evolve only *because* the father's authoritative narrative is disrupted by the "daughters" of his own creation.

These "daughters," certain of Faulkner's female characters, seem intimately and mysteriously related to the productivity of Faulkner's narrative in a way that his male characters do not; for their feminine difference from father-author actually creates those bisexual spaces in which difference may find a voice. These "in-between" spaces affirm difference even as they dissolve our traditional notions of the binary construction of gender.

How do we find these spaces between father and daughter in Faulkner's texts? We first may need to rethink the notion of *character* and its relationship to the processes of loss and desire. Recent critical thought about Faulkner has concerned itself with the pervasiveness of loss in his works and the ways in which loss initiates narrative desire in both author and character. John T. Matthews has shown us, moreover, that the tracing of the absent person or thing in Faulkner's works often has the effect not of reconstructing that which has been lost, but instead of setting into motion a fluid and creative play of differences, which, in their very creativity and playfulness, dissolve the possibility of reconstruction or retrieval of the lost one or thing.[4] Loss thereby triggers the desire to tell stories about what has been lost, a narrative desire that in turn is both absorbed and regenerated in its own playful explorations of the infinite and mysterious spaces left by the absent one or thing. As we know, these processes, as they signify *both* fragmentation and creativity, disorder and expansiveness—as they become themselves by differing from themselves—produce characters who are other to themselves; they are split, fragmented, disordered. They move between what is present and what is absent, and they tell stories of their own inability to cohere, out of their interior differences.

We may think, then, of a Rosa Coldfield as a network of desires and productions rather than the unified, coherent fiction we call "character." Rosa is indeed the example par excellence of the poststructural subject, who, as Houston A. Baker, Jr., points out, is not capable of "speaking" out of wholeness and autonomy, but rather is instead a code that is always in the process of deconstructing and producing itself.[5] At the base of such a description is the Derridean notion of the subject's unconscious as a pattern of differences, a "radical alterity" that is unexplainable.[6] This symbiosis of loss and desire that theorists call the subject replays itself in processes that take shape as character, for example, as the Miss Rosa whose narrative desire both plucks out and reweaves the pattern of a culture that has, at once, denied her humanity and propelled her to produce it through imagination. Rosa speaks in those spaces between her own absence and presence as a speaking subject—that is, between what she is not and what she is. She becomes what Julia Kristeva would call a "questionable subject-in-process," one who makes and remakes herself through the utterance of her desire for her own presence.

Rosa's insistent talk may thus be heard, as Kristeva might say, "not [as] the discourse of a repudiated subject, but of one searching for the laws of its desires, operating as a hinge between immersion in the signifier and repudiation (it is neither one nor the other), its status unknown."[7] What I am suggesting, then, is not just the *presence* of absence in Faulkner's narrative but the necessity of that absence to the character's ability to speak the text's difference. The subject must not be whole, for to be whole is to be silent. It is only by negotiating the economy of loss and desire that the subject learns to speak what is not. Rosa Coldfield must have lost her *"world of living marriage"* before she can speak, through her loss of it, its inherent contradictions—its difference within.

Where we may listen to Faulkner, then, may be in those spaces of difference that create and are created out of the tensions of loss and desire, and the inevitable rending that their utterance produces. If we think in the sexual terms of the oedipal model, we may construe this space of desire and loss as the space between the father and the daughter, in this case, between the male author and the female character. This is the space of sameness *and* otherness. Both the father and the daughter may desire the difference of the other, but their sameness constructs desire as incestuous. To "have" the father, the daughter must lose him, and vice versa.

Here, I would hasten to add, I am not positing worlds of female loss and female lack, as Elaine Showalter describes the androcentric assumptions of Freudian and Lacanian psychoanalysis,[8] but instead am suggesting that we take Luce Irigaray's and Jane Gallop's lead in "reading" psychoanalytic theory in deconstructive ways.[9] What is at stake in our reading of Faulkner is not the father-author's creating of the daughter-character in terms of the authority he possesses. The more interesting and problematic question is: How does man create "character" coded as woman, the "daughter" whose narrative desire and sheer force lead the father-author to relinquish the authority of the word, and thereby create a new kind of narrative process arising from the interplay of difference? In these cases, woman created by man initiates *the difference within* that can make the male text speak against itself; and so becomes, as Alice Jardine says of woman in Western culture and metaphysics, all that "disturbs the Subject, Dialectic, and Truth."[10] By listening to the difference of the feminine, then, we may converse with the spaces between Faulkner and, for example, Caddy Compson, and many of his other female characters as well, as an area of "in-between" in which male creator and female created are present in an ever-heightening tension that generates narrative process. How does the feminine of Faulkner's text rise to speak difference from the position of subject? How does the father's daughter become woman? This is a process that Hélène Cixous's concept of bisexuality may clarify. In Cixous's schema the term *bisexuality* does not mean neuter.[11] It is, to the contrary, the *exacerbation* of male and female elements in the writer and hence in the writing. Such writing is in a permanent state of tension; it is generated and regenerated by the interaction between the feminine and the masculine, between self and other (in the familial model, between the father and the daughter). It does "not annul differences but stirs them up, pursues them, increases their number." In such writing there is an "in-between" that is "infinitely dynamized by an incessant process of exchange from one subject to another."[12]

Faulkner seems to interact in such a way with some women characters of his own creation, his same-yet-other "daughters" whose disruptive female voices articulate *even as they differ from* his male artistic consciousness. Within what I would describe as bisexual spaces in Faulkner's writing—spaces in which this exchange described by Cixous occurs—that consciousness moves from maleness to bisexuality by allowing, as Cixous says, the mutual and engaged presence of both sexes and through this "self-permission," the "multiplication of the effects of the inscription of desire" in the narrative process itself.[13] How, then, do we approach the connection between the male creator and the creative process and desire of these female voices? How does the feminist reader reread the father? Instead of wresting textual mastery away from the male author as Patricinio P. Schweickart suggests, perhaps we should ponder his divisibility and his interaction with the feminine of his own creation.[14] After all, the poststructural rethinking of subjectivity applies not only to the process we call *character,* which, as Cixous tells us, is inevitably disordered and "unanalyzable,"[15] but to the *writing subject* as well, the author who disappears into the spaces of the text and must be read out of those spaces.

Michel Foucault suggests that writing "is primarily concerned with creating an opening where the writing subject endlessly disappears" and enlists us in the examination of "the empty space left by the author's disappearance." We should, he says, "attentively observe, along its gaps and fault lines, its new demarcations, and the reapportionment of this voice; we should await the fluid functions released by this disappearance."[16] In some of Faulkner's texts this "opening" of the text is, I believe, "the daughter" herself—that is, woman; and the interface between Faulkner, the text's father, and this space of authorial effacement evolves within that bisexual space Cixous calls "the in-between . . . infinitely dynamized by an incessant process of exchange from one subject to another." As Faulkner the writing subject disappears into the rhetoric of the text, the created "daughter" emerges with her own language of desire and loss and subversion and, of course, creativity. Within this bisexual space, the daughter's creative voice is engendered by paternal absence, the father's vanishing—that is, his repudiation of authority, and, just as important, *his willingness to vanish,* to disappear into that opening as his text moves beyond its own boundaries and goes . . . somewhere else.

It has been observed, accurately and perceptively, that Faulkner wrote out of his own experience as a white Southern male in a patriarchal culture. Yet we know also that, paradoxically, Faulkner's texts both explore and explode the boundaries of culture through creative probings of their limits and nuances. It is this disruptive freedom of mind, this willingness to differ from itself in infinitely various ways, that we may find reverberating through Faulkner's narrative and its creative female voices. Within certain bisexual spaces of narrative, then, Faulkner relinquishes the mantle of the Lacanian "symbolic father," which, as Robert Con Davis points out, is "the agency of law."[17] He relinquishes the power of the phallus—the authority of the subject presumed to know—to *woman,* the female subject who thus becomes not only the created but also the creator.

I should point out here that, within this bisexual space, my reading of Faulkner offers an opposite conclusion to that of André Bleikasten, who sees fatherhood and sonship in Faulkner as "deeply involved in the *writer's* venture and relate back to his maddest desire: the desire to seize the authority of an original *author*—the authority, that is, of an origin, a founder, a father."[18] To the contrary, I find that Faulkner's texts achieve their greatest "power" (and I use that term advisedly) when they *give away* power and control, often to the subversive creativity of female subjects—the daughters who are the difference within and who become, as Jardine would say, "woman-in-effect"—all that signify "those *processes that disrupt symbolic structures in the West*."[19]

I need to define what I mean by female creativity. Sally Page and Cleanth Brooks view the "creativity" of Faulkner's female characters as inextricable from their reproductive and nurturing functions. Considered in this light, these women characters indeed *must be* either creative or destructive, for their "creativity" must reproduce and nurture the validity of the patriarchal universe in which they live, or it becomes destructive to that milieu. In this paradigm, "woman" becomes the created, the *image* of creation—but not the creator, the doer, the maker, the *agent* of creation.[20] The creativity I will converse with is a different thing altogether: it resides within the female subject who remakes herself and the world through imagination. It is a process engendered by desire that always seeks more than it has, a force from *within* the feminine space rather than one postulated by patriarchal expectation. Born out of sexual difference, it emerges out of the tension between Faulkner's male creative consciousness and its subversive feminine voice that undercuts its own discourse as it expands into new and unknown spaces. It is the bisexual space of Faulkner's texts.

What happens to these female subjects, then, is the same thing that seems to have happened to Faulkner as he created them and their responses to the world. Their creative impulse (and his as irrevocably linked to theirs) transforms the artistic consciousness by temporarily extending its creative boundaries into a new process of interaction that both derives from and intensifies sexual difference at the same time it questions its binary construction. Faulkner does this by allowing the female subject's capacity for creation to remain open and productive. Some of these characters, because of desire engendered by loss, enter what Derrida calls "the play of *différance*." They create new meaning through the disruption of presence, by taking the risk of "meaning nothing."[21] This ability to "play" without seeking center or boundary we find in such diverse characters as Rosa Coldfield, Temple Drake, Charlotte Rittenmeyer, Joanna Burden, Caddy Compson, and Addie Bundren. Tensions between denial and desire, the father and the mother, rigidity and flexibility, repression and sexuality give birth to the disrupted and disrupting female subject's narrative desire and by extension to Faulkner's insistence upon play, upon the plasticity of experience, upon the power of the human mind to break down rigidity and boundary.

If we consider what it means to "play" in the Derridean sense— that is, to disallow the necessity of closure, to defer meaning indefinitely—then we may wish to expand our notion of *character* still further to conceptualize female characters as feminine texts that defer themselves, and differ from themselves, ad infinitum. Their imaginative capacities may have morally negative results; yet their creativity is nonetheless a freeing force for their own psyches, which have been squeezed, compartmentalized, and devalued because of gender.

Emily Grierson "plays" creatively by subverting paternal and societal restraint. She not only breaks the law of the father. Within her own physical space, the bedroom, she subverts the signifiers of marital love—the rose-shaded lights, the tarnished hairbrush, the discarded clothing. She thereby creates new meaning for herself, within the repressive margins of the patriarchal order—inside the father's house.

Addie Bundren insists upon her own subjectivity: "I would be I," she says and she inscribes her different text in an inescapable way. She knows that one never gets to the end of words, that the search for a center is fruitless, that language is not representative but constitutive. What she speaks and thus what she creates is her own sexuality. As Foucault's *The History of Sexuality* shows us, sexual desire is the stimulus for "a regulated and polymorphous incitement to discourse."[22] In response to the deadening force of the father's law, which decrees her to a living death, Addie redesigns her desire into the images of beautiful "garments which we would remove in order to shape and coerce the terrible blood to the forlorn echo of the dead word high in the air."[23] She becomes woman writing her own body, and as Cixous says, "her flesh speaks true. She *inscribes* what she is saying because she does not deny unconscious drives the unmanageable part they play in speech."[24]

Joanna Burden insists, above all, upon the *process* of her subjectivity, the narrative desire to invent and reinvent herself. It is the very multiplicity of her creativity, her insistence upon "playing it out like a play,"[25] which so frightens and alienates Joe Christmas. She must deny her austere past, "the frustrate and irrevocable years" of the father's law, and re-create herself insistently, compulsively, unilaterally. If we continue to think of the female character as a text, we may see that Joanna Burden *becomes* multiple texts of desire: sexuality, jealousy, religiosity. Her narrative desire propels her to reinvent herself variously, yet that same desire deconstructs those texts of herself as part of the ongoing process of invention. In this sense she is not so different from Lena Grove, who is herself the disruptive feminine process *outside* cultural codes, who, like Joanna, is a female subject propelled by loss and desire. Between these two female texts, which are *each* both disruptive and productive, we feel the force of Faulkner's narrative desire in continual process and motion.

But how to read process and motion? Caddy Compson has been thought of as a silent text constructed by her brothers, "a blank screen" imprinted by male fear and desire.[26] I would suggest that we try to "hear" Caddy Compson as the feminine voice of difference within male discourse, as the counter-narrative that speaks the possibility of play. If we can imagine Caddy as the space of woman's multiple and generative libidinal energies, a space that cannot be fixed or mastered, "this sex which is not one," as Irigaray would say, then we may begin to hear her voice from within the folds of Faulkner's text and from within our willingness to be absorbed into the concentric and bisexual spaces *between* the "manifest text" of Faulkner's male creative consciousness and the "unconscious discourse" of its own feminine subjectivity.[27] And so Caddy is never really silent, for her "silence" itself speaks.

Although she speaks as a girl within Benjy's mind, Caddy's voice carries the referential weight of the position of the mother, whose very acts of giving birth, of gestation and nurturance, dissolve the otherness of the other. In Benjy's section Caddy speaks the evaporation of ego boundaries and so creates the difference of maternal space, what Kristeva calls "the *unsettling process* of meaning and subject" rather than "the coherence or identity of either *one* or a *multiplicity* of structures."[28] In many of the scenes created in Benjy's memory, Caddy encloses him within this maternal space that transcends the teleologies of time and distance, and thus becomes their counter-narrative:

"Why, Benjy," she said. She looked at me and I went and she put her arms around me. "Did you find Caddy again?" she said. "Did you think Caddy had run away?"[29]

In such scenes Caddy's voice undercuts some of the very meanings of *The Sound and the Fury,* which, as we have been shown, is indeed about the effects of time and loss.[30] For what Caddy's voice says out of the maternal space created for it in Benjy's mind is precisely *opposite* to what Benjy's narrative as a whole seems to be saying—that originary plenitude can never be regained, that creativity and play have given way to despair, rigidity, meaningless order—to sound and fury signifying nothing.[31]

Let us listen to the Caddy of Quentin's section: "let me go I've got to catch him and ask his let me go Quentin please let me go let me go" (*The Sound,* 202). Here Caddy rises from the repressiveness of Quentin's discourse to speak her desire for Dalton Ames, for entry into a libidinal economy that allows her to give, to spend herself excessively, to play creatively within that half-light between self and other, much as she did within the maternal space she created within Benjy's discourse. At the same time, she speaks *from* Quentin *to* Quentin of the feminine within himself—that which he, entangled in a cultural narrative already written for him, can but desire and grieve for. To embrace the force that is Caddy, "the force and movement which displaces lines,"[32] we may conceive of her character as pervading this section in an organic way—enfolding, burrowing into, and playing within Quentin's mind. Paradoxically she both exceeds and is confined inside his discourse. She is like one of the items Quentin keeps packing in his bag; he tries to squeeze her subjectivity into the objective position required to "pack it away." Of course he fails. The constricted space cannot contain her or her voice. She speaks out of the deepest and darkest spaces of his unconscious, and her voice is a powerful challenge to despair. With jarring force, her voice erupts from the darkness of Quentin's mind, as in his memory of the dungeon in a childhood book. In this intriguing and paradoxical bisexual space, "the dungeon," as Noel Polk has emphasized, is indeed "Mother herself."[33] Caroline Compson's lack of love has created the dark place from which Quentin cannot free himself. It is a dungeon *built by the mother* and it cannot be escaped, for it is the place of the unconscious where fear lives. It is not only threatening; it is terribly and tragically destructive. Yet the feminine differs from itself: the daughter differs from the mother. Within Quentin's memory rises the voice of Caddy who would become a man, a *king*, in order to *"break that place open and drag them out,"* so as to *"whip them good"* (215).

Within the male mind, then, we see maternal space both as dungeon, the place of castration and anxiety, and as the avenue of escape from it. This is surely the "in-between" of Cixous's theoretical imagination, and one of multiple levels and voices. Within Faulkner's male creative consciousness and its multiple subjectivities we find another male creative consciousness and *its* multiple subjectivities, who are *female* and *both* inhibiting (mother) and freeing (Caddy), and moreover in conflict over the status of the male unconscious and so constituting its difference within.

The Caddy of Jason's section continues to speak the language of difference. Filtered through the alembic of Jason's obsessive ("Once a bitch always a bitch") insistence upon male authority, her voice speaks the tragic results of the cultural objectification of the female subject and the disastrous effects of a system of barter that makes women commodities. Because she is both a sign, a commodity, and a speaker of signs, an exchanger, she cannot negotiate in Jason's phallocentric economy. She cannot get what she wants, nor can she return to being the valuable commodity, a virgin, that she once was. She is therefore doubly trapped in male discourse. Hers is a voice to which feminist readers are particularly attuned, for it is the voice of female subjectivity struggling within a cultural text that seeks its silencing. It speaks out of a tight place and it speaks panic and sorrow and loss. "Oh God, oh God," it cries out (261). To listen is painful and terrible, for what we are hearing is the daughter of patriarchal culture speaking loss, speaking what it means to be denied subjectivity and access to one's own desire.

How do we continue to hear Caddy as she fades from our vision in "the moving wall of grey light," into such a yawning chasm of lostness that she seems actually to "disintegrate into minute and venomous particles, like dust . . ."? (*The Sound,* 330). Neither Dilsey who endures nor Quentin who escapes can "say" the Caddy whose plurivocity is the difference that female subjectivity and the force of woman create within Faulkner's text. Yet, as Matthews so persuasively reminds us, *The Sound and the Fury* is about the intimate and mysterious relation between loss and articulation.[34]

Might we ourselves, then, create Caddy through the "grey light" of our own loss of her as the book draws to a close? Might her voice have moved from the space within her brothers' male discourse to another more nebulous (but still bisexual) space between literary text and feminist reader? *For I can still hear Caddy Compson.* She is the voice of alterity to the long list of failed men of Faulkner's Appendix. She speaks in the voice of Melissa Meek who, "trembling and aghast at her own temerity," bursts into Jason's thriving masculine domain and forces him to look upon the face of the woman whose life he negotiated as loss to attain it. If we read the Appendix as this space between text and reader, Caddy still may be heard as the disruptive feminine voice that seeks to give and save and love, and thus speaks the text's difference from itself. Whatever else *The Sound and the Fury* may be and do, surely it leaves us in the space of difference. When we permit ourselves to hear Caddy's voice as it creates this difference, we allow ourselves to enter that opening in the text that Faulkner disappears into, but leaves Caddy's voice to guide us toward.

We may begin conversing similarly with other of Faulkner's female characters—for example, with Rosa Coldfield and Charlotte Rittenmeyer, as feminine texts whose presence creates bisexual spaces in Faulkner's writing. In *Absalom, Absalom!* and *The Wild Palms* these are spaces in which difference mysteriously generates unexpected stories that allow narrative to speak against itself and so to attain a power and tension that it would not have reached other-wise. Rosa Coldfield's telling and retelling of the Sutpen story becomes in the Foucaultian progression of desire, repression, and discourse a cultural necessity—"something akin to a secret whose discovery is imperative, a thing abusively reduced to silence, and at the same time difficult and necessary, dangerous and precious to divulge."[35] This is the sense of things we have from Rosa: that what she thinks she knows, or desires to know, is indeed both dangerous and precious. She is the hysterical woman who reads the inexplicable repressiveness of masculinist ideology articulated in the shared cultural narratives of Thomas Sutpen, Mr. Compson, Quentin, and Shreve. Together these patriarchal narratives, with their culminative authority, devalue woman and silence women who, like Rosa, speak difference from the position of subject.

The men of *Absalom, Absalom!*—even Quentin himself—eventually shut Rosa Coldfield up because they cannot stand the sound of her voice, which so shrilly, insistently tells the story of their own cultural madness. Even silenced, she becomes the uncanny feminine sign of what must be repressed by such a culture in order for it to function. Yet, at the same time, Rosa's creativity, her narrative desire to tell what she has lost, can be linked to the narrative process of *Absalom* itself—its refusal to end, its gaps and ruptures, its own sense of loss.

If we converse with Rosa, we must converse with the ambiguity and anguish of her creativity. She knows the power of the flesh but she must repress her own desire and render it into talk, for her desire to enter the sexual world of *"living marriage"* is always prohibited in a culture that denies white female sexuality, and it is transformed into what Cixous has called the initial act of female creativity: Rosa "unthinks the unifying, regulating history that homogenizes and channels forces."[36] Matthews points out that Rosa must continually defer her desires and thus speaks the loss she feels.[37] I would go on to say that, as a female subject striving to speak her desire in a milieu that denies its existence, Rosa both disrupts and re-creates the racist and sexist culture in which she exists. She creates, for example, the disturbing and terrifying memory of herself and Clytie on the stairs of Sutpen's Hundred; yet she destroys the human recognition she receives in that encounter with her denial of female connection ("*Take your hand off me, nigger!*").[38] She knows the power of the flesh but she must repress her own desire and render it into discourse. She speaks her loss from a feminine space that disrupts patriarchal culture, yet she cannot help but speak her culture as well, with its complex and pain-filled polyphonies of racial and sexual repressiveness.

Rosa Coldfield thus speaks difference in two senses. She herself is the feminine text of difference within patriarchal culture—that which it must deny in order to maintain its systems—*at the same time* her actions cement patriarchy's fixity and rigidity. Her voice conveys her difference from the father, but it also reveals that she is still his daughter. She is trapped in history. Her feminine voice is that of the hysteric, described by Catherine Clément as one "whose body is transformed into a theater for forgotten scenes, [and who] relives the past, bearing witness to a lost childhood that survives in suffering." For Rosa, as for the hysteric, "this is history that is not over";[39] nor, as Faulkner tells us through the text that is Rosa, will it ever be. "Was" can never be "was," and cultural narratives continue to imprint themselves even upon their own deconstructors. Faulkner creates Rosa Coldfield, and himself, as makers of differences, but also as those who are ever in the process of being bound by their culture even as they are eluding it.

Charlotte Rittenmeyer extends the discourse of love beyond cultural codes, creating it as a living thing that is itself an ongoing process of deconstruction and regeneration. Love does not fail, she tells Harry; it is people who fail. In its very excessiveness, in its tendency to "flood" over cultural boundaries the same way the Mississippi River floods the landscape in "Old Man," Charlotte's desire problematizes the binary structure of *The Wild Palms* by mediating the very motion of difference in this watery bloody book. Her feminine "flooding" leads us into the bisexual spaces, the fluid fluctuations, in Faulkner's writing that allow us a way of reading (and thinking) outside binary opposition, a means of dissolving either/or, male/female, active/passive systems. Her desire speaks the difference within this binary narrative, the possibility of *something else*. Such a possibility implies a connection between woman as a desiring subject and the ways in which Faulkner's art floods beyond its own self-constructed levees.

As Faulkner creates female creativity, then, and compels female subjects to "unthink" the world, we feel his participation in their creative processes. As writing subject, (s)he disappears into the text's bisexual opening between male author and the feminine of his own imagination. When this happens, Faulkner the writing subject is able to become father and daughter of his own text. Faulkner's style and meaning, his narrative desire, become immersed in these female subjects, who(m) he himself has made yet also *is*. Gayatri Spivak's tracing of the position of woman in Derrida's schema seems to articulate the meaning of this immersion: as the image of "originary undecidability," woman can "occupy both positions in the subject/object oscillation."[40] Female characters in Faulkner's texts may be both subject and object in the sense that he creates them, yet in a mysterious way also permits his own subjectivity to become entangled with theirs. They and he are neither daughter nor father, but *both* together, at once.

If we think of the process of the feminine as the space of disruption in these and other of Faulkner's texts, as their difference within, and the female subject, the *woman character,* as the discursiveness of that space, as the rebellious unconscious of patriarchy, then we may begin to reread the father-author within those bisexual spaces of his own creation. And within the synergy between feminist reader and male text, we may find Faulkner in the unexpected "in-between" as he becomes both father and daughter of his own text, as he creates *and participates in* the daughter's own tracings of paternal absence, her female subjectivity and her narrative desire, *her* creative negotiations of the spaces left by the father.

Notes

I wish to thank Beth Kowaleski-Wallace and Patricia Yaeger for their many important contributions to the development of this essay.

1. Barbara Johnson, *The Critical Difference: Essays in the Contemporary Rhetoric of Reading* (Baltimore: Johns Hopkins University Press, 1980), 4.

2. Luce Irigaray, *This Sex Which Is Not One,* trans. Gillian C. Gill (Ithaca: Cornell University Press, 1985), 31. In "The Laugh of the Medusa" Hélène Cixous argues that, "far more extensively and repressively than is ever suspected or admitted," writing is generated by a libidinal and cultural economy which is marked as masculine and which, because of exaggeration and oppositional thinking, often has become "a locus where the repression of women has been perpetuated" (249). The idea of excessiveness and expansiveness being marked as feminine pervades the thinking of Cixous, Irigaray, and Julia Kristeva, influenced as they are by psychoanalytic theory. Woman nourishes life, Cixous writes; she gives without measuring how much; she creates "an 'economy' that can no longer be put in economic terms" ("Laugh of the Medusa," 264). Likewise, Irigaray argues that woman's libidinal plurality creates a feminine discourse of desire that replenishes itself, that is "always something more" (*This Sex,* 29). And similarly, Kristeva writes that it is probably necessary to be a woman to push theoretical reason beyond its limits and thus to create a linguistics of "heterogenous economy," which is capable of "accounting for a nonetheless articulated *instinctual drive,* across and through the constitutive and insurmountable frontier of *meaning*" (*Desire in Language,* 146). (See subsequent notes for full citations.)

3. See, for example, *Faulkner in the University,* eds. Frederick L. Gwynn and Joseph L. Blotner (Charlottesville: University of Virginia Press, 1959), 4–5, 77–78, and *Faulkner at West Point,* eds. Joseph L. Fant III and Robert Ashley (New York: Random House, 1964), 48–49.

4. John T. Matthews, *The Play of Faulkner's Language* (Ithaca: Cornell University Press, 1982), 20–21. In *Faulkner's Rhetoric of Loss* (Austin: University of Texas Press, 1983), Gail Mortimer argues that Faulkner's protagonists respond to loss by erecting various kinds of defenses, which allow them to feel that they are exerting control upon "the dissolution that is the normal state of things" and that Faulkner's rhetorical strategies mirror the tensions between control and lack of it (4–5). In this schema women represent a lack of control and a projection of male fear. They become "distorted or mythicized beings, the projection of a masculine consciousness at its most vulnerable" (122). To the contrary, I am suggesting that loss and desire are productive generators of the narrative process, which is itself linked to the feminine in Faulkner's texts.

5. Houston A. Baker, Jr., *Blues, Ideology, and Afro-American Literature: A Vernacular Theory* (Chicago: University of Chicago Press, 1984), 1.

6. Jacques Derrida, *Speech and Phenomena and Other Essays on Husserl's Theory of Signs,* trans. and intro. David B. Allison, preface Newton Garver (Evanston: Northwestern University Press, 1973), 152.

7. Julia Kristeva, *Desire in Language: A Semiotic Approach to Literature and Art,* ed. Leon S. Roudiez (New York: Columbia University Press, 1980), 120.

8. Elaine Showalter, "Feminist Criticism in the Wilderness," *Critical Inquiry* 8 (Winter 1981): 195. This essay has been reprinted in Showalter, ed., *The New Feminist Criticism: Essays on Women, Literature, and Theory* (New York: Pantheon, 1985), 243–70; and Elizabeth Abel, ed., *Writing and Sexual Difference* (Chicago: University of Chicago Press, 1982), 9–36.

9. See, in particular, Gallop's *Feminism and Psychoanalysis: The Daughter's Seduction* (Ithaca: Cornell University Press, 1982) and *Reading Lacan* (Ithaca: Cornell University Press, 1985); Irigaray's *This Sex Which Is Not One,* previously cited; and *Speculum of the Other Woman,* trans. Gillian C. Gill (Ithaca: Cornell University Press, 1985).

10. Alice Jardine, *Gynesis: Configurations of Woman and Modernity* (Ithaca: Cornell University Press, 1985), 183.

11. I should add that Cixous's "bisexuality" differs from androgyny, defined by Carolyn Heilbrun as that which "suggests a spirit of reconciliation between the sexes." See *Toward a Recognition of Androgyny* (New York: Knopf, 1964), x.

12. Hélène Cixous, "The Laugh of the Medusa," in *New French Feminisms: An Anthology,* ed. Elaine Marks and Isabelle de Courtivron (Amherst: University of Massachusetts Press, 1980), 254.

13. Cixous, "The Laugh of the Medusa," 254.

14. Like Judith Fetterley, who positions herself as a "resisting reader" of some male texts, Schweickart argues that the woman reader must struggle against the text for mastery: "Taking control of the reading experience means reading the text as it was *not* meant to be read, in fact, reading it against itself" (50). See Fetterley, *The Resisting Reader: A Feminist Approach to American Literature* (Bloomington: Indiana University Press, 1977); and Schweickart, "Reading Ourselves: Toward a Feminist Theory of Reading," in *Gender and Reading: Essays on Readers, Texts, and Contexts,* eds. Elizabeth A. Flynn and Schweickart (Baltimore: Johns Hopkins University Press, 1986), 31–62.

15. Cixous, "The Character of 'Character,' " *New Literary History* 5 (1974): 387.

16. Michel Foucault, *Language, Counter-Memory, Practice,* eds. Donald F. Bouchard and Sherry Simon (Ithaca: Cornell University Press, 1977), 116, 121.

17. Robert Con Davis, "Critical Introduction: The Discourse of the Father," in *The Fictional Father: Lacanian Readings of the Text,* ed. Davis (Amherst: University of Massachusetts Press, 1981), 2.

18. André Bleikasten, "Fathers in Faulkner," in *The Fictional Father,* 144–45. In the same volume Thomas A. Hanzo seems to be saying the same thing about narrative in general and Dickens in particular when he argues that, just as the Lacanian term "phallus" produces meaning, so "it is the principle of paternity that may be said to govern narrative, as well as other

modes of the generation of meaning" ("Paternity and the Subject in *Bleak House*," 47).

19. Jardine, *Gynesis,* 42.

20. See, for example, Sally Page, *Faulkner's Women: Characterization and Meaning* (Deland, Fla.: Everett/Edward, 1972), 16, and Cleanth Brooks, "Faulkner's Vision of Good and Evil," *Massachusetts Review* 3 (Summer 1962): 697. In an analysis of *Absalom, Absalom!* Thomas Lorch carries this androcentric model to the extreme by arguing that the novel "presents male aspiration and will and the passive, enduring, absorbent Female in more closely balanced conflict than we find in Faulkner's other novels." Thomas Sutpen is Faulkner's most powerful male figure, Lorch finds, but his destruction is wrought by society and women, who "absorb and stifle his creative spark." "Female nature" in Faulkner's fiction is "necessary and good," but only "because it provides the living material for the male to shape and elevate." See "Thomas Sutpen and the Female Principle," *Mississippi Quarterly* 20 (Winter 1967): 38–41.

21. Derrida, "Implications: Interview with Henri Ronse," in *Positions,* trans. Alan Bass (Chicago: University of Chicago Press, 1981), 14. Matthews has applied the Derridean model in his previously cited and illuminating study of the structures of Faulkner's language and argues that the language of the narratives "produces meaning from *différance*" and hence "meaning arises from the lack of authoritative, unique, absolute, or central significance" rather than from any sense of conclusiveness or closure (*The Play of Faulkner's Language,* 31).

22. Michel Foucault, *The History of Sexuality,* trans. Robert Hurley (New York: Vintage, 1980), 1: 34.

23. Faulkner, *As I Lay Dying* (New York: Vintage, 1964), 167.

24. Cixous, "Sorties," in *The Newly Born Woman,* eds. Catherine Clément and Cixous, trans. Betsy Wing, foreword Sandra M. Gilbert, Theory and History of Literature Series, vol. 24 (Minneapolis: University of Minnesota Press, 1986), 92. Also in "Laugh of the Medusa" Cixous posits the concept *l'écriture féminine,* the writing of the female body, so as to transcend a masculine libidinal economy that lies at the heart of Western thought and literary practice. As Ann Rosalind Jones points out in her essay "Writing the Body: Toward an Understanding of *l'écriture féminine,*" Irigaray and Kristeva share Cixous's opposition of women's bodily experience "to the phallic-symbolic patterns embedded in Western thought." The immediacy of that experience "promises a clarity of perception and a vitality that can bring down mountains of phallocentric delusion. Finally, to the extent that the female body is seen as a direct source of female writing, a powerful alternative discourse seems possible: to write from the body is to re-create the world" (366). See Jones's essay in *The New Feminist Criticism,* 361–77. *L'écriture féminine* may indeed be seen as a response to the question posed by Sandra M. Gilbert and Susan Gubar in *The Madwoman in the Attic* (New

Haven: Yale University Press, 1979): "If the pen is a metaphorical penis, from what organ can females generate texts?" (7). In *Of Woman Born* (New York: Norton, 1977), however, Adrienne Rich, like the French feminists, envisions woman's writing of the body in more general terms, as touching "the unity and resonance of our physicality, the corporeal ground of our intelligence" (62). See Showalter, "Feminist Criticism in the Wilderness," and Jones for assessments of what they perceive as theoretical problems in the concept of *l'écriture féminine*.

    25. William Faulkner, *Light in August* (New York: Modern Library, 1967), 244–45.

    26. Bleikasten, *The Most Splendid Failure: Faulkner's* The Sound and the Fury (Bloomington: Indiana University Press, 1976), 65.

    27. I am using Robert Con Davis's terms to describe Lacan's model of narrative as a split process that "never reaches a point of stability or wholeness" and therefore "poses a serious threat to the empirically-based tradition of interpretation as a transparent and focusable lens, an open subjectivity, through which a detached investigator peers into a stable (possibly pictographic) narrative structure." See "Introduction," in *Lacan and Narration: The Psychoanalytic Difference in Narrative Theory*, ed. Davis (Amherst: University of Massachusetts Press, 1981), 857.

    28. Kristeva, *Desire in Language*, 125.

    29. Faulkner, *The Sound and the Fury* (New York: Vintage, 1963), 50. Subsequent references will be cited in the text.

    30. In his influential essay "Time in Faulkner: *The Sound and the Fury*," Jean-Paul Sartre says that the true subject of the novel is the human dilemma of being placed in time. See *William Faulkner: Two Decades of Criticism*, eds. Frederick J. Hoffman and Olga W. Vickery (East Lansing: Michigan State University Press, 1954), 180–88. Douglas Messerli focuses upon Caddy as "the *character* of time" (37), and finds that "in her pure dynamism, in pure becoming is life itself without human order" (41). Messerli's essay provides a summary of other thinking on the subject of time in the novel. See "The Problem of Time in *The Sound and the Fury*: A Critical Reassessment and Reinterpretation," *Southern Literary Journal* 6 (Spring 1974): 19–41.

    31. More optimistically, Matthews finds that loss opens the way to "the fun of writing" and its continual deferment, its "play of failures" (*The Play of Faulkner's Language*, 73).

    32. Derrida, *Writing and Difference*, trans. Alan Bass (Chicago: University of Chicago Press, 1978), 28.

    33. Noel Polk, in his essay by the same name, points out that the image of Caroline Compson as a jailer is reinforced by her carrying of the keys to the house. Her whining and general repressiveness make "of the house itself a prison, the grounds a fenced compound." See "The Dungeon Was Mother Herself," in *New Directions in Faulkner Studies,*

258 Minrose C. Gwin

eds. Doreen Fowler and Ann J. Abadie (Jackson: University of Mississippi Press), 62.

34. Matthews, *The Play of Faulkner's Language,* 65.

35. Foucault, *The History of Sexuality,* 1:35.

36. Cixous, "The Laugh of the Medusa," 252.

37. Matthews, *The Play of Faulkner's Language,* 124.

38. Faulkner, *Absalom, Absalom!* (New York: Modern Library, 1966), 140.

39. Clément, "Sorceress and Hysteric," in *The Newly Born Woman,* 5–6.

40. Gayatri Spivak, "Love Me, Love My Ombre, Elle," *Diacritics* (Winter 1984): 24.

*Where the Absent
Father Went*
Alcott's Work
James D. Wallace

My interest in "Louisa May Alcott and the Absent Father" grows
out of a particular readerly situation that I should explain at the
outset. I did not read Alcott in my youth; instead, I first encountered
Little Women when I read it to my daughter, then ten years old, a
few chapters a night as a bedtime story. In that circumstance, I was
naturally interested in the adoration with which the entire family
spoke of the father, read his precious letters, dreamt of sending him
presents, and longed for his return. I longed for it, too, anticipating
the warm portrait of a wise, loving father nourishing the expanding
sphere of his daughters' encounters with the world, encouraging
the development of their individual talents, quieting their recurrent
anxieties over poverty and the tyranny of their rich aunt—an idealized Victorian portrait, to be sure, but one that would embellish
and confirm the ties I felt to my own daughter as night after night
we made our way through the novel.

I hardly need say how disappointed I was. After precipitating
the chief familial crisis of part 1 of *Little Women* and the supreme
sacrifice of Jo's hair, Mr. March disappears permanently from the
reader's ken. More present in his absence than in the flesh, Mr.
March loses all influence and importance once he has been reclaimed
from the public world of the Civil War, and the role of the father,
insofar as it can be said to exist at all in *Little Women,* devolves

on the kindly but vague Professor Friedrich Bhaer, whom Alcott conjures into the novel as the neutralizer of all that is energetic and engaging about Jo March.

The puzzle of the absent father is only intensified when we turn to the Alcott thrillers collected in *Behind a Mask* and *Plots and Counterplots*. In those wild stories, designed, like Jo March's, for "harrowing up the souls of the readers,"[1] the absent father returns with a vengeance, but he is dismembered, so to speak, and distributed over a wide range of characters: in "Pauline's Passion and Punishment," the weak and treacherous Gilbert Redmond; in "A Whisper in the Dark," Sybil's sinister uncle; in "A Marble Woman," the Hawthornian manipulator, Bazil Yorke, and his mysterious model, Germain; in "Behind a Mask," the stupid Sir John Coventry. In tale after tale a young woman, always an orphan in one sense or another, enters into a struggle for erotic ascendancy with an older man who both harbors some secret grudge against the female sex and holds the key to the woman's future.

In their representation of the pitched battle between the sexes, Alcott's works are far from unique to nineteenth-century culture. Rather, they contribute to a broader and more critical examination of the nature of relations between men and women in American society. The works of Fanny Fern, Harriet Beecher Stowe, and Elizabeth Stuart Phelps, among others, constitute an aggressive critique of the ideology of the domestic sphere, an ideology that gave such sweeping powers to men and so closely circumscribed the arena of women's competence that it ended by structuring *all* male-female relations as essentially those between a father and his daughter. This "universalization" of sex roles led to a curious depersonalization of the male characters in women's fiction; in novels by Fern and others, the father is diminished or eliminated as an actual character, but his avatars, the eroticized representatives of his power and oppression, multiply and diffuse, and the woman's task becomes that of discovering, among alternative versions of the father, the one who will admit her equality and allow her autonomy. Eventually the father's power becomes so abstract that it is disembodied altogether and is represented as some pure form of authority—the authority of "The Law," of "Religion," of "Medicine"—and the tradition finally culminates in the feminist separatism of Mary E. Wilkins Freeman, Sarah Orne Jewett, and Charlotte Perkins Gilman, who entered into an imaginative analysis of what today would be called "patriarchy," who concluded that male-female relations were simply too tainted to be saved, and who created imaginative utopias purified of the presence of men.

Within this tradition, Alcott's career is paradigmatic. Her important novel *Work* marks two essential developments toward a fiction of feminist separatism and resolves the puzzle of Alcott's earlier treatments of the father. First of all, the novel's protagonist negotiates among paternal avatars for the relationships that will allow her to overcome her world-weariness, continue her work, become a mother, and gather to her all the women whose lives have flowed into the same course as hers. With this plot, *Work* signals the point at which the institutionalized separation of male and female into distinguishable cultures enters fully into American literature; never before had any writer faced so resolutely that social fact. Second, in *Work*, as in Alcott's other fiction, the figure of the father is abstracted and depersonalized; the father disappears behind generalized forces and powers as Alcott begins an analysis of the forms of patriarchal power and privilege. For the first time, patriarchy is represented not as the oppressive authority of an outmoded religious or political orthodoxy, but as the capacity of language itself to abstract and as the quality of mind that reduces experience to rote formula, empty rules of conduct, fatuous propriety. In *Work* the father *principal* dissolves to a patriarchal *principle;* both men and their discourse are analyzed as tropes for patriarchy.

In the balance of this essay, I want to consider how *Work* gropes toward a critical understanding of and challenge to the way a privileged group of language users, men, employs its peculiarly masculine discourse as an instrument of patriarchal power. Alcott's strategy is essentially to present a "coming to consciousness" deviously, through devices of displacement, transference, "splintering" of the father's image, scattering of him among avatars, giving new discursive substance to "his" word. Against the hegemony of masculine discourse Alcott puts into play three successive versions of or possibilities for a feminine discourse—first a discourse of housewifery, second an erotic language of the flowers, and last a mediating language of women's liberation—in an attempt to create a language that could fully embody, comprehend, and give a voice to women's experience. Although she cannot finally resolve the question of what language women must discover, Alcott nevertheless offers a provocative analysis of the disappearance of the father into linguistic abstraction.

The protagonist of *Work,* Christie Devon, begins her life of labor as a maid in an exemplary fortress of domesticity. It is a realm created by and for the serenity of the Bronson Alcotts of America, a realm in which the exposure of masculine discourse will accrue special meaning.[2] The husband in the household, Mr. Stuart, is "bent on making his way in the world at any cost" and "absent from morning till night," while his wife is the haughty queen of her domain: "She made a royal progress through her dominions every morning, issued orders, found fault liberally, bestowed praise sparingly, and took no more personal interest in her servants than if they were clocks, to be wound up once a day, and sent away the moment they got out of repair" (25). Christie does her work well, but her dissatisfaction with the pretensions of the Stuart home finds expression in her appetite for racy novels like *The Abbot* and erupts emblematically when, because of her reading, she sets fire to the house: "In the attic Christie was discovered lying dressed upon her bed, asleep or suffocated by the smoke that filled the room. A book had slipped from her hand, and in falling had upset the candle on a chair beside her; the long wick leaned against a cotton gown hanging on the wall, and a greater part of Christie's wardrobe was burning brilliantly" (31–32).

Aroused from her stupor, Christie is "a little hysterical" and laughs at the efforts to douse the flames. Mrs. Stuart fires her on the spot: "She must go, Horatio, she must go! I cannot have my nerves shattered by such dreadful scenes. She is too fond of books, and it has turned her brain" (32–33).

A number of important cultural themes converge on this comic catastrophe. As a maid in a bourgeois household, Christie represents the dangerous forces of the instinctual life within the rigorously maintained consciousness of the domestic household: she associates with the black cook who had been an "insurmountable obstacle" (20) to all other applicants for her job; she cleans her employer's boots and rubbers, although at first she objects to the "degradation" of the task and declares, "I won't submit to it" (22); she finds a stock of novels in the Stuarts' attic "by a sort of instinct as sure as that which leads a fly to a honeypot" (29). Alcott presents all these touches as signs of Christie's no-nonsense approach to the world of work and its necessities, but within the fastidious proprieties of the Stuart household, Christie represents dirt, the lower orders, manual labor, and all that "language of the nether world" that emanates from "below stairs."[3] In addition, the falling book that has set fire to her cotton gown is a literalized image of the cliché that novel-reading *inflames the imaginations* of young persons (especially young women) and renders them unfit for their stations in life.[4] Even more damning is the fact that Mrs. Stuart locates the real peril not in the pernicious effects of novel-reading, but in the love of books itself: "She is too fond of books, and it [i.e., that fondness] has turned her brain." The mere *desire* to read makes a maid dangerous to the domestic fortress—or, by implication, makes any human being dangerous to the persons unfortunate enough to be living in the same household (or community or society). Alcott has in fact produced her own version of the "volcano" poems of Emily Dickinson, in which the hidden fires of the volcano function as images of an explosive, erotic inner force that threatens to detonate the placid conventions of the family and society: "Vesuvius at Home."[5]

Christie's other jobs through this section of *Work* are similarly harassed with projections of her own desire to explode the containing domestic sphere. As a governess, she reads *Jane Eyre* while fending off the advances of a homegrown Rochester; as a companion, she helps a young woman, the victim of a hereditary madness, to submit quietly to her fate; as a seamstress, she befriends a fallen woman, Rachel, and quits when her friend is fired. Her only venture outside the domestic sphere, as an actress, confronts her with the jealousy of another friend, and in the end Christie is literally driven from the stage when a piece of falling scenery hits her on the head. Finally, the tension between desire and duty combines with poverty and a lingering illness to bring Christie to the point of suicide: the consequence of Christie's struggle to come to terms with the domestic sphere is exhaustion and death.

This conflict between individual and society, between the erotic and the civilized, between the urges of the instinctual life and the rigors of rationality, is implicit in the very theme of *Work*, a theme proclaimed by Christie's announcement in the novel's opening sentence: "Aunt Betsey, there's going to be a new Declaration of Independence" (1). Christie seeks that independence in a series of stages built around the work experiences available to American women in the mid-nineteenth century: servant, actress, governess, companion, and free-lance seamstress. Most of these episodes reconstitute Alcott's earlier attempts to write about her work experience— "How I Went Out to Service," *The Rival Prima Donnas,* "Love and Self-Love"—but the later novel is notable for its lack of sensationalism, its matter-of-fact treatment of themes such as jealousy or seduction, representing the gradual broadening of Christie's experience toward a comprehensive perspective on the conditions of American women. The initial theme of independence gradually gives way to its contrary, Christie's realization that human life requires interdependence, and she ends by working for the dream of a community of women based on mutual love and support.

The concept of independence Christie originally sought depends, like the political life of her nation, on a rational discourse of contractual obligation, the Lockean discourse of the benevolent patriarchy that enabled the Declaration of Independence. This discourse, however, is also the discourse of the domestic sphere, the discourse against which the "language of the nether world" has set its seductive, inflaming voice. One of the fundamental projects of *Work*, then, is the search for another discourse, one better suited to embodying and conveying women's experience and yet one that will not burn down the figurative house. In December of 1861, as she began the novel that would become *Work*, Alcott wrote in her journal, "All the philosophy in our house is not in the study; a good deal is in the kitchen, where a fine old lady thinks high thoughts and does kind deeds while she cooks and scrubs."[6]

At the outset of Alcott's novel, this theme of the philosopher in the kitchen is treated comically, as Christie's aunt counsels her while reading a cookbook:

> Aunt Betsey curiously interlarded her speech with audible directions to herself from the receipt-book before her.
> "I ain't no right to keep you, dear, ef you choose to take (a pinch of salt). I'm sorry you ain't happy, and think you might be ef you'd only (beat six eggs, yolks and whites together). But ef you can't, and feel that you need (two cups of sugar), only speak to Uncle, and ef he says (a squeeze of lemon), go, my dear, and take my blessin' with you (not forgettin' to cover with a piece of paper)." (*Work,* 3–4)

At this level, feminine discourse is an accidental though peculiarly apt juxtaposition of worldly advice to the particulars of "woman's sphere," a juxtaposition that provides an ironic commentary on broader notions of "experience" and "authority." The aunt's speech consists of a paternal discourse that defines a series of operations (verbs), but the objects of those operations are withdrawn or repressed, and in their places appear objects of the maternal discourse, the discourse of nurturing and oral satisfaction. "I ain't no right to keep you, dear, ef you choose to take" ought to be completed with "your destiny into your own hands." The parenthetical substitution, "(a pinch of salt)," points both to the difficulty of the goal Christie has set herself (she is choosing to take salt instead of sugar) and to the pretentiousness of her declaration (take it with a pinch of salt). The other substitutions work in the same way: Christie could be happy if only she would learn to take the bad with the good; Christie wants nothing but the sweetness of two cups of sugar; whatever Uncle Enos says will be a squeeze of fresh lemon; Christie's adventures will be covered with the paper that forms the text of *Work.* Unconsciously and with comic precision, Aunt Betsey's interlarded speech deflates Christie's declaration, characterizes her place in the family, satirizes the role of the patriarchal Uncle Enos, and forecasts the transformation of Christie's ambition.

Yet for all its good sense, humor, and pertinency, Aunt Betsey's philosophy remains acutely marginalized by its context and its reception. On the one hand, Aunt Betsey herself is perfectly innocent of what she has said: "Christie's laugh echoed through the kitchen; and the old lady smiled benignly, quite unconscious of the cause of the girl's merriment" (*Work,* 4). On the other hand, her discourse remains enclosed and contained by parentheses, embedded in but separate from the paternal discourse in exactly the same way that the domestic sphere is embedded in and contained by the wider field of masculine activity in America. As a model of the "high thoughts and good deeds" of the philosopher in the kitchen, Aunt Betsey's speech suggests that, so far from the all-pervasive influence ascribed to them by the ideology of the domestic sphere, women have no power in the world at large except the power to parody and subvert the reasoning of men.

This discourse of housewifery yields, in the middle section of the novel, to an erotic discourse based on Christie's ability to interpret for David Sterling the language of the flowers he nurtures in his greenhouse—a language expressive of what is essential to Christie's sense of self and of a transition in her quest for "independence." This floral discourse ramifies from the conditions of Christie's recovery after her attempted suicide; she passes from the care of Mrs. Wilkins, a comfortably comic maternal figure, to that of the minister Thomas Power, whose suggestive name is confirmed by sermons in which he alternates between acting the "stern judge" and the "pitiful father" (213). Mr. Power entrusts Christie to David Sterling as a flower to a gardener: "David is a good gardener. I often send my sort of plants here, and he always makes them grow and blossom sooner or later" (251). David himself is a kind of combination of Professor Bhaer and Henry David Thoreau, a flute-playing naturalist with a "certain paternal way . . . which rather annoyed her at first, and made her feel as if he thought her a mere girl, while she was very sure he could not be more than a year or two older than herself" (236). Christie's understanding of the language of the flowers thus becomes a means of negotiating between the paternal forces that have taken control of her life.

Like Aunt Betsey's feminine discourse, Christie's is bound by the patriarchal. Working in David's conservatory, she begins to sing Herrick's "To Violets" because, as she explains to him, "my father used to say that when we went looking for early violets, and these lovely ones reminded me of it" (232). Later she tries to master the botanical nomenclature for ferns but finds the language too remote from her own experience: " 'I can't go on so much longer,' she thought despairingly. 'Polypodium aureum, a native of Florida, is all very interesting in its place; but it doesn't help me to gain self-control a bit, and I shall disgrace myself if something doesn't happen very soon' " (290–91). Both these instances of patriarchal discourse serve to mark her increasing conflict over her relationship with David, who is given, as she notes, to "making flowers bloom double when they ought to be single" (252). While she is certainly attracted to him, she also is determined to maintain the independence for which she has struggled so valiantly and which has cost her so dearly. Neither Herrick nor botany holds the possibility of any resolution of that conflict.

Between these two instances, Christie explicates an alternative language of the flowers for David, who confesses, "I can grow the flowers, but not read them" (233). Preparing bouquets for a German cotillion, she designs emblems for newly engaged girls, lovers, soldiers, spinsters, sharp-tongued women, and so on; when David has to prepare flowers for a dead baby, Christie adds snowdrops and frail ferns, "just the graceful touch here and there which would speak to the mother's sore heart of the tender thought some one had taken for her dead darling" (235). The narrator of *Work* insists that David, as a man, "liked reasons for things; a trait often very trying to feminine minds" (265). To this rationality Christie adds the electric feminine touch that communicates without words and reaches into the deepest recesses of hidden emotion. In order to explain her own character and ambitions to David, she self-consciously uses the symbol of the morning glory: she wants only to "climb up as far and as fast as I can before the frost comes" (259), and in the different colors of the flowers she locates her "childish fancies," "girlish dreams," pain, happiness, love, passion, and holiness—the entire history of her life (260).

Yet because of its nature as a mediation within patriarchal discourse, the language of the flowers, like Aunt Betsey's feminine discourse, takes Alcott's narrative into a cul-de-sac, the same dead end that plagued Alcott in finishing *Little Women*. In the earlier novel, Alcott had bowed to reader expectations and married off Jo to Professor Bhaer despite her desire to leave her heroine single. The logic of the language of the flowers points to the same end, for the whole tradition of Western poetry (invoked here in Herrick's "To Violets") is thoroughly eroticized, and the imagery that surrounds Mr. Power's transfer of Christie to David's care, the latter's tender cultivation of the ailing plant, and Christie's shy blossoming, all conspire to make marriage, the enclosure of Christie within the conventional domestic sphere, the only possible conclusion to this passage in her life.

The Civil War provided Alcott with the means to satisfy both her reader's expectations and her own ambitions for her heroine: David and Christie marry, and within three hours he departs for the army. Christie (like her creator) serves as a nurse in an army hospital, they meet just often enough for her to become pregnant, and then David is killed. Martha Saxton, noting the brevity of this marriage, has remarked, "Louisa finally came to terms with nonsexual love and respect between men and women, but she couldn't go beyond into speculation on marital relations."[7] Such a conclusion seems difficult to justify with respect to an author willing to speculate on the marital relations of Meg and John in *Little Women* or those of the Bhaers in subsequent novels. That something quite different is at stake in *Work* is suggested by the fate of Philip Fletcher, Christie's most ardent and persistent wooer, who loses an arm in the war and, in this symbolically castrated state, gives up trying to make Christie marry him in favor of becoming a loyal and supportive friend. Rather than refusing to speculate on marital relations, Alcott used the happy intervention of the Civil War to remove or to curb the dominating masculine presences that threatened to return Christie to Aunt Betsey's parenthetical condition. The war to free the slaves also frees Christie, supplies her with the opportunity to rise to the top of her profession, and bestows "upon her the only honors left the women, hard work, responsibility, and the gratitude of many men" (384).

And yet, like Mr. March, the absent father in *Little Women,* Sterling seems somehow to become more present in his absence than he was in his presence. Sitting in his room one day, Christie is startled by a "breath" of music "so airy, sweet, and short-lived that no human voice or hand could have produced it." What seems at first a spirit's voice proves to be the wind, "whispering in David's flute that hung beside the window." Christie had always called the flute "David's voice," and in subsequent months she hears it often: "whether the wind touched the flute with airy fingers or it hung mute . . . it sung to her songs of patience, hope, and cheer, till a mysterious peace came to her, and she discovered in herself the strength she had asked, yet never thought to find" (411–13).[8] What Alcott represents is precisely the moment when David Sterling ceases to be a human being of measurable limitations and becomes the force of a benevolent patriarchy. That Christie dwells continually with "David's voice," that it speaks whether or not the flute sounds, that David's picture, "faded cap and sheathed sword" (424) hang on the wall within to draw Christie's gaze— all these indicate that the disembodied Sterling has become a spiritual force of great power. If this force, unlike the living Sterling or other patriarchs of the novel, does not actually *do* anything, it nevertheless frees Christie from the need to deal with men for the rest of her life.

The final movement of *Work,* then, is toward a vision of liberation, a community of women based on mutual support and nurturing, and freed from the marital forms, domestic restrictions, and commercial interests of patriarchal society. When Christie, now forty years old, goes back to visit her Uncle Enos, she explains that she gives two-thirds of her earnings to her mother-in-law and sister-in-law. Enos, who has always been something of a miser, objects:

"That ain't a fair bargain if you do all the work."
"Ah, but we don't make bargains, sir: we work for one another and share every thing together."
"So like women!" grumbled Uncle Enos, longing to see that "the property was fixed up square." (419)

Christie's extended family, to which the concepts of "bargain" and "property" are alien, forecasts the novel's last image: Christy, her daughter, and all the women she has befriended, joining hands around a table and pledging themselves to work for the advancement of women: "With an impulsive gesture Christie stretched her hands to the friends about her, and with one accord they laid theirs on hers, a loving league of sisters, old and young, black and white, rich and poor, each ready to do her part to hasten the coming of the happy end" (442).

This last image is not, however, achieved without still more difficulties with a conflict between the rigors of patriarchal language and the needs of women. At one point Christie attends "one of the many meetings of working-women, which had made some stir of late," but instead of a harmonious blending of powers by women with common interests, she finds every woman "eager to tell her special grievance or theory." The workingwomen display "ignorance, incapacity and prejudice," while the upper-class women who have come to help them act with "unconscious condescension" (425). Christie listens to three speakers with quite different but equally useless perspectives on the plight of women. The first, like Margaret Fuller, delivers a "charming little essay on the women of antiquity" and projects an "Ideal Republic, where each did the task she liked, and was paid for it in liberty, equality, and fraternity." Unfortunately, this speaker's classical allusions and philosophical themes are lost on her audience, who mutter that "I don't see how it's going to better wages among us *now*." A second speaker fires "the revolutionary blood in their veins" to demand the vote, though the vast majority of the women are quite "unfit" for it. A third, a "statistical extinguisher," produces so grim a report on madness, starvation, suicide, capitalist exploitation, and the increased cost of living among working women that "despair was visible on many countenances, and immediate starvation seemed to be waiting at the door to clutch them as they went out" (426–27).

The point of these scenes is that philosophical idealism, political oratory, and statistical economics, all forms of abstraction and languages of patriarchal power, can neither provide appropriate analysis of nor speak to the needs of working women. All the "natural" barriers of class, caste, race, education, and so on, barriers so important to the Uncle Enoses of the world, are products of these masculine discourses: instead of unity, they promote confusion, dissension, and despair.

At this critical juncture, Christie arises to speak. Everything that has happened to her, every element of her experiences, her character, and even her genealogy, combines to insure her success as a speaker: her training as an actress gives her "self-possession, power of voice, and ease of gesture"; her experience with labor bonds her to the other workingwomen, "for the same lines were on her face that they saw on their own, her hands were no fine lady's hands, her dress plainer than some of theirs, her speech simple enough for all to understand"; she has a "subtle magnetism of character" that "has a universal language which all can understand." In short, Christie finds that she possesses a discourse uniquely qualified to mediate between the radically disparate wings of the women's movement, in which she becomes actively involved for the first time; unlike the other women at the meeting, she can speak *for* the workingwomen *to* the "ladies" in a language both groups understand and find fully expressive of the legitimate aims of the movement. Though the narrative attributes this ability to the fact that she has inherited a combination of her father's gentility and her mother's practicality, it is perfectly clear that Christie owes none of her accomplishments to heredity, that her experience with work has been the preparation for her new role.

Christie is the perfect mediating voice of the women's move-ment, capable of bridging the gap between upper class and working class, of giving voice to the experience and needs of every kind of woman. The power of this voice stems from assimilation of the abstract qualities of her father's "name" (a name appearing now for the very first time in this novel) to the activity of her mother, a sexual difference essentially the same as that at the beginning of the novel between the dour rule of Uncle Enos and the cheerful nurturing of Aunt Betsey, but here at last Christie has found a way to combine the forces of the two, to free the feminine discourse from its parentheses, and invest it with the authority of the masculine. Such a combination not only "liberates" the female voice but also overcomes every other social barrier separating women from each other: "Such women were much needed and are not always easy to find; for even in democratic America the hand that earns its daily bread must wear some talent, name, or honor as an ornament, before it is very cordially shaken by those that wear white gloves" (430).

Alcott's recognition of the problem of patriarchal power did not, of course, insure a fully liberated or liberating text. In a number of ways, *Work* is frustrating for the modern reader. First, Alcott never specifies the mediating language that Christie uses to surmount difference and forge her sisterhood; the scene of her great triumph, which would seem to cry out for dramatic representation, is reported in brief summary, and we never hear Christie's new voice. It is evident that Alcott does not know what that voice would sound like, and that the fantasy of a mediating woman's voice, which ought by virtue of much labor to be Alcott's own, is only fantasy after all.[9]

Second, for all their doubts about the way they have been treated by the men who own the factories, run the wars, and father their children, Christie and her sisters are very much committed to laboring on in an improved version of their male-dominated society. When a married friend asks what she can do for the advancement of women, Christie tells her to "make Harry's home as beautiful and attractive as you can; to keep all the elegance and refinement of former times, and to add to it a new charm by setting the fashion of common sense" (436). There is certainly nothing here to alarm a Catherine Beecher—or a Bronson Alcott.

Perhaps the most telling token of the fact that male authority remains dominant despite the feminism of *Work* is an illustration that appears on the final page of the modern reprint of the novel. It shows Christie, her daughter, and her friends joining hands around a table in anticipation of "the happy end." But the wall displays David Sterling's picture (he seems to be gazing at Christie), and directly above Christie's head hang his cap, bayonet, and sword, poised like Newton's compass in the well-known engraving by William Blake, as if in the act of drawing the circle in which the women sit: the martyred spirit of Sterling authorizes the cause of feminism. The illustrator seems to be reassuring Alcott's readers that there is nothing disturbingly radical in the novel after all. Nor is this illustration at all alien to the spirit of the novel. When Christie rises to address the women's meeting, she attracts attention because of her connections to the male world: "she was known to many as Mr. Power's friend, David Sterling's wife, or an army nurse who had done well" (427).

Despite these hedgings of her theme, however, Alcott accomplished a number of important points in *Work*. In her representation of her own experiences, she did obliquely give a voice to the aspirations, trials, needs, and hopes of workingwomen in America, even if that voice was only reported in the third person; her exploration of those themes entailed the process by which a man becomes a trope for patriarchy, by which an active principal becomes a dominating principle; her investigation of patriarchy led her to analyze language as a source of power and the differences between masculine and feminine discourses as a measure of gender relations in her nation. In tracing Christie's growth from a discourse engaging the mother-daughter relation, to that of woman-man, to the final woman-women, Alcott measures Christie's growth from the domestic to the political sphere, from a narrow concept of personal independence to the vision of independence for all women (and, by implicit extension, for all *persons,* since, as Margaret Fuller argues, the principle of liberty cannot be better understood and more nobly interpreted until it is extended to women).[10] In the end, this is the political vision of *Work*. The final image of three generations of women gathered round a table and pledging themselves to the hope that "the coming generation of women will not only receive but deserve their liberty, by learning that the greatest of God's gifts to us is the privilege of sharing His great work," incidently but definitely excludes all the father surrogates of the novel and projects a vision of a community of women based on neither utopian principles nor capitalist competition but on the common recognition of the principle of liberty.

Notes

1. Louisa May Alcott, *Little Women* (1868; repr. New York: Bantam Books, 1983), 327.
2. Louisa May Alcott, *Work: A Story of Experience* (1873; repr. New York: Schocken Books, 1977). This edition has nineteenth-century illustrations by Sol Eytinge and a modern introduction by Sarah Elbert. All references will be cited parenthetically.
3. For an excellent discussion of the maid as a figure of transgression, see Peter Stallybrass and Allon White, *The Politics and Poetics of Transgression*

(Ithaca: Cornell University Press, 1986), 149–70. The phrase "language of the nether world" is from Walter Benjamin's memory of the family maid in his *Reflections: Essays, Aphorisms, Autobiographical Writings,* trans. E. Jephcott (New York: Harcourt Brace Jovanovich, 1978), 44, quoted by Stallybrass and White, 150.

4. In *Little Women* Professor Bhaer compares a popular weekly of sensational stories to "gunpowder," and comments, "I do not like to think that good young girls should see such things" (333).

5. This phrase is from Dickinson's poem #1705 in *The Complete Poems of Emily Dickinson,* ed. Thomas H. Johnson (Boston: Little, Brown, 1960). The volcano was a favorite image for Dickinson; see poems #175, 601, 1146, 1225, 1677, and 1748. The weekly for which Jo writes her sensational stories in *Little Women* is the *Volcano.*

6. Ednah Dow Cheney, *Louisa May Alcott: Her Life, Letters and Journals* (Boston: Roberts Brothers, 1889), 124.

7. Martha Saxton, *Louisa May: A Modern Biography of Louisa May Alcott* (1977; repr. New York: Avon Books, 1978), 358.

8. In fact, this section of *Work* echoes "Thoreau's Flute," the poem Alcott had written some ten years before at the time of Thoreau's death, and provides a link between the concept of Transcendental pantheism and the spirit of patriarchal culture:

> To him no vain regrets belong
> Whose soul, that finer instrument,
> Gave to the world no poor lament,
> But wood-notes ever sweet and strong.
> O lonely friend! he still will be
> A potent presence, though unseen,—
> Steadfast, sagacious, and serene;
> Seek not for him—he is with thee.

(quoted in Saxton, 289–90)

9. Alcott's own attempts at feminist dialogue often met with resistance from other women, and Alcott was a poor persuader: "So hard to move people out of the old ruts. I haven't patience enough. If they won't see and work I let 'em alone and steam along my own way" (quoted in Saxton, 391).

10. See, for example, *Woman in the Nineteenth Century* (1845; repr. New York: Norton, 1971), 24–25.

14 *Engendering the Literary Father, or, The Law-of-the-Mother*
Adrienne Auslander Munich

The father of my title refers to the patriarchal hero and, by extension, the patriarchal literary tradition as it originates in classical epic. I focus on Virgil's Aeneas as the father of this tradition, not to ignore Homer's heroes, but rather to emphasize the hero's specifically literary shaping. Virgil revised his oral precursor, creating "Father Aeneas," as the poet calls him at the beginning of the epic (*Aeneid* II, 2). The Latin epic focuses on the construction of a kind of man, defining him as a father suited to founding imperial Rome. Virgil's text presents this male figure as necessary for the cultural creation of an admirable male genealogy, the beginning of a new history. The epic also raises questions about the cultural cost of placing so much value on Aeneas's achievement of a depersonalized manner of fathering. In the course of abandoning his wife Creusa and his beloved Dido, the hero learns not to cry, indeed, not to feel. In the end, he not only becomes a valiant but heartless warrior, he also becomes a murderer. In what follows I trace the birth figuration engendering the father who in turn has spawned the progeny of patriarchal texts.

By celebrating himself as poet as well as his subject in the initial phrase, "Arms and the man, I sing,"[1] Virgil self-consciously imposes values on the past to write the hero as a man identified with his arms. The epic opening could be construed as announcing itself as a story about the battle exploits of the man and about the battle he fights to constitute his self as a specific genre of masculinity. That kind of hero's weapons are his attributes—extensions of his heroic identity. "Man is for the sword," Tennyson's king in *The Princess* proclaims, explaining this male gendering of arms in a poem explicitly addressed to preserving conventional gender-roles. Without his sword this kind of hero cannot truly prove himself. The king defines the sword, the arm, as a synecdoche for man. Phallic (not essentially but by royal proclamation), it defends and defines the law-of-the-father.

But another attribution of the sword within the epic tradition beginning with Homer and carried through in Virgil, although less attended to, contests the phallocentric interpretation. To notice the Other, which we might call the matricentric interpretation, raises to consciousness the multivalent meaning of those arms. By "matricentric" here I mean to define a province not as an entity separate from paternal rules but as an empowering state that imprints significant marks on the shared culture and definitively shapes it. By considering selected texts of the tradition, I want to highlight certain tropes authorizing the text, thereby to question binary categories privileging the father. By attending to the patriarch's mother, I wish to reveal complicitous maternal law in the textual articulations of the fathers.

As a dominant model in European canon formation, the *Aeneid* can properly be considered as fathering the traditional concept of the hero. The text supports this originating fiction by referring to Aeneas as "man" (*vir*) in distinction to other males—youths and old men—with whom Virgil juxtaposes him.[2] In this epic of the founding of a patriarchal empire and the price of constructing a male hero suited to found such an empire, the common word *vir* becomes an epithet for the hero, unquestionably masculine and a father-worshiper. The heroic image inspiring generations to patriarchal veneration is that of the father of Rome carrying on his back his aging father out of burning Troy while holding fast to the hand of his son. That image may be taken as a paradigm for Western literary tradition, interpreted as the blessing and law of the father.

From another perspective, however, the image could be understood as the burden of (enfeebled) patriarchal need:

> So I resigned myself, picked up my father,
> And turned my face toward the mountain range.
>
> (Fitzgerald II, 61)

This image of paternal lineage returns as proof of the hero's virtue when Dido, about to kill herself, bitterly remembers Aeneas's faithlessness, his broken pledge to her:

> This is the right hand, this the pledge of one
> who carries with him, so they say, the household
> gods of his land (*patrios*), who bore on his shoulders
> his father weak with years.   (Mandelbaum IV, 823–26)

In Dido's remark, Virgil emphasizes the priority of the fatherland and the father over the attractions of woman. But the poet also offers evidence that this priority occurs by default, not by choice. By carrying the father, Aeneas leaves only his own footprint, an impression of male unity. The literary canon presents itself in this single file, masterpiece following masterpiece, the later carrying traces of the earlier on its textual back. To achieve greatness Aeneas bears the burden of a moribund father. Conventional readings forget that this emblem of patriarchal tradition implies not only filial piety but also paternal fragility.

In contrast, Aeneas's mother needs no carrying and will never age. As Venus, immortal originator of desire, she cannot grow old, cannot die, although her importance can be denied, repressed, or made monstrous. Condemned to be enthralled by a vision of eternal desire, mortal men can only win venerean simulacra, substitutes for the object of desire. Like male gods who force themselves on mortal women, this female goddess takes the man she desires. Aeneas was conceived from Anchises' seduction by Venus in mortal disguise. This myth of engendering balances male desire against an equally libidinous female desire, imagining a female deity who hides herself at will. To confront yet avoid the implications of a seductive Venus who is also maternal complicates this originating text.[3]

As counterweight to the burden of the father, Virgil presents an equally apt emblem for Aeneas's creation. In book 1 the hero yearns after his mother, desiring her evanescent presence. In the beginning of the epic Venus appears to her grown son's eyes as still young and attractive, as if the two were appropriate sexual partners rather than mother and son. Virgil arranges their first meeting in a scene that could be understood as an allegory of male desire. Aeneas has landed in Carthage after being harried at sea by the wrath of an unappeasable Juno. He goes out to reconnoiter and, in the middle of the forest, a place of mystery, he encounters his mother disguised as a young, powerful, free maiden:

> Then suddenly, in front of him,
> His mother crossed his path in mid-forest,
> Wearing a girl's shape and a girl's gear—
> A Spartan girl, or like that one of Thrace,
> Harpalyce, who tires horses out,
> Outrunning the swift Hebrus. She had hung
> About her shoulders the light, handy bow
> A huntress carries, and had given her hair
> To the disheveling wind; her knees were bare,
> Her flowing gown knotted and kirtled up.
>
> (Fitzgerald I, 14–15)

From the son's viewpoint, the mother is ever young, ever desired, a maiden with her own weapons. The poet also figures this desire as willed by the mother who wishes to appear as young and desirable to her son and who controls the terms of her encounter with him. Although he has known she is a goddess, Aeneas recognizes the prime object of his desire as his own mother only at the moment when she is about to vanish, calling to her in a poignant tone that we could understand as the son's frustration with his mother's inaccessibility:

> When she turned,
> her neck was glittering with a rose brightness;
> her hair anointed with ambrosia,
> her head gave all a fragrance of the gods;
> her gown was long and to the ground; even
> her walk was sign enough she was a goddess.

And when Aeneas recognized his mother,
he followed her with these words as she fled:
"Why do you mock your son—so often and
so cruelly—with these lying apparitions?
Why can't I ever join you, hand to hand,
to hear, to answer you with honest words?

(Mandelbaum I, 573–84)

In portraying the son's desire for his mother, Virgil also figures the mother's desire for her son.[4] In the showing forth of the goddess, we read of a scene of mutual desire, banished from discourse as an impossible conversation. Trying to reconstruct his early maternal bond, Aeneas's plaintive question is childlike; to the son, his desire promises more than it can deliver. Aeneas wishes for a conversation that cannot happen. In the gendered hierarchy of his creation, the mother is represented as more powerful than the father, but it is the father's patrimony he is obliged to conserve. The consequence of what he misses—honest words with his mother—as we shall see, constructs a hero who buries this longing for a maternal conversation and who defines himself in terms of his paternal lineage. Because he cannot have this conversation, he turns into a distant father, a man who cannot be spoken to. He turns into an imperial hero.

Aeneas's development involves the loss of his common humanity. His wife, Creusa, initially follows the emblem of patriarchal tradition "in the background," but she is left behind with the complicity of her own ghost who counsels the hero to forget her for the sake of his mission and his goddess-mother who urges him to stop complaining and get on with his task. Until recently, interpreters of that tradition have followed this complicitous "female" advice in the name of a unitary vision.

In what follows, I should like to ignore mannerly convention to reconstruct a different maternal imperative as it augments the father's literary voice. In order to demonstrate only two of the elements in a complex generic past, I trace two ways that the hero as father is created by means of the mother's buried voice. In the first I limit my attention to the symbolic burial of the nurse in *Aeneid* 7, and in the second I trace the epic engendering of arms as a mutual desire for maternal words, the fragmented conversation that seems absent from epic tradition but that exists in the margins of the text as a sign of a suppressed presence.[5] Bringing the patriarchal imperative into poststructural revision as the law of the father involves a radical repression of a fuller language. The remainder of this essay attempts to call attention to some of those notable words of the cultural script.

Burying the Nurse

At the end of book 6 Aeneas has emerged from the underworld through the Ivory Gate, the gate of false dreams. The first half of the epic is over, with Aeneas encountering the past and putting it behind him. Virgil recommences his poem, but before he invokes the Muse, Erato,[6] Aeneas performs one ritual—he buries his nurse, Caieta—and escapes one peril—he sails safely past Circe's isle. Although the events seem irrelevant and even misplaced, we may understand them as symbolic representations of the hero's reaction to mothering, of Aeneas's longing for a maternal relationship, of the mother longing for intimacy with him, and of the hero's symbolically bypassing his too dangerous desires for maternal relationship.[7] In the one event, the nurturer Caieta represents a mother who sustains a helpless infant. In the other, Circe represents the mother as a seductive witch whom he escapes.

The nurse's burial takes place in a scant four lines and seems incongruous at the beginning of a book in which war becomes an inevitable movement toward irrational violence. There may be a symbolic connection between this particular burial and the ensuing violence of book 7, all of which is initiated by females:

> In death, you too, Aeneas' nurse, Caieta,
> have given to our coasts unending fame;
> and now your honor still preserves your place
> of burial; your name points out your bones
> in broad Hesperia—if that be glory.
>
> (Mandelbaum VII, 1–5)

Two contradictory explanations could be suggested for Virgil's placing this passage in a prominent place, stopping the action to honor a nurse. Aeneas possibly idealizes his nurse here, denying her destructive power. The short passage buries her and honors her very quickly by giving her name to a geographical location.[8] Symbolically, she is no longer a part of Aeneas's inner topography but becomes external as a geographical place. This interpretation is supported by ensuing murderous events in book 7, all inspired by destructive female forces, imagined as emanating from the underworld. After Caieta's burial Juno makes her famous pronouncement: "If I cannot move the gods above, I will move the spirits of Hell" (*"Flectere si nequeo superos, Acheronta movebo;"* VII, 312). Consequently, Allecto, the Fury, inflames Queen Amata. The peaceful establishment of Rome is doomed, and the epic ends with Aeneas murdering Turnus. Aeneas has buried the dangerous, murderous mother, but becomes murderous himself in doing so.

Burying the nurse can also symbolize Aeneas's suppressing his own identification with the female nurturing mother for the sake of his constructed masculine identity. In this psychoanalytic description of maturity, the male must distance himself from his own body, the body most connected to its nurturing source. Aeneas's symbolic action is a paradigm for Freud's splitting his own mother from his own nurse in order to deny the fury and power of the nurturer. Jim Swan describes the Freudian definition of male identity as a consequence of idealizing an unsexual mother and debasing a nurse, at once seductress and punisher of the boy's sexual impulses. Swan's description of Freud's concept of maturity is equally relevant to Virgil's construction of his hero's masculinity:

Maturity (that is, *masculine* maturity) means being well defended against one's past, which amounts to the same thing as having a strong capacity for resisting identification—since identification is "the earliest expression of an emotional tie" to which one "regresses." In effect, Freud's picture of maturity is of a man driven to outrun his own personal history—driven, that is, to outrun identification with his own body, which, *historically,* originates in identification with the body of his mother, the original unity of mother and infant.[9]

In Aeneas's wanderings he is driven to outrun his personal history, externalized as relinquishing the desire to found another Troy. The war in book 7 is a cultural sign of Aeneas's aggression as a magnified response to his frustration at having to become a certain kind of father: distant, unfeeling, capable of aggression and destruction in the name of a greater good. Aeneas memorializes his nurse but buries the knowledge of what his nurse represents *to his own body,* paying nonetheless the price of thereafter being false to a part of his human potential. He will no longer be capable of loving a great queen, such as Dido. One reason Aeneas issues from the gate of false dreams at the end of book 6 immediately before he buries Caieta is that he never again will know of his yearning to hold hands and to exchange words with his mother. He outruns his identification with his nurturant body and therefore "fathers" the "masculine" Roman race.

Although contradictory, both interpretations of Caieta's burial help us to understand the complex texture of tradition; keeping them both in mind may bring to view the footprints I have been hoping to uncover. It may help in this detective work to consider Virgil's unexplicated reference to the burial of Caieta as a buried allusion to earlier nurses in the classical tradition, a tradition that Virgil is consciously exploiting and revising to create his own text. The allusions suggest the dual nature of the nurse/mother, both loving and murderous.

In the *Odyssey* Odysseus's nurse, Eurykleia, possesses dangerous knowledge of the hero. Returning to claim his patrimony, the disguised Odysseus vainly pulls away from his nurse as she is about to bathe his scarred thigh, but she instantly reads the sign of the hero's identity that is connected to his naming (according to his maternal line) and to his vulnerable body:[10]

> *You are Odysseus!* Ah, dear child! I could not
> see you until now—not till I knew
> my master's very body with my hands!
>
> (Fitzgerald XIX, 380)

Aeneas must bury signs that he is not impervious. In the first half of the epic we see him crying, mourning his losses, longing for what cannot be recovered, and loving but abandoning Dido. Unlike Odysseus, he cannot return home, and, to assure the impossibility of return to an earlier self as to an earlier locale, he represses the nurse's kind of bodily knowledge, closing off his identity from himself so that he can live in a world in which no one, least of all himself, recognizes his scars.

If Eurykleia harbors powerful knowledge of the male's external body, Orestes' nurse, Cilissa asserts an essential but ultimately a more intimate claim upon her charge. In Aeschylus's *The Libation Bearers* she appears on stage at a crucial moment, and, introducing a domestic tone to the most ritualistic play of the *Oresteia*, separates nurturing from maternity, nurse from mother. Presenting an intimate sketch of infant care, Cilissa claims that her subjugation to the absolute but unpredictable demands of the infant forges a bond to the child that gives her precedence over the mother. She describes her knowledge of the law of the infant's insides:

> Red from your mother's womb I took you, reared you . . .
> nights, the endless nights I paced, your wailing kept me
> moving—led me a life of labor, and for what?
>   And such care I gave it . . .
> baby can't think for itself, poor creature.
> You have to nurse it, don't you? Read its mind,
> little devil's got no words, it's still swaddled.
> Maybe it wants a bit or a sip of something
> or its bladder pinches—a baby's soft insides
> have a will of their own. I had to be a prophet.[11]

Cilissa claims the child's primary allegiance over the biological mother because of their primal communication. Her prophetic knowledge of the baby's guts makes the nurse an embarrassing presence to a grown man. She brings the smells of the nursery into the ritual drama, proving herself the natural if not the biological mother. Separated from speechless maternal laws, Clytemnestra cannot claim the laws of the mother. Her subsequent appeal for mercy by baring her (nursing) breast to her son seems a monstrous mockery of maternity. Like Venus she seems more a seducer than a mother. Splitting mother from nurse in *The Libation Bearers* justifies matricide.

Equally ominous consequences result in the *Aeneid* from splitting off aspects of the mother, only the splits are multiplied and none provide comfort. Venus opposes Juno but she is equally vindictive, as her treatment of Dido indicates. As maternal fragments Caieta and Circe are opposed, but perhaps symbolically linked. After burying the nurse, Aeneas sails apparently unharmed past Circe's shores, but then accepts from King Latinus a team of horses:

> Grown from immortal stock and snorting fire.
> Their sire was that stallion crafty Circe
> Stole from the Sun, her father, and put to stud
> With a mortal mare, getting a bastard breed.
>
> (Fitzgerald VII, 205)

Although Circe does not turn Aeneas into a beast, he receives her beasts, whose lineage resembles his own vexed engendering.[12] As soon as Aeneas accepts the horses, Juno vows in rage to move the female forces below. Virgil represents the repressed female forces represented in Caieta's burial, naturally so, since they are fragmented aspects of Aeneas's own repressed "female" self, projected onto supernatural female beings.

Aeneas buries his fear of being killed by these maternal representatives. Juno tries repeatedly to kill him, using counterparts, both mortal and immortal. In the maddened Queen Amata, Virgil presents a mortal variant of the seductive mother. Her name associates her with Venus, and her passion for her daughter's suitor, Turnus, suggests incestuous passions, more explicit but parallel to those of Venus for Aeneas.[13] Another female force from the underworld, Allecto, is so repulsive that even her father hates her. Allecto drives the mothers wild, prodding Amata "with a Bacchic goad" to a fevered frenzy—the Bacchic goad reminding us of Agave, the mother in Euripides' *Bacchae* who tore her son to pieces and then wanted to devour him.

The nurse in Euripides' *Medea* adds to the other relationships between mothers and nurses the conjunction of murderous mothers and dangerous marriage. This nurse challenges a pious view of nursely protectiveness, opening the play with her concerns about Medea's sons but identifying herself with Medea. In asking the nurse to keep secret her murderous plots, Medea appeals to the bonds of sisterhood as opposed to motherhood:

> Say nothing of these decisions which I have made
> If you love your mistress, if you were born a woman.[14]

So effective is her plea woman to woman that we do not hear from the nurse again. The murderous mother silences the nurturant nurse and murders her sons.

Not only does the *Aeneid* intensify examples of the murderous mother, book 7 alludes to *Medea* in a way that connects dangerous mothers with the perils of marriage. In describing the flame around the head of Aeneas's future bride, Lavinia, Virgil verbally echoes Euripides' description of the flames that consumed the bride Jason abandoned Medea for, his new bride, a princess, like Lavinia. Aeneas's new wedding is thus associated with child murder. In burying Caieta, Aeneas represses his fears associated with women, with mothers, and with brides.

The destruction evoked by allusions to the nurse balances Aeneas's generative triumph in founding the race of Rome. In the epic's last scene Turnus pleads for mercy, but Aeneas sees on him the belt of Pallas, a surrogate son, whom Turnus had killed in battle, taking the belt as a trophy. On the belt is depicted the murder on their wedding night of fifty bridegrooms by their fifty brides, the Danaides. The myth portrayed on the belt is a version—condensed and multiplied fiftyfold—of Aeneas's buried fear. Virgil has shown Aeneas's susceptibility to visual representations when he weeps before the murals of the Trojan War in Dido's palace. Moved by the story pictured on the belt, Aeneas identifies with vengeful Juno rather than with his father, Anchises, who counseled him in the underworld to spare the conquered. Aeneas responds to the scene of female fury on the belt, which warns men of the dangers of the bridal bed. In a fit of rage expressing repressed terror at the murderous power of sexual women, man defends himself by reflecting back that fury he fears, murdering Turnus, the bearer of that representation, and sending him to the underworld—Allecto's realm—in the text's final words, "to the shades below" (*sub umbras*).

Engendering Authority

To further complicate the origins of Aeneas's murderous rage at the end of the epic, it is well to remember that he receives his weapons as his mother's gift. I turn, then, to examine the forming of the hero by the efforts of the mother. Tracing this pattern reveals the hero as being constructed from the mother's repressed desires and the mingling of those wishes with the desire of her son to hold hands with her as an equal and to have a real conversation.

Although the king in Tennyson's *The Princess* claims for men the right of the battlefield and the right to bear arms, in epic tradition the mother arms the hero. The mother's gift imparts special privilege to the hero's authority. In addition, the mother's role in creating the weapon-wielding hero is linked by figures of copulation, gestation, and birth. Nurturing arms turn to murderous ones.

The pattern of associating a story of arms-making with human birth begins in the *Iliad*. Achilles' mother, Thetis, is also figured as Hephaistos's second, "good" mother, who nurtures the smith-god at first for peaceable means until her mortal son requires implements of war. Hephaistos acknowledges his great debt to Thetis because she saved him when his "brazen-faced" mother rejected a lame child. Catching him at the time of his great fall, Thetis becomes Hephaistos' deliverer from a disastrous birth and symbolic mother of a more benign existence. With the help of Eurynome, daughter of Ocean, Thetis nurtured the god of the forge in a cave for nine years. There, the lame god forges only domestic and intricate decorative objects: "pins that bend back, curved clasps, cups, necklaces" (Lattimore XVIII, 401). Hephaistos fondly remembers those years:

> working
> There in the hollow of the cave, and the stream of Ocean
>   around us
> went on forever with its foam and its murmur. No other
> among the gods or among mortal men knew about us
> except Eurynome and Thetis. They knew, since they saved me.
>   (Lattimore XVIII, 401–5)

Protected from the world of gods and men for nine years in a cave, Hephaistos remembers this site in suggestively prenatal terms, telling his story as a myth of uterine generation and creativity.

When Thetis comes to ask him to make her son's new weapons, the god of the forge is aided by strong female spirits:

> These are golden, and in appearance like living young
>   women.

There is intelligence in their hearts, and there is speech
  in them
and strength, and from the immortal gods they have learned
  how to do things." (Lattimore XVIII, 417–20)

Inhabiting an idealized community of women, Hephaistos does
Thetis's bidding and will make implements of destruction for her,
but he decorates the shield with a different life, where war is a
defensive necessity in the whole fabric of essential communal events
rather than the definition of male heroic life. When the miraculous
arms are finished, the hero's mother delivers them to her son,
emphasizing that they issue from her desires:

Accept rather from me the glorious arms of Hephaistos,
so splendid, and such as no man has ever worn on his shoulders.
(Lattimore XIX, 10–11)

In the *Aeneid* Virgil expands upon Homer's suggestive birth
imagery by conflating Thetis's approach to Hephaistos with Hera's
seduction of Zeus in *Iliad* 14. Aided by Aphrodite, Hera beguiles
Zeus:

He gazed at her, and as he gazed desire
veiled his mind like mist, as in those days
when they had first slipped from their parents' eyes
to bed, to mingle by the hour in love. . .
    Soon the Father,
subjugated by love and sleep, lay still.
Still as a stone on Gargaron height he lay
and slumbered with his lady in his arms.
(Fitzgerald, *Iliad* 339–41)

Zeus, the seduced "father" in the *Iliad,* becomes Vulcan, father of
Aeneas's arms. Like Thetis, Venus pleads to the smith-god, her
husband, and like Hera, she seduces him in order to convince him
to work her will:

I do come now, begging your sacred power
For arms, a mother begging for her son.
The daughter of Nereus moved you, and Tithonus'
Consort moved you by her tears to this.
(Fitzgerald, *Aeneid* VIII, 243)

Venus suggests that it is feminine appeal and certainly not the male god's own interest in war that moves him to making weapons. Without that sexual inducement, he might not make arms at all. Venus does not trust her words alone, and in her bridal chamber "All of gold, putting divine desire / In every word," she seduces Vulcan:

> The goddess spoke and wrapped her snowy arms
> This way and that about him as he lingered,
> Cherishing him in her swansdown embrace.
> And instantly he felt the flame of love
> Invading him as ever; into his marrow
> Ran the fire he knew, and through his bones,
> As when sometimes, ripped by a thunder peal,
> A fiery flash goes jagged through the clouds.
> His wife, contented with her blandishment,
> Sure of her loveliness, perceived it all. (Fitzgerald VIII, 243)

Virgil's love scene, expanding upon Homer, suggests that in order to make arms, you first have to make love. Vulcan, however, does not understand the linking of sex with weaponry, telling his wife that she confuses pleasure with business:

> Why do you go so far
> Afield for reasons? . . .
> You need not beg me for these gifts. Have done
> With doubting your own powers!   (Fitzgerald VIII, 243)

Nonetheless, Vulcan participates in the ritual:

> He said no more,
> But took her in his arms as she desired
> And gave himself, infused in her embrace,
> To peace and slumber.   (Fitzgerald VIII, 244)

Virgil makes clear that both sexual desire and desire for weapons originate with Venus, not Vulcan, who is passive but willing. Well before dawn, Vulcan arises to make the arms, and Virgil compares this work to a poor weaver-woman who must rise early to work in order to maintain her family "all to keep chaste / Her marriage bed and bring her children up." Making murderous weapons is tied to chaste marriage, childrearing, and homemaking. Creation and destruction are metaphorically linked—making of arms and babies, making of weapons and housekeeping. In the figure of the weaver-wife and mother, making weapons is also associated with the woman's task of weaving.[15] Venus fathers the arms while Vulcan mothers them.

Like Virgil's Aeneas, Alfred Tennyson's Arthur fathers an empire of sons, knights of the Round Table. Tennyson grafts the Virgilian epic to Arthurian romance in *Idylls of the King*, selecting from Arthurian sources those elements about arms that suggest birth metaphors similar to his epic precursors, but his figures of engendering are sterile, less certainly heroic, the Virgilian reversals even more multivalent and ungendered. By excising Arthur's miraculous wresting of the sword from the stone, Tennyson focuses on its connection to the Lady of the Lake, who represents Arthur's repressed (indeed, submerged) mother. The epic tradition of the mothering of armaments appears as an involuted and fragmented presence. Tennyson described the first and last of his *Idylls of the King*, the parts in which the sword figures prominently as about "the awfulness of Birth and Death." In "The Coming of Arthur," sword and king are crowned together in the language of birth:

> I beheld Excalibur
> Before him at his crowning borne, the sword
> That rose from out the bosom of the lake. [16]

Then, in "The Passing of Arthur," it is clear that the sword is coexistent with Arthur's heroic life. Not only is it "borne" aloft at his coronation but he is born as a hero when he takes it from the lake. Finally, Arthur's mortal life cannot end until Excalibur is returned to the Lady of the Lake. The arm is Arthur as king and hero.

At Arthur's coronation, the Lady of the Lake and Merlin stand near each other, linked symbolically as King Arthur's heroic parents. As surrogate father Merlin bears Arthur to the Round Table, setting him up as king, while the Lady of the Lake creates and delivers Excalibur. Tennyson makes clear that the Lady knows more subtle magic than Merlin, her powers both more complex and less overt:

> Clothed in white samite, mystic, wonderful.
> She gave the King his huge cross-hilted sword.
>
> ("The Coming of Arthur," 284–85)

Like the miraculous cloth she wears, the Lady of the Lake is possessed of a complex and miraculous texture, a subterranean power, not visible but associated with creativity. As mother to the sword, she is also supernatural mother to Arthur, as Merlin is his supernatural father.

Unlike the classical precursors, however, these epic parents engender nothing together. Tennyson turns the epic mother (already reduced to an "arm," a significant pun in the context of the maternal/martial pattern I have been tracing) into a good Lady of the Lake and a bad Vivien.[17] The Homeric Ocean, lapping around the womb where the productive, creative forging took place, is here a lake beneath which the good mother lives and on which she walks. This Lady of the Lake is described in terms reminiscent of Hephaistos's memories of his nine years in Ocean's cave:

> a mist
> Of incense curled about her, and her face
> Wellnigh was hidden in the minster gloom;
> But there was heard among the holy hymns
> A voice as of the waters, for she dwells
> Down in a deep; calm, whatsoever storms
> May shake the world, and when the surface rolls,
> Hath power to walk the waters like our Lord.
>
> ("The Coming of Arthur," 286–93)

This Lady makes the weapon herself, with no male partner, but Tennyson, like Homer, retains temporal suggestions of birth:

> Nine years she wrought it, sitting in the deeps
> Upon the hidden bases of the hills.
>
> ("Morte d'Arthur," 105–6)

While this Christlike woman mothers the sword, Tennyson transforms Malory's Ninian or Nimue into the serpentine Devil, Vivien. Separate from miraculous, subtle parthenogenesis, Vivien seduces a willing Merlin, as Venus seduced Vulcan, but hers is a sterile mockery and reversal of engendering. Rather than giving birth to anything, Merlin is unborn—enwombed (because he is still alive)—in the hollow of a tree. Then, in the sword's return to its submerged mother, the deflected sexuality surfaces in an allusion to the *Aeneid*. When Bedivere stands at the marge of the lake, deciding whether or not to return the sword, Tennyson alludes to Aeneas's indecisiveness in leaving Dido (*Aeneid* IV, 285): "This way and that, dividing the swift mind" ("The Passing of Arthur," 228). In its return the sword is thus associated with the romance element in Virgilian epic tradition. Furthermore, the white samite arm, mysterious and wonderful, is clothed in the same fabric as Vivien, who wears an alluringly transparent gown of samite. Although the Lady of the Lake and Vivien were not the same character in Tennyson's sources, they were both Ladies of the Lake. Making the relatively good Nimue into the wholly wicked Vivien, and a shadowy but good Lady of the Lake, clothed too in samite, Tennyson suggests connections between the two Ladies of the Lake as two aspects of the epic mother who engenders male heroic authority.

Arms and the mother, as an epic tradition, claim that envied function of women to give birth and appropriate it for war. Arms are given miraculous authority by linking them with miraculous birth. Tennyson fragments without undermining the fantasy of the sword-bearing mother, denies the mother's desire for her son and for masculine power, but blames the entire downfall of Camelot upon an adultery between Queen Guinevere and Arthur's first knight (son) Launcelot. Thus figured, the mother's conveying of power is conditional; the sword is symbolic of her authority, only interpreted as phallic in a phallogocentric culture, which cannot otherwise figure this kind of maternal authority.

The epic tradition I have been tracing affirms that the voice and the written language of the mother exerts a great, even decisive, force in the canonical creation of the hero as father. The course of the sword's engendering—from the virtual origins of the tradition in Homer to its repression and consequent greater, though generally unacknowledged presence, in Tennyson—pays tribute to the extraordinary influence of the mother. Although I have only pointed to maternal traces here as a problem to be further explored in all texts, it seems to me that they are evidence of an interdependency of voices, a mutual speaking that needs decoding if we are to understand the relatedness of cultural creation and destruction.

As it surfaces in Tennyson's transformation of Arthurian tradition to a predominantly Virgilian model, the inscription of the mother's voice determines the life span of Arthur's heroic age. Excalibur, the named arm of the mother, contains on it two commandments, written on its blade by the Lady of the Lake:

> the blade so bright
> That men are blinded by it—on one side,
> Graven in the oldest tongue of all this world,
> "Take me," but turn the blade and ye shall see,
> And written in the speech ye speak yourself,
> "Cast me away!"   ("The Coming of Arthur," 299–304)

With its coded threat of blinding as the punishment of the son's desire for the mother (and the mother's desire for the son), the bright sword contains a coded history of language. Although the meaning of maternal words is only suggested, the mother commands the most ancient and most recent tongues of all this world. Mother language encompasses and commands the history of written words. Although they are vatic words and not the conversation desired by Aeneas, the words on Excalibur are the Commandments, not of the Lord but of the Lady. In the same way as engendering epic arms depends upon the law-of-the-mother, the authorizing of heroic prowess is tied to a mysterious but inexorable female realm, "the awfulness," as Tennyson states, "of Birth and Death." Because the text inscribes without interrogating the words of this female power, the Lady's commandments require further exegesis. As Aeneas buries the potential seductive violence of Caieta, so the sword and its maternal arm are once again buried in Tennyson's Arthurian legend. But its commandments signify a longer conversation that is now, in this collection of essays for one, beginning to be heard and recorded.

Notes

I thank Christine Froula for originary conversations, Lauren Taaffe for classical ones, and Susan Squier and Helen Cooper, whose collaboration on a project on women, literature, and war helped refine my thoughts. Sections of this essay appear in a different form in a co-authored article, "The Con[tra]ception of the War Text" from *Arms and the Woman: War, Gender and Literary Representation,* published by University of North Carolina Press.

1. Except for the most familiar opening of the *Aeneid,* rather than presenting the Latin with a literal but unpoetic translation, I have chosen different modern translations according to the one that seems to me closest to the sense I wish to emphasize. In each case, I cite the translator, for the *Aeneid,* either Fitzgerald or Mandelbaum; for the *Iliad,* Lattimore or Fitzgerald, for the *Odyssey,* Fitzgerald. For Fitzgerald, the Arabic numeral refers to the page number, for Mandlebaum and Lattimore, the line number.

2. "Aeneas remains the only major character consistently portrayed as an active adult, a *vir,* from start to finish, with no evident signs of lingering youth or impending old age. From the very first line of the poem it is clear that the designation *vir* will belong especially to him" (Gregory Elftmann, "Aeneas in his Prime: Distinctions in Age and the Loneliness of Adulthood in Vergil's *Aeneid,*" *Arethusa,* 12 [1979]: 193).

3. Centuries of commentary have avoided this significant passage, but I cite a relatively recent critic, William S. Anderson, *The Art of the Aeneid* (Englewood Cliffs, N.J.: Prentice-Hall, 1969), to indicate that the subject perhaps has been too threatening to male commentators, at least up to the present moment: "Before he [Aeneas] gets far he encounters a huntress—or rather Venus his mother, who seems to him a huntress. It is a poignant meeting, for Aeneas does not realize until too late that he is talking with his mother, and she refuses to present herself directly. Why this should be so has never been clearly articulated by critics, and possibly it is better to leave the question to the reader's imagination" (26). Splitting women into types—the femme fatale on the one hand and the blessed mother on the other—forms cultural models rendering the interpretation of Virgil's Venus an unprintable subject, fit only for the privacy of the "reader's imagination."

4. By focusing on male desire, interpretations of Sophocles' *Oedipus Rex* have too often ignored the possibility of Jocasta's desire for her son. Influenced by object relations theory, notably Melanie Klein's portrayal of the mother from the infant's perspective, Julia Kristeva's attention to Bellini's paintings of madonna and child imagines an iconography of maternal possessiveness and filial rage. See "Motherhood According to Giovanni Bellini" in *Desire in Language,* trans. Leon S. Roudiez (New York: Colum-

bia University Press, 1982), pp. 237–70, esp. fig. 6 and 10. The view of the desiring mother and the child's view of the devouring mother, I suggest, fuels some of Virgil's figures of primitive female energies, split images of nurses and furies.

5. Christine Froula, "The Daughter's Seduction: Sexual Violence and Literary History," *Signs* 11 (1986): 625–28, presents the first example of a somewhat different excluded conversation, this one between Helen and Priam, with the father controlling the words by not hearing the daughter's words.

6. There has been much debate over why Virgil invokes Erato, translated by Fitzgerald as "Muse of All Desire." In terms of my argument it seems at least symbolically appropriate that the poet invokes the muse of erotic desire. No other classical Latin poet mentions her, but Plato calls her the muse of love poetry in the *Phaedrus*. Why does Virgil mention her at the stage of his poem in which the wanderings are over and the war begins? I suggest that buried desire impels the rest of the poem. For another view, see F. A. Todd, "Virgil's Invocation of Erato," *Classical Review* 45 (1931): 216–18.

7. I consider the nurse as a surrogate, symbolic, mother, an interpretation supported by Ovid's epitaph to Caieta in which he calls Aeneas the son of his nurse: "Here I Caieta, Saved from Greek flame, was burned with proper fire / Through my dear son's devotion."

8. Of the many theories about the murderous impulses of the nurturing mother, the ones influencing my thinking are Adrienne Rich, *Of Woman Born: Motherhood as Experience and Institution* (New York: Norton, 1976); Dorothy Dinnerstein, *The Mermaid and the Minotaur: Sexual Arrangements and Human Malaise* (New York: Harper & Row, 1976); and Philip E. Slater, *The Glory of Hera: Greek Mythology and the Greek Family* (Boston: Beacon, 1968).

9. "*Mater* and Nannie: Freud's Two Mothers and the Discovery of the Oedipus Complex," *American Imago* 31 (1974): 9–10.

10. For a discussion of this passage, see Eric Auerbach, "Odysseus's Scar," *Mimesis* (Princeton: Princeton University Press, 1953) and, more relevant to the connection of scarring and naming, George E. Dimock, "The Name of Odysseus," *The Hudson Review* 9 (Spring 1956): 52–72.

11. Aeschylus, *The Libation Bearers,* trans. Robert Fagles (New York: Viking, 1975), 735–45; the ellipses are in the text.

12. Swan describes the distant man in ways that apply to Aeneas. The rational, independent, authoritative man *distinguishes* himself from the irrational, passive, dependent woman. For him, anything "irrational" or "passive" or "dependent" in himself is felt as a threatened loss of identity, becoming "like a woman." Thus the woman, in a situation like class conflict, threatens the man with the reality of his own repressed (and projected) irrationality, passivity, and dependence (25). Identifying with an authoritar-

ian father resolves anxiety about being engulfed and annihilated by an overwhelming "bad" mother—who is the dialectical mirror-image of the man's own overwhelming and frustrated oral needs (29). To wage war the warriors perform rites in which they assimilate symbolically the powers of feared, envied, and *excluded* women, and one of these rites, I suggest, is the burial of Caieta.

13. John W. Zarker, "Amata: Vergil's Other Tragic Queen," *Vergilius* 15 (1969): 2–24.

14. Euripides, *The Medea*, trans. Rex Warner, *The Complete Greek Tragedies*, eds. David Grene and Richmond Lattimore (Chicago: University of Chicago Press, 1955), 87.

15. See Ann Bergren's corrective of Freud's essentialist statement about the importance of woman's weaving as a skill developed to compensate for her lack of a penis: "Language and the Female in Early Greek Thought," *Arethusa* 16 (1983): 69–90.

16. "The Coming of Arthur," 295–97, *The Poems of Tennyson*, ed. Christopher Ricks (London: Longmans, 1972). References to this edition will be cited by title and line number in parentheses in the text.

17. S. E. Holbrook, "Nymue, The Chief Lady of the Lake in Malory's *Le Morte Darthur*," *Speculum* 53 (1978): 761–77.

15   *Reading the Father Metaphorically*
Beth Kowaleski-Wallace

> When a woman attributes all aggression, all thrust for power, to men alone, she gives her own potential violence to her oppressor, making him more loomingly omnipotent than any actual man ever was. Such self-denying feminists create a gargantuan oppressor who never existed in life. It seems wisest for women to forfeit dreams of purity—which are patriarchal in origin—in order to gain for ourselves the best possible lives in an imperfect world.
>
> Nina Auerbach, "Engorging the Patriarchy"[1]

Nina Auerbach's analysis of the "dangerous nostalgia for the gorgeousness that has traditionally been part of our [female] oppression" is bound to be provocative. Auerbach asks feminists to consider an uncomfortable truth about ourselves—that we sometimes prefer to assume that aggression belongs to men alone and that we are simply (to use Juliet Mitchell's phrase) "the pure who are purely put upon."[2] Auerbach sees a danger in the feminist tendency to deny the existence of female aggression; in making men into "the enemy" who oppresses women, we perpetuate the myth of our own victimization and embody patriarchy as an unconquerable force. To displace the "thrust for power" onto men may be a convenient way to schematize gender relations, since it is surely easier and more appealing to isolate women from the messiness of patriarchy. We should like to believe that, as victims, we have been only the recipients and never the initiators of violence. In the end, however, such schematization cannot be satisfactory, since the historical participation of women in patriarchal strategies belies a dualistic model of the male oppressor and his female victim.

Auerbach's commentary has special relevance for a feminist project of rereading the father. Often employed as a metaphor for patriarchy itself, the father has been a particularly powerful figure in many feminist analyses; like the gargantuan oppressor in Auerbach's example, he has oftentimes seemed unconquerable, and the daughter who "attributes all aggression, all thrust for power" to her father creates precisely that "loomingly omnipotent" man Auerbach describes. Such a daughter perpetuates the myth of her own victimization while subscribing to patriarchal notions of female purity. Thus, extended to the father-daughter relationship, Auerbach's critique facilitates our understanding of a more consistently complex relationship between women and their fathers. Moreover, her critique inevitably challenges us to reexamine our assumptions about the father's oppressive "influence" over his daughters' lives.

That the father's power owes something to a reading that renders him as metaphor for patriarchy may be an uncomfortable idea for feminists, and yet I would argue that we have habitually read the father metaphorically. In considering the father, our tendency has been to scrutinize the individual father as the *substitute* for patriarchy with its oppressive effects, and we have implied that if only we could remove the influence of the father from his daughters' lives, we could remove the effects of patriarchy itself. This notion is, of course, deceptively simple and at the root of our frustration with patriarchy, for even if the individual father could be "abolished," patriarchal influence would not cease to exist. Nonetheless, in feminist criticism of the father-daughter relationship, the father (whatever the dimensions of his individual character) often continues conveniently to represent a dynamics of patriarchal oppression. And so, a project designed to expose the father, to render him human, fallible, and real—in short to concretize what a process of metaphoric comparison can make obscure—begins to make him less omnipotent. But such a project must also make us self-conscious about what it means to read the father metaphorically.

Here I should like to explore the consequences resulting from the practice of "reading the father metaphorically"—that is, of reading the father as if he stands for something else—and I should like to supplement that practice with an additional one in which the father is read synecdochically. But first, a definition of terms: in this context, "reading the father" is not merely a process of interpretation, but also a process whereby meaning or signification is *projected* onto his figure. My objective, then, is not so much to decipher the father, as it is to analyze the interpretive practices whereby he accrues meaning in feminist critical practices. I contend that those interpretive practices are neither free nor undetermined, for in our quest to "read the father" we are bound by a series of linguistic conventions with profound consequences for our relationship to patriarchy.

Rehearsing the parameters of Roman Jakobson's famous essay on metaphor and metonymy, Frederick Jameson reminds us that language is a substitute that replaces something else: "and it does so either by saying what the content is *like* (metaphor), or describing its content and its contours of absence, listing the things that border around it (metonymy)." Metaphor, as is commonly argued, works by substitution; it replaces one signifier with another, and condenses meaning, making selections *in presentia*. It is made possible by the equivalence of a series of signs. In contrast, metonymy works by association; it displaces meaning, and makes connections *in absentia*.[3]

As a "signifier," the father has been historically subject to special processes of signification: the father has rarely been *treated* as "empty signifier" but almost always as something more.[4] The process of "reading the father metaphorically" has turned him into a phenomenon that we only now, perhaps, can begin to understand. We might begin by examining some of the reasons behind the conflation of the individual father with patriarchy itself: How and why have we come to assume that the father stands in for patriarchy? What are the consequences of such a reading?

The impulse to read the father metaphorically emerges, quite simply, out of our need to articulate the experience of our oppression. As Jameson reminds us, language works by one of two ways—in this case, metaphor tells us what patriarchy is *like*. It gives a recognizably "human" face to an abstract form that seems so inexorable. Working by means of resemblance, metaphoric readings give us a sense that we are finally able to comprehend, to take hold of, the elusive force that enthralls us. History complies with this process of metaphoricity, for indeed the behavior of the historical, individual father—particular paternal prerogatives exercised and abused—suggest, on a smaller scale, the workings of patriarchy. It may well be the case that feminist critics have found literary biography so impelling precisely because of the apparent coincidence between the behavior of individual fathers and the wider patterns of patriarchal oppression. Biographical criticism of women writers, "daddy's girls," in particular, seems to offer feminist critics a fortuitous opportunity to explore representational "case studies" of paternal denial and repression exercised on the personal level. Biographical criticism, in other words, seems to confirm the appropriateness of reading the father metaphorically.

I should like to explore one such case in which the practice of reading the father metaphorically has dominated the biography of a woman writer. In an era heavily populated with "daddy's girls," the Anglo-Irish writer Maria Edgeworth (1768–1849) stands out as a particularly forceful example of a father-identified daughter.[5] Few literary daughters have invested themselves so willingly in their father's work; few have dedicated themselves so readily to the implementation of his philosophies. And few have been so self-effacing. Though she herself was the author of well over twenty volumes, Maria Edgeworth insisted that her literary achievements paled alongside those she had accomplished as her father's "partner." Surely, then, here is a situation ripe for reading the father metaphorically, since the pervasive influence of Richard Lovell Edgeworth over his impressionable daughter *must* tell us something about the devastating impact of patriarchy as embodied in this most problematic father . . . or does it?

With few exceptions, literary history has not been kind to Richard Edgeworth. In Gilbert and Gubar's comprehensive survey of nineteenth-century women writers, for example, Richard emerges, once more, as a man whose overbearing personality dominated his daughter's career. Registering their skepticism over recent attempts to vindicate this father, Gilbert and Gubar assert, "The portrait of

Richard Edgeworth as a scientific inventor and Enlightenment theo-
rist who practiced his pedagogy at home for the greater intellectual
development of his family must be balanced against his Rousseauis-
tic experiment with his first son (whose erratic and uncontrollable
spirits convinced him that Rousseau was wrong) and his fathering
twenty-two children by four wives, more than one of whom was an
object of his profound indifference."[6] From this implicit criticism
of Edgeworth's personal eccentricities, Gilbert and Gubar move on
to a discussion of his negative hold over his daughter's affections
and, more importantly, over her intellectual development, a development they believe to have been thwarted (though not entirely
repressed) by Richard's decidedly patriarchal intellectual prefer-
ences.

Published in 1979 as a part of a sustained feminist critique, Gilbert
and Gubar's assessment of this particular father-daughter interaction
reiterates the comments of several nineteenth-century feminist critics who considered Richard as the living embodiment of an oppressive, patriarchal tradition. Here, for example, is the judgment of
Helen Zimmern. Writing in 1883, she translated Richard's authority
as the voice of patriarchy itself: Maria Edgeworth "did not write
from the inner promptings of genius, but because it had been
suggested to her by patriarchy." Similarly, Emily Lawless wrote in
1904: "Even when not actually guiding her pen—a piece of parental
prescription of which [Richard] was perfectly capable—in spirit he
hovered over it." And "that he was in essentials one of the best-
intentioned of fathers is certain, yet few bad, few merely indifferent
fathers, have inflicted upon a gifted son or daughter worse injuries,
from an intellectual point of view, than he did. He not merely
accentuated, he actually lifted into the light of solemn duty, what
was by nature the most serious of Maria Edgeworth's failings—a
lack, namely of imagination."[7]

For Zimmern and Lawless, Richard's behavior is merely symptomatic of patriarchy in general. The effect is precisely to designate
Maria's father as the omnipresent "gargantuan oppressor" Auerbach
describes: if Richard never actually wrote for his daughter, he could
not help writing "through" her, appropriating her body and soul,
as patriarchy has always appropriated the efforts of women who

remain defenseless against this appropriation. Thus Richard's paternal power is the power of patriarchy itself, a power not merely familial, localized, or personal, but indeed monolithic in its effects. By extension, Richard stands for any patriarchal figure who has impeded the more imaginative, creative, and "feminine" impulses of his daughter.

In contrast to this perspective are the comments of several twentieth-century women critics who rejected a reading that reduced Maria Edgeworth to the status of a ventriloquist's dummy. The entire purpose of Marilyn Butler's definitive biography published in 1972 was to disprove the notion that the daughter had no autonomy from her father or that she suffered from being under his tutelage. Through meticulous textual research of Edgeworth's letters and manuscripts, Butler sought to demonstrate that Richard's influence was neither as pervasive nor as "damaging" as earlier critics had charged. Similarly, Elizabeth Harden's analysis, published in 1984, typifies an approach arguing that Edgeworth was made the better novelist through contact with her father's more "rigorous" masculine intellectual world. From her father's approach as a scientist, she writes that Maria Edgeworth

developed an analytic, detached, impersonal habit of thinking, characteristic of most of her fiction. But what was a liability to her fashionable tales became an asset to her Irish fiction. . . . Her detailed, literal reporting of her father's Irish world would make her seems much more significant as a novelist and much more relevant to her generation than any of her contemporaries. The freedom with which Edgeworth shared this experience with his daughter was finally his greatest gift of all.[8]

Despite their very different assessments of Maria Edgeworth's career, these two groups of representative critics—Gilbert and Gubar, Zimmern, Lawless versus Butler and Harden—essentially preserve the notion of the father's supremacy. At issue here is the *nature* of his influence— inhibiting or enhancing? prohibitive or productive?—and not the basic *fact* of his presence. We could say that, from either perspective, the father remains steadfastly a metaphor for patriarchy: the idea that Richard embodies a patriarchal tradition remains more or less intact, while the critics disagree fundamentally about what Richard's status meant for his daughter.

If Butler and Harden are undisturbed by the persistent effects of Richard Edgeworth's involvement with his daughter's career, their position stems from their own implicit investment in patriarchy and in the father who serves to represent it. Clearly critics like Butler and Harden seek to preserve the mythic stature of a patriarchal literary culture, and they therefore endorse the father's cultivation of his daughter's more "masculine" inclinations, while remaining unconcerned about the repression of Maria's more "feminine" tendencies.

Unlike Butler or Zimmern who reveal their own inclination as "daddy's girls," feminist critics obviously commit themselves to the exposure of patriarchy and to the more negative implications of a strong paternal presence. Here the "real" facts of Richard Edgeworth's life appear to yield adequate evidence substantiating a theory of patriarchal excess and supporting a view of his daughter as victim: for example, a man who in his *Memoirs* recorded so superficially the death of his first wife in childbirth (one contemporaneous critic wrote "If the family cat had died in kittening, the circumstances could not be noticed with less ceremony" [cited by Butler, 111]), a man who married four times in all, the last time to a woman one year younger than Maria herself, siring twenty-two children in the process, a man so obviously dependent upon the efforts of women for the advancement of his own purposes, a single man so capable of so many "transgressions," deserves our aspersion, since all of patriarchal abuse can be summed up in the biography of this particular father. Surely here the indications of daughter's victimization will surface most clearly.

Yet a feminist reading that thus indicts Maria's father on the basis of his behavior serves to condemn not only him, but *all fathers* who have participated, to a greater or lesser extent, in Richard's abuses. Though the details vary a bit here or there (not all fathers take four wives, though many share Richard's impatience with the mother's world of domesticity), in context Richard serves as a convenient scapegoat for *any* daughter who has ever felt herself in any way victimized by paternal authority. Like the biography of many "daddy's girls," Maria Edgeworth's life affords feminist critics the occasion to project and focus their anger and indignation against patriarchy. If Maria Edgeworth seems to have been relatively defenseless against her father, we can be angry for her, but our anger serves not only her biography, but our own as well. We lament not only the frustrated and thwarted dimensions of her creativity, but our own unrealized potential, which we feel to have been similarly restricted by patriarchy.

Thus, as we can see from this example, several consequences follow from the practice of reading the father metaphorically: such a reading substitutes one abstract sign—"patriarchy"—with yet another signifier—"the father," which can become equally universalized, allowing for the projection of (rightful) daughterly anger and the focus on a scapegoat. Yet does such scapegoating help advance our understanding of the father-daughter relationship? How, for example, does reading the father metaphorically account for the daughter's tendency to identify so strongly with the father, even when his masculine inclinations involve her in behavior so antithetical to her own feminine interests? Feminist psychobiography answers this question by enhancing the terms of the metaphor: to the daughter the father can also represent "autonomy" and "freedom," as suggested by the following anecdote from Edgeworth's biography.

In the early days of her infancy and girlhood, Maria rarely saw her father, though she later claimed to remember little of her time with her mother, except approaching her deathbed for a farewell kiss. Butler records that Anna Maria's death was followed by a bout of angry, self-destructive acts, and violent behavior. According to Edgeworth's biographer, when her father appeared at the climax of one such incident, the effect of his presence was overwhelming. According to family records: "Suddenly she heard a voice which she says she has a distinct recollection of thinking quite different and superior to any she had heard before—and the doors being opened she saw a gentleman in black and her imagination was instantly struck with the idea of his being sublimely superior to all she ever saw before" (Butler, 46).

Challenging us on several levels, this passage seems ripe for metaphoric reading; here the father seems to represent "autonomy" and "freedom," experiences not characteristic of Maria's experiences at home, as Richard appears to offer Maria an escape from the deadly claustrophobia associated with her mother's domestic life. In this reading, Maria Edgeworth's early and thorough identification with her father, her very willingness to write "as if she were her father's pen" (Gilbert and Gubar, 151), surfaces as the inevitable consequences of her recognition of the "options" (either succumb to suffocating domesticity, like her mother, or join her father in his worldly pursuits) before her. Yet feminist psychobiography also insists upon the consequences of such identification.

In an often cited essay, for example, Jane Flax, describes the ensuing psychological crisis experienced by the "daddy's girl" like Edgeworth. She writes that in order to identify with the father, "the daughter must give up her own preoedipal tie to the mother, and often take on the father's contemptuous devaluation of and contemptuous attitude for the mother and, by extension, for women as a group."[9] Theorists like Flax posit the result of a woman writer's identification with her father as a profound *self-division,* which makes it impossible for the woman writer to embrace her mother within herself; in taking on the "phallic" task of her father's discourse, the woman writer becomes divided against herself. In Edgeworth's case, the persistence of infantile dependencies, as well as profound self-doubts, seem to suggest the symptomatic signs of her self-division.

I should like to consider for a moment the assumptions upon which Flax's scenerio must rest, for her approach implicitly asserts a particular model of psycho-sexual development, one that is rarely articulated, though it is often central to an Anglo-American critique of patriarchy. Behind such accounts of the woman writer's troubled psycho-sexual development, a development that unfolds in response to the father's metaphoric potential as "autonomy"—lies the important presumption of the possibility of another kind of "self," a self that—in contrast to she who is divided against herself—can attain wholeness, integration, completeness, and "autonomy." While Flax's theory implicitly endorses the "autonomous self" as the preferable goal for the daughter, it simultaneously identifies the "divided self" who emerges from under the experience of paternal seduction as the *product* of patriarchy. Moreover, Flax's description of the father's negative hold over his daughter, of his offer to remove the daughter from the domestic enclosure that later becomes another kind of betrayal, leads her to intimate the existence of what we might call the "normative daughter"—the daughter we *could* or *should* be—whose trajectory would somehow differ from that of the "daddy's girl": her discussion makes little sense unless predicated upon the notion that the woman writer could somehow *do otherwise* than to implicate herself in a paternal seduction. To be sure, the feminist critic cautiously withholds judgment on the woman who succumbs to such tragic self-division, for the point is to locate a failure in patriarchal relations, not in the daughter herself. Still, such a reading implies that the daughter's tragic self-division would not exist if the father's untimely appearance did not initiate a process of female self-alienation.

Other feminist critics have suggested, however, that the idea of an "autonomous self" that enjoys "wholeness," "integrity," and completeness may itself be patriarchal.[10] The often regretted "fall from oneness" imagined as the fate of the child who originally enjoys a preoedipal symbiosis with the mother is not, according to these critics, the "product" of patriarchy, but rather an inevitable consequence of the process whereby we grow into maturity. Juliet Mitchell argues that, far from being a consequence of "paternal betrayal," the sense of division associated with movement away from the mother—or experience of "the gap" between self and other—"is the field of communication or 'language.' " For a Lacanian critic like Mitchell, the sense of being "split" (also known as castration) is an inevitable part of what it means to be *human:* "To be human is to be subjected to a law which decentres and divides: sexuality is created in a division, the subject is split; but an ideological world conceals this from the conscious subject who is supposed to feel whole and certain of sexual identity."[11] Such a reading thus rejects the notion of the autonomous or "normative" daughter who potentially enjoys "autonomy" while challenging our tendency to read the father as the specific agent of our "self-division."

In other words, the process of reading the father metaphorically, whether as "patriarchal oppression" or as "the principle of autonomy," tends problematically to perpetuate the idea of a "normative" daughter. In addition, reading the father metaphorically leads to inordinate emphasis on biographical particulars that are considered the ultimate witness to patriarchal imprinting. This is not to suggest that we should deny the important particularities of any one paternal body. Nor is it to overlook the very real impact of any father who embodies certain cultural norms. Rather, it is to insist that the individual father's presence cannot be our only concern if we are to understand the full workings of patriarchy. Working characteristically *in presentia*, metaphor draws attention to the father *who is there*, but a metaphoric reading should not obscure the "father" who is present even when notably absent. The full extent of the father's influence does not depend upon his presence, as Juliet Mitchell explains: "For whether or not the actual father is there does not affect the perpetuation of the patriarchal culture within the psychology of the individual; absent or present, 'the father' always has his place. His actual absence may cause confusion, or, on another level, relief, but the only difference it makes is within the terms of overall patriarchal assumption of his presence. In our culture he is just as present in his absence" (232).

The usefulness of a perspective like Mitchell's becomes especially apparent when applied to biographical situations illuminating a dynamics of paternal absence *and* presence. In the specific case of Maria Edgeworth, such a dynamics complicates the task of reconstructing Richard's influence over his daughter. Let us return to the passage with which we began our metaphorical reading. As recorded by Harriet Butler, Maria's half sister, in 1838—*twenty-one years after his death*—the incident of Richard's first appearance has been doubly refracted through a magnifying lens, and the effect of that lens is to remind us that the father's presence is never merely transparent: Maria "reads" the details of her life backward to find the first confirmation of her subsequent conviction of her father's ultimate importance, while, in the family annals, the half-sister perpetuates not only the moment of recognition itself, but also her sister's sacred "recollection" as testimony to her father's greatness, an idea to which she herself remains dedicated.

In other words, what's being remembered or recollected here is not so much the individual father's presence as it is the history of a daughterly investment in the symbolic dimensions of that paternal presence. Framed as hyperbole (a man "so sublimely superior to all she had ever seen before"), stylistically structured to emphasize retrospectively the dramatic impact of the moment, Maria's description evokes not necessarily the individual father, for one could argue that Richard Edgeworth has been all but obscured by the rhetoric of the passage. Rather, through memory the individual father is associated with everything that the daughter has come to value within the patriarchy itself. The intended effect of this memorial is to make the now absent father once more present for all his "daughters," yet the distorting effect of memory undermines this effort to re-create presence. Here memory and language play an important part in the reconstruction of the father who emerges the sum total of all his daughters' investments in him.

Emphasizing the ways in which the father has been reconstructed *in absentia* in this passage suggests, in other words, that synecdoche operates alongside metaphor in this passage: here language works by association in order to evoke the father's full power, a power that resides beyond the paternal body itself. While reading the father metaphorically directs our attention back to the individual father, daughterly investment in patriarchy often takes us beyond the figure of the father himself, and "reading the father synecdochically" seems most appropriate when circumstances suggest such an investment For example, in a passage later canceled from her father's *Memoirs,* Edgeworth described the effect of her father's correspondence sent to her while she was away at school: "His power of exciting early affection and ambition to deserve his approbation was great—It is the first and best power a preceptor & parent can possess. I never can forget the delight & pride I felt in receiving letters from him when I was at school.—The direction—The handwriting within— even the breaks erasures & blots are present to me" (Butler, 57).

Locating the father's power in the act of paternal writing itself, the daughter gives us a situation whose full significance depends upon our ability to read synecdochically. This passage shifts our attention away from the father's immediate presence to indications of that presence, as a third term—that of writing—intercedes in the process of reading metaphorically. It is no longer simply the case that the father "stands for" something else. In recalling not her father but the effects of his letters, Edgeworth pointedly remembers the effects of a series of signifiers that lack determinate meaning, signifiers that fail to tell us what the father's language specifically "represented." What she recalls is not the *content* of any particular letter, the explicit message of any patriarchal missive, but the "letters" themselves, both literally and figuratively. The handwriting is composed of letters that leave exposed the "breaks erasures & blots," absences that paradoxically signal paternal presence. The father is evoked here not by means of continuity but contiguity, as the remembered letters approximate paternal presence without actually substituting for it.

This censored passage intimates, furthermore, the desiring nature of the daughter's relationship to the paternal body, since the "breaks erasures & blots" seem to promise the daughter a glimpse of that which has been disembodied in paternal speech, perhaps the human and fallible father. A kind of voyeurism occurs here: revealed is the daughter's preoccupation with the exposure of paternal authority, as "breaks erasures & blots" suggest the undoing of the father's power as an author. Such marks signal the moment when Richard's "authority" temporarily lapses, yet ironically the daughter savors this moment precisely because it tantalizes her by exposing paternal fallibility. If such a fascination suggests an aggressive impulse toward paternal authority, it also suggests a longing, for to cherish such marks is to perpetuate the notion of the father's accessibility. Furthermore, the "breaks erasures & blots" are ultimately the reminders of the father's own "castration," of a symbolic wounding that belies the myth of his paternal omnipotence. In this excerpt, far from offering the literary daughter the illusion of autonomy or "wholeness" through participation in paternal discourse, the father's marked and "violated" letters suggest that the authority of authorship is continually susceptible to what Edward Said calls "molestation."[12]

That Edgeworth later chose to excise this passage from her father's memoirs suggests, among other possibilities, a tendency to protect her father against further exposure. Revealed through this act of omission is the thoroughness of a daughter's investment in the myth of paternal inviolableness. But such an act also suggests the impulse to protect herself, for in recording her obsession with the lapses of writerly authority, she unmasks the limitations of writing itself, a limitation of profound significance to the daughter as well as the father. Referring to Juliet Mitchell's definition of what it means to be human, we could say that the "breaks erasures & blots" that disturb her father's text are reminiscent of the "gap" associated with the "field of language," and the daughter's own "castration" (in the sense that Mitchell uses that word) is evoked by means of this attention to her father's status as author.

Edgeworth's manner of reading her father's writing, a reading that (as we have seen) necessitates censorship, resembles other kinds of problematic feminist readings of the father and the language that represents him. All daughters are similarly voyeurs—simultaneously attracted to and horrified by the possibility that the father's power might *not* be inviolable, and we implicitly fear the very possibility that the signifiers representing him might be empty: Where can we locate the source of our oppression if not in the power of the father and his language? Like Edgeworth, we seek to protect *ourselves* by perpetuating the myth of paternal omnipotence, since our own "castration" is made most apparent when we are forced to recognize the limitations of the father and his language. In the service of "reading the father metaphorically," we repress the partial nature of our own experience. If neither "wholeness" nor "autonomy" can be part of the human experience, then it is not the father who blocks or denies us access to such completion, for "wholeness" is not his to give us. To unduly fix our attention on the father as the catalyzing agent of the "gap" is to deviate from the more rigorous analysis of patriarchal mechanisms. Again, this does not mean that we should repress the specific details of a destructive sexual politics directed at particular women, but that we must always consider the individual father in terms of his fuller relationship to the structure we call patriarchy.

In conclusion, adding synecdoche to a reading of the father brings us to the recognition that, as Auerbach insists, we live as imperfect subjects in an imperfect world. In revising our way of seeing and reading the father, we revise our way of thinking and interacting with him. We learn to be wary both of that "man in black" who seems to appear out of nowhere and of our own imaginations, which insist on rendering him "so sublimely superior" to all we have ever seen before.

Notes

1. Reprinted in *Historical Studies and Literary Criticism,* ed. Jerome McGann (Madison: University of Wisconsin Press, 1985), 235. I wish to thank Janet Grey, James Wallace, Helena Michie, and Patsy Yaeger for their insightful comments and observations of earlier drafts of this essay.

2. Juliet Mitchell, Psychoanalysis and Feminism (New York: Random House, 1974), 362.

3. Frederic Jameson, *The Prison House of Language* (Princeton: Princeton University Press, 1972), 122–23. Roman Jakobson, "Two Aspects of a Language: Metaphor and Metonymy" reprinted in *European Literary Theory and Practice,* ed. Vernon W. Gras (New York: Dell Books, 1973), 121. I recognize that metaphor is often paired with metonymy, yet in choosing to privilege synecdoche over metonymy, I mean to emphasize precisely the ways in which the father stands in as a *partial* representation for the *whole* process of patriarchy. In other words, to insist on synecdoche is to preserve the notion of an essential relationship between the part and the whole.

4. Whether Lacan's "critique of the signifier" extends to a critique of the paternal metaphor has, of course, been the subject of rigorous debate among feminists. Some of the most sophisticated argument on this topic is to be found in the work of Jane Gallop (in *The Daughter's Seduction* [Ithaca: Cornell University Press, 1982]), Jacqueline Rose and Juliet Mitchell (in *Psychoanalysis and Feminism; Jacques Lacan and the école freudienne* [New York: Norton, 1985]; and *Women: The Longest Revolution* [New York: Pantheon, 1984]). Useful discussions of Lacan's writings on metaphor and metonymy—with their implicit privileging of metaphor—are to be found in Anthony Wilden, *Speech and Language in Psychoanalysis,* trans. Anthony Wilden (Baltimore: Johns Hopkins University Press, 1968), 238–49, and Ellie Ragland-Sullivan, *Jacques Lacan and the Philosophy of Psychoanalysis* (Urbana: University of Illinois Press, 1986), 233–63.

5. For further anaylsis of Maria Edgeworth's status as a "daddy's girl," see my book on patriarchal complicity in the lives and works of Hannah More and Maria Edgeworth.

6. Sandra Gilbert and Susan Gubar, *The Madwoman in the Attic* (New Haven: Yale University Press, 1979), 147.

7. Helen Zimmern, *Maria Edgeworth* (London: W. H. Allen, 1883), 34, and Emily Lawless, *Maria Edgeworth* (New York: Macmillan, 1904), 19.

8. Marilyn Butler, *Maria Edgeworth: A Literary Biography* (Oxford: Oxford University Press, 1972). Elizabeth Harden, *Maria Edgeworth* (Boston: G. K. Hall, 1972), 21–22.

9. Jane Flax, "Mother-Daughter Relationships: Psychodynamics, Politics, and Philosophy," in *The Future of Difference,* eds. Hester Eisenstein and Alice Jardine (Boston: G. K. Hall, 1980), 37.

10. See, for example, Juliet Mitchell, *Women: The Longest Revolution,* 238–39, or Toril Moi, *Sexual/Textual Politics* (New York: Methuen, 1985), 66–67.

11. *Women: The Longest Revolution,* 240 and 277.

12. Edward Said, *Beginnings: Intention and Method* (New York: Basic Books, 1975), 83–84.

Afterword
My Father's Penis
Nancy K. Miller

When I was growing up, my father wore what we called string pajamas. Actually, I only remember his wearing the bottom part of the pajamas, which as their name suggests, closed with a tie at the waist. (On top he wore a ribbed, sleeveless undershirt, tucked into the pajama bottoms.) The pajamas, made of a thin cottony fabric, usually a shade of washed-out blue, but sometimes also striped, were a droopy affair; they tended to bag at the knees and shifted position at the waist with every movement. The string, meant to hold the pajamas up at the waist, was also meant to keep the fly— just an opening in the front—closed. But the fly, we might say today, resisted closure and defined itself instead by the meaningful hint of a gap.

As my father wandered through the apartment in the early mornings, occupied in a series of ritualized activities (watering the plants, making my sister and me eat breakfast before we left for school and regularly burning the toast, bringing my mother coffee in bed, drinking his own truly awe-inspiring combination of orange juice and buttermilk, shaving, and performing indeterminate wanderings that can only be characterized properly by the Yiddish verb, *draying*), this almost gap continually caught my eye. It seemed to me that behind this flap lay something dark, maybe verging on purple, probably floppy, and definitely inaccessible. I also thought it was hairy in there; I was pretty sure I had glimpsed hair (he had hair everywhere on his back and shoulders, why not there).

I don't think I really wanted to see it—"it" had no name in my ruminations—but there was a peculiar way in which its mysterious daily existence behind the slit in the pajama bottoms loomed large in my prepubescent imaginary as somehow connected to the constant tension in our family, especially to my mother's bad moods. Growing up, I had only the vaguest notions of sex; I can still remember my utter astonishment when, sitting on the living room couch, I learned at age fourteen from my mother that a penis had to become "erect" to enter a vagina (I had never really thought about *how* the *man's* penis—in the redundant but always less than instructive language of hygiene classes—gets into the *woman's* vagina). So that years later when in college I finally had a look at my first penis (this was no small surprise), I realized that I had never visualized the thing to myself at all.

Almost forty years after the scene of these memories, I find myself again, as a middle-aged, therapized intellectual, thinking about my father's penis. Years later, living alone after my mother's death in the same apartment, my father, stricken with Parkinson's disease, shuffles through the room *draying*. Boxer shorts have replaced the string pajamas, but the gap remains the same and it's still dark in there. But it's not the same: I have seen his penis. I have even touched it: one day when his fingers had grown so rigid he couldn't, as he puts it, "snare" his penis. He wanted to go to the bathroom; it was late and I wanted to go home; so looking and looking away, I fished his penis out from behind the fly of this shorts and stuck it in the urinal; it felt soft and a little clammy.

Shirley, the nurse's aide who takes care of my father, reported one day that when she arrived at the apartment in the morning, she had found my father in the kitchen "bare-bottomed" and cold. "His—was blue," she said (her slight Caribbean accent made the word hard to understand over the phone); "I rubbed it until it turned pink. Then he felt better." Rubbed his *penis?* But what else, in the vicinity of a bare-bottom, of two syllables, could have gone from blue to pink? Did it respond to her rubbing? Become erect? The mystery returns. What do I know? Shirley and I talk about my father, his care. The apartment, despite her efforts, smells of urine. There's no missing this penis-effect. One day, in the middle of eating dinner, his back to me, he demands his urinal from Shirley, which he uses while at the table. Shirley buys him new boxer shorts on 14th Street. Six dollars, she says. Apiece, I ask? No, three *Fruit of the Loom* in a package.

This is the condition of his remaining at home (he gives me a pained look at the mention of going to a "home" that silences me): to get out of bed and make it to the bathroom without falling, or to use the urinal that hangs like a limp penis from the walker he despises (he shows his superiority to his infirmity by carrying the walker in front of him instead of leaning on it). When these solutions fail, Ellen, the neighbor who brings him his daily *New York Times,* says "He peed himself" (my father always talks more elaborately about the "difficulty of urination," of responding in time to the "urgency of its call"). The newspapers (now like the *New Yorkers* to which he maintains his subscription, and which remain unopened in their plastic wrappers) pile up unread in the living room; I throw them away in my weekly sweep through the apartment.

In "Phallus/Penis: Same Difference" (great title) Jane Gallop writes: "The debate over Lacan's and, beyond that, psychoanalysis's value for feminism itself centers on the phallus. Yet the *phallus* is a very complicated notion in Lacan, who distinguishes it from the *penis*. The distinction seems, however, to resist clarification." For a while after touching my father's penis, I went around thinking smugly I would never again confuse penis and phallus, boasting that I had transcended the confusion. Phallus was the way my father used to scare me when I was growing up: tearing sheets of paper out of the typewriter because I hadn't left wide enough margins; throwing me across the room in rage because I had been talking endlessly on the phone to a girl friend when the hospital called to say his mother was in a coma; knocking me down in an elevator for staying out late with my boy friend in college; making me break a date with a cab driver (but Daddy, he's *Jewish,* the son of a cantor!) I had been picked up by in London when I was eighteen. Penis was that dark-veined, heavy thing hanging between emaciated, unexpectedly hairless and elegant thighs, against strangely elongated, even darker, balls. It made problems for me, but they were finally prosaic, unmediated by concepts and the symbolic order. My father doesn't have the phallus; no one does, Lacan said. But, Gallop writes in *The Daughter's Seduction,* "the need, the desire, the wish for the Phallus is great. No matter how oppressive its reign, it is much more comforting than no one in command." So now I decide, say no, and yell; I am responsible for the rest of his life ("it's for your health and welfare," he used to say); maybe I, failing the penis, have my chance at the phallus.

Months after I write "My Father's Penis" I come into my father's room. I think I have put an end to all this speculation (phallus, penis, the law of the father, castration, etc.) but when I see him sleeping naked, stretched out like a dilapidated Endymion across a hospital bed, I can't resist. I move closer to see what is going on. I want to take a good look this time. His hand is resting in his lap, his penis tucked away, hidden between his thighs. Maybe, he doesn't have a penis after all, what then? I don't seem to know anymore: I mean I know what it looks like, but I'm still not sure what it is that I've seen.

I can remember seeing, some time ago, the call for papers for this collection of essays. Although I didn't feel personally engaged by the project then—I wasn't "working on the father"—I recall being intrigued but also made a little uneasy and impatient by the notion of "The Father's Breasts," as Patricia Yaeger enlists the language of Sharon Olds's images for her theoretical enterprise. I'm not sure what made me uncomfortable, the imagination at work in Olds's tropes or the implications for feminist theory of this new, revised father figure: giving up on sheer antagonism; giving the father back a body we seemed to have forgotten he had (first the mother, then the father: would we never get out of the family?). But since I had nothing to contribute, I didn't pursue the issue further and proceeded to forget about the volume and the project.

When I wrote "My Father's Penis" last summer, I had been thinking more about penises than fathers. A friend of mine, who is an art historian, had done a slide-show lecture on representations of the penis in painting, and I conceived my piece originally as a kind of footnote to her panoply of members—the geriatric extension of her taxonomy. I was also writing in the aftermath of an intensely difficult teaching experience in which the question precisely of "experience" in feminist theory had been challenged with what I will call, despite its familiar vagueness, a certain phallic insistence. When it then became a question of publishing "the penis" (it seems impossible to invoke the title or its content without getting derailed by catachresis) in *Refiguring the Father*, it seemed to me that I had found a proper home for it: that the fragmentary essay, because of its mixed origins, born of the troubled intimacies of the autobiographical penis and the theoretical phallus, had unexpectedly come full circle—from "My Father's Breasts" to "*The* Father's Breasts" to "My Father's Penis" and back.

What is most interestingly at stake for me in this collection of essays is that tension between the "my's" and "the's," between the anecdote of experience and the theory that depends upon it, between the body in theory and its resistances in practice. I have found myself wondering whether the attention in these essays to the cracks in the metaphorics of intact authority that we have deployed in our representations of the paternal regime—the "breaks, erasures & blots" Beth Kowaleski-Wallace foregrounds in her call for a synecdochal poetics of reading—is somehow symptomatic of a shift of emphasis in feminist inquiry. Is there a way in which these rereadings of patriarchy as vulnerable text can be seen as a response to the paradoxes of the current moment in which a newly empowered academic feminism encounters a renewed political conservatism that celebrates the family circle of home? As we begin to take the measure of what it has meant to live in the Reagan era, with its sublime indifference to what lies outside the nostalgia of home, there is a certain urgency in also understanding the insecurity of the father's places. Perhaps in face of the homeless we confront the violence that inheres in the assumption of a continuity between paternal zones of power—domestic borders—and the dominion of metaphor.

Feminist theory has alway found its material in the material of experience thought to remain unfigured by patriarchal empire: the others' side of dominative practice. In the idea of *Refiguring the Father*, which proposes a new look at that material, we have the chance to question our own tropes of patriarchy and the politics of their effects.

Notes on Contributors

Joseph A. Boone is the author of *Tradition Counter Tradition: Love and the Form of Fiction,* in addition to several articles. Associate Professor of English at Harvard University, he teaches courses on the nineteenth- and twentieth-century novel and on gender-related topics. He is currently writing a book entitled *Sexuality and Narrative: Issues in the Psychology of Sex and Self in Modern Fiction,* from which his article in this collection is excerpted.

Vanessa D. Dickerson, Assistant Professor of English at Rhodes College, teaches Victorian, Afro-American, and women's literature. She is currently at work on a book on black women novelists.

Irene Fizer is a National Mellon Fellow in the Humanities in the Comparative Literature Graduate Program at the University of Pennsylvania.

Jerry Aline Flieger is Associate Professor of French at Rutgers University, where she teaches literature, critical theory, and women's studies, specializing in feminist psychoanalytic theory. She has published extensively on topics relating to psychoanalysis, feminism, and literature, and is the author of two forthcoming books: a monograph on the work of Collette analyzed from a Lacanian perspective, and a study of the relationship of Freud's joke theory to postmodern and poststructuralist concepts of textuality.

Susan Fraiman teaches English and women's studies at the University of Virginia. Her essay is part of a larger work on narratives of female development impeded or undone.

Susan M. Griffin, Associate Professor of English at Louisville, is the editor, with William Veeder, of *The Art of Criticism: Henry James on the Theory and the Practice of Fiction,* and the author of several articles on James. She is currently completing a book on visual perception in late James and has recently begun work on the position of the adolescent in Victorian culture.

Minrose C. Gwin is Associate Professor of English and codirector of Women's Studies at Virginia Polytechnic Institute and State University. She is the author of *Black and White Women of the Old South: The Peculiar Sisterhood in American Literature,* and a forthcoming feminist study of Faulkner.

Heather Hathaway is a graduate student at Harvard University. She received a B.A. from Wesleyan University and is currently pursuing a Ph.D. in the History of American civilization, concentrating on Southern and Afro-American history and literature.

Linda Kauffman has written numerous articles on nineteenth- and twentieth-century British and American fiction, and is the author of *Discourses of Desire: Gender, Genre, and Epistolary Fictions.* She is presently writing a sequel, *Special Delivery: Epistolary Modes in Modern and Postmodern Fiction.* She has also edited a collection of critical essays entitled *Gender and Theory: Dialogues on Feminist Criticism.* She teaches literary criticism, critical theory, and modern literature in the English Department at the University of Maryland.

Beth Kowaleski-Wallace has written a book on patriarchal complicity in the lives and careers of Hannah More and Maria Edgeworth. Her essay "Milton's Daughter: the Education of Eighteenth-Century Women Writers" won the Florence Howe Prize, awarded by the Women's Caucus of the MLA, in 1985. She teaches in the English Department at Simmons College.

Helena Michie is an Assistant Professor of English at Brandeis University. She is author of *The Flesh Made Word: Female Figures, Women's Bodies,* and has published numerous articles on feminist theory, feminism and psychoanalysis, and nineteenth-century literature.

Nancy K. Miller is Distinguished Professor of English at Lehman College and the Graduate Center, CUNY. She is the author of *The Heroine's Text: Readings in the French and English Novel, 1722–1782* (1980) and *Subject to Change: Reading Feminist Writing* (1988), and editor of *The Poetics of Gender* (1986). She co-edited with Joan DeJean "The Politics of Tradition: Placing Women in French Literature," *Yale French Studies* 75 (1988).

Adrienne Auslander Munich, editor of *Browning Institute Studies: An Annual of Victorian Literary and Cultural History,* teaches at State University of New York at Stony Brook. Her recent work on feminist theory includes a coedited collection, *Arms and the Woman: War, Gender, and Literary Representation,* and a book, *Andromeda's Chains: Gender and Interpretation in Victorian Literature and Art.*

Nancy Sorkin Rabinowitz received her Ph.D. from the University of Chicago in 1976 and has been on the faculties of Kirkland and Hamilton College since 1974. Her published work includes articles on Charlotte Brönte, Margaret Drabble, and Margaret Ayer Barnes, as well as Aeschylus and Euripides. She teaches comparative literature and women's studies.

James D. Wallace, Director of American Studies at Boston College, is author of a book on James Fenimore Cooper, *Early Cooper and His Audience,* and of a number of articles on American Fiction.

Patricia Yaeger is Associate Professor of English at Harvard. She is the author of *Honey-Mad Women: Emancipatory Strategies in Women's Writing* and is at work on a project entitled, "Dirt and Desire: The Grotesque in Southern Women's Fiction."